FROM

The Saturday Evening Post

ADVENTURES OF THE MIND: *Second Series*
(1961)

ADVENTURES OF THE MIND: *First Series*
(1960)

LOREN EISELEY: *An Evolutionist Looks at Modern Man*
JACQUES BARZUN: *The Misbehavioral Sciences*
WILLIAM S. BECK: *The Riddle of Life*
PAUL TILLICH: *The Lost Dimension in Religion*
J. ROBERT OPPENHEIMER: *The Mystery of Matter*
EDITH HAMILTON: *The Lessons of the Past*
ALDOUS HUXLEY: *Drugs That Shape Men's Minds*
ARTHUR M. SCHLESINGER, JR.: *The Decline of Heroes*
EDITH SITWELL: *The Poet's Vision*
D. W. BROGAN: *The End of Empire*
HANS SELYE: *What Makes Basic Research Basic?*
HERBERT READ: *Art and Life*
FRED HOYLE: *When Time Began*
LEWIS MUMFORD: *How War Began*
AARON COPLAND: *The Pleasures of Music*
MARTIN CYRIL D'ARCY: *The Varieties of Human Love*
JAMES R. NEWMAN: *Einstein's Great Idea*
S. I. HAYAKAWA: *How Words Change Our Lives*
CLEMENT GREENBERG: *The Case for Abstract Art*
WALTER GROPIUS: *The Curse of Conformity*
BERTRAND RUSSELL: *The Expanding Mental Universe*

These are BORZOI BOOKS
published in New York by ALFRED A. KNOPF

ADVENTURES OF THE MIND

[*Second Series*]

ADVENTURES

OF

THE MIND

FROM

The Saturday Evening Post

Edited by Richard Thruelsen and John Kobler

19   61

ALFRED·A·KNOPF   *New York*

L. C. catalog card number: 59–11691

THIS IS A BORZOI BOOK,
PUBLISHED BY ALFRED A. KNOPF, INC.

FIRST EDITION

ACKNOWLEDGMENTS

For permission to reprint the following essays, the editors wish to thank:

Prentice-Hall, Inc., for "The Challenge of Being Free" by Henry Merritt Wriston from *Goals for Americans*, © 1960 by The American Assembly, Columbia University.

Curtis Brown, Ltd., for "Screwtape Proposes a Toast" from *The World's Last Night* by C. S. Lewis, Harcourt, Brace and Company, © 1959 by Helen Joy Lewis.

Harcourt, Brace & World, Inc., for "Why Marx Failed Here" by Clinton Rossiter, subsequently published in Mr. Rossiter's book *Marxism: The View from America*, © 1960 by Clinton Rossiter.

The World Publishing Company for "The Final Answer" from *The Son of Man* by François Mauriac, translated by Bernard Murchland, © 1960 by The World Publishing Company.

Acknowledgments

Holt, Rinehart and Winston, Inc., for "In Praise of Waste" from *Nature and Man's Fate* by Garrett Hardin, © 1959 by Garrett Hardin.

Cambridge University Press for "The Conflict of Cultures" from *The Two Cultures and the Scientific Revolution* by C. P. Snow, © 1959 by C. P. Snow.

"Battle Cry for Book Lovers" by Robertson Davies subsequently appeared in an expanded version as "A Call to the Clerisy" in Mr. Davies's book *A Voice from the Attic*, published by Alfred A. Knopf, Inc., © 1960 by Robertson Davies, © 1960 by The Curtis Publishing Company.

For permission to quote the poetry in "The Act of Language" by John Ciardi, the editors wish to thank:

Random House, Inc., for lines from "In Memory of W. B. Yeats" from *The Collected Poetry of W. H. Auden*, © 1940 by W. H. Auden.

Holt, Rinehart and Winston, Inc., for lines from "Two Tramps in Mud Time" from *Complete Poems of Robert Frost*, © 1949 by Henry Holt and Company, Inc.

Houghton Mifflin Company for lines from "Ars Poetica" from *Collected Poems* by Archibald MacLeish, © 1952 by Archibald MacLeish.

Oxford University Press for lines from "Felix Randal" from *Poems of Gerard Manley Hopkins*, © 1948 by Oxford University Press, and for lines from "Aereopagus" from *Ten Burnt Offerings* by Louis MacNeice, © 1953 by Louis MacNeice.

Stanley Kunitz for lines from his "Deciduous Branch," © 1944 by Stanley Kunitz. Harcourt, Brace & World, Inc., for lines from "The Ruins" from *Goodbye Earth and Other Poems* by I. A. Richards, © 1957 by I. A. Richards.

For permission to quote the poetry in "The Making of a Poem" by C. Day Lewis, the editors wish to thank:

Harper & Brothers for "The Gate," "The New-Born," and lines from "Final Instructions" from *Pegasus and Other Poems* by C. Day Lewis, © 1957, 1958 by C. Day Lewis.

Introduction

The second volume of selections from *The Saturday Evening Post* series, *Adventures of the Mind*, owes its existence not only to the enthusiastic reception of the first collection of twenty-one essays but also, and more directly, to the remarkable response this 3-year series of articles has evoked from *The Post's* readers. That response, in turn, is a direct indication of the earnest desire of a growing number of Americans to participate in the profound and exciting progress man is making in extending the horizons of his knowledge.

The forty essays in this book reflect the extension of our intellectual boundaries in many directions and at many different levels. Donald J. Hughes leads us inward to the infinitely complex worlds of subatomic particles, while A. C. B. Lovell takes us outward to the giant spiral galaxies in their enigmatic recession from the observable edge of the universe. Earl A. Evans shows us how biologists are unravelling the secret of life itself; and Jesse Greenstein lets us look into the hot interior of a star. The essays by Henry M. Wriston and John Kenneth Galbraith illuminate a quest of a different kind, the nation's new strivings for a sense of purpose, both moral and material. Owen Barfield ponders the moods of meaninglessness and alienation which pervade our lives as a result of the revelations of science and the impact of the midcentury technological revolution.

Although the essays appearing here deal with such apparently disparate subjects as nucleonics and the inspirational processess of the poet, they have a common wellspring. For the poet working at his craft and the physicist exploring the heart of matter both belong to the community of creative thinkers. While each may deplore the modern-day estrangement of the scientist and the humanist, an estrangement eloquently outlined by C. P. Snow in his essay, "The Conflict of Cultures," an even greater gulf has increasingly separated these creative workers from the millions of us who are almost wholly preoccupied with the problems of day-to-day living.

It was in an attempt to help bridge this gap between the intellectual and the intelligent layman that the *Adventures* project was launched in the spring of 1958. For some time the editors of *The Post* had, like many others, been keenly aware of the increasing emphasis in American life on entertainment. Paradoxically, this trend in the press, radio, and television toward the superficial and the transitory was occurring in a decade of scientific and intellectual discovery. But as the researcher, the scholar, and the artist advanced further and further into the realms of new knowledge and abstract thoughts, the concerned layman found himself less and less able to follow.

Linked with this frustration were the problems of national survival, of emergent nationalism among the underdeveloped countries, of the world wide population explosion, and what we have come to call the crisis in education. Faced by such challenges, millions of thoughtful citizens found themselves plagued with a sense of bafflement and uncertainty in a time of awesome problems which they, as voters, taxpayers, and wielders of opinion must ultimately help to solve.

The *Adventures of the Mind* series has addressed itself to these problems and many more. A number of them are discussed in this volume, in each case by acknowledged experts in the field. Barbara Ward outlines the dilemma of a world divided between rich and poor nations. Stefan Possony explains Russia's uses of semantics as a weapon of conquest. J. D. Williams sets forth the implications of a rapidly multiplying human race on a finite globe. Morris Kline gives us a lucid exposition of the nature and power of mathematics. Jacob Bronowski urges us to adopt the morality of science. C. Northcote Parkinson asks, "Can Democracy Survive?"

Introduction

For each of the forty contributors to this volume the *Adventures* series has been a means to bridge the gap of understanding between the specialist and the inquiring citizen. For the non-specialist, the essays stand as invitations to join the researcher, the scholar, and the philosopher on the frontiers of thought. It is the editors' hope that this book will help them in their common effort.

THE EDITORS

Contents

Contents

ADVENTURES OF THE MIND

HENRY M. WRISTON

[*Photograph by Ollie Atkins*]

Henry Merritt Wriston is president emeritus of Brown University, president of the Council on Foreign Relations and president of the American Assembly at Columbia, a group formed to study national problems. Doctor Wriston was educated at Wesleyan University and Harvard. After teaching history at Wesleyan, he became president of Lawrence College in Appleton, Wisconsin, in 1925. Doctor Wriston was president of Brown from 1937 to 1955. In February 1960 President Eisenhower appointed Doctor Wriston chairman of his Commission on National Goals. This article is excerpted from the Commission report and represents solely the views of the author. Prentice-Hall published the report in 1960 under the title, Goals for Americans.

The Challenge of Being Free

BY

HENRY M. WRISTON

The acid test of successful democratic government is the degree of effective liberty it makes available to the individual. That criterion establishes an order of values. Self-fulfillment is placed at the summit. All other goods are relegated to lower orders of priority; even security and comfort must have less consideration.

The principle is easy to state. Its application requires a continuous exercise of judgment and will. For there is a perpetual tension between the particular and the general, between individual tastes and social necessities. Indeed, that is characteristic of life itself. Centuries ago Aristotle observed that man is a social animal. Each person has both particular and general interests, individual wants and social needs. When the general interest is overaccented, freedom declines and may disappear; first controls, then paternalism supervene. On the other hand, if individual interest utterly neglects social needs, anarchy is the end result. The consequence of either extreme is loss of liberty.

There has been a kind of uneven historical rhythm in the degree to which the state managed the lives of its subjects, some-

3

times leaving them alone to a great extent, at other times intervening in even trivial matters.

For some brief periods in history it has seemed that tensions between the state and the individual were slight. One can say relatively slight, but never absent; *laissez faire* was not a policy; it never existed even as a tenable theory. It is a fantasy. The nearest responsible men came to that concept was in the aphorism, "That government is best which governs least." Even that statement was cast in relative, not absolute, terms. It was fully applicable only in brief moments when all good things—freedom, security, comfort—seemed to exist concurrently. Such eras in history have been rare and short-lived. Normally the tensions between liberty and other values we cherish are more acute. Often they rise to the point of conflict. In a society so completely and complexly organized as ours, in a world so interdependent and so disturbed, the choice between individual desires and social necessities becomes difficult.

It is made needlessly difficult when the basic value of freedom—human dignity—becomes confused with either wealth on the one hand or hardship on the other. Neither comfort nor hardship measures human dignity. Economic determinism belongs to the Communists; let them have it. Dignity does not consist in being well housed, well clothed and well fed. Gandhi never lost dignity. In the deepest sense of the word he never lost security when he lived in prison, was clothed with a loincloth and subsisted on goat's milk. Other men of "royal" blood have lived in luxury, yet had no shred of self-respect and deserved no respect from others. Dignity does not derive from a man's economic situation, nor from his vocation. It does not require a white-collar job or any other status symbol. It rests exclusively upon the lively faith that individuals are beings of infinite value.

Abraham Lincoln had great insight in these matters. He had experienced abject poverty. He had worked as a common laborer. His education was the product of his own untutored determination. And he said, "It is difficult to make a man miserable while he feels he is worthy of himself and claims kindred to the great God who made him." In our reconsideration of the

4

"great truths" of the Declaration of Independence, we need to be reminded of these things, lest our perspective should become distorted.

Because of the increasing pressures of man against man in this shrunken and crowded world, there has been an increasing number of compulsions upon the individual, designed to require him to do things for the general welfare as well as his own benefit. The most inevitable is taxes—usually joined with death as the only absolutely unavoidable occurrence. The power to tax involves the power to destroy. In less extreme forms it is the power to redistribute wealth and reshape society, either to protect the individual or destroy his incentive and impair his initiative.

One of the commonest compulsions is school attendance. Its purpose is to develop the individual and protect society. Compulsory vaccination is a health measure—with like dual purpose. Social security is calculated to protect the individual in his old age, or his survivors if he dies, and by making him share the cost, shields society from his possible dependence. Many other examples could be cited. Each is defensible when it does not inhibit essential free choices and when nonperformance would involve danger, needless cost or disadvantage to others. Those are the tests of the boundary between liberty and license; one man's freedom should involve no tresspass upon others' rights to life, liberty and the pursuit of happiness. They also mark the boundaries between freedom of the individual and paternalism on the part of the state.

At any given moment the decision regarding how far the state should intervene turns upon the current—and dominant— estimate of man's capacity to accept the bitter with the sweet. If the judgment accentuates his courage and strength, liberty will summon all his energies—physical, mental, moral—to wrestle with inescapable, and often intractable, problems. If opinion stresses his weakness, there will be a demand that government make choices for him and care for him. That process, carried too far, puts comfort before freedom, government above the individual.

5

The dilemma is perpetual in history; it is new neither in form nor in substance. When the Declaration and the Constitution were being framed, Europe had rulers known as "enlightened" or "benevolent" despots. A good example was Prince Karl Frederick von Baden. He had many virtues—he developed agriculture and commerce, he sought to improve education, he reformed the administration of justice. Clearly he was enlightened. He was also benevolent; he held it to be the duty of his government "to teach his subjects even against their will how to order their domestic affairs" and "to make them, whether they liked it or not, into free, opulent and law-abiding citizens."

At that time, the dominant economic theory was mercantilism. Characteristic of that system were economic planning and social engineering in extreme forms. The government was to tell citizens what to do: "It is in its hands to guide them away from error into the right path and to teach them, even against their own wills, how they are to institute their households." The all-powerful, paternalistic state was familiar to the founders of this nation. With determined purpose they turned away from that ideal to establish a new order. Much later Dostoevski summed up the matter in a few words; he held even "tragic freedom" preferable to "compulsory happiness."

History is replete with manifestations of the acuity of that remark. When the issue is posed in sharp relief, the choice may be hard, but it is clear. From the standpoint of physical comfort and well-being, many slaves were better off before they were freed and had to fend for themselves. Yet none is so ethically blind as to use this as a defense of slavery today. The black men of Africa cannot manage their economies, their public-health measures or many other things so well as the Europeans did for them; but that they prefer tragic freedom to paternalism no one can doubt.

Usually the issue is less dramatically posed. We have been living in an era of moral fatigue. The characteristic historical tone of American life has been optimistic. Disillusionment when two world wars brought no peace, when, instead, allies turned (in both instances) into enemies, the reaction that always follows war's sacrifice, and the shock of the great depression—all these combined to daunt our faith and supplant ebullience with pessimism.

In the mood stimulated by these shattering events, human misery came to seem more terrible than human freedom seemed beautiful. The individual was lowered in the scale of values, and society exalted. For a brief time technocracy—the ultimate in materialistic determinism—had a great vogue and was offered as a "modern" substitute for liberty under democracy.

More generally, men were referred to as "social units." A report to the President of the United States said that "the development of social technology" was "imperative." There were demands in influential places for "social engineering." Those are mechanistic concepts; they deal with individuals not as unique beings of diverse gifts and infinite worth, but as structural units to be built into a planned society.

Fortunately we hear less of this subversive doctrine today, but other causes of tension have arisen to take its place. One is concern over competition with the manipulated economy of the Soviets, which has led to much talk of the "more efficient use" of "manpower" under the aegis of the government. Often this concept is pressed so far as to constitute an assault upon appreciation of the individual as free and self-directed. When the "manpower program" proceeds beyond information and counsel toward direction by authority, the basic doctrine of our nation is countered.

During the mood of doubt regarding our system—which often went so far as to assert that we had no ideology—trespass upon individual rights could make subtle progress, and the inversion of values could proceed in small but successive and cumulative steps. Security could be exalted above freedom, and intellect become suspect; checks upon thoughts and words instead of deeds were made to seem reasonable and necessary. Item by item, government was called upon to make choices that had belonged to individuals. Some reforms were essential; some went too far.

It must be emphasized that the rapidly growing Federal Government was by no means the only organization that tended toward submerging the individual. This is made abundantly clear

7

by the fact that a large share of recent Supreme Court cases involving the Bill of Rights arose from actions of the states, cities and lesser governmental units, such as school boards.

Moreover, the tendency to overwhelm the individual appears also in private organizations, which, like government, have grown greatly in size and influence. A business corporation may be so bureaucratized that only an "organization man" can survive. Corporate policy may oppose taking "controversial" positions on public questions or actively participating in a political party, particularly one not favored by the management. In dozens of intangible ways such policy may restrict freedom. All sorts of devices, even including "benefits," may reduce the mobility of the individual and virtually tie him to his place of occupation. The tendency of every organization to eat up its members is perennial and must be fought every step of the way.

Unions were organized to protect the individual because he was in an adverse bargaining position facing the power of a corporation. But a union may go far beyond its essential service. By making membership compulsory and collecting dues by checkoff, sharp limitations are laid upon voluntarism. Sometimes insistence upon uniform wages, seniority rights, work quotas, featherbedding "rules" and many other devices accentuate the losses in individuality arising from machine production instead of offsetting them. The union may curb merit increases and promotions; it may impair incentives. When the leader establishes an effective dictatorship, it is an assault upon freedom. Then the individual is a tool, not a master, as in the democratic process he has a right—and an obligation—to be. When his vote is sought to be delivered as a bloc, it is an attempt at invasion of his basic civil rights.

A school can be an enemy of freedom if its discipline is too harsh, if its curriculum is too narrow or is dominated by some dogma. If it seeks to indoctrinate instead of stimulating originality of thought, it is at war with its own reason for existence. A church which curbs political action, which interferes with matters beyond faith and morals likewise becomes a barrier to liberty.

8

When any of these things happen, the state, itself curbed by the Bill of Rights, must curb the new threat. Paternalism upon the part of the state is vicious. It is no less intolerable on the part of a private organization. There is no doubt that in the 1960's the individual needs to be shielded from the tyranny of organizations. Any institution—political, social or economic—that tends to stifle individual initiative or prevent individual innovation is a force for making the United States second rate and regressive.

The Bill of Rights was not designed for corporations. Free enterprise is only one fruit of liberty, not its root; property and business exist for the benefit of individuals and have no inherent rights. Protecting individuals from the state did not destroy the state; it merely forced government to live with the democratic process. Protection from private threats to individuality will not destroy corporations or unions or schools, though they would have to conform to democratic requirements. Change is the order of life. As private institutions grow with change, they can meet changed circumstances.

The basic natural resource of the United States is its people. It follows inescapably that the first national goal to be pursued—at all levels, Federal, state, local and private—should be the development of each individual to his fullest potential.

The "Negro problem" is the most conspicuous area for dramatic new advance. It is man made and can be man ended. Problems in race relations are not unique to the contacts of Negroes and whites. From time immemorial "stranger" was equivalent to "enemy." Tensions have always been more difficult to eliminate when physical differences accentuated the distinction. It is one of the triumphs of civilization when that ancient prejudice is erased. That it is possible to overcome prejudice is plain upon the record. Different races live together in amity and effective co-operation in many parts of the world. Hawaii offers a conspicuous American example—peoples of many tinctures of skin, backgrounds of history and varieties of culture dwell together in peace.

The first unalienable right, without which the other two

have no meaning, is the right to life. A truncated life will not do; men are entitled to life in all its fullness—length, breadth, depth. Yet, for a Negro, life expectancy at birth is 7.6 years less than for a white man. At age twenty the life expectancy of a Negro is still 5.9 years less than for a white. Clearly the difference does not arise wholly from higher infant mortality. This startling discrepancy between Negroes and whites is largely caused by inferior education, poorer living conditions, inadequate dental, medical and surgical attention. Those deficiencies are the direct consequence of curtailment of unalienable rights. Negroes who have had equal advantages in housing, education and medical care have the same expectation of life as whites. That fact shows how needless is anything less.

A tremendous economic loss is involved. The working years of a colored person are roughly 12 to 15 per cent less than they should be. In terms of the production of goods and services—the growth of the economy—that is a waste we cannot afford. The loss runs far beyond what those raw figures indicate.

Failure to give the Negro equal education condemns men to remain common laborers though they have a much higher potential. The Department of Labor lists more than 5000 professional and skilled occupations. Most are effectively closed to Negroes. There is a glib explanation—"They do not meet the standards." So far as it goes, that is unquestionably true. But the deeper truth, the overriding truth is that they have been deprived of proper preparation to meet the standards. Talent is distributed across the human race without respect to national boundaries, race, sex or any other classification. No competent study ever found one race inferior in social, political, economic or cultural potential.

The loss in human satisfactions runs far deeper than the economic; it is beyond calculation. When people are denied fulfillment, it is trespass upon the unalienable right to pursue happiness, to find for oneself the deeper satisfactions of self-realization.

Moreover, the political consequences are desperately bad. Needless barriers inevitably create and constantly multiply bitterness against a system which not only tolerates but ensures frustration. Whatever is done, at any level—public or private—to continue to foment resentment lays the ax at the root of the system of government to which we are committed.

Democracy, to be viable, requires a large measure of consensus. To continue deliberately to impair that consensus among citizens is folly. The danger is increased manyfold when some have defied prejudice, broken through barriers and secured higher education, gaining capacity for articulate leadership. They give voice to what have been mute discontents. They give direction to programs to attain the equality supposedly guaranteed by their citizenship. We have reason to be thankful that, thus far, action is nonviolent, that the new leaders counsel peaceful measures.

When it is urged that Negroes are not "socially acceptable," the statement misses the point. People are not born with social grace. It comes from education, training, environment—the whole atmosphere surrounding youth. The product is the result of the process. It is not reasonable to deny a proper environment and then complain of the consequences.

The first and dominant goal with regard to the "Negro problem" is to treat men and women as individuals and pay no attention to their pigmentation. The time has come—almost too late—for a massive and sustained effort to meet this issue at every level—Federal, state, local, economic, social, personal. Like every other citizen, the Negro must be not only allowed but helped to fulfill his potential.

This goal is necessary not only in justice to the Negro but for the sake of the moral integrity of us all.

Democracy is the political aspect of the assertion of the supreme importance of the individual. It is predicated upon the measureless riches that arise from the variety of his inventiveness. The fertility of the individual mind is one of the mysteries of the universe. The source and manner of production of ideas no philosopher, no metaphysician, no scientist has ever been able to fathom. Somewhere, out of the void, that which did not exist before leaps into the mind of man. In freedom, each thinker and every doer has the right to self-expression in vocation and avocation. Liberty puts the maximum reliance upon self-discipline.

This goal touches the foundations of democracy. From the first, it was realized that popular government required an educated citizenry. The declaration in the Northwest Ordinance of 1787 is classic: "Religion, morality and knowledge being necessary to good government and the happiness of mankind, schools and the means of education shall forever be encouraged." What was necessary then is doubly essential today.

The United States is the largest, most diverse and most complex political structure ever to seek to manage its affairs by the democratic process. When achieved, that method of government is the most rewarding. But government at all levels has become so complex and problems so multifold that, to attain success, citizens must command greater intellectual resources than their forebears. Because the position the United States holds in the world is so influential, the success of the democratic process here is vital not to the United States alone but to all the world.

The political necessity for the fullest, most competent and most continuous education should be obvious. When any citizen, for whatever reason, is deprived of this development, it is a denial of one of his unalienable rights. It is a subtraction from the viability of our democracy. It is a threat to the rights and well-being of the rest of us. Every incompetent citizen is a menace to the freedom of all.

The economic argument is not primary, but it is exceedingly strong. Endless talk of the need for capital and machinery obscures the far more vital need for brains. To promote economic growth it is necessary to think not only in terms of what the Federal Government can do, or what private capital can do, not merely in terms of law and regulation and investment. Far more vital are the development and exploitation of the innate capacities of people to the fullest degree. The most severe limitations upon the expansion of the economy are deficiencies and rigidities in the skills of the work force.

We have learned to glorify management; it receives special training at many levels and large rewards. The research scientist, with his long years of preparation through arduous discipline, is at last recognized as essential to a growing economy. We are witnessing, dramatically, the shrinking need for the common laborer. Yet some of the crafts and professions—including teaching—pursue restrictive practices which deny many competent people access to their skills. Apprenticeships are limited to give a false "security" to current practitioners. In the guise of "standards," exclusion from professions is common. Restrictions should fall; the first way to expand prosperity and to attain maximum economic growth is through the building of a larger reservoir of people with higher competence.

The fullest development of every individual is hindered by underestimating the potential of a majority—women. They own much of the wealth of the nation; but in its management, in the direction of policies concerning it—not to say in the political operations which determine the atmosphere in which wealth is created—they are still discriminated against. At a time when women constitute nearly a third of the labor force, it makes no sense, from the standpoint of an expanding economy, to apply social sanctions which limit their earning power and deprive the economy of their executive abilities, their capacity for scientific research and even their higher technical skills. The union of family life and career is possible to a degree never before conceivable. Yet barriers of pride and prejudice are needless hurdles for the woman to surmount.

As political and economic reasons point to the need for greater personal development, so also does military security. It is irresponsible to talk as though arms, munitions and money were primary. Estimates of defense requirements in terms of "hardware" offer a classic case of preparing for the wrong war. The first, and vital, necessity is more people of transcendent capacity and skill.

The importance of scientific and technical skills is appreciated. But they will not be enough. Indeed, by themselves, untempered by the humanities and social studies, they may heighten danger. We need people with such sophisticated knowledge and such calm judgment that no mass excitement could trigger an unnecessary war.

The twentieth century has seen Fascism and Nazism. Both were manifestations of mass hysteria—men were literally carried away from normal behavior. Victory in war over those institutions did not eliminate the danger of recurrence. Exaltation of one-man "leadership" leans in that direction. The urgent need is for widely distributed, not overcentralized, leadership and in many different fields. Many people must play important roles, lest the democratic process be ultimately prostituted to dictatorship.

Political strength, economic growth and security of the nation unite in demanding personal development. Social considerations make the same demand. An underdeveloped citizen —physically, mentally, morally—is not an energizer, but a burden upon society. The vast growth of hospitals for the chronically ill and of prisons for the hardened criminal stresses that fact.

While schools are being improved, there must also be a massive assault upon whatever handicaps man physically—all the way from prevention of prenatal injuries to the postponement of senescence. This puts in right perspective medical and surgical advances, availability of hospitals, the provision for adequate relaxation and recreation to repair the ravages of exertion and restore energy. In the closely intercommunicating world of today infections fly across land and sea; the protection of the individual is not only a local or even a national concern. It is an international obligation of urgent importance. Inescapable inferences for foreign policy flow from the concept of every individual developed to his highest potential. Statistics on the loss of human resources by physical incapacities show that the scope of this concept is broad enough to challenge a myriad of talents.

The effectiveness of democracy—the most rewarding and most difficult form of government—rests not alone upon knowledge and judgment, but upon character. Only the morally mature individual will be determined to do away with slums, end corruption and help lift the load from the poverty stricken at home and abroad. Only through moral sensitiveness can there be escape from the smugness that wealth and comfort breed. Moral sense resists avarice and self-seeking. It stimulates that concern for his fellow men by which society escapes disintegration, while giving the individual maximum play for his talents, tastes and interests.

With the combination of these elements, physical, intellectual and moral, man rises to aesthetic appreciation—to culture. Without awareness of beauty, life is barren even in the midst of luxury.

Once the individual as a physical, intellectual and moral integer is put at the center, the acceptance of tyranny, the tolerance of totalitarianism and the readiness to exploit the ignorant and the poor have been made impossible. In a word, democracy becomes not only viable but absolutely indispensable.

All these considerations suggest the true character of education; it is the life-long process of growth—physical, mental, moral, aesthetic. It is not primarily training, though training is part of it. Central are the stimulation and the discipline of the individual. This does not require every individual to be a scholar. The wisdom of the world is not confined to the learned; often it is found in the perceptive experience of those whose schooling has not carried them into "higher education." Their shrewd insights on public as well as private matters are part of the historical record of progress.

There is no such thing as "mass education." Every use of the phrase is a denial of a vital reality; education is a wholly individual process. The life of the mind—despite all pressures to invade it—remains a private life. It occurs in each person uniquely. We do democracy no service in seeking to inhibit thought—free, wide-ranging, hazardous.

The American system is built upon the thesis that conformity is not the way to progress. Without independence of mind there is no freedom for the individual. Therefore education should never over-accent "adjustment." Whenever that emphasis is dominant, it is a deliberate effort to defeat the infinite variety that enriches society and the world.

15

The educative process should never be distorted by the nation's "need" for scientists, or engineers, or doctors, or any other specific profession or skill. Whenever counseling and curriculum stress vocation primarily, they underestimate needs just as vital, though not statistically conspicuous. The nation needs philosophers, poets, artists, critics and a thousand other sorts of people—in numbers which "manpower analyses" can never estimate.

Education and its objectives defined in these terms involve no less concern with classrooms, equipment and teachers in adequate supply. But there must be vastly more concern to develop schools devoted to growth. It is not enough to pass child-labor laws and compulsory-attendance laws to keep young people off the labor market and immure them. The need is for challenge and stimulation.

If we make effective self-discipline in freedom the chief educational goal of the '60's, we shall bring a fresh perspective to all our tasks. It would be a clean break with the materialistic determinism of the Soviets. It would establish the moral stance of the United States before the world. It would give us a vastly more efficient society.

No one can doubt that our nation started with extravagant objectives. Its success was so conspicuous that many people regarded progress as inevitable; some even called it "automatic." At that point, what had been a manifestation of will and hard work and confidence became a complacent reliance upon factors other than effort and dedication.

Two world wars and the great depression rudely shattered such smugness. The pendulum of opinion swung too far in the opposite direction, and many doubted that there was any such reality as "progress." The ebullient optimism of the nineteenth century gave way to the pessimistic outlook of the mid-twentieth.

It is time to strike a new balance. The revolution in industry and agriculture wrought by science and technology has revealed unlimited possibilities for progress. The amazing economic recovery of Western Germany illustrates that dedication, skill and hard work still make progress possible. The process is not even; we do not move forward on all fronts at once. Indeed, while advancing in one area, we may retrograde in another. Nor is the pace steady. Progress comes in surges. In science it is sometimes called a "breakthrough," which must be followed by tedious and unglamorous consolidation of the new position.

For some years now, organization has seemed to mean more than individuals. The program of national defense has been so huge that stress has been on "teamwork." Even in science, group enterprises have seemed dominant ever since the Manhattan Project produced the atomic bomb. Industry has become huge and corporate; unions have developed in size, structure and resources. Politics has seemed to depend more on organization than upon ideas.

The moment is ripe to remind ourselves once again that ideas come from individuals, that progress stems from ideas. In the same way, morals are the exclusive possession of individuals. Phrases like group morality cloud the reality rather than help clarify it. Ideals are the combination of individual imagination, intelligence and moral clarity. Leadership, if the word has any meaning at all, is a characteristic which inheres in individuals who have energy, faith and ability in unusual degree.

There are many legitimate goals for the United States. None of them—literally none—is attainable without the intelligence, courage and industry of individuals. The central goal should be a renewal of faith in the infinite value and the unlimited possibilities of individual development. Whatever constitutes a barrier to a man's unalienable rights should be swept away. Nothing whatever should curb his right to life—as long, as full, as rich as life can be. Liberty is his because of his manhood; in liberty the infinite richness of his contribution to the life of others is facilitated. The pursuit of happiness is an endless quest; in it no one can "deliver the goods" to the individual, though the environment can be vastly improved. He must seek it for himself.

Walt Whitman was the poet of America. He summed up the goal in a characteristic poem, *By Blue Ontario's Shore:*

17

I swear I begin to see the meaning of these things!
It is not the earth, it is not America, who is great,
It is I who am great, or to be great—it is you up there or
*   anyone;*
It is to walk rapidly through civilizations, governments, theo-
*   ries,*
Through poems, pageants, shows, to form great individuals.
Underneath all, individuals!
I swear nothing is good to me now that ignores individuals.
The American compact is altogether with individuals,
The only government is that which makes minute of individuals,
The whole theory of the universe is directed to one single indi-
*   vidual—namely to You.*

Further reading:
Konvitz, Milton R. and Clinton Rossiter: ASPECTS OF LIBERTY.
    Ithaca: Cornell University Press; 1958.

Becker, Carl L.: DECLARATION OF INDEPENDENCE: A STUDY
    IN THE HISTORY OF POLITICAL IDEAS. New York: Vintage
    Books; 1942.

Wallich, Henry C.: THE COST OF FREEDOM: A NEW LOOK
    AT CAPITALISM. New York: Harper & Brothers; 1960.

Whitehead, Alfred North: ADVENTURES OF IDEAS. New York:
    New American Library of World Literature, Inc.; 1955.

Hayek, F. A.: THE CONSTITUTION OF LIBERTY. Chicago: Uni-
    versity of Chicago Press; 1960.

Hand, Learned: SPIRIT OF LIBERTY: PAPERS AND ADDRESSES
    OF LEARNED HAND. New York: Vintage Books; 1960.

STEPHEN SPENDER

[Photograph by Jacob Lofman]

Stephen Spender, British poet, author and critic, has achieved fame in many literary genres. He published his first volume of verse in his teens. At Oxford, he belonged to a group of brilliant young poets that included W. H. Auden, C. Day Lewis, and Louis MacNeice. In recent years, however, he has turned increasingly to prose. During the 1930's Spender became a convert to Communism. He has described his subsequent disillusionment in a book titled The God That Failed. *In addition to producing short stories, critical analyses, and his autobiography,* World Within World, *Spender has translated both German and Spanish poetry. He is a frequent visitor to this country as a lecturer and teacher. Since 1953 he has been co-editor of the international monthly,* Encounter.

The Connecting Imagination

BY
STEPHEN SPENDER

I could be bounded in a nutshell and count myself a king of infinite space," boasts Hamlet and immediately cancels the claim with the qualification, "were it not that I have bad dreams."

He expresses the predicament of the individualist ever since the Renaissance: priding himself on the independent, self-sufficient world of his individuality and, in the same breath, bemoaning that he is not, cannot be, himself, because the history of his time has got under his skin and undermined the foundations of the world inside the nutshell skull.

The foul vapors of the court of Denmark, the metaphysical promptings of his father's ghost, made it clear to Hamlet how he should act. But, from his own point of view, his action had a purpose other than revenge or a *coup d'état* in Denmark. He wanted an external world which would not threaten the unity of his self-perfecting inner world. The bad dream, outside his control, was the outsideness of history—outside, but also the nightmare inside us all. He had to put his soul in jeopardy and take that leap into the external world to right the time, in order to create the conditions where his inner world could be himself.

We frequently are told that Hamlet is divided between the contemplative man and the man of action. But fascinating as his character is, I think it is his predicament—also our predicament—which really preoccupies and involves us. We are the spectators of the fluctuations of the drama of the inner life of a prince (essentially the prototype of the inward person who wishes to develop the qualities of his aloneness), with the outward circumstances which do not merely condition but also have actually become in part his inner life. In watching Hamlet, however little we may feel outselves to be the prince of Denmark, somehow we are spectators of our own souls placed in any history. The heroes of Joyce's *Ulysses*, E. M. Forster's novels, T. S. Eliot's poems might all agree that history is a nightmare from which they would awake.

In Hamlet's case, the vaporization of his kingdom of infinite space is by the condition of Denmark. In our case, it is the capsule of the vision of the destruction of everything, which the H-bomb has neatly inserted in the head of each one of us. The bad dream dethrones us from being ourselves.

The relationship of inner world to outward history varies, of course, from age to age and decade to decade even. Much modern literature and art express nostalgia for some selected past which was more favorable to the self-perfecting individual than today appears to be, because in some longed-for and envied past, outward circumstances seemed to confirm his own inner values. The nostalgia which the aesthetes at the end of the last century felt for the Athens of Pericles and the Florence of the Renaissance was doubtless because men like Pater and Ruskin thought that in those times the shining city was a polished mirror in which the man of ideals could see reflected the image of his own soul.

And certainly, in one respect, no age could be less a mirror of the whole man than our own, even if we have certain very definite advantages over those envied Athenians and Florentines. For our external world of too large social units, of utilitarian consumer goods, of bureaucratic organization, of total threats and total promises, is adjusted not to the high demands of a society in which every man is able to develop his own uniqueness but to the lowest-common-multiple demands of one in which everyone is the same. The modern world has tremendous power of good or of evil for all of us. But it is not scaled to the pulse and feeling and senses of the flesh-and-blood individual genius or lover of genius.

Thus it happens that a good many persons, among them the liveliest and most perceptive of several recent generations, revolt against the impersonality and abstractedness of the whole modern world of production based on generalized statistics. To them, what it creates, or invents, seems as repulsive—and ultimately the same, even—as the results of its destructive powers. Destruction is an explosion in which we have to die, but construction in the modern world of ever-accelerated change is a nonstop explosion in which we have to live. Life becomes, for those who hate explosion, the egotistic search for their lost egos. The beatniks, with their renunciations of all the results of materialism, their perverse religiosity, their resort to drugs and violence to stimulate in them sensations of which they feel they have been robbed, are the most recent example of an attitude of total rejection of modern life by modern art which began with Baudelaire in the last century.

The seeming irresponsibility of yesterday's Dadaists and today's beatniks is what one might call a kind of serious unseriousness, a refusal to accept a world in which science and politics have undermined the long-term inward aims of life, which are those of the individual. For the potential of destruction in modern life is the obverse of mass production. And so long as what produces can, still more effectively, destroy us all, the inner life of modern Hamlet in his nutshell skull is vaporized by the nightmare of the external world.

Until the second half of the present century the chief antagonist of everyone alive was his own death. This made his own existence seem pointless and yet gave point to existence; for without personal death there is no point in doing anything with life. One would dawdle through eternity. But the person who knows he has to die may seek to discover significance for himself and others, to make his mark, to jump from the interior of his own being onto that external ship carrying living memories to the future, which is civilization. But if civilization itself is doomed to extinction within a calculable space of time, then the future has, as it were, been cut away from under our feet. And from now on, each one of us has to double the certainty of his own death with the possibility of the death of civilization. Nor is there the voice of any ghost of Hamlet's father to obey, nor wicked uncle to kill, which would put the time to rights. Personal death gives life significance, if, paradoxically, we allow our minds to dwell on it and, at the same time, determine to live as though we were immortals.

This attitude to our personal death provides us with the example of how to confront the destruction of the world, which already, so far as ourselves are concerned, will be extinguished with our own deaths. We have to act as though civilization would continue forever. If we are incapable of this, we can comfort ourselves by remembering that many civilizations have already vanished, and that the early Christians lived from day to day in expectation of the certain end of the world, and yet produced many things of value, including great art. We may even fix our minds on the thought suggested by science fiction, that consciousness is not unique to our planet. If there are no human beings on Mars, from now on it will become necessary for us to invent them.

Nevertheless, even if we banish the idea of the Big Bang from our minds, it remains true that the existence of so much concentrated mechanical power in the hands of a few men has greatly widened the gap between the overshadowed life of personal values and the impersonal realities of forces made available by science. Public morality seems to have become separate from personal values. It is still possible to consider that another person may be "human" and, therefore, open to an appeal to understand a private problem. But the impersonal forces are like some inexorable god, not really even under the control of the high priests who minister to it. It seems almost too much to expect this god to spare the lives of the world's millions of inhabitants and of their millions more children.

So it is scarcely possible today to think that anyone could, like Hamlet, feel the call to impose his personal vision upon the state for the sake not just of the external order but of the personal vision itself. Perhaps what ultimately undermines religion in the modern world today is the sense that it is impossible to imagine a savior. Doctor Schweitzer serves as a reproach, but our confidence in him is shaken when we hear that he refuses the most up-to-date methods of medicine in his hospital. We like him, but we have greater faith in penicillin than in healers. Gandhi was effective, and perhaps now ranks among the several hundred Hindu gods, but this is only because India is so "backward" and because in the last two decades of the British raj, British loss of faith created a power vacuum in which a saint could lead an effective movement of nonresistance. If we try to imagine a situation in which personal qualities would again make themselves felt as public ones, we are likely to find ourselves thinking of a world in which all the machines have been destroyed, and where a few humans are left wandering through a world of ruins. In their hatred of machines, the minds of some artists have played dangerously with the idea of such a holocaust.

So in modern circumstances there tends to be an ever-widening split between public morality and personal standards. The public sphere consists of the vast impersonal forces, some of them working for the general good and others for the general destruction. People who value personal relationships, affection, discriminating taste, tradition and sensibility naturally enough support what they regard as the constructive, rather than the destructive, side in the war of the impersonal forces. They are against war and in favor of feeding and clothing the multitudes. But in the world divided between East and West, even this choice is not easy, because both sides, while opposed to each other, nevertheless stand for what they believe to be progress. That two sides, both having ultimate goals which are similar, can yet be prepared to destroy the world in order that the one may not be overcome by the other, shows how far power has overreached the scale of individual human values. Neither side can, in fact, be the instrument of that which individuals on both sides, all over the world, want, because the impersonal forces are so powerful.

And so it happens that we live in a world where those who

wish to perfect their own individuality tend to accept the situation of a life divided into two compartments—one of personal living and the other of the impersonal forces. On the one hand are personal relationships, marriage, children, friends, culture and travel. On the other hand, the struggle of history which, in its effect of making social ciphers of us all, regards the individual simply as a unit who gives of what he has to the state and receives from it, in return, protection and various benefits. We pay our taxes, vote, worry and try to appease the impersonal forces, while at the same time preserving a life apart from them, something in us which says "I." Among human generations there probably has been none in which people have insisted on their "individuality" so much as we in the West do today. Yet this individualist who says "I" is only a half person; the part inside himself has been saved from that other half outside which is yet also inside, because it is the bad dream that stops him from being king of infinite space. The inner world is threatened by the external state which vaporizes the life inside the nutshell skull.

Individuals worry a good deal today about what makes them real. They go to the psychoanalyst to discover whether they are real or unreal. What makes a personal real? The sense of existing *in* his own body *with* his own mind and within a community. This is exactly what many persons today lack; they are cut off from half themselves.

Many also feel convinced that in the past, in more intimate, more personal communities—like those of the New England settlers and of the English cities from which these came—men were more real. Their relation with the life around them was a flesh-and-blood relationship, heartfelt and less abstract. Radii spread, as it were, from the isolated individual to a circumference of the community in times of the kind described in the novels of Jane Austen or Nathaniel Hawthorne.

Nevertheless, we are committed to the world of impersonal forces, and there seems no foreseeable political solution of the problem of the estrangement of the individual from the society in which he lives. We should not, for that reason, however, make the attempt to return to the past of organic communities.

Nor should we become paralyzed, hypnotized or drugged in a gesture of refusal to regard ourselves as anything but ourselves, as in any way responsible to society, like the beatniks. We probably have to accept the idea of the separation of private from public worlds. But, at the same time, we have to bridge the gulf in our imaginations if we cannot do so within the social structure.

Poets, novelists and artists have been telling us, in various ways, for more than a century that we must do this. I am chary of saying that poets have a message; yet if they do have one it is this: that modern man must once more connect the separate worlds of personality and society, and that this can be achieved through an effort not so much of the will as of the imagination.

Perhaps the first poet to declare this was Shelley in his famous essay on the *Defence of Poetry*. In this essay Shelley analyzes very exactly the relationship of people at the beginning of the 1800's to the emergent world of scientific inventions. He points out that systems of economics, centralized government and industrialization tend to become a kind of circumference developing by their own automatism of accumulating knowledge and removed from the true center of human needs and the significance which gives life spiritual value. "We must imagine that which we know," wrote Shelley, foreseeing a world in which men would make great advances in specialized knowledge and in applying its results, without understanding the effects that these activities were having on human beings. Shelley foresaw that the world of science and material advance might become divorced from the centers of individual values.

The English novelist E. M. Forster, wrote a series of novels which might with justice be regarded as demonstrations, in terms of contemporary English life, of the failure of the British ruling classes to apply Shelley's injunction of imagining that which they knew. *Howards End* is the study of a successful businessman, Henry Wilcox, head of what Forster calls the "tribe of Wilcoxes," who despises every attitude but such as he considers practical, and lives in a world of "telegrams and anger." The Wilcoxes' lives become entangled with those of Margaret and Helen Schlegel, two girls who consider that friendship, kindness to one's employees, music, poetry, art and, beyond these, an awareness of "invisible values," provide standards for actual day-to-day living which are sacred and must never be betrayed. Their association with the Wilcoxes sets a devastating analysis of the Wilcox tribe and all they stand for. Forster shows how, under Henry Wilcox's gospel of practical good sense, there lies nothing but panic and emptiness, and that in practice it produces the obtuse actions which led to the decline of England, even in terms of money and power.

The "message" of *Howards End* is "only connect." In 1910 Forster could still think that if men at the head of affairs could "imagine that which we know," there was hope even for the Wilcoxes—redeemed by the Schlegels. Nor should one dismiss this as the dream of an idealist. The background to the events related in *Howards End* is the rivalry between the then British and the then German empires. And who, looking back, can regard the First World War as a triumph of hardheaded realism? Was it not, rather, the record, written in the blood of the world's youth, of failure of imagination and neglect of "personal relations"?

A *Passage to India* depicts the effects of the failure of imagination, which have resulted in making personal relations impossible, and which therefore leaves a situation in which the only remedy for violence and unending hatred is political surgery. The English officials described in Forster's novel are conscientious, scrupulous and just, according to their lights, but they treat the Indians as their inferiors, the "natives."

As long as the English remain in India, personal relations between Indians and English are impossible. That they have become so is a measure of what is ultimately failure of imagination. Not that in a situation where the British were occupying India such a situation was not inevitable. But with imagination and understanding a better solution might have been found. And if, after all, the leaving of India by the British was a much less unfortunate affair than other like episodes in recent history, this may at least in part be due to the effect on both Indians and British of Forster's plea for personal relations and the life of the imagination.

Forster's conclusion, at the end of A *Passage to India*, is that it is impossible for an Indian and an Englishman to trust each other as friends until the British have left India. But it would be also true to say that if the English had treated the Indians as persons, the British might have stayed in India; perhaps not as occupiers, but as equals.

Fifty years after *Howards End* it is too late to hope that the connecting imagination might save an empire or, indeed, solve the political problems made by the impersonal forces. But it is not too late to bridge the gulf between the person as person and as social unit within the inner world of individual life. For the modern individual is divided within himself between an over-subjective "I" and an oversocialized "he."

The split was always implicit, of course, through the dichotomy of the I/he double aspect of each man's existence. To myself I am "I"; to others I am "he." Within the circle of my family and a few friends, I am able to enter into the "I" aspect of half a dozen people, but beyond that, everyone is "he" and "she" —whom I cannot think of as being "I."

In the past, as I have pointed out, societies tended to recognize the "I" aspect of men and not to treat them simply as social concepts. The "I" was expressed within the "they" in the architecture of cathedrals, like great arrows directing the souls of men upward to heaven, carrying all those "I's" up to that "You" who cared equally for all of them as his children. The cathedrals, expressing a shared belief, were built also by anonymous hands, those of all the able-bodied community. The modern situation, in which social awareness penetrates individual consciousness and divides it into two separate subjective and objective halves, has been brilliantly described by D. H. Lawrence:

> It seems to me that when the human being becomes too much divided between his subjective and objective consciousness, at last something splits in him and he becomes a social being. If man loses his mysterious naïve assurance, which is his innocence; if he gives too much importance to the external objective reality and so collapses

in his natural innocent pride, then he becomes obsessed with the idea of objectives or material insurance; he wants to insure himself, and perhaps everyone else: universal insurance. The impulse rests on fear. Once the individual loses his naïve at-oneness with the living universe, he falls into a state of fear and tries to insure himself with wealth. If he is an altruist, he wants to insure everybody and feels it is the tragedy of tragedies if this can't be done.

What Lawrence says about the individual is surely true, though I do not agree with his rejection of "social insurance." We are surely committed to progress which consists of caring for people who have never before been cared for, and we must somehow combine this with strengthening individual values.

Lawrence thought that society could be redeemed through a new attitude toward sexual relations between men and women. This is not so ridiculous as it sounds, so crudely stated. He saw that the estrangement of modern people from society leads often to the total isolation of the individual, even within marriage, where people may have very little true relation with each other. By confronting them with the basic reality of marriage—sex —he would break down this separateness. What Lawrence was really doing, perhaps, was fortifying the "personal relations" of E. M. Forster with modern psychology.

However, one should not reject writers like Forster and Lawrence because their conclusions seem too demanding, or ineffective, nor even when they seem simply wrong. The remedy such writers offer is not so important as the fact that they have imagined our predicament and stated it in terms in which a philosopher, or even a statesman, can translate it into terms of their thinking—and even of action. When the poet or novelist tells us what things are like and how people behave, he may be a genius. When he tells us how to act, he is probably no wiser than ourselves who read the newspapers. Einstein was a genius as a physicist, an amateur as a violinist and a child as a politician. The art of the novelist and poet helps us to chart our place on the map of our time, though the writer may tumble when he instructs us how to get to the next place.

Today literature and art are perhaps the only bridges we have left. The religious can still command faith, but they cannot connect the modern experience of a man living in this world of science and power with the traditional past. They can only set aside the world and direct our thoughts to eternity. But poems, novels, paintings and sculpture can interpret the changes happening in the world of machinery, inventions, discoveries and revolutions as changes which are happening inside men's souls. When Picasso painted his famous picture of the bombing of the little Basque town of Guernica during the Spanish Civil War, we not only had a terrifying realization of the screaming horror of a cellar in a village when the bombs are falling all around but we also knew, more significantly, the modification which takes place in the individual sensibility when someone reads of such an event. Appalled as the spectator of *Guernica* may be, it is better to be appalled than to be indifferent.

In fact, one cannot really be indifferent to anything that happens, and of which one knows, that debases the human condition. Either one refuses to be affected by it, in which case one has hardened one's heart and becomes something less of a human being, or one faces the horror, in which case one keeps alive a little of that hope which ultimately might transform the human condition.

We live then in a world divided between statistical facts and personal experiencing. Generalizations derived from statistics tell us certain things: that people will be happier if they have better plumbing, more food, refrigerators, television sets. But the final test of such things is the effect they have on inner lives. Imaginative truth is individuation: the experience of the circumference of external history by the centers which call themselves "I." Statisticians and sociologists cannot tell us much about the individual—even when individuals are the whole population. We do know, of course, that the hungry should be fed. We do not know whether television sets and automobiles make people happier. Partly we do not know, because it takes a man of genius to define what happiness is.

Art, because it imagines the individual within a given situation, reaffirms the "I" in each one of us and opens up the possibility of a life where people do not merely live in better conditions, but where they really might be themselves—their better selves.

If civilization is to survive, nothing is more important than that the gap between real life—the life of the experiencing and feeling individual—and the external world of technological advances should be bridged. For as Max Born, the German physicist, pointed out, scientific "progress" just as much as scientific destruction, is a kind of explosion and threatens men's souls almost as much as it threatens their bodies.

In our part of the world we can still use a symbolism which refers to the love and the values of the human personality without regard for the state. There are enough warnings—from India yesterday, from the rest of Asia, and still more, from Africa today—that there is a sense in which the writing of men of imagination, such as Forster, may still suggest a line of conduct that "pays" better than the so-called realism of politicians and that if we do not use our imaginations, there are continents and civilizations to lose. Still more important than this practical consideration, however, is the fact that unless we use the imagination, the nutshell kingdom of infinite space which is human individuality will be subject to diminution as people become, in their external lives, ever more absorbed into the tasks of progress. It is possible, then, that the artist has a task in our time: to resist the temptation to withdraw into subjectivity. And his public also has a duty: not to neglect—indeed to respect and encourage—the life of the imagination.

It seems to me that the bridges which cross the gulf of interior and exterior worlds can, today, be made only by men who have the power to imagine vividly and create in novels, poems and paintings our situation. In the West we still have the freedom to build bridges. In totalitarian countries, when such men become too powerful the politicians attempt to stop their creative warnings. This struck me forcibly in Moscow recently. I went to visit the studio of a famous artist, a sculptor much feted by the authorities. After he had shown me statues of Lenin, Maiakovsky, Gorki and other heroes of the people, just before I left, he hesitated, and then said in a rush of confidence, "I am now going to show you something I really care about. But this cannot be shown till after my death, and then only if a great disaster happens." He went to the end of the studio and drew back a curtain, revealing, unfinished, an immense statue of Christ.

Further reading:

Spender, Stephen: WORLD WITHIN WORLD. New York: Harcourt, Brace & Company; 1951.

Shelley, Percy Bysshe: "The Defence of Poetry" in SELECTED POETRY AND PROSE OF SHELLEY. New York: Modern Library, Inc.; 1951

Lawrence, D. H.: SELECTED LITERARY CRITICISM. New York: The Viking Press, Inc.; 1956.

Orwell, George: 1984. New York: New American Library of World Literature; 1954.

SIR GEORGE THOMSON

[*Photograph by Eugene Kammerman*]

Sir George Paget Thomson, one of the world's leading atomic physicists and Master of Corpus Christi College at Cambridge, is the Nobel Prize-winning son of a Nobel Prize-winning father, Sir J. J. Thomson, who contributed largely to the discovery of the electron. Sir George's award was won for his work on Electron Diffraction, which proved that electrons, though particles, behave as waves. During World War II, Sir George headed a British committee which, in 1944, reported favorably on the prospects of an atom bomb. After the war, he participated in theoretical work on the possibilities of obtaining nuclear power from heavy hydrogen.

What You Should Know About Physics

BY

SIR GEORGE THOMSON

To understand our twentieth-century world and the changes which are shaping our lives, every intelligent man and woman should enjoy a cultural familiarity with the basic principles of modern physics. This obligation should not be confused with the precise and detailed knowledge needed by the technical student or the working scientist. For the layman, it is only necessary that he should appreciate the thoughts that are basic to physics and the kind of concepts that are used to understand it and that he be familiar with the general principles to which these concepts lead.

I should like to justify my opening statement. The most important benefit from such a cultural familiarity is the introduction which the principles of physics constitute to the philosophical revolution which is gradually permeating our culture —to a new pattern of thought which rephrases man's relationship with the universe around him. A second valuable consequence is the opportunity of observing the creative scientific mind at work—an adventure worth the time of anyone interested in the dynamics of our contemporary society. And, lastly, an acquaintance with these principles provides a measure

37

of understanding of the procedures, the gadgetry—from synthetics and television to spaceships——and the limitations of modern scientific research.

This article is an attempt to explain the kinds of factual order which scientists have achieved in the three centuries since Galileo, the world's first experimental physicist. I will not attempt to describe the facts involved, as many of them are too technical for a discussion of this nature. I shall try to illustrate the basic principles by examples, by classifying them and by showing the relationship between the principles and the theories which incorporate them. As working theories in physics are framed in mathematical terms, this effort will involve translation and interpretation, with all their attendant hazards.

The principles and theories of physics are stated in terms of concepts. These concepts are the real heart of physics. Though some of these concepts may now seem obvious, it is well to remember that their origin often demanded a tremendous effort of creative thought. The history of physics shows that all progress is indissolubly tied to these conceptual discoveries. Without them, research flounders. With them, our knowledge expands at an explosive rate. Consider the history of the single concept of force.

Until the time of Galileo, in the latter half of the sixteenth century, force was thought to be something that maintained the motion of a body. By an act of genius, Galileo reversed this concept. Instead of asking what preserves motion and calling that force, he asked what changes motion. This something that changed the motion of a body he called true force. His concept later became the basis for Newton's dynamics and thus the foundation for all progress in physics until the early part of this century.

To appreciate the daring that Galileo's conception demanded, it should be remembered that until October 4, 1957, when the first Sputnik was put in orbit, all objects which man set in motion stopped moving almost immediately unless something was done to keep them moving. This stoppage occurs, of course, because there is always some sort of frictional force which kills motion unless it is offset by some other driving force.

Galileo's conceptual feat was to question the apparently obvious and decide that true force is not motion itself, but what changes motion.

To illustrate some of the other basic principles of physics, I will first examine two which are related—the conservation of electric charge and the conservation of energy. I will then consider three theories of light, to show how more sophisticated theories can complement simpler theories without replacing them. The related principles of indeterminacy and probability will be considered, with some observations on their dramatic effect on contemporary philosophical thought. This will be followed by an example of how one concept, called entropy, has been formulated in two different ways to give us two theories which are apparently different, but actually equivalent. Finally, I will discuss a unique principle—that of atomicity, or natural units.

The concept of conservation demands a prefatory note. It is curious that a number of physics' most important discoveries are not how to do things, but discoveries that there are some things which can't be done. These apparently negative affirmations are sometimes called principles of impotence. Two examples are (1) that it is impossible to construct a perpetual-motion machine and (2) that nothing can go faster than light.

These principles of impotence have a strong attraction for the physicist. Their appeal is partly aesthetic, for, in appearance at least, they have the grandeur of simplicity. An even greater appeal may stem from man's innate desire for security and permanence—for in most cases a principle of impotence asserts that something is unchanging, that it cannot be created or destroyed. This, in the language of physics, means that it is conserved.

CONSERVATION OF ELECTRIC CHARGE

To Benjamin Franklin, more than anyone else, physics owes the idea of the conservation of electric charge. The early experiments with electricity generated by friction were both intriguing and bewildering to the experimenters. They discovered that a glass tube that had been electrified by rubbing could pick up light objects—objects which might later be repelled by the same tube. Moreover, these effects could sometimes be transmitted a certain distance over strings or wires. The true nature of the forces causing these effects, however, eluded the early experimenters.

Franklin was the first to state clearly that rubbing the glass tube transfers something present in all bodies from one to another, so that one body acquired that part of the "something" given up by the other body. From this arose the concept of positive and negative charges of electricity, equal in quantity and opposite in charge. In essence, this implies the idea of something which is unchanging in quantity—something, that is, which is conserved. Thus, if positive electricity is created in one place, an equal, negative charge, or quantity, must occur elsewhere. This establishes a kind of double-entry system in nature's accounts; charge can be transposed, but can be neither created nor destroyed.

Franklin's concept of conservation is one of the few early principles of physics which have not had to be altered to fit the revolution of thought introduced by the relativity and the quantum theories. This principle, which explained the simplicities of what happened to the glass tube, is equally useful in accounting for the electrical complexities of nuclear physics.

Electrons and protons are atomic particles which carry a natural unit of charge. The electron is very light, with a charge that is by convention negative; the proton, 1838 times as massive as the electron, carries an equal, positive charge. Further, even when we create electrons out of space and energy, this charge is still conserved. When we make an "ordinary" electron with its negative charge, it brings with it a companion electron of positive charge. This positive electron does not last long in ordinary matter—perhaps a billionth of a second—but when it disappears it takes with it an ordinary electron with a negative charge, so that there is no net loss or gain in the matter of charge. Thus nature enforces one of the great principles of physics.

CONSERVATION OF ENERGY

Though the principle of the conservation of energy was the great creation of nineteenth-century physics, its origins can be found in an earlier century. Galileo hypothesized an experiment which proved that a marble rolling down one slope and then up another could never reach a point higher than its original elevation. Under ideal conditions, Galileo showed, however, that the marble would reach a height equal to its original elevation. This is what we now think of as conservation of energy in its simplest form. The energy of position which the marble possesses—because of its elevation—is transformed into energy of motion as it rolls down, and then back to energy of position as the marble rolls up the opposite slope.

The nineteenth-century physicists proved that there were many other forms of energy besides those of motion and position. There is, for example, electrical energy—which can be turned into a form of energy we call heat. Energy in any form observes all the requirements of the conservation principle and can, indeed, be changed to other forms of energy. When a bullet imbeds itself in a target, the heat released through the impact will be equivalent to the energy of motion of the bullet.

During the present century our concept of the conservation of energy was expanded immeasurably when Einstein postulated that mass is a form of energy. (Mass, in this context, should be thought of as a measure of inertia, which is a body's fundamental resistance to any change in its motion.) Einstein proved that a system of bodies loses mass when it loses energy and, conversely, gains mass when it gains energy. To oversimplify, this is somewhat like saying that the faster a body travels, the bigger it gets. In everyday life this effect is unobservable because of the relatively small velocities involved. In nuclear physics this principle is of great importance; by using its corollary we can tell, from the masses of atoms, what energy they can yield. Actually, a very small amount of mass corresponds to a great amount of energy—less than one twenty-eighth of an ounce of mass would produce the Hiroshima explosion.

SIR GEORGE THOMSON

THREE THEORIES OF LIGHT

Let us now consider the three theories of light, which introduce the paradox that scientific principles can be something other than either true or false. They can be true, in other words, to a degree.

The ray theory of light says that light goes in straight lines called rays. These rays, however, can be reflected by a mirror or refracted at a transparent surface such as water. The Greeks knew about the laws of reflection; the laws of refraction were established early in the seventeenth century.

The wave theory of light, conceived by Huygens of The Hague late in the seventeenth century, says that light is a wave motion in some sort of ether. This ether, at first thought to be an elastic substance which permeated all matter, later came to be considered as something which acted electromagnetically. The wave theory was placed on a firm mathematical basis early in the nineteenth century and until recently was accepted by physicists as the principle which best explained the properties of light.

During the early years of this century the extraordinary behavior of X rays and of various types of radiation from hot solid bodies forced on physicists a new set of ideas called the quantum theory. The quantum theory supposes that the action of one body on another occurs, not smoothly and uniformly, but by discontinuous steps. Light is emitted and absorbed in discrete packets—the energy of each packet being determined by the wave length, or color, of the light. In considering the properties of light the quantum theory combines this new concept with elements of the ray and the wave concepts and certain revolutionary assumptions of quantum mechanics which introduce the element of indeterminacy into man's conception of the universe.

It would be logical to suppose that the ray theory would have been replaced by the more accurate wave theory, and this, in turn, by the more sophisticated quantum theory. Such, however, has not been the case. Not only has the ray theory survived in teaching; it has continued to be the basis for the design of most optical instruments. Although rays and waves are different conceptions, they lead, in most cases, to the same practical results, and the ray theory is easier to handle mathematically by the man who wants, for example, to design a new camera lens. When necessary, the wave theory can be employed to correct a design made through use of the ray theory. The quantum theory of light, in turn, is used in relatively few optical problems—one case being the design of photoelectric cells. In designing the shapes of lenses and mirrors, the quantum theory gives the same results as the wave theory.

The interesting point here is that we have three theories of light, each with a different conceptional basis. Each theory gives us a different explanation of light. Yet, in a sense, all these theories are valid, and all continue to be used. The reason for this seemingly unnecessary triplication is that the theories form a group of progressively improving accuracy but diminishing convenience. The less sophisticated theories survive because of their convenience.

Does this mean that physicists are insincere in their pursuit of truth and prefer convenience to accuracy? This may sometimes be true, but the moral implication is unjust. No existing theory in physics is completely true in the sense that it can correctly answer every possible question relating to its content. When nothing is completely accurate, it seems legitimate to weigh degrees of accuracy against degrees of convenience.

INDETERMINACY

Some thirty years ago a German physicist, Werner Heisenberg, discovered a principle of impotence of a new type. Instead of saying what one cannot *do*, the principle of indeterminacy states what one cannot *know*. This principle derives from the fact that physics deals with observations and that the act of observation may alter what is observed.

In many cases, particularly where the objects under scrutiny are large, this observational effect can be unimportant. An example of this situation is Newton's theory of gravitation, which predicted how the planets would move around the sun. It was not necessary to consider the effect of the observer upon this phenomenon; light, the medium for observation, does exert force, but the force of sunlight on a planet is negligible compared with the force of gravitation.

We face a different situation with atoms and their particles, such as electrons. In this case the "push" given by light is all-important. The argument here involves two stages. The first is that we cannot see the electron unless it gets a push corresponding to at least one quantum of light. One quantum is the smallest measure of light that can produce an effect, and if the light does not affect the electron, the electron will not affect the light and will remain invisible.

Though one quantum of light is enough to disturb an electron, it gives us but a limited amount of information. We would like to know, for example, whether electrons in an atom are moving or at rest. This demands that we observe an electron at successive moments—to see if it has moved. But if the quantum of light used in the first observation disturbs the electron, how can we tell whether the change of position seen in the next observation is the result of natural motion or the result of the push by the light which enabled us to make the first observation?

To answer this question we must allow for the push of the first quantum of light. In order to do this we obviously must know the force and direction of that initial push. This introduces the second stage of the argument; the quantum theory says the push is random—so you can never allow for it.

From this reasoning it is apparent that the motion of electrons—and this is just one example of the application of the principle of indeterminacy—is essentially unknowable. The problem here is not one of perfecting the design of microscopes. The impossibility of knowing, in this case, is inherent in the nature of light.

The perceptive reader will have recognized that Heisenberg's indeterminacy principle introduces a revolutionary philosophical concept which affects the corpus of western culture. Newton's world, which provided the intellectual climate for the growth of the natural sciences until the beginning of this century, was an ordered world of cause and effect, of strict determinism. Every sparrow's fall was ordained; the limits of knowing lay within man himself. It was this rocky, mechanistic barrier of logic that gradually alienated man's spiritual and intellectual compulsions. Indeterminacy, in implementing the quantum theory, has now introduced the element of chance, of potentiality, of the unknowable, into the most precise of man's investigations of the universe. The results of this change in our thinking are unforeseeable.

PROBABILITY AND ENTROPY

The impossibility of complete knowledge is closely related to the probability element which occurs in some of the physical laws that depend upon the quantum theory. As with the profits of Monte Carlo and the actuarial statistics of insurance companies, probability turns into a virtual certainty when enough independent events are considered. In nuclear physics, since the quanta of action are small, all actions concerned with more than a few atoms involve large numbers of quanta. Despite this, the element of probability must always be considered. No prediction is quite certain—it is only probable in some degree. The probability element also plays a part in other branches of physics. One of these is the kinetic, or motion, theory of gases. Gas is composed of molecules—each, in turn, composed of a few atoms—which move about in the space occupied by the gas, colliding with one another and with the walls of the containing vessel. Normally these molecules travel many times their length between collisions. The collisions exert force on the walls of the containing vessel. This force is the pressure of the gas.

Though the kinetic theory of gases explains many of the properties of gases under various conditions, it has one special characteristic which bears upon our consideration of probability. It is a theory of chaos—the probability of chaos, if you like. The measure of this probability is a quantity called entropy. The kinetic theory assumes that the molecules move at random in the sense that any particular molecule is just as likely to be going one way as another and is just as likely to be in any

45

particular region of the containing vessel as in any other of equal size.

What is odd is that precisely this assumption of chaos, as measured in terms of entropy, leads to exact mathematical conclusions concerning the pressure of the gas on the walls of the containing vessel and the proportion of the molecules having different speeds. (The kinetic theory also assumes that the conservation of energy is obeyed in the molecular collisions.) The average kinetic energy of the molecules turns out to be proportional to the temperature of the gas. The ideal chaos, if one may use such a phrase, is the most probable state of the gas. After the molecules in the gas have made a few collisions— actually, they will make many billions a second—they will have lost all "memory" of their former state, even if it happened to be an ordered one.

The process I have just described may be compared to shuffling a deck of cards. If the cards are initially arranged in suits they will soon cease to be so, but if they are in a random distribution it is extremely unlikely that the shuffling will sort them into suits. There would, however, be nothing contrary to nature in such an event. Perhaps, in the history of cards, such an orderly rearrangement of the fifty-two cards has occurred a few times. In even a small quantity of gas, on the other hand, there are millions of millions of molecules to be sorted, and the probabilities become even more overwhelming. The chance of any measurable quantity of gas departing for long from a random state is wholly negligible. The behavior of gas is thus governed by its strong tendency to take up the most probable, which means the most random, arrangement. The measure of this probability is the entropy of the gas.

Considerations of probability and entropy in the arrangement of the molecules of gas turn out to be closely related to similar concepts derived, by different methods, from the study of steam engines.

Heat is a form of energy, but while the energy produced by a steam engine can be wholly converted into heat—through the friction of a brake, for example—the heat supplied to the engine cannot be wholly converted into energy. Even in an "ideal" engine, with no friction, only a definite fraction of the heat given to the steam in the boiler can be transformed into usable mechanical energy. This fraction, which measures the efficiency of the "ideal" engine, depends solely upon a pair of temperatures—the temperature of the boiler and the temperature at which the steam is either condensed or rejected into the surrounding air.

The governing principle here is Rudolf Clausius' second law of thermodynamics, which states that heat of itself cannot pass from a colder to a hotter body. From this principle, combined with the conservation of energy, one can prove by pure logic that the efficiency of the engine is never 100 per cent and calculate what it will be for any particular pair of temperatures.

From Clausius' principle another approach to entropy was established. For it is possible to prove that when heat is transferred from one body of a system to another, the entropy of the system increases. Thus, when the hot, fast molecules at one end of a steam-filled tube exchange position and energy with the slow, cold ones at the other end—as they would—we find that the entropy of the steam increases. This is equivalent to saying that the state of the molecules becomes a more probable, more random one.

Thus from two different approaches—from the kinetic theory of gases and from thermodynamic theory—we have evolved a reasonable understanding of probability and the quantitative uses of the measure we call entropy. Interestingly, while entropy is a hypothesized quantity, it is very useful in the mathematics of physics, for we know that when entropy increases, the available energy of a system decreases. What may appear to be pure theory has many practical applications—considerations of probability and entropy bear strongly, for example, on the present attempt to make energy by nuclear reactions in heavy hydrogen gas.

NATURAL UNITS

We have seen that physical theories are, basically, ways of calculating facts of experience and putting these facts in or-

47

der so that one can predict what will happen in the future and design devices to bring about the effect one wants. Some physical theories transcend this function in that they have the power to suggest new discoveries. These fruitful concepts seem to come to life and to apply more widely than anticipated, in the way that characters of a novel sometimes take charge and insist on behaving quite differently than the novelist intended.

An outstanding example of this evolutionary process is the theory of atoms. As late as the end of last century the purists in the philosophy of science maintained that the concept of atoms was an unjustifiable one. Following a tradition as old as the ancient Greeks, atoms were reinvented by John Dalton in 1803 to account for the laws that express the proportions by weight in which elements combine to form chemical compounds. The purists, who took the view that nothing not directly observed should enter a scientific theory, maintained that since all that was observed was proportion by weight, only these proportional weights—called "combining weights"— should be considered, to the exclusion of atoms.

Fortunately, the more experimentally minded physicists continued to think of atoms. They found that the "atoms," contrary to the Greek view, had parts—electrons, protons and neutrons. Atoms are now as real to the physicist as grains of wheat to the farmer. He knows their arrangement in many thousands of substances; in many experiments they can be counted individually, and their paths, when they go fast enough, can be traced on photographic plates and in gases. It has recently become possible actually to see in an electron microscope the rows in which atoms are arranged in crystals.

The existence of natural units, of which atoms are one example, seems to be the most fundamental of all physical discoveries. At the basis of physics are electrons, protons, neutrons and quanta, not to speak of the strange particles which Oppenheimer discussed in an earlier article of this series ("The Mystery of Matter," by J. Robert Oppenheimer, ADVENTURES OF THE MIND, The Saturday Evening Post, July 5, 1958). All these are units by nature. One cannot have two and one third electrons! Further, they build patterns which them-

48

selves have unitary properties. For instance, six protons and six neutrons form the nucleus of carbon, which gathers to itself six electrons to form a normal carbon atom. More rarely there are seven or even eight neutrons instead of six to form a carbon isotope, but never six and a half.

Carbon atoms, with those of hydrogen, oxygen and nitrogen, are the units that build up a vast variety of molecules. Though various, these molecules are chemical entities which can be separated out and purified. Here we have two stages of patterns based on integers, for each molecule consists of integral numbers of the various kinds of atoms which compose it—just as each atom consists of integral units of its particles.

Carrying this classification a step further, we can envision the cell as a unit or organic structure which parallels the unit atoms and the unit molecules of which it is composed. In their turn, cells form individual organisms, or parts of organisms, such as the leaves of a tree. There are a vast number of almost identical leaves on an oak tree, each composed of a vast number of cells, and the oak tree itself will be one of a species containing a vast number of individuals.

This principle of unit numbers, or atomicity, is different in kind from the principles of impotence we have considered. For one thing, it seems more fundamental to the nature of matter. It links in a common frame the billions of nebulae, each with their billions of stars, with the electrons and the atoms, with the cells of our bodies and with the individuals of our own and other species of living creatures. It recalls the saying of the mathematician, Leopold Kronecker, "God made the integers and man made all the rest."

The universe thus seems to be a place where a vast number of a few kinds of units form patterns based on whole numbers. These patterns change from time to time, on a scale which ranges from the minute to the cosmic. These changes are the events which the physicist tries to predict. When the scale is small, he can only assign probabilities of action. On a larger scale, when many units are concerned, these probabilities become virtual certainties by the operation of the statistics of larger numbers. Even in such cases, however, we are dealing

49

in principle only with the highly probable. The rigid determinism to which all physical happenings were once held accountable is no longer tenable. In its place there now stand the shadow of probability and the shade of what is perhaps never to be known. But, as the nineteenth-century physicist, James Clerk Maxwell, observed, "It is a universal condition of the enjoyable that the mind must believe in the existence of a law and yet have a mystery to move in."

Bachman, C. H.: PHYSICS, A DESCRIPTIVE INTERPRETATION.
New York: John Wiley & Sons, Inc.; 1955.
Blackwood, O. H. and others: OUTLINES OF ATOMIC PHYSICS.
New York: John Wiley & Sons, Inc.; 1955.
Bohr, Niels: ATOMIC PHYSICS AND HUMAN KNOWLEDGE. New
York: John Wiley & Sons, Inc.; 1958.
Peierls, R. E.: THE LAWS OF NATURE. New York: Charles
Scribner's Sons; 1956.
Heisenberg, Werner: PHYSICS AND PHILOSOPHY. New York:
Harper & Brothers; 1958.

WILLIAM SNAITH

[*Photograph by Arnold Newman*]

In an age of specialization William T. Snaith of Weston, Connecticut, is an anachronism—a universal man. His activities as president of Raymond Loewy–William Snaith, Inc., industrial designers, scarcely begin to absorb his creative energies. A prolific painter, he has exhibited in three New York galleries and the Whitney Museum's annual show. Yachtsman and owner of Figaro III, *he won first place, Class C, in the 1956 Bermuda Race and second place, Class B, the following year in the transatlantic Newport-Santander Race. He is an architect, scenic designer, university lecturer (Yale, Cornell, Penn State), musicologist, madrigal singer, chess player, and the father of three sons by the former Elizabeth Colman, an alumna of the Jooss Ballet school. In addition, the versatile Mr. Snaith is currently writing an opera libretto based on the* Oresteia *of Aeschylus.*

The Anguish
of Modern Art

B Y

WILLIAM SNAITH

I t is deplorable that the cult of worship which surrounds so much of modern art demands total dedication. Even to raise questions involving the conflict between rationality and emotion, communication and technique, is regarded by the hierophants as heresy. Challenges to authority generate a heat as intense as that of the discussions among certain learned medieval monks as to the sex of angels. In such a highly charged atmosphere the search for truth and objectivity is inhibited, especially when the high priests of modern art defend their cult with metaphysics as obscure as a lot of modern painting.

Yet it should be possible to say that modern man is being cut off from one of his spiritual sanctuaries by the relentless evolutionary process of modern art, and still maintain the conviction that art has a valid purpose in our culture.

At present, I believe, art has turned away from its historic role as a communicator of beauty and human emotion that can reach and move most men. It now addresses itself to an elite; it is a Coney Island mirror of an alienated society. But despite his loss of universality the artist has gained an awesome technical and intellectual power, which may yet produce a new age of aesthetic communication. Meanwhile, we are living in the long night of torment of that creation. We must try to look at modern painting with objectivity as well as love. We must reject both cant and the principle of stability desirable in other areas of our society.

It would be tragic if art, that godlike language by which man has been able to transmit to man truth and beauty, should become a mystic ritual open to only a chosen few. In our Organization Society, with its technological estrangements, we find it increasingly difficult to turn to art for consolation and reassurance. We find instead that a great deal of contemporary art is incomprehensible and forbidding. The personal interpretation of nature, as in the recent past, is being replaced by a private set of ideographs, a kind of calligraphy, to which the ordinary man has no key. Communion with and enjoyment of the art of his time are being denied to him; art is becoming an instrument of alienation.

The late Spanish philosopher Ortega y Gasset wrote: "If a man dislikes a work of art but understands it, he feels superior. If, on the other hand, he dislikes a work of art but does not understand it, he is humiliated and angry. Through an act of incomprehensibility the work of art has compelled the average citizen to realize that he is incapable of receiving the sacrament of art and is blind and deaf to pure beauty. The mass of man, accustomed to ruling supreme, feels that an art for the privileged aristocracy of the finer senses endangers their rights as men."

The modern artist, driven by a search for individuality in a mass society, has revolted with such violence that he is in danger of losing contact altogether with that society. To achieve self-expression, as every artist must, he contrives a set of rules rooted in technique and couched in a private language. Obviously, every work of art involves technique. But what we now see emerging is a pattern of creative motivation derived from the technological rather than the communicative characteristics of art. Communication requires a subjective effort on the part of the beholder. But art has become an aesthetic Rorschach experience.

To a degree all the arts reflect a shift in motivation and emphasis. In an earlier period of music, for example, the composer was paramount. His communicative power was the fulcrum of musical enjoyment. The musical heroes were Bach, Beethoven, Mozart, Brahms. Later came the era of the virtuoso, with interpretation the high point of musical experience. From content the emphasis had shifted to performance. Connoisseurs traded memories of Elman, Heifetz, Hofmann and Toscanini.

Though the supremacy of interpretation has not yet declined, a new set of values is arising—the electronic transmissions of sound. Countless thousands huddle over the oscilloscopes of their hi-fi sets, or listen intently to the balance of stereo sound flowing from their twin batteries of tweeters and woofers. Inexorably technique pervades and alters every realm of the spirit.

The problem of communication is, of course, the timeless problem of art. The poet Horace advised the artist, "If you want me to weep, you must first grieve." Horace touched the essence of communication. It is self-evident that to evoke response to his grief or joy or anger, the artist must convey his emotion in an understandable language. That language may be complex and varied; understanding may require an experience shared with the artist, or a subconscious identification. But whatever the mode of expression, it cannot be isolated from the past. Art, like literature and music, reflects changing mores, subject matter and techniques. Each generation, in its need to establish itself as the ultimate flowering of civilization, may attempt to bury the immediate past. But the past is a restless ghost. History is not discontinuous; the frontiers of change remain blurred.

Thus, no stage of aesthetic development occurs in a vacuum. A painter cannot approach his canvas as though nothing had gone before, and accept a new doctrine without consciousness of the old. The past insistently intrudes upon the present, offering a standard of comparison to the observer and a challenge to the artist.

The drive for self-expression has been central and continuous throughout the history of art. We see it, despite the rigid formalism, in the Egyptian wall paintings, with their exacting laws of proportion and composition. We see it in the swirling arabesques of the baroque. And we see it in the intellectualized painting of today. The artist's basic drive remains constant; only the emphasis changes, and it is the contemporary phase of this change which imperils communication.

Among the major means of communication through painting have been what we may call naturalism, formalism and symbolism. Naturalism, the most direct means, embraces all those representative paintings of recognizable objects—trees, clouds, the beauty of women, ships and shoes and sealing wax —which provide the onlooker with instantaneous recognition and conscious experience. These are the simple mechanics of naturalism. More importantly, however, in this kind of painting the artist communicates his individual vision of nature. Sometimes our visible world is remade in his vision. It is difficult to look up a narrow Paris street toward the dome of Sacré Coeur, without subconsciously composing it as Utrillo did. There is a delightful story of Whistler and his passion for painting the Thames. At a gallery a woman came up to Whistler and said that she had come to the show on a bus along the Thames. "It was a whole series of Whistler paintings!" She exclaimed. "Yes, madame," Whistler replied, "nature is creeping up."

Formalism, in simplified terms, is a visual narrative method by which the artist conveys an image of something perhaps never seen, but which strikes chords of response in man's heritage of history, allegory, literature. The quality of the response to this kind of painting depends upon the knowledge and experience of the perceiver. In one who feels intensely about the Crucifixion, a painting of the Crucifixion which parallels or increases his emotion has enormous communicative impact.

A third major element of communication calls into play a symbolical or intuitive range of perception. Here comprehension requires identification of a symbol, such as the dove representing the Holy Ghost, or a halo indicating saintliness.

Symbolic painting also includes that area of human understanding in which the symbols stimulate an analogous though

HENRI MATISSE: *Piano Lesson*. 1916
MUSEUM OF MODERN ART, NEW YORK
MRS. SIMON GUGGENHEIM FUND

VASILY KANDINSKY: *Composition* (3). 1914
MUSEUM OF MODERN ART, NEW YORK
MRS. SIMON GUGGENHEIM FUND

EDVARD MUNCH: *Jealousy.* 1896
MUSEUM OF MODERN ART, NEW YORK

not directly recognizable experience. The sensual, emotional and intellectual capacities combine to evoke a subjective response through association, color or form. Such a response stems either from a primitive, instinctive surrender to the emotion inherent in the symbol, or from an extreme of sensibility to or knowledge of the implications of the symbols and how the artist has used them.

Although the elements of communication should be subdivided for accurate definition, during the last fifty years the mainstream of artistic creativity has been concentrated in symbolism. The modern artist, oppressed on the one hand by the weight of a magnificent tradition and on the other by the unnerving representational precision of a new technology—photography, gradually retreated into symbolism as an unchallengeable area of expression, and there developed an intensely personal iconography.

The great change in the kind of emotion and thought to be communicated began with the liberation from the idea that art was a mirror of nature or even an aesthetic comment upon it. The freedom thus gained gave rise to a yeasty period of exploration in theory, form and technique. In this revolutionary atmosphere two important movements arose, one in France, the other in Germany. While both broke incisively with the past, they took quite separate directions.

In France Cézanne, Seurat, Matisse, Van Gogh and Gauguin, among many others, explored a multiplicity of new methods and theories. There was no cohesive school. The artists were rampantly individual. While the period was pervaded by strong, bright colors, many painters used shadowy coloration. Ambroise Vollard, the art historian, tells of a man who sought to punish his wife, presumably for infidelity, by making her look at a Cézanne nude as proof of the inherent repulsiveness of the flesh. A phlegmatic Englishman, confronted by a particularly tenebrous painting by Rouault hanging among the brighter examples of his contemporaries, lighted a match, peered at the picture, blew out the match and murmured, "Good night."

Despite their rejection of traditional representation, the artists of the period actually heightened and intensified communication by their liberated treatment of color, form and selection of detail. The French painters, however, concerned themselves with aesthetic rather than human problems, a trend which persists in modern French painting today.

In Germany, the new spirit was manifested by a group called the Blue Riders, after a painting by Vasily Kandinsky, one of its leaders. From this group evolved a movement known as Die Brücke (the bridge), which influenced most of the important pre-World War I German and Scandinavian painters. With their search for a new form of artistic expression they reflected a deep concern for human problems. They denounced man's reliance on a technological civilization as spiritually lazy and self-indulgent. About 1910 German modern painting began to be called expressionism. Again, unlike the later developments

FERNAND LÉGER. *Three Musicians*. 1944
MUSEUM OF MODERN ART, NEW YORK
MRS. SIMON GUGGENHEIM FUND

PIET MONDRIAN: *Composition in White, Black, and Red.* 1936
MUSEUM OF MODERN ART, NEW YORK
GIFT OF ADVISORY COMMITTEE

in French painting, German expressionism grappled with human rather than aesthetic problems. Its goals were concisely defined by the Norwegian, Edvard Munch, who wrote, "I want to show men who breathe, feel, love and suffer." In his own work Munch observed this credo with embarrassing candor. There is the portrait of his friend, the writer Przybyszewski, for example, entitled *Jealousy*. The writer, painted a bilious green, glares out of the foreground. Behind him his wife, quite naked, painted in red, stands beside her lover, clad in black. Munch and the playwright Strindberg, we now know, both loved Przybyszewski's wife. Strindberg won her favor. The painting is Munch's cry of anguish.

The French artists, meanwhile, concentrated more and more on technical problems. Though they acknowledged the importance of human emotions in art, they at first stressed their individual aesthetic emotions. Eventually they concluded that aesthetics should not be involved with emotion at all, but motivated and disciplined by pure intellectuality. At this point art proliferated into cubism and numerous other theoretical deviations—all of them intellectual explorations.

Cubism, the most radical break with the past, had its roots in Cézanne's last explorations into the geometry of nature. There was no single kind of cubism, but there was one paramount rule underlying all kinds: a picture was to be constructed with known elements of reality, though without sensual or psychological expression; communication was to be achieved solely by the play of pane, color and line.

The founders of cubism were Pablo Picasso and Georges Braque. These two, while employing somewhat similar means, brought to the art quite dissimilar personalities and purposes. Picasso approached his problems with a vibrant truculence. It was his avowed purpose to destroy what had gone before and start afresh. Two statements of his are revealing. As an illustration of his affirmative intuition, he said, "I do not seek, I find." Asked to explain his painting, he replied, "Do you ask a bird to explain its song?"

Braque was a more lyrical, sensitive artist, seeking to build up from the past. Yet he said, "I like the rule, the discipline, which controls and corrects emotion." It was almost a definition of the motivation of cubism. Again, "The subject is not the object of painting, but a new unity, the lyricism that results from method."

In terms of communication cubist pictures consisted of dimly recognizable subject matter arranged in planes that preserved the validity of the two-dimensional surface while obeying a restriction later set down by Jean Cocteau, "A picture is not a window."

Gradually, with freedom of expression, all recognition of the object was abandoned. New schools sprang up on all sides. In Italy, futurism; in Switzerland and New York, Dada; in Holland, *De Stijl* (The Style). This last was the most coldly intellectual of them all. To Piet Mondrian, one of its leading exponents, external reality and chance disturbed the "true reality." He reduced form to areas delimited by right angles made up of verticals and horizontals, and reduced his paints to white, black, red, yellow and blue. Mondrian's art has left an indelible imprint on modern architecture.

But under the stylistic restraints imposed by such cold intellectuality, artists grew restless. Their need for self-expression drove them to seek something more personal, and within their own psyche they discovered a new wellspring of vitality. Painting became the product of liberated personality. Its source was the artist's inner being.

Now the floodgates stood wide open, and there poured forth a torrent of personal expression, much of it originating at a psychological level. Significant in this era was the work of the surrealists, Salvador Dali, Yves Tanguy, and Max Ernst. With impeccable technique they portrayed a vision of a subconscious world which impressed some people by its power, but left the bulk of mankind wondering if it was art or nightmare. Painting has since diverged from this direct exploration of the artist's neuroses, but to a great degree it is still motivated by the artist's inner self rather than by the problems of humanity.

Communication, then, is no longer the primary interest of the modern artist. What he strives for is to induce a subjective response in the onlooker. Yet this loss of communication does

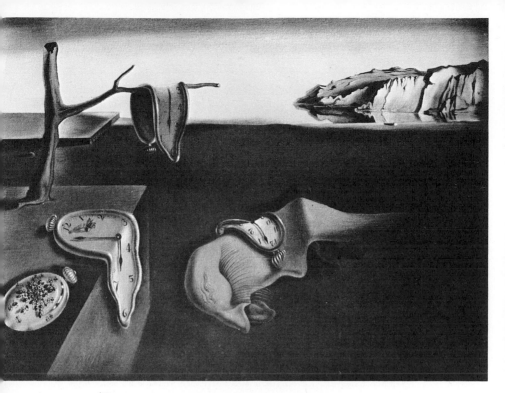

SALVADOR DALI: *The Persistence of Memory.* 1931
MUSEUM OF MODERN ART, NEW YORK

not arise primarily from the technical complexities of the new aesthetic. In the relatively rare instances when the modern artist desires to communicate, a strange aesthetic imposes no unscalable barrier to understanding and feeling. Rather, by identification with a human emotion, he effects a heightened response. A masterly example is the large oil painting by Picasso titled *Guernica*. Painted in 1937 for the Spanish Loyalist Government as an exhibit in its pavilion at the Paris World's Fair, it combines contemporary aesthetics with political comment. Picasso was emotionally committed to the Loyalist cause. The painting is his reaction to the bombing of the small town of Guernica by German planes flying for Franco. Yet the painting is in no sense reportorial.

The multiplicity of stations for the eye in its perspective, or rather lack of perspective, eliminates the sensation of reality. The distortion of familiar objects, the unexpected use of symbols such as a light bulb and a bull, does not facilitate communication. But it is this very distortion, in the dying horse, the screaming mother, the dead child, that heightens the sense of agony, the horror of sudden death from the sky. In the extreme delineation of muscular and emotional tension, conveyed by deliberate dehumanization of the mother, we can almost hear her screams.

To many, this picture communicates more emotion about Guernica than all the words and photographs ever published, such is the artist's great compassion and dreadful anger. To be sure, the picture does not communicate emotion to everybody in the same degree, but it powerfully affects a large number of people. That many can be made to feel intense emotion through an aesthetic medium indicates that artist and layman can again be brought together in common humanity.

Another modern painter able to communicate within the framework of the new aesthetic was the late Paul Klee. In a mood quite apart from the thunder of Picasso, gentle, poetic, almost childlike, he infused his canvases with a sense of magic and wonder.

In his *Twittering Machine*, he depicted a preposterous contraption, consisting of spidery lines in a seemingly logical mechanical order. From one side projects a crank, a birdlike device perches on the top, and we know at once that when the crank turns, the whole foolish machine will come joyously to life, and the bird will twitter away. Indeed, the spidery delicacy of the drawing seems to be atwitter already. We begin to hear it.

I have chosen these two examples because, though diverse in style and subject, both evoke a universal human response. Despite strangeness of language and symbol, they move us. As long as the artist strives for communication, he has the right to demand that we try to understand him. For art is a language, expressing feelings impossible to express in any other way, and language is a communication by mutually understood symbols. While one may respond to a painting without being able to explain the response, if these symbols become too remote, the language places an excessive burden on the auditor, and may

PABLO PICASSO: *Guernica.* 1937
MUSEUM OF MODERN ART, NEW YORK
ON LOAN FROM THE ARTIST

lead him to a subjective re-creation distinct from the original intent.

The dilemma is not readily resolved. It is an age-old artistic problem. Its chief source arises from the artist's need to express individuality. Today he no longer subscribes to Da Vinci's doctrine: "A good painter is to paint two main things, namely man and the working of man's mind."

In his search for self-identity the artist has ranged far from an exclusive concern with man. His ever-present imperative has been the search for personal style. Nothing is as tyrannical as a reigning style. It is a juggernaut destroying everything in its path. It brushes aside former styles which were equally imperative. This is not a new phenomenon. It is difficult to remember that a public eager for the new deserted Cimabue for Giotto. A reigning style gains great support from those who fearfully withhold criticism because they remember the fate of the critics who scoffed at Cézanne and the impressionists.

The drive for originality is inherent in the search for style. The German painter Arnold Böcklin said: "True art consists of nothing more than an eternal fight against the existing." Inevitably, in the assessment of a man's work, originality receives higher praise than any other aspect. Art is hunted by its originators. To the ordinary man the trail blazers remain a source of personal inspiration. But to the artist, with his creative ego drives, they are a challenge to blaze new trails.

Originality as a value cannot be underestimated. Without it there would be a conformity so stultifying as to strangle art to death. But the drive for originality creates problems in communication. When the artist wholly disassociates himself from the past, he leaves man bereft of any consciousness of his artistic heritage. Amid the profusion of modern art, too many painters bid for attention by piling sensation on sensation. Excessive value is placed on surface characteristics, on sheer technique. Stridency and cleverness increase to the detriment of potential beauty, serenity and profundity.

The ordinary man, confronted with so much originality, feels bewildered and excluded. He is struggling hard as it is for comprehension and control over the daily pressures of life. Art's

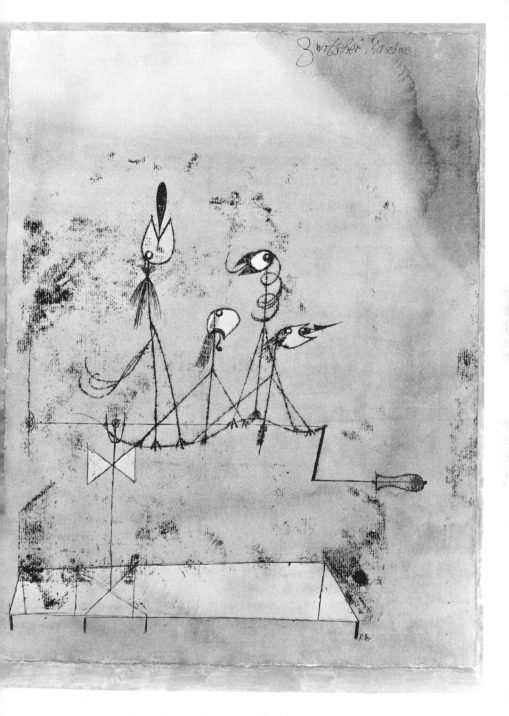

PAUL KLEE: *Twittering Machine.* 1922
MUSEUM OF MODERN ART, NEW YORK

self-conscious obscurity further frustrates his craving for stability. Here, then, is a tragic polarization—the artist passionately striving to express himself in a strange tongue, the average man unable, if not unwilling, to understand him.

We have witnessed a violent exchange between the supporters and detractors of the canvases chosen to represent American art in the United States pavilion at the Brussels Fair. These entries were chosen from the school of abstract expressionism, originally an American phenomenon, typified by the late Jackson Pollock, Willem DeKooning, Franz Kline and Robert Motherwell. The painters of this school describe their work as an act of self-discovery. Their method closely approximates automatism. Though recognition is totally absent, considerable visual impact is achieved through bold form, strong color contrast and a rugose, tactile quality. Strong and violent, the effect offers limitless scope for subjective response.

At least two of the painters, Pollock and Kline, developed highly personal, easily identifiable styles. Pollock constructed his paintings from a semicontrolled fall of paint, dripping and throwing it on the canvas with a physical vigor quite evident in the final result.

Kline creates an impenetrable ideography by slashing at huge white canvases with crude black strokes. This simplified organization in these big areas produces a feeling of great strength. The size of the canvas is in itself important, because the simple idea gains power by enlargement. The effect is inescapable. The sheer violence compels subconscious response. But it communicates nothing whatever of humanity. Undeniably original, forceful and spontaneous to the point of improvisation, it remains incomprehensible to all but a small audience. It is a private art. Moreover, no sooner stated than it has been stated once for all. To keep repeating it, as the abstract expressionists do, must be an act of considerable will, since each time they must re-energize the spontaneity.

In his recent book, *Conversations with Artists*, Selden Rodman quotes Adolph Gottlieb, an abstract expressionist, as follows: ". . . the abstract expressionist says to the public, 'You're stupid. We despise you. We don't want you to like us—or our

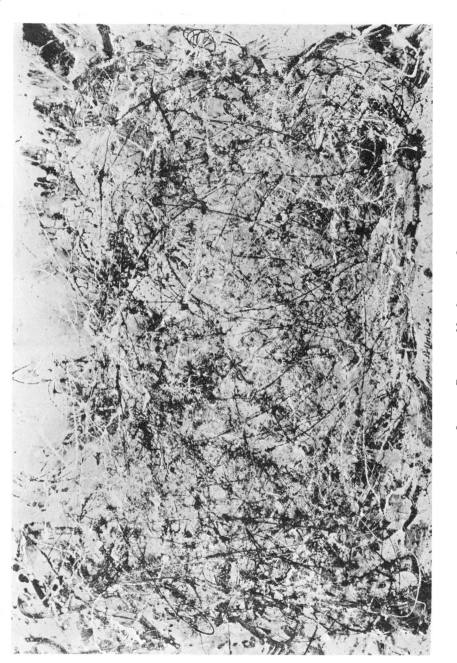

JACKSON POLLOCK: *Number 1*. 1948
MUSEUM OF MODERN ART, NEW YORK

art.'" And again, "'I'd like more status than I have now, but not at the cost of closing the gap between artist and public. I'd like to widen it!'" It is probably unfair to tar all abstract expressionists with Mr. Gottlieb's brush. Nevertheless, his remarks reflect the withdrawal of many a contemporary artist.

At the same time such capacity of the new aesthetic to evoke response, however indefinable, cannot be dismissed. It holds the promise that if artists re-establish communication, they will have the means to do so with an energy and directness never before possible. For the moment the prevailing isms seem to record a private anguish—the travail of artists trying to rid themselves of everything they know in the attempt to find a new beginning.

Unfortunately the economics of art hamper the serious artist so seeking. Cults arise whenever a painter seems to have achieved some daring new position. It may be merely a transitory stage en route to real discovery, but the museums and private collectors clamor for a picture just like the one which created the stir in the first place, thereby freezing the artist in the middle of his quest. To free himself from this kind of acceptance takes enormous will and profound conviction, to say nothing of a sustaining vision of the future.

As for the ordinary onlooker who sincerely wants to understand, it is difficult to view this torment in paint dispassionately. He must be very wise indeed not to take a more or less fixed position. But by taking an inflexible position, by rejecting all but one kind of understanding, he lends support to what is essentially arbitrary and antiartistic.

With his infinite variety of experience, man cannot be limited to a single standard of understanding. Bias in favor of one language should not be allowed to impose judgment upon another. But perhaps art, after all, has run its course as the universal communicator, and is to remain a ritual practiced by the few. Perhaps another medium will replace it as man's solace and inspiration. I cannot believe it. I do not want to believe it.

If painting is once more to speak to and for mankind, the desire for communication must be re-established. Somehow a measure of comprehension must be added to today's total reliance on subjective emotional response.

The highest order of artistic experience is participation in the creation of art. Since this lies beyond the capacities of most men, the next highest experience is that which comes from understanding the origins, rationale and emotions of creation. Without that understanding, experience belongs to the artist alone in his study. It is my hope and my faith that we have not lost forever the sublime joy of what Bernard Berenson describes as "that flitting instant so brief as to be almost timeless when the spectator is at one with the art."

Further reading:

Baudelaire, Charles: THE MIRROR OF ART. New York: Doubleday & Company, Inc., Anchor Books; 1956.

Berenson, Bernard: AESTHETICS AND HISTORY. New York: Doubleday & Company, Inc., Anchor Books; 1954.

Fry, Roger: VISION AND DESIGN. New York: Meridian Books, Inc.; 1956.

Ortega y Gasset, José: THE DEHUMANIZATION OF ART. New York: Doubleday & Company, Inc., Anchor Books; 1956.

Read, Herbert: THE PHILOSOPHY OF MODERN ART. New York: Meridian Books, Inc.; 1955.

Panofsky, Erwin: MEANING IN THE VISUAL ARTS. New York: Doubleday & Company, Inc., Anchor Books; 1955.

Rodman, Selden: CONVERSATIONS WITH ARTISTS. New York: The Devin-Adair Co.; 1957.

MORRIS KLINE

[*Photograph by Jacob Lofman*]

Dr. Morris Kline, author, scientist and professor of mathematics, is director of the Division of Electromagnetic Research at New York University's Institute of Mathematical Sciences. For the past ten years his chief interest has been the relationship of geometrical optics to electromagnetic theory. Among his patents is a radio meteorological telemetering system which transmits weather information from a balloon to an automatic ground-tracking station. It is currently in use by the Armed Forces. Doctor Kline once built his own radio sets, a diversion he's abandoned because "electronics is getting too complicated for me."

The Meaning
of Mathematics

B Y

MORRIS KLINE

Mathematics is undoubtedly one of man's greatest intellectual achievements. In addition to the knowledge which the subject itself offers, its language, processes and theories give science its organization and power. Mathematical calculations dictate engineering design. The method of mathematics has inspired social and economic thought, while mathematical thinking has fashioned styles in painting, architecture and music. Even national survival depends today upon progress in mathematics. Finally, mathematics has been a major force in molding our views of the universe and of man's place and purpose in it.

The paradox of how such an abstract body of thought can give man an ever-widening and deepening grip on the physical world and work its influences on almost all phases of our culture tantalizes the nonmathematician. We propose therefore to examine the nature of mathematics and to see why the subject possesses such astonishing effectiveness.

The distinguishing feature of mathematics is its method of reasoning. By measuring the angles of a dozen or so triangles of various shapes and sizes a person would find that the sum in any one triangle is 180 degrees. He could then conclude by inductive reasoning that the sum of the angles in every triangle is 180 de-

77

grees. One can also reason by analogy. The circle plays about the same role among curves that the sphere does among surfaces. Since the circle bounds more area than any other curve with the same perimeter, a person might conclude that the sphere bounds more volume than any other surface with the same area.

Reasoning by induction and by analogy calls for recourse to observation and even experiment to obtain the facts on which to base each argument. But the senses are limited and inaccurate. Moreover, even if the facts gathered for the purposes of induction and analogy are sound, these methods do not yield unquestionable conclusions. For example, though cows eat grass and pigs are similar to cows, it does not follow that pigs eat grass.

To avoid these sources of error, the mathematician utilizes another method of reasoning. He may have the fact that $x - 3 = 7$ and wish to find the value of x. He notes that if he adds 3 to both sides of this equation he will obtain $x = 10$. May he perform this step? He knows that equals added to equals give equals. He knows also that by adding 3 to both sides of the original equation he is adding equals to equals. Hence he concludes that the step is justified. The reasoning here is deductive. As in the present case, so in all deductive reasoning the conclusion is a logically inescapable consequence of the known facts. Hence it is as indubitable as these facts.

Since deduction yields conclusions as certain as the initial facts, the application of this process to known truths produces new ones. The latter may then be used as the premises of new deductive arguments. Every conclusion so obtained may not be significant, but the end result of ten or twenty such arguments could be. If so, it is labeled a theorem. The series of deductive arguments which lead to the theorem is the proof.

Though mathematical proof is necessarily deductive, the creative process practically never is. To foresee what to prove or what chain of deductive arguments will establish a possible result, the mathematician uses observation, measurement, intuition, imagination, induction or even sheer trial and error. The process of discovery in mathematics is not confined to one pattern or method. Indeed, it is in part as inexplicable as the creative act in any art or science.

The requirement that mathematical reasoning be deductive was laid down by the Greeks. The Greek mathematicians were also philosophers and as such were concerned with truths. They saw clearly that only deductive reasoning could supply certainties. By recommending mental exploration of the riches contained in some available truths, a most reasonable people carved out a new intellectual world and made reason a vital factor in western culture.

The plan to obtain truths by deduction presupposes some initial truths. These the Greeks found in the domains of number and geometrical figures. It seemed axiomatic that equals added to equals should yield equals, that the whole is greater than its parts and that two points determine a straight line. Hence mathematics was built on the axioms of number and geometry. Mathematicians as mathematicians do not reason about forces, weights, sound, light, chemical mixtures or the goal of life.

There were other reasons for the decision to concentrate on number and geometrical figures. The triangle formed by a piece of land and the triangle formed by the earth, sun and moon at any instant are both subsumed under the abstract geometrical concept of triangle. Study of the properties of this concept would yield knowledge about these two physical triangles and about hundreds of others in one swoop. What the Greeks saw, in other words, was that number, size and shape are fundamental properties. In fact, the Greeks believed that the universe was mathematically designed, and so the phenomena of nature could be understood only in terms of number and geometry.

The third feature of mathematics is its highly symbolic language. There is, however, nothing deep or complicated about this language, for it is only a shorthand and, in fact, an easier one to learn than that employed by stenographers. Such symbols as $+$ for addition, x for an unknown quantity, and x^2 for x times x, are, of course, well known. Letters are used for several purposes, and the context usually tells us what is intended. Suppose, for example, we take a famous mathematical statement which describes the result of some experiments made by Galileo about 350 years ago: The number of feet which an object falls in any given number of seconds is 16 times the square of the number of seconds it has been falling. Symbolically this statement is written as $d = 16t^2$ wherein t stands for any number of seconds and d the corresponding distance fallen in these t seconds. Thus, if an object falls for 5 seconds, simple arithmetic shows that it has fallen 400 feet.

Why is symbolism used so extensively? Brevity, precision and comprehensibility are the three major reasons. The brevity is apparent. Precision is aided because many important words of ordinary discourse are ambiguous. The word "equal," for example, can refer to equality in size, shape, political rights, intellectual abilities or other qualities. Hence the assertion that all men are born equal is vague. As used in an expression such as $d = 16t^2$, the equals sign stands for numerical equality. The comprehensibility gained through symbolism derives largely from the fact that the mind easily carries and works with symbolic expressions, but has considerable difficulty even in carrying the equivalent verbal statement.

Our discussion of the method of proof, subject matter and language of mathematics gives some indication of its nature. It is but a step from this point to see some of the sources of the power of mathematics. Number and geometrical figures, and the relationships built on these abstractions, such as formulas, embody the essence of hundreds of physical situations. Any knowledge acquired about these abstractions is many times more potent than that acquired about any particular situation, just as any fact applicable to all men is more powerful than a fact about John Jones. A second source of strength derives from the reliability of deductive proof. Hence the conclusions derived by the Greeks are still acceptable as logical consequences of the axioms and will be a thousand years from now.

But the power of mathematics rests on still another ground. The mathematician is the professional reasoner who devotes his life to learning what has been accomplished in his subject and to extending the results by new reasoning. Moreover, all of the results obtained by one generation are passed on to the next, and this one carries on from where the preceding generation left off. Each generation adds a story to the structure.

To appreciate the full power of mathematics we must examine its role in science. In the seventeenth century, when modern science was founded and received its first great impetus, several major physical laws were obtained by induction and experimentation. Of these we shall be concerned with the second of Newton's three laws of motion and with Newton's law of gravitation. These laws involve a few, by now, common concepts—force, mass and acceleration. Newton's second law of motion states that any force applied to a mass gives it an acceleration, and the quantitative relation among the amount of force F, the amount of mass m, and the amount of acceleration a is

(1) $F = ma$.

The Newtonian law of gravitation states that any two pieces of matter in the universe exert a force of attraction or gravitational force on each other and that the quantitative expression for this force is given by the formula

(2) $F = \dfrac{G\,m\,M}{r^2}$.

In this equation F is the amount of force exerted; m is the amount of mass in one body; M is the amount of mass in the second body; r is the distance between these bodies; and G is a constant, that is, the same quantity no matter which masses are involved and whatever the distance between them.

These laws concern force, mass and acceleration, which are physical concepts, and the obtainment of relationships among such quantities is the task of the scientist. However, formulas (1) and (2), regarded in and for themselves, are merely algebraic equations relating variables, and it is legitimate to ask the mathematician whether he can draw upon his stock of theorems and processes to deduce new significant equations from (1) and (2). He can. He observes first of all that it is mathematically correct to write formula (2) in the form

(3) $F = m\left(\dfrac{G\,M}{r^2}\right)$.

He then compares (1) and (3) and observes that the two formulas have the same algebraic form. Moreover, formula (1) applies

81

to any force and so, in particular, applies to the force of gravitation. Since the quantity which multiplies m in (1) is acceleration, the quantity which multiplies m in (3) must also be acceleration. That is, the acceleration which the gravitational force F between M and m imparts to m is

$$(4) \quad a = \frac{G M}{r^2}.$$

Next let us apply this formula to a particular situation. Let M denote the mass of the earth. Equation (4) now gives the acceleration which the gravitational force of the earth imparts to any other mass, the acceleration which causes the mass to fall if released from a point above the surface of the earth. It is a fact that the earth acts as if all its mass were concentrated at the center. Then for objects near the surface of the earth the quantity r in (4) is the radius of the earth. The quantity G, as noted above, is a constant under all conditions. Hence, all quantities on the right side of (4) are constant no matter which mass m near the surface of the earth is involved. We may conclude that all bodies fall to earth with the same constant acceleration, a famous result which Galileo discovered experimentally, but which we have deduced from the second law of motion and the law of gravitation.

Now, says the mathematician, we can go a step further. If the quantities a, G and r in (4) are known, then (4) may be regarded as a simple first-degree equation in the unknown M, and M can readily be calculated. For, correct algebraic steps yield that the mass M of the earth is

$$(5) \quad M = \frac{a r^2}{G}.$$

Let us see if we do know the several quantities which appear on the right side of (5). Since the acceleration of all bodies falling to earth is the same, one could take any falling body and measure its acceleration. This quantity had been measured by Galileo and is 32 feet per second each second. The quantity G is a constant under all conditions. It can be and has been measured many times in a laboratory where the conditions are at the experimenter's convenience. Its value is 1.07 divided by 1,000,000,-

ooo. The value of the earth's radius r can be determined by a simple application of geometry and was first obtained by the Greek Eratosthenes about 250 B.C. This radius is 4000 miles or 4000 × 5280 feet. After the known numerical values are substituted for a, G, and r in (5) one finds that

(6) $M = 131 \times 10^{23}$ pounds.

(The symbol 10^{23} stands for the product 10 × 10 × 10 . . . containing 23 factors.) The mass of the earth is a staggering number, but what is more staggering is how easily one finds it.

With essentially such simple tools, Isaac Newton, his contemporaries and his immediate successors calculated the masses of the sun and the several planets, the paths of comets, the motion of the moon and the rise and fall of the tides. In particular, Newton showed that the Keplerian laws of planetary motion, which Kepler had obtained merely by induction from data, were logical consequences of the laws of motion and the law of gravitation. Thus the key laws of the heliocentric theory of planetary motion, which up to that time were unrelated to any basic physical principles, received indisputable support.

The work we have just described belongs to celestial mechanics, a field which has come to the fore again to treat the motion of satellites. It was followed by the construction of equally majestic theories for light, sound, electricity and magnetism, electromagnetic waves (which comprise the radio waves, the very existence of which was predicted mathematically); the flow of fluids and gases as applied to the design of ships and airplanes; relativity, atomic structure, molecular structure (now basic in modern chemistry); the biological science of mathematical genetics and the statistical treatment of social and medical problems. In all these domains the union of mathematics and science has been most fertile.

The contributions of a special, functional language and the deductive processes are a small part of the mathematical largess. Science seeks to obtain knowledge of the physical world, but that knowledge would be useless if unorganized. A mass of disconnected results is no more science than a collection of bricks is a house. The major results of scientific work are theories. In each of these, hundreds of results are organized in a deductive structure very much like Euclidean geometry. At the head of the structure are basic physical principles which play the role of axioms. From these axioms the various laws of any one theory are deduced. The large and overriding fact is that the entire structure of a scientific theory is held together by a series of mathematical deductions. The mortar which binds the bricks, or individual laws, one to another is mathematical deducibility. A scientific theory is, so to speak, a branch of mathematics whose axioms state quantitative relationships among physical concepts, whose structure is a series of mathematical deductions and whose theorems are mathematical affirmations about these concepts.

Mathematics plays still another role in science. The central concept in the most impressive and most successful body of science, mechanics, is the force of gravitation. This force, when exerted by the earth, pulls objects to the earth and, when exerted by the sun, keeps the planets in their paths. What is the mechanism by which the earth and the sun exert their respective attractive forces? Newton had considered this very question and, having failed to answer it, uttered his famous "I frame no hypotheses." The history of this subject is extensive, but the upshot of it is that no explanation of the action of the force of gravitation has ever been given.

What then do we know about the force of gravitation? The answer is formula (2) above. We have a quantitative law which tells us how to calculate this force and from which we can deduce how bodies will move, what paths they will take, and where they will be at particular instants of time. We have not a shred of insight into the physical nature of the force itself; it can with full justification be regarded as sheer fiction.

In the Newtonian age mathematics mounted the steed of science and took the reins in its own hands. Since the seventeenth century the physical behavior of nature has become less and less clear despite the vast expansion of the sciences, and mathematical laws have become the essence and goal of science. The mathematical conquest of science has by now proceeded so far that in our own century the late Sir James Jeans, the noted astronomer and physicist, claimed that the mathematical description of the universe *is* the ultimate reality. The pictures and models we use to assist our understanding are a step away. We go beyond the mathematical formula at our own risk.

While mathematical physics was growing to manhood, mathematics began to exert a formative influence on numerous other branches of our culture. Revival of interest in the physical world caused the Renaissance painters to abandon the unrealistic, highly symbolic style of medieval painting and to seek a veridical depiction of nature. To solve the problem of presenting on a flat surface scenes which would create the same visual impression as the three-dimensional world itself, the painters created a methematical system of perspective painting. This introduction of depth, solidity, mass and consequent realism is the key contribution to Renaissance painting.

The mathematical treatment of matter in motion engendered the now famous philosophical doctrines that every phenomenon in the universe can be reduced to matter and motion, that all matter, including man's body, follows invariable and immutable mathematical laws, that man's will is bound fast, and that thought is but a mechanical reaction to material sensations impressed on the brain through the sense organs. Inspired by the success of the mathematical method in the physical sciences and enthusiastic about the power of reason exercised through mathematics, leading eighteenth-century thinkers undertook a rational approach to social problems and launched the sciences of government and economics. The spread of this same rational spirit freed man from superstitions and groundless fears and permitted him to breathe in a more tolerant atmosphere.

The proliferating demands of science, which first became urgent during the seventeenth century, stimulated an enormous expansion in mathematics proper. To obtain a deeper appreciation of the nature of modern mathematics we must look into these more recent developments. The mathematics which the Europeans possessed by 1600 consisted of algebra, Euclidean geometry and the beginnings of trigonometry. In the seventeenth century the need to study curves—whether the paths of light through lenses, the paths of cannonballs, the paths of ships at sea, or the paths of the planets—prompted René Descartes and Pierre de Fermat to create an algebraic method of representing curves so that algebra could be used to deduce the properties of curves. This creation is known as co-ordinate or analytic geometry.

The need to calculate varying velocity, force, pressure and other physical quantities in problems of celestial mechanics as well as in navigation and gunfire was met by the creation of a new concept, the concept of a limit, and a new method called differentiation. This is the substance of the differential calculus. To obtain the sum of an infinite number of small quantities, for example, the sum of the gravitational forces which each bit of earth exerts on some external mass, the integral calculus was created.

The calculus was the beginning of a series of new branches commonly grouped under the name of analysis. Differential equations, infinite series, differential geometry, the calculus of variations, functions of a complex variable and vector and tensor analysis are but a few of the subdivisions of analysis. The domain of algebra was likewise extended to include such abstractions as complex numbers, vectors, hypernumbers, matrices, abstract sets and the theory of structures of algebra known as abstract algebra. Projective geometry, non-Euclidean geometry, algebraic geometry and topology joined Euclidean geometry.

The major motivation for all these creations was to further the leading physical studies of the eighteenth and nineteenth centuries—the strength of beams in structures, the motion of ships, the flow of the tides, the development of steam as a source of power, the generation and utilization of electrical power, the improvement of optical instruments, ballistics and dozens of other new or growing scientific interests. But we should not overlook the fact that mathematicians enjoy the creative mathematical activity itself, the intellectual challenge, the satisfaction of accomplishment and the beauty of proofs and results. Given the themes suggested by physical problems, mathematicians develop these far beyond the needs of science, often to find that they have anticipated other needs or have unintentionally supplied the concepts and frameworks for new physical theories.

While the proliferation of mathematics is a phenomenon of our modern culture, an even more startling development has been the realization that mathematics is not an aboslute, all-embracing truth, or description of reality, in the sense that man had until recently thought it was. For 2000 years the axioms of number and geometry were accepted as self-evident truths. Since the theorems are logically necessary consequences of the axioms, the theorems, too, were believed to be incontrovertible truths.

The creation of non-Euclidean geometry had the unintended effect of thrusting mathematics off this pedestal. Historically, non-Euclidean geometry was the result of attempts to find a simpler version of the Euclidean parallel-line axiom which postulates, in effect, that through any point in a given plane there is one, and only one, line parallel to a given line. In the course of this research, mathematicians deliberately adopted an axiom on parallel lines which contradicted Euclid's axiom. From this new axiom and the remainder of Euclid's axioms they proceeded to deduce theorems. They expected to arrive at inconsistencies within the new geometry; that is, they expected to find some theorems contradicting others because they had started with an axiom, which, so they thought, denied the truth. But these contradictions failed to appear!

The supreme mathematician of the nineteenth century, Karl Friedrich Gauss, was the first to see the handwriting on the wall. He realized that Euclidean geometry could no longer be regarded as the only geometry of physical space and that a non-Euclidean geometry might do as well. Further, his efforts to test experimentally which of the geometries, Euclidean or non-Euclidean, fits the physical world better, ended in failure. The situation became even more unsettled when Bernhard Riemann created additional non-Euclidean geometries. The potential applicability of all the non-Euclidean geometries was increased when mathematicians recognized that the physical "straight" lines used in the most weighty scientific work are not stretched strings or rulers' edges but paths of light rays. Since these paths are generally not straight, the geometry whose axioms fitted their behavior and the behavior of figures formed by such "lines" could very well be one of the non-Euclidean varieties. The mathematicians were ultimately forced to admit that there was no reason to believe in the exclusive truth of any one of these geometries. When the theory of relativity made use of a non-Euclidean geometry, the point was driven home.

Some mathematicians sought refuge in those portions of mathematics which rest on the number system and maintained that these at least offer truths. However, this thesis is also indefensible, for we now see more clearly that while the arithmetic we ordinarily use fits the common situations involving quantity, there are other arithmetics and their algebras which fit other situations. To mention a trivial example, an alternative arithmetic fitting a real situation is used when we state that four hours after nine o'clock the hour will be one o'clock rather than thirteen o'clock.

A word of comfort here to the nonmathematician who fears that he may have learned the rudiments of arithmetic and geometry in vain—or suspect that my earlier statements concerning the validity of mathematical processes are now contradicted. "Two plus two equals four" is still a valid deduction from the axioms of arithmetic just as the theorems of Euclidean geometry are still valid deductions from Euclid's axioms. However, the arithmetic and geometric conclusions can be applied only where experience tells us that the axioms are applicable. Thus we shall still use the fact that 2 dollars plus 2 dollars are 4 dollars, but not that 2 raindrops added to 2 raindrops are 4 raindrops. Two raindrops plus 2 raindrops make a puddle. Again, if we mix 2 cubic inches of hydrogen and 1 of oxygen, we obtain not 3 but 2 cubic inches of water. Philosophically this suggests that "truth" in mathematics, as in all human processes, is a many-faceted thing.

Recognition of the shattering fact that mathematics, which had always been regarded as the anchor of truth and as conclusive evidence that man can attain truths, rests on pragmatic grounds was a direct result of the nineteenth-century questioning of man's assumptions concerning the physical world. Mathematicians had believed that the assumptions or axioms—and therefore the logical consequences—were truths. It was now realized that such axioms are man-made inferences based on limited sense data and are only approximations of what happens in the physical world. In fact, the word "axiom" should now be taken to mean assumption, rather than self-evident truth. We continue to use the axioms and conclusions, even though they are not truths, because they do offer some highly useful knowledge about the physical world—the best knowledge, in fact, that man possesses.

Oddly, though truth, the most prized possession of mathematics, was taken from it, the subject emerged richer for the loss. Axioms palpably untrue had led to geometries which proved useful. This experience justified the exploration of any system of axioms, however unpromising for application it might seem at the outset. Mathematics, which had been fettered to the physical world, passed from serfdom to freedom.

There is no doubt of the positive value of the new freedom. From the unrestricted play of mathematical imagination have come and will continue to come systems of thought which may prove to be far more valuable in representing and mastering the physical world than could have come from concentration on the two original systems of number and Euclidean geometry. So it was, when Einstein needed to know the structure of a particular four-dimensional, non-Euclidean geometry, that he found the information at hand.

Examination of the newer mathematics reveals another gradual change in its nature. The early concepts of mathematics, the whole number, the fractions and the several geometrical figures, were clearly suggested by immediate experiences. Mathematicians later found themselves developing and applying such abstract extensions of the idea of number as irrational, negative and complex numbers. Because they did not at first understand these new types of numbers or recognize their usefulness, even the greatest ones resisted their introduction. Having worked for centuries with numbers and geometrical figures which were suggested directly by physical objects, mathematicians had implicitly and unconsciously concluded that their concepts must be "real." What was involved in the acceptance of new types of numbers was a sharp break from concepts grounded directly in experience. Mathematicians have since learned the deeper meaning of the statement that mathematics is an activity of the human mind and now grant that any concept which is clear and fertile should be explored whether or not it has an apparent physical basis.

Paradoxically, to obtain insights into the physical world, we must plunge deeper into human minds, consider abstractions that are remote from reality, and explore the implications of axioms that not only transcend but even appear to deny our sense impressions. Though recourse to higher and higher abstractions seems regrettable, the case for it was superbly stated by the distinguished philosopher, Alfred North Whitehead: "Nothing is more impressive than the fact that as mathematics withdrew increasingly into the upper regions of ever greater extremes of abstract thought, it returned to earth with a corresponding growth of importance for the analysis of concrete fact. . . . The paradox is now fully established that the utmost abstractions are the true weapons with which to control our thought of concrete fact."

The pleasures and pains of mathematical activity have been recommended largely on the ground that they help us to achieve knowledge of the physical world. Why do we seek this knowledge? The ultimate goal of scientific activity is man himself. He wants to know the meaning of his own life and seeks the answer by attempting to understand the world in which he finds himself.

Mathematics mediates between man and nature, between man's inner and outer worlds. What mathematical concepts and methods have achieved in rationalizing nature have yielded our clearest and most weighty scientific doctrines. When solely for mathematical reasons Copernicus and Kepler adopted a new mathematical scheme by which to organize the observations of the heavens and placed the sun rather than the earth in the center, they caused man to recognize that he was an insignificant creature whirling through vast spaces rather than the central figure in the drama of nature. When Newtonian mechanics revealed a universe firmly controlled by definite mathematical laws and functioning both in the past and in the future to no end other than the fulfillment of mathematical laws, man had to cope with the implication that he was without will or purpose. If more recent creations such as quantum theory have cast in doubt the bleak, mechanical, deterministic implications of earlier theories and have given man some hope of reinstatement in an important role, it is still true that his outlook is confined and directed by mathematical chains of thought.

Science provides the understanding of the universe in which we live. Mathematics provides the dies by which science is molded. Our world is to a large extent what mathematics says it is. This body of man-made abstractions, wherein as Bertrand Russell put it, we never know what we are talking about nor whether what we are saying is true, this practical tool, model of all intellectual enterprises, and essence of our knowledge of nature leads through science to man himself.

Further reading:
    Eddington, A. S.: THE NATURE OF THE PHYSICAL WORLD. New York: Cambridge University Press; 1932.
    Kline, Morris: MATHEMATICS IN WESTERN CULTURE. New York: Oxford University Press; 1953.
    Kline, Morris: MATHEMATICS AND THE PHYSICAL WORLD. New York: Thomas Y. Crowell Company; 1959.
    Sawyer, W. W.: PRELUDE TO MATHEMATICS. Baltimore: Penguin Books, Inc.; 1955.
    Sutton, O. G.: MATHEMATICS IN ACTION. New York: Dover Publications, Inc.; 1959.

C. S. LEWIS

[*Photograph by Wolf Suschitzky*]

Clive Staples Lewis, professor of medieval and renaissance English literature at Cambridge University, has been described as possessing "the rare gift of being able to make righteousness readable." Since the publication of Doctor Lewis's The Screwtape Letters in 1942, the book has become a satirical classic—one of those rare works that approach the problems of Christian morality with both grace and humor. Screwtape, the writer of the letters, is a senior devil who gives his nephew, Wormwood, a junior devil, an advanced correspondence course on how to corrupt human souls. As Screwtape here reappears as an after-dinner speaker, we repeat Doctor Lewis's earlier admonition to his readers: ". . . the devil is a liar. Not everything that Screwtape says should be assumed to be true even from his own angle."

Screwtape Proposes a Toast

BY

C. S. LEWIS

(The scene is in Hell at the annual dinner of the Tempters'
Training College for young Devils. The principal, Dr. Slubgob,
has just proposed the health of the guests. Screwtape, a very
experienced Devil, who is the guest of honor, rises to reply.)

M r. Principal, Your Imminence, Your Disgraces, my
Thorns, Shadies and Gentledevils: It is customary on
these occasions for the speaker to address himself chiefly to
those among you who have just been graduated and who will
very soon be posted to official Temperships on earth. It is a
custom I willingly obey. I well remember with what trepidation
I awaited my own first appointment. I hope and believe that
each one of you has the same uneasiness tonight. Your career is
before you. Hell expects and demands that it should be—as
mine was—one of unbroken success. If it is not, you know what
awaits you.

I have no wish to reduce the wholesome and realistic element of terror, the unremitting anxiety, which must act as the

lash and spur to your endeavors. Yet at the same time I would wish to put before you a moderately encouraging view of the strategical situation as a whole.

Your dreaded principal has included in a speech full of points something like an apology for the banquet which he has set before us. Well, Gentledevils, no one blames *him*. But it would be vain to deny that the human souls on whose anguish we have been feasting tonight were of pretty poor quality. Not all the most skillful cookery of our tormentors could make them better than insipid.

Oh, to get one's teeth again into a Herod, a Henry the Eighth or even a Hitler! There was real crackling there; something to crunch; a rage, an egotism, a cruelty only just less robust than our own. It put up a delicious resistance to being devoured. It warmed your inwards when you'd got it down.

Instead of this, what have we had tonight? There was a municipal authority with Graft sauce. But personally I could not detect in him the flavor of a really passionate and brutal avarice such as delighted one in the great tycoons of the last century. Was he not unmistakably a Little Man—a creature of the petty rake-off pocketed with a petty joke in private and denied with the stalest platitudes in his public utterances; a grubby little nonentity who had drifted into corruption, only just realizing that he was corrupt, and chiefly because everyone else did it? Then there was the lukewarm Casserole of Adulterers. Could you find in it any trace of a fully inflamed, defiant, rebellious, insatiable lust? I couldn't. They all tasted to me like undersexed morons who had blundered or trickled into the wrong beds in automatic response to sexy advertisements, or to make themselves feel modern and emancipated, or to reassure themselves about their virility or their normalcy, or even because they had nothing else to do. Frankly, to me who have tasted Messalina and Casanova, they were nauseating. The Trade Unionist garnished with sedition was perhaps a shade better. He had done some real harm. He had, not quite unknowingly, worked for bloodshed, famine and the extinction of liberty. Yes, in a way. But what a way! He thought of those ultimate objectives

so little. Toeing the party line, self-importance, and above all
mere routine, were what really dominated his life.

But now comes the point. Gastronomically all this is deplorable. But I hope none of us puts gastronomy first. Is it not,
in another and far more serious way, full of hope and promise?

Consider first the mere quantity. The quality may be
wretched; but we never had souls (of a sort) in more abundance.

And then the triumph. We are tempted to say that such
souls—or such residual puddles of what once was soul—are
hardly worth damning. Yes, but the Enemy—for whatever inscrutable and perverse reason—thought them worth trying to
save. Believe me, He did. You youngsters who have not yet been
on active service have no idea with what labor, with what delicate skill, each of these miserable creatures was finally captured.

The difficulty lay in their very smallness and flabbiness.
Here were vermin so muddled in mind, so passively responsive to
environment, that it was very hard to raise them to that level of
clarity and deliberateness at which mortal sin becomes possible.
To raise them just enough; but not that fatal millimeter of "too
much." For then, of course, all would possibly have been lost.
They might have seen; they might have repented. On the other
hand, if they had been raised too little, they would very possibly
have qualified for Limbo, as creatures suitable neither for
Heaven nor for Hell; things that, having failed to make the
grade, are allowed to sink into a more or less contented subhu-
manity forever.

In each individual choice of what the Enemy would call the
"wrong" turning, such creatures are at first hardly, if at all, in a
state of full spiritual responsibility. They do not understand
either the source or the real character of the prohibitions they
are breaking. Their consciousness hardly exists apart from the
social atmosphere that surrounds them. And, of course, we have
contrived that their very language should be all smudge and
blur; what would be a *bribe* in someone else's profession is a *tip*
or a *present* in theirs. The job of their Tempters was first, of
course, to harden these choices of the Hellward roads into a
habit by steady repetition. But then—and this was all-important

—to turn the habit into a principle, a principle the creature is prepared to defend. After that, all will go well. Conformity to the social environment, at first merely instinctive or even mechanical—how should a *jelly* not conform?—now becomes an unacknowledged creed or ideal of Togetherness or Being Like Folks. Mere ignorance of the law they break now turns into a vague theory about it—remember they know no history—a theory expressed by calling it *conventional* or *puritan* or *bourgeois* morality.

Thus gradually there comes to exist at the center of the creature a hard, tight, settled core of resolution to go on being what it is, and even to resist moods that might tend to alter it. It is a very small core; not at all reflective (they are too ignorant) nor defiant (their emotional and imaginative poverty excludes that); almost, in its own way, prim and demure, like a pebble or a very young cancer. But it will serve our turn. Here at last is a real and deliberate, though not fully articulate, rejection of what the Enemy calls Grace.

These, then, are two welcome phenomena. First, the abundance of our captures; however tasteless our fare, we are in no danger of famine. And secondly, the triumph; the skill of our Tempters has never stood higher. But the third moral, which I have not yet drawn, is the most important of all.

The sort of souls on whose despair and ruin we have—well, I won't say feasted, but at any rate subsisted—tonight are increasing in numbers and will continue to increase. Our advices from Lower Command assure us that this is so; our directives warn us to orient all our tactics in view of this situation. The "great" sinners, those in whom vivid and genial passions have been pushed beyond the bounds and in whom an immense concentration of will has been devoted to objects which the Enemy abhors, will not disappear. But they will grow rarer. Our catches will be ever more numerous; but they will consist increasingly of trash—trash which we should once have thrown to Cerberus and the hellhounds as unfit for diabolical consumption. And there are two things I want you to understand about this. First, that however depressing it may seem, it is really a change for the better. And secondly, I would draw your attention to the means by which it has been brought about.

It is a change for the better. The great—and toothsome—sinners are made out of the very same material as those horrible phenomena, the great saints. The virtual disappearance of such material may mean insipid meals for us. But is it not utter frustration and absolute famine for the Enemy? He did not create the humans—He did not become one of them and die among them by torture—in order to produce candidates for Limbo; "failed" humans. He wanted to make saints, gods, things like Himself. Is the dullness of your present fare not a very small price to pay for the delicious knowledge that His whole great experiment is petering out? But not only that. As the great sinners grow fewer and the majority lose all individuality, the great sinners become far more effective agents for us. Every dictator or even demagogue—almost every film star or crooner—can now draw tens of thousands of the human sheep with him. They give themselves—what there is of them—to him; in him, to us. There may come a time when we shall have no need to bother about *individual* temptation at all, except for the few. Catch the bellwether, and his whole flock comes after him.

But do you realize how we have succeeded in reducing so many of the human race to the level of ciphers? This has not come about by accident. It has been our answer—and a magnificent answer it is—to one of the most serious challenges we ever had to face.

Let me recall to your minds what the human situation was in the latter part of the nineteenth century—the period at which I ceased to be a practicing Tempter and was rewarded with an administrative post. The great movement toward liberty and equality among men had by then borne solid fruits and grown mature. Slavery had been abolished. The American War of Independence had been won. The French Revolution had succeeded. Religious toleration was almost everywhere on the increase. In that movement there had originally been many elements which were in our favor. Much atheism, much anticlericalism, much envy and thirst for revenge, even some rather absurd attempts to revive paganism, were mixed in it. It was not easy to determine what our own attitude should be. On the one hand it was a bitter blow to us—it still is—that any sort of men who had been hungry should be fed or any who had long worn chains should have them struck off. But on the other hand there was in the movement so much rejection of faith, so much materialism, secularism and hatred that we felt we were bound to encourage it.

But by the latter part of the century the situation was much simpler and also much more ominous. In the English sector—where I saw most of my front-line service—a horrible thing had happened. The Enemy, with His usual sleight of hand, had largely appropriated this progressive or liberalizing movement and perverted it to His own ends. Very little of its old anti-Christianity remained. The dangerous phenomenon called Christian Socialism was rampant. Factory owners of the good old type who grew rich on sweated labor, instead of being assassinated by their workpeople—we could have used that—were being frowned upon by their own class. The rich were increasingly giving up their powers not in the face of revolution and compulsion, but in obedience to their own consciences. As for the poor who benefited by this, they were behaving in a most disappointing fashion. Instead of using their new liberties—as we reasonably hoped and expected—for massacre, rape and looting, or even for perpetual intoxication, they were perversely engaged in becoming cleaner, more orderly, more thrifty, better educated and even more virtuous. Believe me, Gentledevils, the threat of something like a really healthy state of society seemed then perfectly serious.

Thanks to our Father Below the threat was averted. Our counterattack was on two levels. On the deepest level our leaders contrived to call into full life an element which had been implicit in the movement from its earliest days. Hidden in the heart of this striving for liberty there was also a deep hatred of personal freedom. That invaluable man Rousseau first revealed it. In his perfect democracy, you remember, only the state religion is permitted, slavery is restored, and the individual is told that he has really willed (though he didn't know it) whatever the government tells him to do. From that starting point, via Hegel (another indispensable propagandist on our side) we easily contrived both the Nazi and the Communist states.

Such was our counterattack on one level. You who are mere beginners will not be entrusted with work of that kind. You will be attached as Tempters to private persons. Against them, or through them, our counterattack takes a different form.

"Democracy" is the word with which you must lead them by the nose. The good work which our philological experts have already done in the corruption of human language makes it unnecessary to warn you that they should never be allowed to give this word a clear and definable meaning. They won't. It will never occur to them that "democracy" is properly the name of a political system, even a system of voting, and that this has only the most remote and tenuous connection with what you are trying to sell them. Nor, of course, must they ever be allowed to raise Aristotle's question: whether "democratic behavior" means the behavior that democracies like or the behavior that will preserve a democracy. For if they did, it could hardly fail to occur to them that these need not be the same.

You are to use the word purely as an incantation; if you like, purely for its selling power. It is a name they venerate. And, of course, it is connected with the political ideal that men should be equally treated. You then make a stealthy transition in their minds from this political ideal to a factual belief that all men *are* equal. Especially the man you are working on. As a result, you can use the word "democracy" to sanction in his thought the most degrading—and also the least enjoyable—of all human feelings. You can get him to practice, not only without shame but with a positive glow of self-approval, conduct which, if undefended by the magic word, would be universally derided.

The feeling I mean is, of course, that which prompts a man to say "I'm as good as you."

The first and most obvious advantage is that you thus induce him to enthrone at the center of his life a good, solid, resounding lie. I don't mean that his statement is false merely in fact—that he is no more equal to everyone he meets in kindness, honesty and good sense than in height or waist measurement. I mean that he does not believe it himself. No man who says "I'm as good as you" believes it. He would not say it if he did. The St. Bernard never says it to the toy dog, nor the scholar to the dunce, nor the employable to the bum, nor the pretty woman to the plain. The claim to equality, outside the strictly political field, is made only by those who feel themselves to be in some way inferior. What it expresses is precisely the itching, smarting, writhing awareness of an inferiority which the patient refuses to accept. And therefore resents.

Yes, and therefore resents every kind of superiority in others; denigrates it; wishes its annihilation. Presently he suspects every mere difference of being a claim to superiority. No one must be different from himself in voice, clothes, manners, recreations, choice of food: "Here is someone who speaks English rather more clearly and euphoniously than I—it must be a vile, upstage, la-di-da affectation. Here's a fellow who says he doesn't like hot dogs—thinks himself too good for them, no doubt. Here's a man who hasn't turned on the jukebox—he's one of those damned highbrows and is doing it to show off. If they were honest-to-goodness all-right Joes they'd be like me. They've no business to be different. It's undemocratic."

Now this useful phenomenon is in itself by no means new. Under the name of Envy it has been known to the humans for thousands of years. But hitherto they always regarded it as the most odious, and also the most comical, of vices. Those who were aware of feeling it felt it with shame; those who were not gave it no quarter in others. The delightful novelty of the present situation is that you can sanction it—make it respectable and even laudable—by the incantatory use of the word "democratic."

Under the influence of this incantation those who are in any or every way inferior can labor more wholeheartedly and successfully than ever before to pull down everyone else to their own level. But that is not all. Under the same influence those who come, or could come, nearer to a full humanity, actually draw back from it for fear of being undemocratic. I am credibly informed that young humans now sometimes suppress an incipient taste for classical music or good literature because it might prevent their Being Like Folks; that people who would really wish to be—and are offered the Grace which would enable them to be—honest, chaste or temperate refuse it. To accept it might make them Different, might offend against the Way of Life, take them out of Togetherness, impair their Integration With the Group. They might (horror of horrors!) become individuals.

Meanwhile, as a delightful by-product, the few (fewer every day) who will not be made Normal and Regular and Like Folks and Integrated, increasingly tend to become in reality the prigs and cranks which the rabble would in any case have believed them to be. For suspicion often creates what it suspects: "Since, whatever I do, the neighbors are going to think me a witch, or a Communist agent, I might as well be hanged for a sheep as a lamb and become one in reality." As a result we now have an intelligentsia which, though very small, is very useful to the cause of Hell.

But that is a mere by-product. What I want to fix your attention on is the vast, over-all movement toward the discrediting, and finally the elimination, of every kind of human excellence—moral, cultural, social or intellectual. And is it not pretty to notice how democracy—in the incantatory sense—is now doing for us the work that was once done by the most ancient dictatorships, and by the same methods? You remember how one of the Greek dictators (they called them "tyrants" then) sent an envoy to another dictator to ask his advice about the principles of government. The second dictator led the envoy into a field of grain, and there he snicked off with his cane the top of every stalk that rose an inch or so above the general level. The moral was plain. Allow no pre-eminence among your subjects. Let no man live who is wiser, or better, or more famous, or even handsomer than the mass. Cut them all down to a level; all slaves, all ciphers, all nobodies. All equals. Thus tyrants could practice, in a sense, "democracy." But now "democracy" can do the same work without any other tyranny other than her own. No one need now go through the field with a cane. The little stalks will now of themselves bite the tops off the big ones. The big ones are beginning to bite off their own in their desire to Be Like Stalks.

I have said that to secure the damnation of these little souls, these creatures that have almost ceased to be individual, is a laborious and tricky work. But if proper pains and skill are expended, you can be fairly confident of the result. The great sinners *seem* easier to catch. But then they are incalculable. After you have played them for seventy years, the Enemy may snatch them from your claws in the seventy-first. They are capable, you see, of real repentance. They are conscious of real guilt. They are, if things take the wrong turn, as ready to defy the social pressures around them for the Enemy's sake as they were to defy them for ours. It is in some ways more troublesome to track and swat an evasive wasp than to shoot, at close range, a wild elephant. But the elephant is more troublesome if you miss.

My own experience, as I have said, was mainly on the English sector, and I still get more news from it than from any other. It may be that what I am now going to say will not apply so fully to the sectors in which some of you may be operating. But you can make the necessary adjustments when you get there.

In that promising land the spirit of "I'm as good as you" has already become something more than a generally social influence. It begins to work itself into the educational system. How far its operations there have gone at the present moment I would not like to say with certainty; nor does it matter. Once you have grasped the tendency, you can easily predict its future developments; especially as we ourselves will play our part in the developing. The basic principle of the new education is to be that dunces and idlers must not be made to feel inferior to intelligent and industrious pupils. That would be "undemocratic." These differences among the pupils—for they are odiously and nakedly *individual* differences—must be disguised. This can be done on various levels. At universities examinations must be framed so that nearly all the students get good marks. Entrance examinations must be framed so that all, or nearly all, citizens can go to universities, whether they have any power or wish to profit by higher education or not. At schools the children who are too stupid or lazy to learn languages and mathematics and elementary science can be set to doing the things that children used to do in their spare time. Let them, for example, make mud pies and call it modeling. But all the time there must be no faintest hint that they are inferior to the children who are at work. Whatever nonsense they are engaged in must have—I believe the English already use the phrase—"parity of esteem." An even more drastic scheme is not impossible. Children who are fit to proceed to a higher class may be artificially kept back, because the others would get a "trauma"—Beelzebub, what a useful word!—by being left behind. The bright pupil thus remains democratically fettered to his own age group throughout his school career, and a boy who would be capable of tackling Aeschylus or Dante sits listening to his coeval's attempts to spell out "A Cat Sat on a Mat."

In a word, we may reasonably hope for the virtual abolition of education when "I'm as good as you" has fully had its way. All incentives to learn and all penalties for not learning will vanish. The few who might want to learn will be prevented—who are they to overtop their fellows? We shall no longer have to plan and toil to spread imperturbable conceit and incurable ignorance among men. The little vermin themselves will do it for us.

Of course, this would not follow unless all education became state education. But it will. That is part of the same movement. Penal taxes, designed for that purpose, are liquidating the middle class, the class which was prepared to save and spend and make sacrifices in order to have its children privately educated. The removal of this class, besides linking up with the abolition of education, is fortunately an inevitable effect of the spirit that says "I'm as good as you." This was, after all, the social group which gave to the humans the overwhelming majority of their scientists, physicians, philosophers, theologians, poets, artists, composers, architects, jurists and administrators. If ever there was a bunch of tall stalks that needed their tops knocked off, it was surely they. As an English politician remarked not long ago, "A democracy does not want great men."

It would be idle to ask of such a creature whether by "want" it meant "need" or "like." But you should be clear. For here Aristotle's question arises again.

We, in Hell, would welcome the disappearance of democracy in the strict sense of that word—the political arrangement so-called. Like all forms of government it often works to our advantage; but on the whole less often than other forms. And what we must realize is that "democracy" in the diabolical sense— "I'm as good as you," Being Like Folks, Togetherness—is the finest instrument we could possibly have for extirpating political democracies from the face of the earth.

For "democracy" or the "democratic spirit" (diabolical sense) leads to a nation without great men, a nation mainly of subliterates, morally flaccid from lack of discipline in youth, full of the cocksureness which flattery breeds on ignorance, blustering or whimpering if rebuked. And that is what Hell wishes every democratic people to be. For when such a nation meets in conflict a nation where children have been made to work at school, where talent is placed in high posts, and where the ignorant mass is allowed no say at all in public affairs, only one result is possible.

The democracies were surprised lately when they found that the Soviet Union had got ahead of them in science. What a delicious specimen of human blindness! If the whole tendency of their society is opposed to every sort of excellence, why did they expect their scientists to excel?

It is our function to encourage the behavior, the manners, the whole attitude of mind, which democracies naturally like and enjoy, because these are the very things which, if unchecked, will destroy democracy. You would almost wonder that even humans don't see it themselves. Even if they don't read Aristotle (that would be undemocratic) you would have thought the French Revolution would have taught them that the behavior that aristocrats naturally like is not the behavior that preserves aristocracy. They might then have applied the same principle to all forms of government.

But I would not end on that note. I would not—Hell forbid!—encourage in your own minds that delusion which you must carefully foster in the minds of your human victims. I mean the delusion that the fate of nations is *in itself* more important than that of individual souls. The overthrow of free peoples and the multiplication of slave states are for us a means—

besides, of course, being fun—but the real end is the destruction of individuals. For only individuals can be saved or damned, can become sons of the Enemy or food for us. The ultimate value for us of any revolution, war or famine lies in the individual anguish, treachery, hatred, rage and despair which it may produce. "I'm as good as you" is a useful means for the destruction of democratic societies. But it has a far deeper value as an end in itself, as a state of mind which, necessarily excluding humility, charity, contentment, and all the pleasures of gratitude or admiration, turns a human being away from almost every road which might finally lead him to Heaven.

But now for the pleasantest part of my duty. It falls to my lot to propose on behalf of the guests the health of Principal Slubgob and the Tempters' Training College. Fill your glasses. What is this I see? What is this delicious bouquet I inhale? Can it be? Mr. Principal, I unsay all my hard words about the dinner. I see—and smell—that even under wartime conditions the college cellar still has a few dozen of sound old vintage Pharisee. Well, well, well! This is like old times. Hold it beneath your nostrils for a moment, Gentledevils. Hold it up to the light. Look at those fiery streaks that writhe and tangle in its dark heart, as if they were contending. And so they are. You know how this wine is blended? Different types of Pharisee have been harvested, trodden and fermented together to produce its subtle flavor. Types that were most antagonistic to one another on earth. Some were all rules and relics and rosaries; others were all drab clothes, long faces and petty traditional abstinences from wine or cards or the theater. Both had in common their self-righteousness and the almost infinite distance between their actual outlook and anything the Enemy really is or commands. The wickedness of other religions was the really live doctrine in the religion of each; slander was its gospel and denigration its litany. How they hated one another up there where the sun shone! How much more they hate one another now that they are forever conjoined but not reconciled. Their astonishment, their resentment, at the combination, the festering of their eternally impenitent spite, passing into our spiritual digestion, will work like fire. Dark fire. All said and done, my friends, it will be an ill day for us if what most humans mean by "religion" ever vanishes from the earth. It can still send us the truly delicious sins. The fine flower of unholiness can grow only in the close neighborhood of the Holy. Nowhere do we tempt so successfully as on the very steps of the altar.

Your Imminence, your Disgraces, my Thorns, Shadies and Gentledevils: I give you the toast of—Principal Slubgob and the college!

CLINTON ROSSITER

[*Photograph by Jacob Lofman*]

Clinton Rossiter, political scientist, historian, and prize-winning author, is John L. Senior Professor of American Institutions at Cornell University. Professor Rossiter took his bachelor's degree at Cornell in 1939 and subsequently received the M.A. and Ph.D. degrees from Princeton University. Among his seven books are Seedtime of the Republic, Conservatism in America and The American Presidency. *The book from which the present article was drawn was published in 1960 by Harcourt, Brace, under the title* Marxism: The View From America. *Professor Rossiter spent the academic year 1960–61 as Pitt Professor of American History at Cambridge University.*

Why Marx Failed Here

BY

CLINTON ROSSITER

The teachings of Karl Marx are holy writ in one third of the world. In the United States they are an anathema. While Marxism has scored astounding triumphs in the most unlikely places, its record in what Marx himself considered one of the most likely places of all is one of stunning failure. Intellectually as well as politically and militarily, America presents an almost solid front against the man, his ideas and his heirs. Quite the contrary to Marx's prediction that the most advanced industrial countries would be the first to make the transit from capitalism to socialism and beyond to communism, this most advanced of all countries has never been insulated so thickly against the appeals of Marxism nor ever behaved in so thoroughly un-Marxist a fashion.

Even among intellectuals, whom Marx expected to be trail blazers of the coming order, he has had few American disciples and not a great many more admirers. As a thinker he is much quoted by social scientists; as a counselor he is simply ignored. The number of conscious Marxists who have raised their voices influentially in American intellectual or political debate is amazingly small; the contribution of these men to Marxist thought has been negligible.

I do not mean to say that the American mind has been untouched by Marx. A pervasive "Marxist" influence has spread all through the American intellectual community in the twentieth century, and many men who would deny flatly any debt to Marx have thought in "Marxist" categories and employed "Marxist" language. Yet in this instance I use the word—as do most historians of the American mind—to describe a general pattern of realistic, antitraditional, collectivist thought rather than a particular source of inspiration. Even if Marx had never lived, this pattern would exist and exert a powerful influence in America—and, it seems hardly necessary to add, so would the income tax and Social Security.

The failure of Marxism as a doctrine is, of course, only one aspect of the failure of radicalism as a political force in the United States. The darling of the world's radicals in the early years of its existence, this country has now become their despair. American writers agree almost unanimously on the social, political and personal causes of the failure of radicalism.

First among these is what historians of the early Republic called "the history and present state of the United States of America." However full of rough spots the history—depressions, upheavals, insurrections, wars, repeated acts of exploitation of men and nature—we have had less than our share of misery and frustration, more than our share of happiness and fulfillment. However full of soft spots the present state—racism, corruption, vulgarity, obscurantism—we are clearly the most fortunate and well-situated of the nations of the earth. The appeals of radicalism have gone unheeded in America because the promises of radicalism have been largely fulfilled. The isms of Europe have foundered, as the German Marxist Werner Sombart once noted, "on the shoals of roast beef and apple pie."

Friedrich Engels, the good Sherpa of Marx's assult on the summit of capitalism, put his reluctant finger on a related reason for the hard times of radicalism in the United States. In a letter of 1892 to Friedrich Sorge, a German revolutionary who had settled down in Hoboken to teach music and spread socialism, Engels complained of the staying power of America's "bourgeois prejudices," which he found to be almost as "strongly rooted in the working class" as among businessmen. He saw clearly, as Marx apparently did not, that the bigness, uniqueness, success and freshness of the American experiment had created a popular state of mind unusually hostile to comprehensive radicalism. If he were alive today, he would see that the hostility has grown to frightening proportions—frightening, that is, to the hopes of Marxist radicalism.

At least part of this hostility is a simple and understandable reaction to the savagery of Marx's judgments on our whole way of life. Upon us, it must be remembered, he unleashed the brunt of his major attack and upon us the attack continues in undiminished violence. Indeed, it almost seems as if Marx were as vibrantly alive and censorious today as he was 100 years ago. We have no social arrangement—our welfare capitalism, the ascendancy of our middle class, the variety of our groups and interests—for which he can say one kind or even understanding word. We have no institution—church, family, property, school, corporation, trade union and all the agencies of constitutional democracy—that he does not wish either to destroy or to transform beyond recognition. We have no ideals or ideas—from the Christian ethic through patriotism to individualism—that he does not condemn out of hand. The essence of Marx's message is a prediction of doom for the liberal, democratic way of life. He announces that prediction not sadly but gladly, not timidly but furiously, not contingently but dogmatically— and, of course, so do his heirs. Khrushchev was a faithful grandchild of Marx when he laid to rest all doubts about our future by promising happily, "We will bury you." This is not the most effective way to persuade the minds of Americans.

Our hostility to radicalism has not, to be sure, prevented our borrowing useful ideas piecemeal from radicals in our midst. A major cause of the decline of the Socialist Party, and of a dozen other radical parties that have orbited crazily around it, has been the cannibalistic tastes of the Republicans and Democrats. Indeed, everything about American politics—the broad appeal of the two major parties, the costs of political campaigning, the widespread refusal to adopt proportional representation, the statutory difficulties of getting on and staying on the ballot in many states—seems to be loaded against the rise and prosperity of third parties.

Not all the troubles of the American Left have arisen from conditions outside the movement. At least two reasons for the failure of radicalism, and especially of Marxist radicalism, were bred in the bone: first, the intense and self-defeating sectarianism of the Marxists and their fellows in dissent, which led Marx himself to complain that the "Yankee Socialists" were "crotchety and sectarian"; and second, the alien stamp, which has been imprinted for at least three generations on the purposes and personalities of most radical groups in this country. Few of our leading radicals have been Americans in birth, interests, inspirations or even language, and this visible fact has nourished the natural xenophobic prejudices of the American mind. The easy identification of radicalism with socialism, of socialism with communism, of communism with Soviet tyranny, and of all these isms with subversion and ungodliness, has wellnigh shattered the hopes of any brand of political radicalism in the United States.

There is, I think, one last nail in the coffin of Marxist aspirations in America, one conclusive reason for our refusal to bid Marx and his followers a decent welcome, whether they have come to us as men of learning or men of action. The fact is that the Marxist ideology, whether in the classical form in which Marx and Engels left it or in the Bolshevized version that holds sway in the U.S.S.R., contradicts flatly almost every principle with which Americans have attempted to explain or justify or purify their way of life. Even if Marxism had encountered none of the other difficulties I have mentioned, it would have held little appeal for the minds of men who had been brought up, however carelessly, in the American tradition. Nothing in that tradition prepares men to share Marx's anger, to accept his advice or to answer his summons—even, to our present disadvantage, to understand his appeal to the less fortunate peoples of the earth. Everything in it, as we learned in the 1930's, forbids most Americans to turn to Marx even in their desperate hours.

Why should this have been so? Why has the giant new theory of the nineteenth century—now the giant new religion of the twentieth—been rudely ignored in one of the few countries for which it was supposed to hold an immediate appeal? Why

114

did we, the people who converted liberalism from a permissive faith into a national monument, shy away skittishly from what Raymond Aron, French political scientist and brilliant critic of Marxism, describes as the "synthesis of all the principal schemes of progressive thought"? Why, even now, do we find it difficult to go to Marx for instruction in those fields in which he was a provocative, if not always trustworthy, teacher? My own answer is that it is not enough to lay out the historical reasons for the failure of Marxism as a basis for political action, nor even enough to prove that our minds are insulated by "bourgeois prejudice" against its collectivist, irreligious, antibourgeois temptations. What we come down to in the end is a fundamental conflict between two bodies of principle, two faiths, two ideologies—if I may use that word in a Pickwickian rather than Marxist sense—a conflict so severe that peace between them has always been and remains today impossible to achieve. More than that, peace between the communist and democratic worlds becomes a far more difficult exercise than the mere adjustment of conflicting economic interests and of suspicious military stances. Ideas do, after all, have consequences.

The contradiction between Marxism and the American tradition shows itself harshly in almost every area over which the human intellect ranges—for example, in psychology, where Marxists talk of human behavior as an infinitely plastic product of social environment, and we talk of indelible qualities that are common to all men everywhere; in sociology, where they insist that the normal relationship among classes is one of exploitation and struggle, and we make much of cooperation and mutual dependence; in economics, which they find to be the domineering influence in the lives and thoughts and values of men, and which we see as only one among three or four primal influences; in history, the wondrous complexity of which they force into a constricting pattern of class struggle and social cataclysm, and which we deal with in terms of multiple causation and mystery; in political theory, which teaches them to fear the power of the liberal state and yet to trust completely the power of the dictatorship of the proletariat, and which teaches us to fear unchained power in the hands of any breed of men;

in the principles of constitutionalism, which they regard as a "bourgeois fraud," and we consider the essence of free government; and above all in philosophy, in the basic ideas with which men approach both the large wonders and the small facts of the world in which they live. Their whole doctrine is grounded on a rigid materialism, and ours is a subtle blend of rationalism, idealism, empiricism and pragmatism—all of these approaches to knowledge which the Marxists despise and deride.

This contradiction is one between tempers as well as between ideas, between *how* as well as *what* we and they think. The Marxist temper, as the American sees it, is zealous, dogmatic, revolutionary, violent, amoral and elitist. It is supremely confident of the rightness and the ultimate triumph of the Children of Light, the proletariat; yet, like the Manichaean heretics of early Christianity, it is strangely obsessed with the sins and the staying power of the Children of Darkness, the *bourgeoisie.* The American temper, in contrast, seems easygoing, pragmatic, tradition-directed, peaceful, moral and democratic. It is supremely confident of nothing except the fact that no group of men, certainly not the Marxists, has a monopoly of truth. It is more Manichaean than it used to be, but it is still far removed from obsession with ideas and forces other than those it calls its own. It is more apocalyptic too, thanks to Spengler, Toynbee and Marx himself, but it still cannot believe that America must bury communism or be buried by it.

When this record of intellectual and spiritual contradiction is fully scanned, it seems to display three deep-cutting, irreconcilable conflicts.

The first arises primarily in the realm of ideas—the head-on collision of monism and pluralism. Marxism is the latest and most presumptuous of all those celebrated systems of thought with which learned men, moved by the doubts and fears of the unlearned, have sought to interpret the world in terms of a single principle. It has an explanation of everything; and to everything it grants one explanation. The whole range of man's behavior is explained in terms of the business of making a living, the whole configuration of society in terms of the class structure, the whole sweep of history in terms of the class struggle, the whole phenomenon of classes in terms of private property. Marxism, in short, is a closed system in which all new facts and ideas are made to conform to a rigid, monistic pattern.

The American tradition, to the contrary, is consciously pluralistic. Its unity is the result of a process through which un-numbered diversities of faith and intellect seek to live together in accommodation, if not always in harmony. Man, history, society, politics, nature—all are explained, to the extent that they can be explained, in terms of multiple causation. Our system of ideas is open to new thoughts and fresh evidence. It has its bedrock beliefs in the dignity of man, the excellence of liberty, the limits of politics and the presence of God; but on these beliefs, even in defiance of the last, men are free to build almost every conceivable type of intellectual and spiritual mansion. For this reason we find it hard to grant much respect to a system of ideas as monistic as Marxism. More to the point, we find it increasingly hard to grant it license, for too much evidence is now before our eyes that monism in the world of ideas leads to absolutism in the world of events.

The second conflict arises primarily in the realm of institutions—the head-on collision of collectivism and individualism. Marx talks of classes rather than of individuals, of systems rather than of persons; he seems to have no respect at all for private man. On both "the individual withdrawn into his private interests" and the family with even a symbolic fence between itself and the community he pronounces a stern sentence of doom. His prescriptions for the society of the future are therefore thoroughly collectivistic. No man, no group, no interest, no center of power is to defy the dictatorship of the proletariat in the period of socialist transition or to remain outside the harmonious community in the endless age of communism. That age would surely be marked by a state of "togetherness" that would obliterate every barrier between man and mankind.

The American tradition is doggedly individualistic. It makes room for the state, for society and for natural and voluntary groups. Yet it leaves a wide sphere to private man, the private family and private groups even in its most socially conscious moments, and it insists on a meaningful, lasting contradiction between the interests of that sphere and those of the commonweal. It is fundamentally a challenge to collectivism at two levels—a challenge in behalf of the free individual, a challenge in behalf of the free group.

The last confrontation is both ideological and institutional —the not quite head-on, yet resounding-enough collision of radicalism with conservatism and liberalism. Marxism is, by almost any standard, the supreme radicalism of all times. It is radical in every sense of that sticky word—because it is revolutionary, because it is extremist, because it proposes to dig down to the roots of all things. It insists that the political and social institutions of the United States and its friends are oppressive and diseased, the values that support them rotten and dishonest; it bids us supplant them with an infinitely more just and benign way of life. So complete is its commitment to the future, so unwilling is it to suffer delay, that it is prepared to force entry into this future by subversion and violence.

The American tradition, like most successful traditions with a broad appeal, is a casual blend of conservatism and liberalism. It is conservative in all the useful senses of that sticky word— because it is cautious and moderate, because it is disposed to preserve what it has inherited, because it puts a high value on tradition as a social force and prudence as an individual virtue. Yet it is liberal too, in most senses of that stickiest word of all— because it is openhanded and openminded, because it really expects the future to be better than the past, because it is interested first of all in the development of free men. Product of a history of ceaseless change and growth, it makes a large place for progress through conscious reform and prescriptive innovation, but not through the kind of revolutionary cataclysm that Marx predicts and prescribes.

In the end, I think, the decisive confrontation of Marxism and the American tradition is one of totalitarianism and liberal democracy. Marx himself was not a totalitarian, for totalitarianism is very much an institutional and ideological phenomenon of the twentieth century, the age of advanced technology and mass man. His teachings, however, were a major intellectual source of the kind of totalitarianism now on display in the

Soviet Union and Communist China. One can find with ease in Marx—as one cannot find with any amount of effort in Jefferson or Lincoln—the seeds of the distinctive characteristics of a totalitarian system: the obliteration of all restraints on political power; the penetration of every nook and corner of the exposed and defenseless society by the restless, dynamic power of the state; the ubiquitous control and direction of the individual; and the manipulation of men and power in pursuit of a millennial ideology. One can find in Marx's words of advice to the revolutionaries with whom he associated—on his own terms, I might add—the seeds of most of the distinctive institutions in such a system: the all-encompassing state, the all-directing party, the permanently conspiratorial elite, the monopoly of the media of communication and of the sources of culture, even the system of organized terror.

Most important of all, he was the spiritual father of the Soviet theory of "democracy," which rests squarely upon the concept of a "scientific" leadership that knows what is good for the people much better than do the people, who cannot in any case be trusted to govern themselves. Marx, like his Russian and Chinese heirs, believed in government not *by* but only *for* the people, and for the people in a sense that makes it unnecessary and even impolitic to consult them about their wishes. His prescription for society was undemocratic in its parts and undemocratic in the whole; and the Marxists of the Soviet Union are, to this extent, his devoted heirs. Small wonder that we have rejected Marxism so flatly as an explanation of the human predicament and as a program for its improvement.

Men who turn their backs on Marxism are still faced with the perplexing figure of Marx himself. We may turn away from him too, I suppose, if we take the position that his person and teachings have been swallowed up so completely by the communists that he is no longer a man to whom we dare or care to listen. On the other hand, we may try to separate the thinker from the revolutionary, the gadfly from the godhead, the critic of capitalism from the plotter for communism, the man of the nineteenth century from the myth of the twentieth, and so go to school with him neither more timidly nor less inquisitively than we do, say, with Machiavelli or Nietzsche or Sorel or Clausewitz or even the Marquis de Sade.

If we do, we will learn many things from him. We can learn them elsewhere, to be sure—from farsighted men who came before him and from able synthesizers who have come after—but no one teaches any of them with such piquancy, or all of them together with such authority as does Marx himself. I think, for example, of his teachings that economic forces exert a profound influence on all aspects of human behavior and social organization, that the course of history is shaped powerfully by the way men organize themselves for production, that neither men nor the ideas they profess can be studied as abstractions apart from the social environment, and that classes constitute one of the most persistent and influential phenomena of society. I think too of his strictures on the social systems of his time, which led him to proclaim that toilsome poverty is not the heaven-ordained state of man, that the forms of democracy are not yet democracy itself, that psychological security is not easily found in an industrial system, that capitalism is bound to have its ups and downs, and that private property is property—but also power.

Most important of all, I think of the lessons we can learn from his bad example and from the even worse example of the tough heirs with whom we will be contending both ideologically and politically—let us hope not militarily—for years to come.

The first of these is that we must not be tempted or bullied by the fierce pressure of events into aping the habits of thought we scorn in the Marxists. Let us not, like them, set forth on any delusive quest for certainty, nor even comfort ourselves with the conviction that we have found it, lest we, too, equate dissent with heresy. Let us not, like them, treat all ideas as if they had social significance, lest we, too, strangle ourselves with the cord of "politicalization." Let us eschew ideology, despise dogmatism and discipline ourselves against extremism. Above all, let us take note of their monumental presumptuousness and make our own advances in the world of ideas and values step by step, hypothesis by hypothesis, test by test, fact by fact.

Second, we must face the communists in the arena of

ideas with our own forces marshaled on the broadest possible front. They have framed the struggle of their world and ours as one between "capitalism" and "socialism," and we have let them get away with it much too long. The issue between us is not that simple. In the first place, their "socialism" is a harsh form of state capitalism, and our "capitalism" is a mixed economy that has been civilized by social controls. Far more important than that veiled truth, however, is the fact that it is not alone our economy that divides us from them, but our free, pluralistic, accommodating patterns of government, social relations, culture, science, education and religion. It is high time that we sought to undo the damage we have let Khrushchev do with his insistence—while we flounder about in our own clichés—that "peaceful co-existence" is an accommodation between socialism and capitalism. We will never put our cause persuasively to the uncommitted world until we make clear how much more encompassing the conflict really is. Our struggle with the communists is one of society against society and mind against mind; our chief strength lies in a tradition that insists, in defiance of our own urges toward dogmatism and obscurantism, that both be kept open.

Third, let us rise serenely above the Manichaeanism that fogs the Marxist view of reality. We must not resolve all the torments of our century into a two-sided struggle between the forces of pure light and the forces of total darkness, lest we ourselves end up in a state of frenzied obsession with the enemy. We must not make as intense a religion of anti-Marxism as they have of Marxism, lest we suffer the fate of those who identify the absence of evil with the presence of good. Only thus can we keep our minds free and flexible.

Most important of all, we must not slide hopelessly into an apocalyptic view of the struggle between their system and ours, lest we slam the door forever on all hopes of an evolution in communism that would make it possible for East and West to live together in a reasonably peaceful world. No one in his right mind would predict such an evolution confidently, but hope may still reign where prediction abdicates. The changes that have taken place in Marxism already should be enough to persuade us that other changes are sure to come, changes perhaps so profound in nature that the Soviet system will be transformed out of all recognition. What would be left over would be Marxism only in name, but that, after all, has been the fate of most of the great isms that have held sway in the world. The apocalyptic promise of Marxism, like that of Islam, might then endure for centuries—unfulfilled and unrepudiated.

All this, of course, is speculation about a distant and enigmatic future. For the present it should be comfort enough to remember that I have been contrasting two faiths, and that like all faiths they claim a great deal more allegiance than they will ever get. If we were perfect, if our grasp on reality matched the reach of our tradition, we could look forward confidently to a free, peaceful, prosperous world. If they were perfect, if they never really doubted Marx's promise that they would inherit the earth, we could look forward to abject surrender or inevitable war. But we, unfortunately, are imperfect democrats, and they, fortunately, imperfect Marxists. In the first of those two facts lies the challenge, in the second the hope of a brighter future for America and for the world.

Further reading:

Hook, Sidney: MARX AND THE MARXISTS: THE AMBIGUOUS LEGACY. Princeton: D. Van Nostrand Co., Inc.; 1955.

Hunt, Robert N. Carew: MARXISM: PAST AND PRESENT. New York: The Macmillan Company; 1955.

Mayo, H. B.: INTRODUCTION TO MARXIST THEORY. New York: Oxford University Press; 1960.

Meyer, Alfred G.: LENINISM. Cambridge: Harvard University Press; 1957.

WILLIAM ALFRED FOWLER

[*Photograph by Gene Lester*]

William Alfred Fowler, professor of physics at the California Institute of Technology and experimental nuclear physicist in that institution's W. K. Kellogg Radiation Laboratory, combines studies of the smallest and the largest—the atomic particle and the universe—to probe the mysteries of the origin of matter. On a national level Doctor Fowler has made important contributions to the development of the proximity fuse, of rocket ordnance and of atomic weapons. Besides participating in international astrophysical discussions, he conducts oenological research here and abroad.

The Origin
of the Elements

B Y

WILLIAM ALFRED FOWLER

Man inhabits a universe composed of matter of almost infinite variety and complexity. Around him, his five primitive senses perceive a welter of endless complication. Even the most commonplace objects in his physical surroundings—a rock on the ground, a cloud in the sky—are clearly not simple in structure or composition. Whether he looks up to the stars or down to the depths of the earth, he sees a chemistry of creation wondrous in its countless forms and variations.

Men of science have long attempted to probe behind this complexity. While searching for the ultimate natural laws, they have also sought the nature and the origin of the fundamental forms of matter—the chemical elements and their basic building blocks. What are the elements? How and when did they come into being? Starting with the basic building blocks, what has been the history of matter which produced the elements which we observe in the world about us?

It has been a fascinating detective story. In the thin skin of the earth's crust, in the meteorites which fall on the earth, in the light from the sun and stars, and in the cosmic rays from outer space lie the clues which tell not only of what the universe is composed but also of the history of the cosmic events which produced the rich and varied forms in which matter appears to us.

The ancient Greeks thought that the fundamental forms of matter—out of which all other forms could be produced—were air, earth, fire and water. In the nineteenth century all matter was found to be composed of atoms of what were termed the chemical elements—hydrogen, helium, carbon, neon, gold, uranium, to name a few. These elements were thought to be immutable—they were the indestructible bricks from which the universe was built.

The twentieth century has changed all this. The nuclear physicist has found that the elements are not immutable. The ancient alchemist's dream has come true in the modern nuclear laboratory. Elements can be transmuted one to the other. These transmutations were first unleashed in the atomic bomb and later in the hydrogen bomb. Controlled transmutations in nuclear-fission reactors supply power for cities and submarines. It is known that these processes take place in stars and serve as the energy source for the light which they radiate—but this is the burden of our story. For the moment we must return to the atoms and what is known about them.

Each atom consists of a very small central *nucleus* surrounded by *electrons*. The mass of the atom is concentrated almost entirely in the nucleus. (By the mass of a physical entity we mean the measure of its inertia or resistance to acceleration.) The electrons move in a cloudlike region which is much larger than the nucleus. If we can imagine an atom magnified to the dimensions of a football stadium, the central nucleus would be the size of a garden pea and the electron cloud would take up the rest of the space.

In ordinary matter, nuclei have a positive electric charge while electrons have a negative charge. (By the charge of a physical entity we mean the quantity of electricity associated with it.) The neutral atom has no over-all charge because the number of negative electrons surrounding the nucleus is just enough to balance the positive nuclear charge. The number of electrons determines almost entirely the commonplace chemical, physical and electrical properties of the atom. Thus these properties depend on the charge of the nucleus. The atoms of one element are distinguished from those of another by the nuclear charge and the corresponding number of electrons. For example, the nuclei of hydrogen have a single positive charge. In the hydrogen atom this is balanced by one negatively charged electron. The nucleus of uranium has ninety-two times the charge of hydrogen nuclei, and this charge is balanced in the uranium atom by ninety-two electrons.

Even when we concern ourselves only with atoms, there is still considerable complexity. For one thing, there are now known to be 102 elements or atomic species—from hydrogen, the lightest, to Element 102, which has nuclei with 102 times the charge of hydrogen nuclei. In addition to the great number of the elements there is another point of complexity. Although the nuclei of a given element all have the same charge, they do not all have the same mass. These differing forms are called *isotopes* from the Greek—*iso*, the same, plus *topos*, place—referring to the fact that they occupy the same place in the periodic table of the elements, a classification of the elements according to their chemical properties. Chemists associated the isotopes of a given element because they had the same chemical properties in spite of their differing mass.

We have identified more than 300 isotopes of the elements found on the earth. Slightly over fifty of these are naturally radioactive. In addition to the 300 naturally occurring isotopes of the elements, it has been possible to synthesize another 900 radioactive nuclei in nuclear reactors or high-energy accelerators. Adding the 300 naturally occurring to the 900 man-made forms, we find that we know of 1200 nuclear species—the hearts of the atoms of the elements. Is this the number of the fundamental units of matter? Fortunately the answer is no!

In 1932 the riddle of this apparent complexity was solved; all nuclei were shown to consist of two still more fundamental building blocks, the *proton* and the *neutron*, collectively called *nucleons*. The proton is the central nucleus of the ordinary hydrogen atom. The proton has a single positive charge and slightly more than one unit of mass in the measuring system used by the nuclear physicist. The neutron also has slightly more than one unit of mass, but has zero electric charge; it is electrically neutral—thus the word *neutron*. Neutrons in a vacuum or free state transform to positive protons and negative electrons—always in combination, to preserve the over-all charge at zero. Inside nuclei, neutrons can retain their own identity and are just as good building blocks as the protons.

Each of the 1200 nuclear species is characterized by a definite number of protons and a definite number of neutrons. For example, there are three variants, or isotopes, of uranium found in nature, all with ninety-two protons, but with 142 or 143 or 146 neutrons. Adding the number of protons and neutrons yields the designations uranium 234, uranium 235 and uranium 238. It is the uranium 235 which serves as the most effective fuel in supplying fission energy in nuclear reactors.

Thus we see that atoms with the same number of protons but differing numbers of neutrons in their nuclei are isotopes of the same element. In ordinary physical and chemical processes isotopes behave alike. In nuclear processes, however, isotopes behave quite differently because of the differing numbers of neutrons. In other words, these differences in isotopes are not important under ordinary circumstances; only in the nuclear laboratory or reactor or at the high temperature and density in the center of stars do the isotopes of an element play their individual nuclear roles.

It is well to emphasize that the relative amounts of the isotopes of one element remain unchanged in most geological processes. The ten isotopes of the element tin, for example, have come down to us unchanged in their relative numbers since they were produced in cosmic events. They tell us of the nuclear history of the universe, and in what follows it will be seen that we have learned to look upon the isotopes of the elements as truly eternal clues.

The proof of nuclear structure comes from experiments in nuclear laboratories. These experiments have shown that all nuclei can be dissociated into neutrons and protons and all can be fused or put together again from these same nucleons. Some progress has even been made in understanding the internal structure of the nucleons, but the story is by no means complete. In most acts of the drama of creation the nucleons may be considered immutable.

This immutability of nucleons is not inviolate. When nuclear collisions occur at high velocity and great energy in the nuclear laboratory, particles called *antiprotons* can be produced in pairs with protons. An antiproton escapes with considerable velocity from the proton with which it is born. In ordinary matter it eventually meets another proton which it annihilates along with itself in a great burst of energy. Similarly, *antineutrons* which annihilate neutrons can be produced in pairs with neutrons. The nomenclature for these new particles is quite literal and graphic—antimatter annihilates matter!

Thus, protons and neutrons can be created and destroyed at high energies. We have pointed out previously that free neutrons and some neutrons in radioactive nuclei can transform to protons along with negative electrons. It is also known that protons in certain other radioactive nuclei can transform to neutrons along with positively charged electrons, called *positrons*. In low-energy interactions, in a world of our kind of matter, protons and neutrons, collectively as nucleons, are stable and immutable. This is in spite of the fact that no previously known laws prevent them from transforming to electrons and other lighter particles with the disappearance of mass and the release of large amounts of energy. For this reason we have to accept another law of nature: Nucleons at low energy are immutable. If this law did not hold, then the universe as we know it would not exist.

With this picture of the structure of the nuclei of the elements in mind, it is natural to attempt to explain their origin by a synthesis starting with the fundamental building blocks, the protons and neutrons. Here we will not attempt to account for the origin of the protons and neutrons. Some cosmologists believe in a steady-state cosmology in which nucleons are constantly being created. Other cosmologists think that the nucleons were created many billions of years ago in a primordial event. Both points of view have the common difficulty that we only know of processes in which nucleons are created in pairs with antinucleons—and antinucleons annihilate nucleons. We

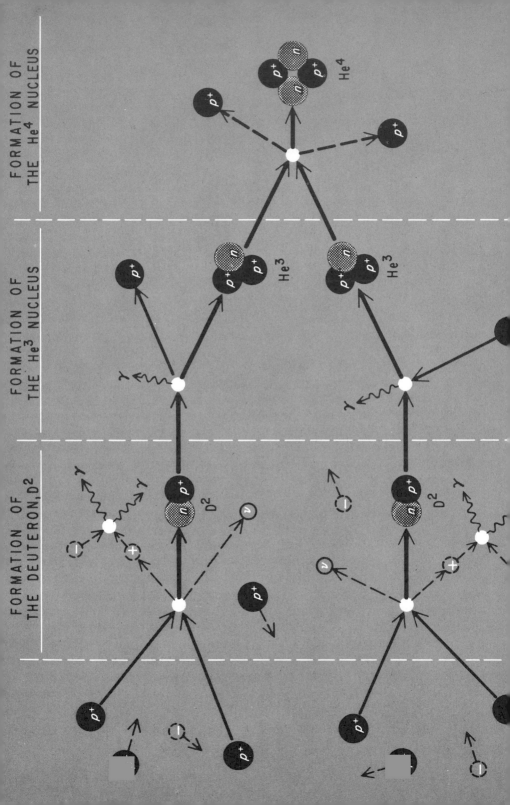

FORMATION OF THE DEUTERON, D² FORMATION OF THE He³ NUCLEUS FORMATION OF THE He⁴ NUCLEUS

THE FUSION OF HYDROGEN INTO HELIUM IN THE INTERIOR OF THE SUN

The fusion of hydrogen into helium is the primary source of energy in stars such as our sun. It occurs in the stages illustrated above. At the high temperature in a star's interior the hydrogen atoms are broken down into protons ● and negative electrons ⊖ all in rapid motion. In a violent collision (left) two protons fuse together to form the deuteron ⊚ which consists of a neutron ⊙ and a proton and has a mass of two units. A positive electron or positron ⊛ and a neutrino ⊕ are emitted in the fusion process. The neutrino escapes directly from the star because it interacts only very infrequently with other forms of matter. The positron soon collides with an electron, and both are annihilated with the appearance of energy in the form of two photons or quanta γ of radiation. The deuteron eventually collides with a proton (middle column) and forms a nucleus of helium with a mass of three units (He^3) and the appearance of more radiant energy. The collision of pairs of He^3 (right) results in the release of two protons and the production of a nucleus of helium (He^4) which has a mass of four units. In this way four protons and two electrons (those annihilated by the positrons) have been converted into one helium nucleus plus radiant energy and kinetic energy of motion. Starting with primordial hydrogen a new element has been produced. Energy is released because the mass balance before and after is not exact. The four protons and two electrons are slightly heavier than the helium. By Einstein's famous law the mass lost is converted into energy. The energy thus produced in the center of the sun travels out to the surface, and is radiated away as light and heat.

live in a world of nucleons. How did our nucleons escape completely from the set of annihilating antinucleons with which they were born? No one knows. But today we can ask and partially answer at least the following question: Given protons and neutrons as the building blocks, how and when were they put together in various combinations to form the elements and all of their isotopes? How did the complexity come to be, starting with the universal simplicity?

Just as there are two antithetic theories of the origin of the nucleons, the continuous creation and the single creation, so there are two divergent points of view concerning the synthesis of the elements beyond hydrogen. In one point of view, physicist George Gamow and his collaborators have appealed to the astronomical evidence for the expanding universe. This evidence shows that the light from other galaxies is shifted in color to the red. A similar shift to longer wave lengths is observed for the radio waves from these same galaxies. These shifts indicate that the distant galaxies are receding from us. The light we receive from them is reddened and the radio waves are lengthened just as the sound from the whistle of a receding train is shifted toward the bass. We also know that the more distant a galaxy the greater its red shift and thus the greater its velocity of recession. The most distant galaxies observable have velocities measured up to one third the velocity of light, which would have them moving away from us at 200,000,000 miles per hour.

Such a recession suggests a primordial "big bang," in which all the matter of our universe was ejected with high velocity from a common region; the galaxies whose matter received the greatest velocities relative to that of our own are now the most distant from us. The distances to the galaxies divided by the velocities as deduced from the red shifts fix the time of the creation. This turns out to be ten to twenty billion years ago.

Holding to the explosive evolutionary cosmology with its expanding universe, Gamow suggested that in the early stages of the expansion the density of radiation and matter was very great indeed and that under these circumstances neutrons rather than protons and electrons were the major constituents of matter. And so, *in the beginning*, Gamow postulates a huge "neutron ball" that promptly began to expand because of its great internal energy. This was the start of the expansion of our universe which we now observe.

We can study in the nuclear laboratory the nuclear processes which took place during the early stages of the expansion. We have mentioned that neutrons in vacuum transform to protons and electrons. This transformation takes time and, in the case of the neutron, the "half-life" is found to be twelve minutes—that is, of a given number of free neutrons existent at a given time, one half transform in an interval of twelve minutes, one half of the remainder transform in another twelve minutes, and so on. Thus, as the primeval expansion took place, neutrons gradually changed into protons and electrons.

Again laboratory observations tell us something relevant. When we produce neutrons in hydrogen gas, rather than in vacuum, they fuse together very rapidly with the protons in the hydrogen atoms; the protons are said to capture the neutrons. We can think of this as happening during the primeval expansion. One of the free neutrons transforms. The proton from this transformation captures one of the remaining free neutrons. The result is the formation of the deuteron, the nucleus of an isotope of hydrogen called "heavy" hydrogen. The deuteron has a mass twice that of the proton or neutron. The first of the nuclear species beyond ordinary hydrogen has been produced.

The deuteron can in turn capture another free neutron to form the triton, a still heavier form of hydrogen with a mass of three units, but still with the single positive electrical charge of the original proton. At this stage, experiments show that one or the other of the two captured neutrons in the triton emits an electron and becomes a proton, leaving a nucleus with two protons—and the remaining neutron—and therefore a positive charge of two units and a mass of three units. This makes the resultant atom an isotope of helium, whose nuclei are doubly charged. A new element has been formed. The common form of helium has a mass of four units, and this comes into being when the helium with three mass units captures a neutron to keep the chain of events going.

Thus, according to this theory, by a succession of neutron

captures, interspersed from time to time by electron emission to form protons, all of the elements were built in a matter of a few minutes during the earliest epoch of the expanding universe. (Naturally there had to be enough electrons from the neutrons to neutralize the protons and produce a universe of neutral atoms.) This picture of the creation and the element-building, followed rapidly by the formation of galaxies, stars and planets, seemed to be demanded by the astronomical evidence when it was proposed some years ago. At that time the age of the universe was thought to be the same as that of the solar system, namely 5,000,000,000 years. This suggested that the elements, the galaxies, the stars and the planets had been created in a relatively short time. Recent research has set the age of the universe as at least 10,000,000,000 years—while the solar-system age remains at 5,000,000,000 years—so a somewhat less hectic early history is now possible, even in this evolutionary picture of cosmology.

There are widely recognized difficulties in the foregoing element-synthesis chain. The most striking difficulty arises from the fact that among all the nuclear species found in nature, none has a mass of five or a mass of eight units. When produced in the laboratory, nuclei with these masses break up again very rapidly. Thus the chain of neutron-capture events—one unit of mass at a time—has two broken links. We are forced to conclude that only the lightest elements could have been produced in the primeval explosion.

We now turn to another point of view—one that has been advocated by several scientists, but primarily by Fred Hoyle (see "When Time Began," by Fred Hoyle, ADVENTURES OF THE MIND, *The Saturday Evening Post*, February 21, 1959). Hoyle and Geoffrey and Margaret Burbidge and I have collaborated in one of the recent studies of the subject. In this point of view the elements beyond hydrogen have been produced in the stars.

All of us have heard the nursery rhyme, "Twinkle, twinkle, little star; how I wonder *what* you are?" But have many of us ever really wondered what is in a star? According to Hoyle, the answer is right in ourselves; because all of the elements in our bodies, all of the elements in the earth and in the sun—all those beyond hydrogen, that is, and even part of the hydrogen—have been at some time or other in the hot interior of a star. We are "star dust." The reader will be skeptical, and so let us turn for confirmation to certain astronomical observations.

Fifteen billion years ago our Galaxy, the Milky Way, was not at all like it is at the present time; it was an enormous mass of hydrogen gas hanging tenuously in space. It was roughly spherical in shape, and it was slowly rotating. Shortly after this mass of gas became separated from the rest of the universe, stars formed from some of the gas, and as they condensed and contracted, their gravitational potential energy was converted into internal thermal energy and into radiant heat and light. Eventually as more and more stars were born, lived and died, the rotation caused the collection of present stars and uncondensed gas to take up the flattened disklike shape of the present Galaxy. What about the individual stars? After a few tens of millions of years of contraction, stars stop contracting and settle down for a relatively long period, constant in size like our sun, during which they emit light uniformly and steadily, again like our sun. How did this stability come about? Where did the energy come from, after contraction and the release of gravitational energy stopped?

Again for the answers we must turn to the nuclear laboratory. There we find that with particle accelerators we can cause pairs of deuterons, the heavy hydrogen nuclei with a mass of two units, to fuse into helium nuclei with a mass of four units. This process is called *fusion*. Several steps are required, but we can produce helium nuclei one at a time with our accelerators. In spite of the valiant efforts of scientists throughout the world— in Russia, in England and in the United States—no one has been able to produce a *self-sustaining* fusion process.

Why should anyone want to do so? The answer lies in the fact that all the masses we have quoted have been approximate. The two deuterons together have slightly greater mass than the helium nucleus they form, and when the fusion occurs, the excess mass is converted into energy. By Einstein's famous equation, one obtains the energy released by multiplying the excess mass by the velocity of light, once and then once again. Thus a large amount of energy results from the small change in mass, and if the fusion process could be made self-sustaining, as is the fission process in reactors, then we could essentially burn as fuel the heavy hydrogen which forms a part of all sea water. We would have a source of energy sufficient for all mankind forever. The unsolved problem lies in the fact that the nuclear *burning* must take place at such high temperature that we cannot build a furnace which will confine and contain the fuel.

The fusion problem has been solved in stars. Because of their size, stars contain a sufficient amount of material so that they can confine nuclear fuel gravitationally, sustain fusion processes and shine on the energy that comes from these processes. Moreover, in the star's early stages of contraction the stellar material is heated until the nuclear processes are triggered by the high temperature. The release of the nuclear energy adds to the violent internal motions, and the contraction of the star is stopped with a delicate balance resulting between inwardly directed gravitational forces and outwardly directed thermal pressure.

Stars, including our sun, have solved another problem. They consist most abundantly of ordinary hydrogen, with practically no heavy hydrogen. It will be recalled that ordinary hydrogen nuclei are called protons. In principle it is known that four protons, each with a mass of one unit, can fuse into a helium nucleus with a mass of four units. Two positive electrons, or positrons, are produced in the process, but these annihilate immediately *in situ* in combination with two negative electrons. Two ephemeral particles with no mass or charge, called neutrinos, are emitted with the positrons. The neutrinos move outward with the velocity of light and escape from the star. The mass balance in the over-all fusion process is not exact, and the mass lost reappears as energy—the fusion of ordinary hydrogen into helium goes on in the deep interior of most stars, and this is the source of their stability and their energy.

The fusion of protons into helium can occur in stars even though protons are all positively charged and mutually repel each other. As a matter of fact, on classical Newtonian mechanics, the fusion cannot occur, because even at stellar temperatures the protons do not have sufficient relative velocities to overcome their mutual repulsion. Sir Arthur Eddington, who proposed hydrogen fusion as the source of energy in stars in 1920, gave a magnificent answer to those who criticized him on classical grounds: "We do not argue with the critic who urges that the stars are not hot enough for this process; we tell him to go and find a hotter place." Eddington's critics were saved from their classical fate by modern quantum mechanics, which governs the behavior of atomic particles and permits fusion to occur even when it is "impossible" on Newtonian mechanics.

We now begin to see the evidence for the role played by stars in the nucleosynthesis of the elements. We can postulate that the Galaxy formed from pure hydrogen and so did the first stars within the Galaxy. As time went on, the internal hydrogen in these stars was consumed, like the fuel in a furnace, and the ash was helium. If the early stars broke up or exploded at this stage, they would contaminate the otherwise pure primordial hydrogen of the Galaxy with helium. Then, any stars which formed at a later state in Galactic history, as our sun did, would contain, as does our sun, not only hydrogen but also helium.

Stars do not necessarily break up after converting their central hydrogen into helium. They may continue their element-building. When the central, hottest part of a star becomes all helium, the hydrogen being exhausted, this new element is truly an ash because it is inert at the temperature, about 10,000,000 degrees absolute, at which the hydrogen was burning. Higher temperatures—about 100,000,000 degrees absolute—are required to burn helium. But now gravity takes over again as the nuclear hydrogen fire goes out. The helium core of the star contracts and raises the temperature to the ignition point for helium. How does the helium burn? This was a great puzzle for many years, but now we know that—in a complicated two-stage process which can be studied only in reverse in the laboratory—three nuclei of helium, each with a mass of four units, can be fused into a nucleus of the element carbon, which has a mass of twelve units. This is, in fact, the most abundant form of carbon which we find in nature. Moreover, the process leapfrogs over the missing links at mass five and mass eight and winds up at mass twelve.

The production of carbon with mass of twelve units in the

helium core of a star which remains stable is followed by a succession of similar building processes until the elements near iron in the periodic table are produced. We know that these processes must terminate near iron, which has been found to have the lowest energy content of all the elements because it has the lowest excess mass in the sense we previously discussed. Thus, the end of the line is reached for the first-generation stars of the Galaxy, formed from pure hydrogen, when they have developed an iron core at their center surrounded by layers of intermediate elements out of still-unconsumed layers of carbon, helium and hydrogen in their cooler outer regions. When the iron core begins to collapse, no further energy can be released. The collapse of the innermost regions becomes catastrophic. The ultimate result is ejection of the outer parts of the star in a gigantic explosion. The super-novae seen by astronomers as "new" stars which flare up to great brilliance in a few days are probably such explosions. New elements, synthesized by the stars as they produce energy through nuclear transformations, are eventually dispersed throughout the interstellar medium in the Galaxy. Thus, stellar systems formed at a late stage of the life of the Galaxy, such as our sun and the earth and the other planets, contain not only the primordial hydrogen of the Galaxy but also heavier elements. This, then, is the origin of the more complicated forms of matter which enrich our surroundings.

The essentials have now been told. There are many more details. In second-generation stars which formed from hydrogen plus the helium, carbon and iron produced in the first stars, nuclear reactions can take place which produce neutrons. Neutrons, which are neutral, are not repelled electrically by other nuclei. Furthermore, they can be captured by iron and other elements to form still heavier elements. The process proposed by Gamow for the synthesis of all the elements in the primordial universe can take place in stars which contain small amounts of iron. There are no broken links in the chain beyond this point, and snythesis up to the stable elements with the heaviest nuclei, lead and bismuth, can take place slowly but surely in stars which are second generation of stars. Following their demise, later-generation stars—our sun would seem to be one of these—form from material containing all of the elements which have stable forms.

What nuclear processes occur in the sun? It is fairly certain that the sun did not produce the heavy elements observed in it and on the earth. The earth and the outer part of the sun which we can see tell us of what the solar system was formed. Our plentiful supply of heavy elements is consistent with the fact that the sun formed relatively late in the Galaxy, long after many other stars had enriched the galactic medium with the products of their internal nuclear transformations. We use the term *enriched*, but this is truly a figure of speech. The material of the sun is still mostly primordial hydrogen, some 75 per cent, and in its hot interior hydrogen is being converted into helium as a source of energy. The sun is middle-aged as a star; about one half of its interior hydrogen is consumed. The sun is about 5,000,-000,000 years old, and in another 5,000,000,000 years it will have developed a large helium core. Then in a relatively short period the sun will produce carbon and heavier elements and eventually die in a final explosive outburst. It will be imperative that our space ventures be successful before that time!

This would all be fine and dandy if it were not for one thing. How were the radioactive elements thorium and uranium produced? They cannot have been produced by the steady neutron-capture process in slowly evolving, second- and later-generation stars which we have previously described. This process reaches to lead and bismuth, which have the heaviest nonradioactive nuclei. Between bismuth and thorium there are many short-lived radioactive elements which spontaneously emit helium nuclei with a mass of four units. This emission more than counterbalances the gain of one unit of mass on capturing a neutron. Obviously the thorium and uranium can only be produced when many neutron captures can occur before radioactive loss. This is somewhat analogous to scooping up water with a sieve—it can be done if one scoops rapidly enough. Rapid neutron captures occur astrophysically only during the explosive stages of stellar evolution. Evidence for rapid-neutron synthesis became available terrestrially in the first hydrogen-bomb explosion at Eniwetok in November, 1952. After the explosion the thermonuclear debris revealed that an isotope of element ninety-eight, named californium, with a mass of 254 units had been produced. Since the heaviest material in the bomb was uranium 238, it became clear that in the intense neutron flux produced in the explosion, the uranium 238 had captured some sixteen neutrons in a very brief space of time to become uranium 254. After the explosion the uranium 254 transformed in a short time to californium 254.

The californium has the unique property that it transforms spontaneously by breaking into two roughly equal parts by the fission process, with an enormous release of energy. The half life for the transformation was observed to be fifty-five days. This is also the half life of the decrease in the light intensity of supernovae after their original flare-up. It has been suggested that californium 254 is produced in supernova explosions and that after the explosion it contributes fission energy to the expanding stellar debris. In some way the light output from the star follows the californium activity, decreasing in time just as the californium disappears. The neutron flux in the supernova is so much more intense than in a man-made bomb that we can think of the californium as being produced from elements such as iron and not from uranium. This permits the possibility that uranium and thorium were also produced in the same manner along with certain isotopes of many of the other elements.

We find uranium and thorium in the earth today because, although they are radioactive, their lifetimes fall in the range of billions of years. Their survival tells of supernova events which happened billions of years ago. Radioactive nuclei remind one of an hourglass—perhaps *aeon*glass would be more apt in this connection. The nuclei which have not transformed are the grains of sand in the top of the glass, those transformed are the grains in the bottom. The action of these nuclear clocks is impervious to all the ordinary cosmic and geologic events to which these nuclei have been subject since their original nucleosynthesis. Thus they can be employed to tell us when they were produced.

The conclusion is that the uranium and thorium in the solar system were produced in stars in the Galaxy over a period which started at least 12,000,000,000 years ago and ended when our system formed some 5,000,000,000 years ago. The stars which explode as supernovae are, on the average, about 3,000,-000,000 years old when they do so, and so we see that our Galaxy must be at least 15,000,000,000 years old, three times the age of our own solar system. It would seem that we have on our hands a problem in cosmic geriatrics. Since Copernicus we have not believed our earth to be central in the solar system; in recent times we have found that our sun is not central in the Galaxy. Now we see that the sun and the earth are not central in time—that is, they did not originate at the beginning of our Galaxy. The last vestige of our primitive geocentric beliefs must be abandoned.

How do we know that the supernova events which are frequently seen at the present time by telescopic observations of other galaxies are really stellar explosions? There have been three such events in *our* Galaxy in recorded history. Johannes Kepler studied one which occurred in 1604; Tycho Brahe made beautiful observations on a previous one in 1572. The most interesting of all is one recorded by Chinese astronomers of the royal court in A.D. 1054. Exactly where they reported the position of the new star in the sky, astronomers now see a tenuous, filamentary mass of gas called the Crab nebula. It looks for all the world like an explosion in space, with the debris now far-flung after travel outward for more than 900 years. The Chinese observed it first on, of all days, the fourth of July, 1054. They called it a "guest" star, visible by day, like Venus. They could see it with the naked eye—they had no optical aids—for two years, and from this we know that they observed the same decreasing luminosity, down by one half every fifty-five nights, which we think is due to the radioactivity of an isotope of californium.

And so we come to the end of the line in element synthesis. The elements which make up the sun and the earth, with the exception of some primordial hydrogen, were formed in the hot caldron of the interiors of many previous stars over an epoch of incredible duration. There is some possibility that some of the material was even made in stars in other galaxies and was spread throughout space. We can speculate that this material condensed into our Galaxy at the time of its formation or even at a later stage.

This would make our sample of homely materials universal on a truly grand scale. It might mean that we do inhabit a steady-state universe and that our sun and our Galaxy, as they die, will contribute material to countless stars and galaxies yet to be formed. If we are truly universal in our physical make-up, it may well mean that the chance of other systems' occurring in the universe with similar intelligent life to ours is immeasurably enhanced. It may be not just "one world," but truly "one universe."

Further reading:
   Gamow, George: MATTER, EARTH AND SKY. Englewood Cliffs, N.J.: Prentice-Hall, Inc.; 1958.
   Lemaître, Canon Georges: THE PRIMEVAL ATOM. Princeton: D. Van Nostrand Co., Inc.; 1950.
   THE UNIVERSE. By the editors of *Scientific American.* New York: Simon and Schuster, Inc.; 1957.

DAVID L. BAZELON

[*Photograph by Philippe Halsman*]

As a member of the United States Court of Appeals in Washington, D.C., since 1949, the Hon. David L. Bazelon has written more than twenty-five opinions on the insanity defense in criminal cases, highlighted by his formulation of a broadened test of criminal responsibility in Durham v. United States in 1954. For these opinions, which have evoked world-wide discussion, the American Psychiatric Association awarded him a certificate of commendation, proclaiming that "he has removed massive barriers between the psychiatric and legal professions and opened pathways wherein together they may search for better ways of reconciling human values with social safety." Dr. Karl Menninger of the famed Menninger Clinic in Topeka, Kansas, describes the Durham decisions as "more revolutionary in its total effect than the Supreme Court decision regarding segregation."

The Awesome Decision

BY

DAVID L. BAZELON

The administration of criminal justice and the extent of individual moral responsibility are among the crucial problems of a civilized society. They are indissolubly linked, and together they involve our deepest personal emotions. We often find it hard to forgive ourselves for our own moral failures. All of us, at some time or other, have faced the painful dilemma of when to punish and when to forgive those we love—our children, our friends. How much harder it is, then, to deal with the stranger who transgresses.

Few of us view punishment realistically. Whether applied to criminals or to our own flesh and blood, we are profoundly confused about punishment. We waver between feeling "he deserves it" and "it will do him good." The first reaction is our immediate emotional response, the second our rationalization after the fact. "It will do him good" can be proved or disproved; it lies within an area of practicality. "He deserves it" is unprovable, a proposition derived from absolutist morality. The latter reflects the retributive theory of justice, whereby appropriate penalties are necessary if only to uphold the moral law. But many people cannot accept this view. They argue that, though punishment may not be defensible in all cases, it cannot be dispensed with because social balance requires the gratification of the need for vengeance. Or they assert that we must punish to deter potential criminals.

Nowhere is the social attitude toward individual moral responsibility more sharply focused and more dramatic than in a criminal court. Here, in the whole process of justice—symbolized by the trial—the full weight of society's official force, moral and physical, is arrayed against a single human being. More often than not, this defendant is one of life's failures— part of the human debris of civilization. Thus, the considerations which govern the determination of his responsibility are a measure of man's humanity to man, or lack of it.

We pride ourselves, and in many respects justly so, on our efforts to insure a fair trial, and so manifest the advance state of our civilization. Yet in an essential aspect of criminal justice we remain backward. We remain backward in the way we deal with the question of responsibility as it relates to mental disease, personality disorganization and the nature of antisocial behavior. Our criminal courts do not generally welcome the psychiatrist with his greatly expanded knowledge of unconscious motivations and environmental conditioning. Instead they cling doggedly to an age-old rule of criminal responsibility which makes modern science irrelevant to the critical question of the defendant's psychic state. In effect, our courts still ask a nineteenth-century question and insist on a nineteenth-century answer.

I refer to the famous formulation of the insanity defense which resulted from the trial of Daniel McNaghten in 1843. This rule—the prevailing law both here and in England for more than a century—requires a jury to consider only whether the defendant knew what he was doing or knew that it was wrong. In relying exclusively on the rational capacity of the mind, this so-called right-wrong test reveals its ancient lineage. It is based on the prescientific view of the human psyche and behavior, wherein the whole story is the eternal conflict between reason and passion. As long as any capacity to know or to reason remains intact, so the theory goes, failure to use it to control the passions constitutes choice, and is therefore culpable. The accused should be punished because he chose to do wrong.

But today we know that a choice of behavior involves the whole functioning human, not just reason alone. We are all painfully familiar with examples of behavior in which the accompanying thought process is only rationalization. Psychiatrists continually come across mentally sick patients who retain substantial reasoning powers. Indeed, one of the commonest symptoms of serious mental disorder is such a dissociation between the rational top of the mind and the emotional underpinnings of the personality.

On January 20, 1843, Daniel McNaghten, a Scottish wood turner, fatally shot Edward Drummond, secretary to the prime minister, Sir Robert Peel, as Drummond was entering a government office in London. The assassin had mistaken the secretary for the premier. "The Tories in my native city have compelled me to do this," he explained later. "They follow and persecute me wherever I go and have entirely destroyed my peace of mind."

The sole issue of McNaughten's trial was insanity. His counsel, Alexander Cockburn, called nine physicians and surgeons to the stand. All testified that the accused was insane. The prosecution entering no medical testimony in opposition, the presiding Lord Chief Justice Tindal directed a verdict of "not guilty, on the ground of insanity." McNaghten spent the rest of his life in mental institutions.

The public reaction was indignant; many people ascribed the shooting to a political plot. Queen Victoria herself protested the verdict. As a result, the House of Lords put several questions to the fifteen judges of England. Their answers have governed the insanity defense ever since throughout most of the English-speaking world. Lord Chief Justice Tindal set forth the McNaghten Rules as follows:

> . . . the jurors ought to be told in all cases . . . that to establish a defense on the ground of insanity, it must be

clearly proved that, at the time of the committing of the act, the party accused was laboring under such a defect of reason, from disease of the mind, as not to know the nature and quality of the act he was doing; or, if he did know it, that he did not know he was doing what was wrong.

The insanity defense had a long history prior to Tindal's formulation. As early as the thirteenth century, British law recognized that "a madman does not know what he is doing." In 1724 Judge Tracy held that insanity was exculpatory if the defendant "doth not know what he is doing, no more than . . . a wild beast." Thirty-six years later the "wild beast test" was abandoned in favor of the defendant's capacity to distinguish between "right and wrong"—the precursor of the McNaghten Rules.

The insanity defense reflects a concept that has pervaded the entire history of the criminal law. We call it the doctrine of *mens rea*, sometimes described as "guilty mind," or "evil intent." It can be traced back to Deuteronomy 19:4–6, "Whoso killeth his neighbor ignorantly, whom he hated not in time past . . . shall . . . live . . ." *Mens rea* is a capsule phrase used, in connection with most crimes, to describe a state of mind which makes the offender blameworthy and so subject to criminal sanctions. Whether this state of mind is a deliberate intent to commit the prohibited act, or some form of negligence, it usually involves ability to anticipate consequences and guard against them. The insanity defense is designed to relieve from criminal liability persons who are incapable of such a state of mind.

The concept of "insanity"—conceived by lawyers, not by doctors—is rooted in this requirement. Originally the insane defendant was thought of as one so obviously bereft of reason that, on the basis of common experience alone, all men could agree that he was incapable of entertaining an evil intent. Through early legal history only total insanity was recognized as a defense, probably because no scientific knowledge existed to differentiate the shadings and gradations of mental disease.

It is ironical that at the very time when psychiatry was beginning to emerge as a distinct medical discipline, antiquated, nonmedical ideas about insanity were frozen into the Mc-Naghten Rules. The law closed the door in psychiatry's face.

It was in 1838 that the American psychiatrist, Dr. Isaac Ray, published his classic *Treatise on the Medical Jurisprudence of Insanity*, attacking the concepts upon which, five years later, the rules were based. In fact, McNaghten's counsel cited Doctor Ray. Other psychiatrists soon joined Doctor Ray in the attack. In this century the chorus of protest has become deafening. Some of the world's leading psychiatrists have refused to testify in court under the distorting limitations of the McNaghten Rules. In a poll taken a few years ago, 80 per cent of 300 American psychiatrists pronounced those rules unsatisfactory, and numerous jurists have agreed. Justice Cardozo flatly stated, "Everyone concedes that the present definition of insanity has little relation to the truths of mental life."

The main criticisms of the right-wrong test are fourfold. First, it misses the point entirely, because whatever "insanity" means, the term refers to abnormal conditions of mind that cannot all be gathered together under the rubrics "know" and "wrong." Second, the test is based on an outmoded theory of faculty psychology—derived from phrenology—that divided the topography of the mind into separate compartments. Modern psychology views a man as an integrated personality, and reason as only one element of that personality and not the sole determinant of conduct. Third, the test poses to the expert an ultimate question involving legal and moral as well as medical issues. Fourth, the test has so strait-jacketed psychiatric testimony that insanity is defined exclusively in terms of extreme psychosis and patent organic deterioration.

What arguments favor the right-wrong test? Chiefly that it reflects traditional morality governing the conduct of normal persons, that it persists historically, that alternative tests are inadequate and, perhaps most important, that many courts ignore the test as often as they apply it. From the juridical point of view, what all this controversy adds up to practically is whether we are to have more and freer psychiatric testimony. With it stated this way, I myself have no hesitance in taking a position solidly in favor of freer and fuller expert testimony.

DAVID L. BAZELON

This is exactly what we did in the District of Columbia in 1955 when the United States Court of Appeals adopted the Durham Rule. Under this new, more liberal rule, a modern and comprehensive body of law governing the adminstration of the insanity defense is being slowly built up on the basis of continuing experience. At the same time the community's fears that great numbers of dangerous persons would be freed to attack again are being put to rest. Nothing of this sort has happened. Defendants acquitted under the Durham Rule have been sent to mental hospitals, many of them for longer periods than they would have served in prison. And they appear to get into less trouble after release than prison convicts.

Although no other court has yet adopted the District of Columbia precedent, it is not an eccentric backwash of American jurisprudence. For one thing, it is an adaptation of a broadened test that the Supreme Court of New Hampshire adopted in 1870. This test, which allowed the insanity plea if the unlawful act arose from mental disease, was fashioned largely under the influence of Dr. Isaac Ray. For another, the Durham Rule reflects a widespread movement among the legal, psychiatric and allied professions to work out alternatives to the rigid spirit of the McNaghten Rules. For example, in 1955 a new test designed to liberalize McNaghten was proposed by the American Law Institute, a leading body of distinguished lawyers, judges and scholars.

To recount the Durham case, on July 13, 1951, twenty-three-year-old Monte Durham broke into a Georgetown home and was caught pilfering clothes. Since the age of sixteen, Durham had been charged with passing bad checks, embezzlement, parole violation, car theft and attempted suicide. Three times he had been committed to mental institutions. Psychiatrists had variously diagnosed him as "psychotic with psychopathic personality" and, oddly, "without mental disorder but with a psychopathic personality."

Following his indictment for housebreaking, he was adjudged of unsound mind and again sent to a mental hospital. Sixteen months later the hospital's superintendent certified that "prolonged psychiatric study has established that [Durham]

150

suffers from psychological illness, but is mentally competent to stand trial. . . ."

As in the McNaghten trial, the sole issue was the mental condition of the defendant. The only medical witness was the Government psychiatrist who had originally found Durham incompetent to stand trial, and his testimony "was unequivocal that Durham was of unsound mind at the time of the crime." The trial judge, who heard the case without a jury, strictly applied the McNaghten test and rejected the psychiatric testimony because the Government doctor declined to answer categorically the ultimate question—did Durham know the difference between right and wrong?

On appeal, Judges Henry W. Edgerton, George T. Washington and I held this was error and, in reversing the conviction, we announced a broader test to be applied in all subsequent cases. We stated that the new rule "is simply that an accused is not criminally responsible if his unlawful act was the product of mental disease or mental defect." Under this test the question would be "whether the accused acted because of a mental disorder, and not whether he displayed particular symptoms which medical science has long recognized do not necessarily, or even typically, accompany even the most serious mental disorder."

Our underlying purpose was to unfreeze the expanding knowledge of psychiatry, as it could be applied to the law, in order to free the psychiatrist from having to make the moral and legal determinations required by the right-wrong test for which he has no special qualifications, and to allow him to address himself to the problems of mental disease and defect, for which he is qualified.

Finally, it was our purpose to restore to the jury its traditional function of applying "our inherited ideas of moral responsibility to individuals prosecuted for crime" under the historically sanctioned precept that "our collective conscience does not allow punishment where it cannot impose blame." But in making the awesome decision as to criminal responsibility, the jury "will be guided by wider horizons of knowledge concerning mental life."

According to the opponents of the new rule, it creates more

problems than it solves. If this statement be amended to read "uncovers" instead of "creates," I would agree. I think that any realistic revision of the insanity formula is bound to reveal difficult problems which have been ignored or suppressed under the McNaghten test. Many psychiatrists, for example, who admit their inability to answer the right-wrong question, follow the mechanical practice of testifying that a psychotic cannot distinguish right from wrong, while an individual suffering from a nonpsychotic mental illness can. They so testify even though such an artificial demarcation has neither a medical nor a legal basis. Under Durham, or any broader test, there will not be the same compulsion to dispose of the issue by means so deviously mechanical—a practice that also wrongly relieves the jury of its duty to decide the case.

I agree with one of the more widespread criticisms of the Durham Rule, that the term "mental disease" cannot be rigidly defined. But that is because it is a dynamic concept undergoing continual redefinition in the course of clinical experience. It is strange logic, however, to conclude from this fact that the complexities behind the term should therefore be ignored or that lawyers should arrive at a definition a priori. We must instead seek out the best current scientific explanations.

Another frequent criticism of the Durham test holds that any serious investigation of the nature of mental illness and its effect on criminal conduct will lead to the conclusion that all criminals are mentally ill. If that is so, then it is high time we found it out. I am flabbergasted that some of the most dogmatic defenders of McNaghten actually believe that all criminals are ill. If true, would this not require a complete reconstruction of our criminal law? At the very least, it would require us to abandon the special defense of insanity and the corollary concept of *mens rea*, thereby overturning our historic system.

A third objection to the new rule is that the resources of psychiatry are not up to the task. This may or may not be valid, but we do know psychiatry has more to give than the law now receives. Until we accept what it has to offer, we cannot discover the actual limitations of psychiatry.

The fourth objection to the Durham formulation is that it is difficult to determine whether a criminal act is "the product of" mental illness. This is true, but I think unavoidable. Other formulations involve the same difficulties—the American Law Institute proposal uses the phrase "as a result of." Moreover, juries solve a similarly difficult problem of causation every day when they decide in personal-injury cases whether it was the defendant's negligence that caused the plaintiff's injury.

But the overriding objection to Durham undoubtedly derives from our deepest feelings about punishment. In the traditional mode of thinking we, the good citizens, feel that they, the criminals, should be punished. So, the argument proceeds, it is just as well that only "slobbering idiots" should be excused, as under the McNaghten Rules. A broader rule is bad just because more criminals would get off.

This objection, based on the felt need to punish, brings us to an issue that transcends legalisms and all merely professional considerations—an issue embracing the whole of society. Here are involved the mutual demands of society and the individual upon each other. Here, within the democratic framework, lies the grand context of criminal responsibility.

Practically speaking, the legal term "insanity" can be defined by the consequences of its use. When pronounced "not insane," the accused is sentenced to prison as a punishment. When held insane, he goes to a mental institution for treatment. This is the practical aspect, what all the theoretical discussion boils down to—punishment or treatment.

Prisons and mental hospitals fulfill a similar function to the extent that both segregate undesirable persons from society. In this sense, both protect society. According to ideal penological theory, punishment reforms; after release the prisoner will behave acceptably, and society will be protected. But in reality the rate of recidivism is high—more than 60 per cent among Federal convicts. Now, it is majestically simple that, since punishment so often fails of its purpose, something else is needed. And this something else is treatment.

Punishment as such, remember, is supposed to fit the crime, not the criminal. When the sentence has been served, the warden of the penitentiary signs a certificate to that effect, and the prisoner rejoins society—even though it may be obvious that the punishment has worked no cure and indeed may have intensified the prisoner's criminal impulses. On the other hand, an inmate of a mental hospital is released only when certified by the staff as cured, or at least not dangerous to himself or others. No psychiatrist, to be sure, is infallible. He may err in his prognosis and recommend release prematurely, with disastrous results to the community. Many state hospitals, moreover, are too overcrowded and understaffed to provide optimum care. But at least the effort is made to exercise responsible medical judgment, whereas the prison warden is called upon to enter no judgment at all except as to parole. Is it not evident that treatment rather than punitive incarceration offers society better protection? So much for the practical aspects.

But as I have pointed out, society tends to waver between the ideas, "he deserves it" and "it will do him good." A somewhat more sophisticated attitude is reflected by the so-called deterrence theory which attempts to merge "he deserves it" and "it will do him good" under the synthetic proposition, "it will do us all good." This theory not only underlies the usual learned arguments against broadening the insanity defense but forms the central theoretical problem of the entire criminal law.

The deterrence theory, like its less sophisticated antecedents, seeks to justify the existing amount of punishment meted out as a means of preserving public order. By imprisoning the criminal, it is contended, we deter others from committing crimes. The prisoner thus becomes a scapegoat. In a free society such use of an individual cannot be justified except by a survival of the "he deserves it" feeling as well as the sanguine belief that his incarceration both serves as a beneficial example to all and does the prisoner good. Thus the ancient views of retribution persist in the deterrence theory.

It seems to me that this theory begs the entire question of justice for the individual. Unlike the retributive theory, it assumes that though punishment may not be right, may be purposeless or downright destructive to the individual, yet it protects society and so is justified. Hence even the mentally ill and hopelessly psychopathic recidivist are sacrificed for the purported social benefit. Thus the individual is degraded—contrary to our democratic ethos.

Unarguably, the maintenance of public order must be backed up by a system of sanctions. Neither law nor morality can sustain itself from generation to generation without the threat of some penalties. Many of us do not steal, not because of a fear imposed from without, but because of an internal control system generated by our mores and traditional beliefs. For most of those who require external controls it is the threat of going to jail, not actual time spent there, that keeps them from stealing. We need sanctions to give substance to the threat. How much actual punishment is required in order to sustain the threat of punishment at an effective level? That is the real problem posed by the deterrence theory. Many of its supporters seem to answer, "Exactly as much as we now have." This strikes me as both too easy and antihistorical. After all, it was not so long ago that whippings and executions, carried out as public spectacles, were considered essential to the preservation of order.

In our society the essential aim of the criminal law should not be to induce mass fear of punishment, but to reaffirm the value of each individual by due process in his conviction and purposeful treatment thereafter. Too often, in our eagerness to protect society, we forget that society is composed of individuals. In a democracy, society or the state is no more than the sum of its individual components. The state exists for the benefit of the individual, not vice versa, as in Nazi Germany or Soviet Russia. Consequently, repressive law can be justified only as an accommodation of the mutual liberties of two or more individuals. The real difference is not always apparent, and at times we may favor one group of individuals over another in the interests of those liberties. But the basic theory does not change. It remains transcendently important. It is perhaps the central thread of continuity in our law.

If we now consider the issue of criminal responsibility on spiritual rather than practical or ideological grounds, we discover an ancient philosophical conflict at the heart of the problem—free will versus determinism. I am not equipped to deal with this great problem as a philosopher or theologian would, but I want to venture one or two observations.

If the question is whether we make real choices, two things are clear—we obviously seem to do so, and some people seem to have a wider choice of action than others. Intellectual, physical and emotional capacity, wealth, social status, all extend or limit the area of choice. Yet, in the eyes of the law, for example, the poor and the rich face the same responsibility to resist the temptation to steal, even though the poor may be overwhelmingly tempted and the rich not at all.

Surprisingly, this free-will-determinism issue is seldom discussed in the practical context of actual choice, but usually on the level of abstract theory. On that level the argument often revolves around the old issue of science versus religion. Freudianism has carried the banner of scientific determinism into the inner sanctum of theology—the human soul. Darwin placed the human animal in nature, and Freud attempted to explain what occurred inside this human animal. His success has been substantial. Freud's concept of the unconscious as a source of motivation, as part of the great revolution it is working in modern thought, has compelled us to reconsider the question of criminal responsibility.

As a result, an expanded category of disease has supplemented or displaced the diminished category of "evil." Evil is not a scientific word. Madmen were once thought to be possessed by evil spirits, and the means of exorcising the devil included torture. If we are not yet prepared to view every juvenile car thief as ill, many of us do feel that his social and economic background may be out of joint and may itself be "ill." The notion of a perfectly personal evil no longer suffices to explain all the events in a human career.

Evil, of course, can only be punished or forgiven. But illness is supposed to be ameliorated or cured. Thus the name we put to our failures makes a difference. We all tend to believe in free will when we entertain hopes for the future, but switch to determinism when recalling our past failures. I suggest we extend the same consideration to the failures of others.

As Hollingshead and Redlich suggested in their study, *So-*

cial Class and Mental Illness, neurosis is something of a class privilege. It is less common in the lower social strata. There are the number of psychotics and psychopaths appears to be greater. According to the Hollingshead-Redlich findings, the neurotic containment of conflict requires certain amenities of life, especially the possession of social values to be preserved. The mentally ill of the poor classes, including many criminals, lack the leisure for inner neurotic torture, and have less to lose by "acting out" their conflicts. Though no conclusive scientific proof exists, the indications are strong that a good deal of criminal behavior should be viewed as a pathological function of marginal socio-economic status. Some 90 per cent of the criminal cases which come before our United States Court of Appeals involving the insanity plea concern indigent defendants. For many people it takes certain minimum advantages in life to "learn how to be good." With those who have clearly failed to learn, it may be that part of the burden of social responsibility shifts from them to us, calling for something better than punishment.

The law is neither a scientific instrument nor an adjunct to any absolute moral doctrine. Our legal system is the way we conduct our business of mediating conflicts, preserving the peace and furthering orderly social development. It thus stands between all opposing forces or conflicting ideologies. In the criminal law and in the administration of the insanity defense the wisdom of the past, including the free-will postulate, meets modern scientific views, including the postulate of causal determinism. The legal process differs from religion in that, being concerned with factual decisions, it cannot utter moral imperatives. It differs from science in that it cannot choose its experimental subject matter, it cannot plead ignorance and it cannot select its hypotheses freely. A court must resolve all conflicts presented to it, with or without adequate knowledge.

The chief inhabitants in the house of the law are the members of the jury. This much maligned body carries the final burden of redressing the social balance. In shouldering the awful responsibility of assessing the degree of another person's responsibility under the law, the jury—that sample of all of us—

needs all the help available. When considering the insanity defense, obviously it needs the help of psychiatric and other scientific experts, given fully and freely. Only then, on the basis of all possible relevant facts and scientific insight, can the jury make its moral judgment, its awesome decision.

In the Durham case we said, "The legal and moral traditions of the western world require that those who, of their own free will and with evil intent . . . commit acts which violate the law, shall be criminally responsible for those acts. Our traditions also require that where such acts stem from and are the product of mental disease or defect . . . moral blame shall not attach, and hence there will not be criminal responsibility."

Thus, within our traditions, the case goes to the jury.

Further reading:

Guttmacher, M. S., and H. Weihofen: PSYCHIATRY AND THE LAW. New York: W. W. Norton & Company, Inc.; 1952.

Lindner, R. M.: REBEL WITHOUT A CAUSE. New York: Grove Press; 1956.

Menninger, Karl: MAN AGAINST HIMSELF. New York: Harcourt, Brace & Company; 1956.

Overholser, W. THE PSYCHIATRIST AND THE LAW. New York: Harcourt, Brace & Company; 1953.

Weihofen, H.: THE URGE TO PUNISH. New York: Farrar, Straus & Cudahy, Inc.; 1956.

Zilboorg, G.: THE PSYCHOLOGY OF THE CRIMINAL ACT AND PUNISHMENT. New York: Harcourt, Brace & Company; 1954.

Freud, Sigmund: BASIC WRITINGS. New York: Modern Library, Inc.; 1938.

Barnes, Harry Elmer, and N. K. Teeters: NEW HORIZONS IN CRIMINOLOGY. New York: Prentice-Hall, Inc.; 1959.

Deutsch, A.: THE MENTALLY ILL IN AMERICA. New York: Columbia University Press; 1949.

ALEXANDER ELIOT

[*Photograph by Larry Fried*]

Alexander Eliot is best known for his monumental art history, Three Hundred Years of American Painting; *yet that work represents only a fraction of his interests. A novelist* (Proud Youth) *and art critic* (Time), *Eliot is chiefly obsessed by what he calls "the ultimate problem: understanding with the heart." Last year saw publication of his* Sight and Insight, *a philosophy of art-in-life and life-in-art. He is now working on* Elements and Kingdoms, *which will explore the wisdom to be gained from direct contemplation of nature.*

Eliot's forebears played distinguished roles in the flowering of New England and Harvard University. He himself makes frequent visits to his home ground, but prefers living in New York City. Eliot travels abroad extensively with his wife and three children for the purpose, he explains, "of trying to rediscover the world with the help of my wife's mind and my children's eyes."

ᒪᒪᒪᒪᒪᒪᒪᒪᒪᒪᒪᒪᒪᒪᒪᒪᒪᒪᒪᒪᒪᒪᒪᒪᒪᒪ

The Sense of Truth

BY

ALEXANDER ELIOT

From the shadow-measuring and tub-sitting of the ancient Greek scientists to antibiotics, cyclotrons and satellites has been a fabulous advance. Where once rode classical thunderheads of intellection, white against the sky, we have dark torrents of numbers and symbols innumerable as raindrops and mingled with the fitful play of man-made lightnings, earthquakes and germs. Near miracles lie stacked like dishes stories high in the brains of giant guardian computers. Yet the loftiest experiments remain those of people. Thomas Jefferson still says more than the bulletins from Cape Canaveral. Christ on the cross flew higher than an astronaut ever will.

Each man that lives is an experiment, self-controlled. He is both crucible and chemist in himself. Let him but open his own heart and mind, and the cosmos pours in upon him. He must distill what he can. To realize this plain fact of the human condition can be like awakening from a dream into real life.

They say that the ancient Greeks put man at the center of the cosmos; but nobody put him there—it is his cosmos. Granting that in thought a man may travel far from his own center, which is the center of his cosmos, and granting even that he may stop off at aesthetic, philosophical, religious or scientific planets far removed from the mother earth of his own experience, experience brings him home; and in himself he remains

161

the center of it all. Therefore aesthetic and philosophical refinement, religious revival and scientific advance can do little to heal our sick culture. A sick culture is made up of sick selves; we have to heal ourselves.

Madness and death—these things we face, and we are too heavily armored to face them. Madness we call a disease, yet our sanatoriums are very like our jails at one end of the social scale and retirement paradises on the other; they are play streets roped off. The symptoms add up to the same old withdrawal from reality.

The idea of killing oneself can have much sweetness. To be "half in love with easeful death" is quite all right subjectively. Let a friend take the plunge, and we are horrified. With death the possibility of human understanding ceases. My friend is gone; I remain with my question. But if he had been run over, say, would I feel so bad? We all get run over sooner or later, one way or another. Since death comes from from another world than our world of the living, it must always have an accidental quality. Yet the ancients called "dying well" the very height of philosophy. Clearly they were not talking about raw courage. The wise man holds his life complete, knows it complete with each passing moment and therefore faces death with equanimity.

Aristotle said that tragedies ought to be concerned with renowned families only. He was speaking of the stage. In real life, however, all those whom we really know and love are heroes to us; they are of noble family, the human family, and their deaths are tragic—because life is tragic, as it is lived now.

The death of a bird does not seem tragic; it has lived its life complete. Those ducks on the pond will take flight again in a day or so; they have a thousand miles or more still to go, and on the way many will be shot down. Couple by couple they swim and feed now in a kind of bliss. Instinct brought them here and will blow them on. Resistless, they ride the winds of instinct, and the winds and they are one, the pond and they are one—it is all one and all complete continually. For just an instant a jet liner, Europe bound, casts its shadow athwart the pond. The people in that plane are borne on the winds of circumstance, not instinct; and if the plane should fall—tragedy.

Thought, like the jet liner, casts its shadow now and then athwart the still and central truth, but only for a moment. Thought travels far and far away. Finally alighting in strange countries, it forgets to trust itself—naturally enough. For the nature of pure brainwork is to be swift, far-reaching and sharply limited.

Who could ever surmise the totality of this pond? What mind could encompass it? Beginning with the day it first began, what have been its weathers and its creatures? What of its microscopic life and its plants? What of all the thousands of men, from Indian times, who stood where I stand now; what have they felt and thought and acted out along the edges of this pond? White water lilies, dark-leaved, ride the wind-purpled pond at rest. We see them as if in a dream, but they are real. There was once a great painter of water dragons who worked only from hearsay. Taking pity on his blindness, a real dragon swam up out of the pond and appeared to the artist—who died of fright.

Life as we live it is tragic because it is unreal. Born to reality, living to penetrate reality, we refuse even to believe in it.

What has been the relation of science to reality? The ancient Greeks paced out certain measurements of earth and built from there. They drew, of course, on Egyptian surveying methods, developed to keep track of the constantly changing relations between the Nile and the land. Underlying all the changes, the Egyptians had found, were certain unchanging geometric principles. These the Greeks refined, clarified and organized. Greek geometry still is taught—more or less by rote—to school children. We learn geometric principles as facts merely, but the Greeks saw them as absolutes, awesomely pure and eternal.

On cloud terraces of mind the Greeks laid the speculative foundations of science. Then there were the medieval and Renaissance alchemists, who failed apparently for lack of rigor. They multiplied their problems in the laboratory as a nervous cook heaps on spices. Often, too, they felt a mystical rapport with their materials and, instead of watching the pot, they would be praying. Modern science rests on more strictly controlled experiments. The bulk of its equipment is designed to eliminate extraneous factors. Moreover, until a few years ago the experimenter himself was considered fairly extraneous to his experiment. But now science is beginning to demonstrate increased respect for human experience—that is, for what happens between the experimenter and the experiment being performed. The eyes of science continue to peer bleakly into laboratory experiments as if from outer space, or now and then peek into a sort of mailbox for messages. Yet the minds behind those chill eyes burn with a newly subjective urgency that no mere data can satisfy.

Calculating machines, which were supposed for a moment to make human calculations comparatively suspect, are proving suspect themselves. Being peculiarly a prey to "noise" or static in various elusive forms, they seldom get precisely the right answer to difficult questions. And when the machine's answer is way off, the question must be rephrased. This requires putting the seer back into science. Only men who can guess very close to hidden truths ask rewarding questions.

What fabulous answers flow to our control rooms! What new worlds appear! The alchemist's old dream is child's play compared to this—not worth the candle. The physicist makes things more potent than gold, and he finds facts past prophesying. Yet he will be the first to point out that not even science can penetrate far into nature. Any man's conceptions are limited, the argument runs, to what his five senses tell him. Truth, pragmatically considered, is what can be proved. Man obviously is far too limited a creature to construct an all-inclusive theory of reality; and even if he had the theory, he could never build a laboratory complex enough to prove it. Science shines ever brighter in an ever-widening darkness, illuminating far more problems than it penetrates. There is such a thing as the scientific predicament.

Also there is such a thing as the sense of truth. What can never be proved in a laboratory may be proved in any moment of a man's own life. Blue is blue and a triangle is a triangle. One can know these things, however, without sensing their truth. The sense of truth comes with human experience in time and space. It comes with growing blue morning-glories or constructing a sailboat. Then, oddly enough, the absolutes of the Greeks, the subjective protoscience of the Middle Ages and Renaissance and finally the strict data processing of modern science all merge in one's mind. So also do the five senses through which reality pours. A man remains his own best chemist and crucible. Acting on this, he has the sense of truth.

An eminent physicist has taken issue with me here. After a recent conversation between us he sent me the following note: "My link with you is through our common belief in the reality of the subjective and the joy of the immediate. We part company when you become abstract and want to give me a sense of truth. To me it is as welcome as an extra head. My own concern is more for beauty. I would rather contemplate a mature oak in the gentle rain than comprehend the chemistry of chlorophyll or the action of gravity."

That is his viewpoint and, with all due respect, I find it a sentimental one—not only sentimental but also symptomatic of our times. Truth and beauty are like brothers; it is we who divide them. The scientist muses dumbly on a tree while the poet wistfully shrugs off simple mechanics and chemistry. The moments when music and meaning merge—when truth and beauty join— are continuous. It is our fault that we feel them so rarely.

A man's best moments embrace two activities at once—the first aesthetic and the second intellectual. Only at such times may he comprehend the chlorophyll in the foliage and the gravity in the rain without losing sight of the vision as a whole. Goethe said that any form correctly seen is beautiful. He had the sense of truth. The old Masonic sign that appears on United States one-dollar bills—the eye in the apex of a pyramid—well symbolizes scientific vision, which is intellectual vision. The sense of truth requires besides this a more sensuous, varied and personal view of nature, which might in its turn be symbolized by the Chinese calligraph for the word "see"—an eye on legs.

The ancient Chinese recognized not four elements but five. They found the same four that Empedocles noted and then inscrutably added wood. I have never seen a reason given for this. Perhaps they wanted five elements to balance the five senses.

And wood carries in itself the principle of growth, which the classical elements, taken separately, lack.

Heraclitus, a father of science as we know it, moved in the opposite direction from the Chinese. He boldly reduced the elements to a primal one—fire. Heraclitus lived in Ionia on the coast of Asia Minor, between Athens and Suss. Presumably then his thought was colored in part by the fire-worshiping Persians. Logical and extreme, he taught that a pond with migrating ducks and water lilies, or an oak tree in the gentle rain, or what you will, are all composed of one and the same fire—that saint and fire are one, that air, sea and land are all ablaze continually, and that humanity is a sort of sparkling.

Physicists find this proposition increasingly plausible and attractive. It has simplicity on its side and also finality. Fire, as Blake sang, "gives its light and gives its heat away." The second law of thermodynamics spells eventual exhaustion—a cold "heat death"—for the entire cosmos.

Mathematically considered, order tends to disorder. Thus, in a famous example, a perfectly stacked deck of cards gets increasingly disrupted when shuffled. Yet scattered seeds will create new order. Here is a conflict which contemporary science tends to resolve in favor of hopelessness. Nature may seem to be a sweet and graceful dancing of life with death; but, science says, the pattern of the dance has all been determined to lead us back through chaos to certain destruction. In classical times such determinism gave rise to stoicism—"Whatever will be will be"— a philosophy for slaves. The latest breed of stoics—"logical positivists"—are, if anything, even less positive and more abject.

Science measures, predicts, exploits and manipulates the course of things. Hence scientists are tempted to consider truth nothing but a conglomeration of things, about which we happen to have ideas. This temptation they generally resist, and for an excellent reason. If truth exists only on the material plane, whence come our ideas? From the realm of illusion?

Religion and philosophy concern the spirit; hence men of the cloth or of cap and gown are tempted to think of truth as a purely spiritual thing, a matter of ideas to which the physical world corresponds. But if the correspondence between spiritual and material be exact, where lies the distinction between them? And if, on the contrary, it be inexact, then is matter false? In the Orient, and sometimes in the Occident as well, the philosophers' answer to this question has been, "Yes, matter is false or, rather, illusory." But as Samuel Johnson demonstrated, a stubbed toe suffices to upset that notion.

Another down-to-earth observation of Doctor Johnson's was that in putting on a pair of pants it makes no difference which leg goes in first. That idea applies precisely to the quest for a sense of truth. One may begin with either material or spiritual reality, so long as one ends with both together. In the end, the sense of truth requires only a firm hold on the fact that the tree in the rain and the tree in the brain are both true—and that each completes the other.

In a surviving fragment Heraclitus noted that all things are determined and that men must act as if they were not. I should like to expand Heraclitus' statement as follows: All mere things, perhaps, are determined. Yet men must act as if *they* were not. So long as any man possesses and acts upon the sense of truth he learns freedom.

> *Look at the rising sun; there God does live,*
> *And gives His light, and gives His heat away,*
> *And flowers and trees and beasts and men receive*
> *Comfort in morning, joy in the noonday.*

The best poets are those who speak comprehensibly of incomprehensible things. Scientists, on the other hand, speak in riddles about things that soon will be understood by all. Science is becoming a cult; let us learn everything we can from it except its pride, obscurity and chill doubts. The scientist is a man of arcane, special and hard-won lore. His heavy load of learning may oppress and darken his mind. To treat him as the rightful custodian of nature would be unfortunate. Nature belongs to all men, as every scientist who has a poet in him knows.

Just as much as science needs poetry, so does poetry need science. The sad fact, however, is that only a handful of scientists "find time" to read Blake or even Shakespeare, and only a handful of poets "find time" to acquaint themselves with the rudiments of physics or biology. The rest let lack of time turn them into half-minded men.

Who are the contemporary poets? Mostly script writers, copy writers, song writers, speech writers, publicists and columnists. Gibbon, describing the secret rot of Rome's Augustan age, remarks in passing that "a cloud of commentators darkened the land." It is the same today. Again, as in Rome, the so-called major poets are more scholars than poets. They look backward. They conclude. This holds for Joyce, for Pound, for T. S. Eliot's "Shakespeherian Rag."

Better a forward-looking science than mere scholarship, and it may well appear, over the years, that the enduring poets of the twentieth century have been men of science. One thinks of Freud and Jung. Dante's *Divine Comedy* is a poem which he intended partly as a treatise. Freud's *Interpretation of Dreams* on the other hand is a treatise which, despite the author's intentions, becomes poetry. What dates in each is like a discarded snakeskin, sloughed off by the living truth.

Man's greatest discoveries are always made in nature—in living nature—by men for whom knowledge and feeling merge. Newton, needless to say, did not invent gravity, he discovered its principle in nature. Yet the run of scientists tend to treat nature as the living proof of science, and this is not the same thing at all. The high-school science student finds himself a million or more light years out in space, and the chances are that he will never return. Meeting experts on every plane except the human, he learns to think of the very elements in which man moves and lives, the very elements of which mankind is shaped, as mere abstractions. There now exist in scientific terminology more than 100 "elements" and about a third as many "elementary particles." Their infinitesimal differences have got to be recognized; meanwhile, they have ceased to be elementary. For me the elementary elements remain the classic ones that I experience.

In chemistry water is H_2O. But H_2O is only a formula relating to water. Water is water, different all the time—in clouds and cups, cascades, birdbaths, puddles, Mississippis, gulfs and mountainous ocean, and in ice cubes and the garden hose. The Navajo Indians have dozens of nouns for water, being a desert people. There is water in the body—rivers of all kinds entwined. Heracles once broke the horn of a river rival, wrestling, and with Apollo's aid, Achilles bore down frothing Scamander. Gentler waters also come to mind—Undine, the water babies and that mermaid who cautioned a little boy to undress lest he get wet. One thinks of baptism, holy drops, and then raindrops racing down a train window, tears, drops of sweat and the pure globes of water carried home like bubbles from a sacred spring.

Or take fire, that holiest of elements, poured into this world from the sun, which is our life. A city man's closest contact with fire may come with lighting cigarettes. Or if the furnace goes out on a winter's day, he may descend for a disgusted look at the ashes. But to know how far one has fallen from the real element, one has only to think of Roman candles and pin wheels when a boy, or in autumn of the live burning of the leaves on the trees. Or one may chance to glance into the sun, or to think of fire-defying heroes such as Siegfried, or that grim Roman who burned off his own hand to prove a point of honor. Joan of Arc knew fire, knew it well. Such nostalgic and heroic associations would be just the beginning of fire conceived as a whole experience. They say that if the sun were encased in ice forty feet thick, it would melt all that ice in a minute. Some calculation! From the "Greek fire" that preserved Byzantium to the razing of Hiroshima, fire has remained the very brow of war. And all the iron sinews of this age are fire-forged. Poets take to the fiery element as naturally as salamanders—Homer, Virgil, John of Patmos, Dante, Milton, Blake. There are the many, many ritual uses of fire, from yule log to Olympic torch. On Persian peaks the Magi nurtured deathless flames. God spoke to Moses from a burning bush. These are but flickering, fiery thoughts.

The whole joy and purpose of living is living—that is, experiencing reality. Children know it well and, in general, they live best. A child's feeling about life is as immediate and ephemeral as life itself. He neither knows nor needs to know that he will die; he lives as if each hour might be his last, and thus he learns more every hour. Whereas we who set ourselves to learn some one thing for future use find it harder every day. Better perhaps to do as the child does and bring everything we have to present experience, to experience in depth.

"Count no man happy," said Solon, "until he be dead." I would count those happy who are happy and also ready for death. To store up riches, fame, power or knowledge unused is to blink away the prospect of death and be made a sad fool at the end. Happiness is a little boy dancing about a lawn sprinkler on a June afternoon.

To see that boy in sun and splash is to know that one has never experienced the Elgin marbles at the British Museum, simply because *they* are indoors. We should have more respect for the interplay of elements and kingdoms in nature. Not only are the marbles themselves such an interplay—between animal and mineral—but they need as well the blessing fires of sun and moon and the waters of heaven. If out of doors they weather away over the centuries, let them.

Museum people frequently refer to their collections as "material," meaning primarily material for scholars. Scholars themselves are material for scholarship, and scholarship in my view is material for one thing only—the deepening of direct experience. Everyone has felt the sudden, sweet, intense delight that comes with first seeing an inspired painting or poem. To derive everything possible from the masterpiece, there must follow hours of contemplation and cool study. One learns as much about the thing as one can and then goes on to speculate, not stopping at knowledge either. Finally one puts all that one has learned and imagined out of mind, to gaze with fresh eyes. Only then can understanding come and delight return to stay.

I have an ancient Athenian coin of silver, a drachma commemorating the Battle of Marathon. The warrior-goddess shines and smiles in my hand. I toss her, and she comes down the owl, symbol of dark, swooping thought. Who sculpted this? Who struck it off? Who has held it and spent it, and for what things? My first still pleasure in the beauty of the coin turns to adventure on the blood-and-silver seas of history. I think of Marathon, the air alive with arrows and the dying runner with his eternal message. I think of Socrates, that hard old optimist, and his teasing ways. He may have held this coin and pressed his thumb to the goddess's lean, smiling cheek. This drachma may have purchased Scythian slaves or ivory from India or perhaps a fat black wineskin, filled with forgetful music, from next door. It was one of a heap in a dooryard game of knucklebones. It stopped a dead man's tongue once; Charon brought it back. And I, coming back to present life now with the coin still in my hand, see it as if for the first and last time. It was beautiful before; but now, how much more beautiful! And more than ever an object. To contemplate a thing deeply and imaginatively will never adulterate that thing in itself. Quite the contrary; put thought away, gaze again upon the thing in itself, and it shines truer than before. Putting the drachma back in my pocket, I close my eyes and watch it rise on the horizon of interior vision. It casts its light upon the waters of my soul. I have experienced this coin, and the experience comprises a totality.

Heraclitus can be known in part, and his thoughts either proved or disproved. But my drachma cannot be known or disproved; it can only be experienced. It is not a thought center but a life center, as mysterious as was the pond with its water lilies and migrating ducks. Both purple pond and silver coin remain forever beyond intellectual comprehension, in their entirety, and yet rest easily within the heart. We can never hope for totalities of knowledge; yet we can have, often, totalities of experience. It is a matter of trusting the experience—not myself, not the object of my experience, but the experience itself.

The sense of truth arises from such trust. For truth is nature, and nature is experience.

Further reading:
Eliot, Alexander: SIGHT AND INSIGHT. New York: McDowell, Obolensky; 1959.
Plotinus: THE ENNEADS (Stephen MacKenna translation). New York: Pantheon Books, Inc.; 1957.

Boehme, Jacob: SIX THEOSOPHIC POINTS AND OTHER WRITINGS. Ann Arbor: University of Michigan Press; 1958.
Nietzsche, Friedrich: THUS SPAKE ZARATHUSTRA. New York: Modern Library, Inc.; 1920.

FRANK A. BROWN, JR.

[*Photograph by Jacob Lofman*]

Frank A. Brown, Jr., Morrison Professor of Biology at Northwestern University, first became interested in the phenomenon of living clocks in 1948. As an endocrinologist studying the action of injected hormones on crabs and shrimps, "We found that something beyond the influences of our ordinary laboratory conditions and procedures was affecting our animals and their reactions. Subsequently, with our study of the fluctuations with lunar and solar periods, the rhythms of life became more fascinating than our former problems." Professor Brown was educated at Bowdoin College and at Harvard. In summer he conducts his research at the Marine Biological Laboratory, Woods Hole, Massachusetts.

Life's Mysterious Clocks

BY

FRANK A. BROWN, Jr.

One of the greatest riddles of the universe is the uncanny ability of living things to carry out their normal activities with clocklike precision at a particular time of the day, month and year. Why do oysters plucked from a Connecticut bay and shipped to a Midwest laboratory continue to time their lives to ocean tides 800 miles away? How do potatoes in hermetically sealed containers predict atmospheric pressure trends two days in advance? What effects do the lunar and solar rhythms have on the life habits of man? Living things clearly possess powerful adaptive capacities—but the explanation of whatever strange and permeative forces are concerned continues to challenge science. Let us consider the phenomena more closely.

Over the course of millions of years living organisms have evolved under complex environmental conditions, some obvious and some so subtle that we are only now beginning to understand their influence. One important factor of the environment is its rhythmicality. Contributing to this rhythmicality are movements of the earth relative to the sun and moon.

The earth's rotation relative to the sun gives us our 24-hour day; relative to the moon this rotation, together with the moon's

175

revolution about the earth, gives us our lunar day of 24 hours and 50 minutes. The lunar day is the time from moonrise to moonrise.

The moon's arrival every 29.5 days at the same relative position between the earth and the sun marks what is called the synodical month. The earth with its tilted axis revolves about the sun every 365 days, 5 hours and 48 minutes, yielding the year and its seasons.

The daily and annual rhythms related to the sun are associated with the changes in light and temperature. The 24.8-hour lunar day and the 29.5-day synodical month are associated most obviously with the moon-dominated ocean tides and with changes in nighttime illumination. But all four types of rhythms include changes in forces such as gravity, barometric pressure, high energy radiation, and magnetic and electrical fields.

Considering the rhythmic daily changes in light and temperature, it is not surprising that living creatures display daily patterns in their activities. Cockroaches, earthworms and owls are nocturnal; songbirds and butterflies are diurnal; and still other creatures are crepuscular, like the crowing cock at daybreak and the serenading frogs on a springtime evening. Many plants show daily sleep movements of their leaves and flowers. Man himself exhibits daily rhythms in degrees of wakefulness, body temperature and blood-sugar level.

We take for granted the annual rhythms of growth and reproduction of animals and plants, and we now know that the migration periods of birds and the flowering periods of plants are determined by the seasonal changes in the lengths of day and night.

In a similar fashion creatures living on the seashore exhibit a rhythmic behavior corresponding to the lunar day. Oysters and clams open their shells for feeding only after the rising tide has covered them. Fiddler crabs and shore birds scour the beach for food exposed at ebb tide and retreat to rest at high tide. The reef heron, though living many miles inland, appears to know when low tide will occur and leaves home each day just at the proper time to take advantage of it.

Synodical monthly breeding rhythms, geared to particular

portions of the year, phases of the moon, and times of solar day, are common among animals inhabiting the sea. These rhythms assure that the eggs and sperm of a given species will be available at the same place at the same time. Each species has its own characteristic breeding time, which is often so precisely scheduled that we can accurately predict its occurrence. If, for example, we should go to the water's edge in Bermuda about an hour after sunset during a three- or four-day period of a summertime full moon, we would witness within a few minutes the mating display of the Atlantic "fireworm." At that time the females swarm to the surface from their burrows in the coral rock and luminesce brilliantly until joined by the males. At the same location, just before midnight either three to four days before or two days after a new moon, the swarming of the males and females of the glassy transparent shrimp, *Anchistioides*, takes place.

Palolo worms of the Southwest Pacific swarm in huge numbers on the nights of the third quarters of the October and November moons, liberating their reproductive elements into the sea water just as the dawn breaks. The breeding behavior of a small California fish, the grunion, is also exquisitely timed. Just after the moment of high tide, on nights from April through June, when the tides are at their monthly highest, these fish arrive at the beach in large numbers and ride the waves onto the sand. The fish quickly dig pits into which they discharge their eggs and sperm. Thus the new generation is able to develop over the period of a month without being prematurely washed out by the surf of the ordinary high tides.

Reproductive rhythms also occur in certain seaweeds. *Dictyota*, a brown alga, produces eggs and sperm on a monthly schedule. All the plants in one area may be synchronized to one phase of the moon, while those in another area will be regulated to another phase. The particular phase appears to be determined in some manner by the local tides.

Lunar reproductive rhythms are not restricted to sea dwellers. The reproductive cycle of the human female, averaging exactly the synodical month, indicates that here, too, exist both solar and lunar rhythms.

Though it might appear that such rhythms are merely the

responses of organisms to rhythmic changes in light, temperature or the ocean tides, this is far from being the whole answer. For when living things, ranging from the single-celled Paramecium to flowering plants and mammals, are removed from their natural habitat and placed under conditions where no variations occur in any of the forces to which they are generally conceded to be sensitive, they commonly continue to display the same rhythms they displayed in their natural environment. The fiddler crab, for example, normally darkens by day and pales by night, runs actively at low tide and rests at high tide. When removed from the beach to laboratory isolation from light, temperature and tidal changes, the crab continues to behave in synchrony with his fellows still free on the beach. The crab somehow possesses the capacity to measure accurately and simultaneously both solar-day and lunar-day intervals without the stimulation of light, temperature and tidal changes.

Seeds persist in their annual sprouting cycle under similar laboratory conditions. This persistent adherence to rhythms with sun- and moon-related periods under conditions in which the organism is isolated from any obvious manifestation of these time cycles strongly suggests that an inherent clock system is probably a universal attribute of life.

Although living clocks appear to function simply and precisely in their regulation of organisms in nature, they present baffling difficulties when they are studied in the laboratory. The inquiring biologist faces a problem comparable to that of an observer in space who tried to figure out the nature of man's artificial clocks by observing the activities of a coastal industrial town. In the daily activity rhythm, some persons would be early risers, others late. Some, the clam diggers, would appear to have a lunar-day timer. The employees of a factory with three equal shifts working around the clock, would appear to have no daily clocks. The general population would appear to have a seven-day clock reflecting no natural terrestrial period.

In studying the living clocks in nature we are confronted with a similar observational limitation; we can analyze the clocks only by observing the rhythmic phenomena they time. We must, in other words, work from what the clock does back to the clocks themselves. This sort of inference is simply illustrated in a study of the common fruit fly.

In its natural habitat, the adult fruit fly normally emerges from its pupal case about dawn. If this process is subjected to laboratory control, with the eggs being laid and allowed to develop in continuous darkness, the young flies will emerge at any time of the day. If the maggot-larvae hatched from the eggs are subjected to even a single light flash during this controlled period of darkness, however, the flies, when they emerge, will come out of their pupal cases at the same time of the day that they were exposed to the light flash. This suggests that fruit flies have operating twenty-four-hour clocks; under natural conditions the clocks of the developing flies are set to local sun time while they are still maggots and alert the flies for emergence at dawn. In much the same way, the lunar-day activity rhythms of such creatures as oysters and fiddler crabs correspond to the tidal times of their local shores.

The adaptiveness of the basic timing system may be illustrated with organisms as unlike as beans and bees. The leaves of beans, which rise and fall in a regular daily sleep rhythm when the plants are kept in a constant dim illumination, may be induced to rise momentarily from their lowered position by a brief light stimulus. This induced behavior will continue day after day at the same time, without further stimulus, if the plants are kept in the same environment. Similarly, honeybees trained to come to a sugar-water feeding station at one or two arbitrarily selected times of day, will persist in this same twenty-four-hour food-seeking schedule for a few days even if the food is no longer provided.

This adaptiveness of daily rhythms is most useful when living things are moved rapidly to a new time belt. When, for example, a person flies from California to England, he arrives in England with his physiological rhythms of waking, body temperature, blood-cell count and hormone secretion still adjusted to the local time of California. It takes at least eight or ten days for these physiological processes to adjust to the new local time. The various processes change at different rates; time of waking shifts fast, requiring only two or three days, while other rhythms shift more slowly. Hence there appears to be a period during which various bodily processes are shifting gears relative to one another.

Recent studies by Dr. Mary Lobban and by Dr. Janet Harker, both at Cambridge University, suggest some possible consequences of having our rhythms out of their ordinary relationships with one another. Doctor Lobban found evidence of stress in some human subjects who, during the protracted daylight of the arctic summer, lived by watches adjusted to indicate recurrent "days" of unnatural lengths. Doctor Harker, working with cockroaches, discovered she could produce tumors by transplanting a hormone-producing neural element, the sub-esophageal ganglion, from animals with their running-activity rhythms set to the usual time of day into animals whose rhythmic changes had been artificially reset (by reversing the natural light-dark cycle) to be twelve hours slow.

It is well established that some animals navigate by the sun, the moon or even the constellations, orienting themselves relative to these objects at an angle which changes systematically with the rotation of the earth. Birds or bees also alter their usual direction of orientation when their natural clocks are reset by cycles of light and darkness to indicate a different time zone. One can even predict the new direction of orientation from the interval by which the timing rhythm has been reset.

This was dramatically illustrated in a recent study by Dr. Max Renner of the University of Munich. Honeybees were trained on the East Coast of the United States to fly northwest to a feeding station at one p.m., Eastern Standard Time. The trained bees were then taken by airplane to the West Coast. The next day, in California, the bees went seeking food about ten a.m., Pacific Coast Time. They were still on Eastern Standard Time. But they adhered to their previously learned sun angle, and now with the morning sun flew off in a different direction— southwesterly. In both cases the sun was, so to speak, in their left eye.

Daily changes of both light and temperature are primarily responsible for resetting natural rhythms to local time. The twenty-four-hour rhythms in an organism's sensitivity to light and temperature facilitate this resetting process. If a plant, for example, is exposed to light during the hours of darkness (when it is sensitive to light), the plant will immediately reset its twenty-four-hour rhythm of light sensitivity. If the plant is then returned to its natural environment of uninterrupted periods of light and darkness, this adjusted rhythm will continue to be re- set by a small amount each day until the plant's light-sensitive and light-insensitive periods match the appropriate periods of night and day. In a similar fashion a mouse's rhythm of light sensitivity is set so that its activity and its running occur at night.

Each species seems to utilize such characteristic sensitivity rhythms. It also seems probable that these same twenty-four- hour cycles of light and temperature responsiveness in some way assist living creatures to measure the changing lengths of night and day and thus adapt themselves to natural annual cycles.

When some animals and plants are kept under controlled conditions of unchanging light and temperature, their daily rhythmic activities are observed to occur, in some cases, slightly earlier, in others, a little later each day. This produces activity rhythms with periods which vary from the twenty-four-hour cy- cle. These latter rhythms also vary somewhat in their periods with changes in temperature and illumination and from one in- dividual to another. Such variations from the twenty-four-hour cycle introduce a fundamental question. Are these variations the product of poor-quality living clocks which run fast or slow? Or are the clocks themselves precise—with the apparent inaccura- cies ascribable to some other cause?

We think we have the answer to why the rhythms often ap- pear to run fast or slow under these unchanging conditions. To the organism placed in the laboratory at a constant level of light and temperature these two factors will continue to have the most impact during the sensitive phase of its twenty-four-hour cycle of responsiveness to the environment. These two factors in effect will appear, therefore, to the organism to show a daily variation, but now the light and temperature cycles will seem to have become inverted. Thus, during the sensitive period of its cycle—which normally falls at night—it will interpret the in- creased effectiveness of the light and temperature as indicating daytime. Employing the same splendidly adaptive machinery it uses in nature to reset its rhythm until the sensitive portion comes to fall in the darker, cooler nighttime, the organism keeps resetting its sensitivity rhythm a little forward, or backward, regularly each day in a futile attempt to adjust to the illusory "day-night cycles."

This simple, reasonable hypothesis, compatible with all our current knowledge, makes it probable that the living clocks are always precise in their timekeeping. The alternative interpretation—that the inaccurate rhythms persisting under controlled conditions reflect inaccuracies in living clocks—is most improbable in view of the precision of the clocks under natural conditions where such resettings would not occur.

BASIC CLOCK QUESTION

Scientists are reluctant to credit a phenomenon for which they see no plausible explanation. As a consequence, evidence for living clocks was for a long time essentially ignored by most biologists. Recently, as our knowledge has become more refined, the phenomenon of timed rhythms was encountered so frequently by investigators in so many areas of biology that the possession of clock systems by living things became tacitly accepted. The problem of the nature of the clock systems had then to be faced.

Man-made clocks are of two general types—those with intrinsic timing and those with extrinsic. Examples of the intrinsic type are the hourglass, the pendulum and hairspring-balance clocks. Intrinsic clocks possess independent timing capacity and are useful any time and any place. Extrinsic clocks, like the sun dial and the electric clock, have no independent timing capacity but depend upon an inflow of timing information. The sun dial depends upon the sun's shadow, the electric clock upon the sixty-cycle alternating current. Extrinsic clocks are sometimes referred to as repeaters.

The basic question concerning the clocks of living things is whether they are intrinsic or extrinsic or whether, perhaps, they are both. This question has long been debated by students of biological rhythms.

The intrinsic-clock hypothesis has been generally favored over the years. This seemed the simplest hypothesis to account for the persistence of behavior of rhythms in unvarying light and temperature—especially the apparent inaccuracies and individually differing periods of the rhythms, their adaptiveness and their persistence in organisms transported long distances eastward or westward.

The extrinsic hypothesis, on the other hand, was questioned because it demanded that living things be sensitive to still unidentified, subtle pervasive factors. Such an hypothesis was radically opposed to the universally accepted concept of "constant conditions" in the laboratory—which postulated that under controlled laboratory conditions we could truly isolate an organism from fluctuations of every factor of the environment to which the organism is sensitive. The organism was deemed insensitive to such factors as magnetic and gravitational changes.

Since the rhythms persist in meticulously controlled "constant conditions," the working hypothesis of most investigators has been that the living clocks are intrinsic. The lengths of their natural periods, it was thought, are inherited and a consequence of fully independent cyclic biochemical transformations which would someday be explained solely in terms of the principles of physics and chemistry. But every investigation based upon this assumption found the living clocks unorthodox in terms of any ordinary biochemical scheme. Though all ordinary metabolic processes are greatly speeded up or slowed down by raising or lowering temperature, respectively, the periods of the clocks seemed generally independent of temperature. Crabs, as indicated by their color change and running habits, continue to measure accurately the periods of the day and the tides whether they are kpet at 54° F. or 77° F.; dried seeds, as shown by testing samples periodically, display the same annual rhythm in their capacity to germinate whether they are stored in a freezer at −8° F. or in an incubator at 113° F. Similarly, none of the drugs known to alter the rate or character of metabolic changes seem to interfere with the accuracy of the basic timer.

Clearly, if the timer is intrinsic, it is a most extraordinary mechanism. But this is exactly what one would expect of any good clock. And if the experimental conditions in which these rhythms persisted were really constant for the organism, the timer had to be intrinsic. On the other hand, if it were proved that laboratory conditions hitherto presumed constant for the organisms were really not constant and that the organisms continued to receive outside rhythmic stimuli despite laboratory controls, a potential timing signal would be available for an extrinsic clock. And such an extrinsic clock could account readily for all the observed properties of the rhythms, including temperature and drug immunities, and the long rhythmic periods which are the same lengths as the geophysical ones.

EXTRINSIC RHYTHMICALITY

It has recently become evident that organisms, even when hermetically isolated under so-called constant conditions, still derive information as to the geophysical rhythms from their environment. Such information must be transmitted by highly pervasive forces hitherto ignored by biologists. Let us briefly consider the evidence for this.

Oysters, collected in New Haven Harbor, Connecticut, were shipped to Evanston, Illinois. Kept in pans of sea water in a dark room, they continued for a time to open their shells widest when it was high tide in New Haven waters. By the end of two weeks the New England oysters had reset their rhythms to open their shells widest at the moon's zenith and nadir positions with reference to Evanston. The oysters maintained thereafter this new schedule throughout the month they were observed. The zenith and the nadir positions of the moon—the two lunar positions on opposite sides of the earth which give rise to twice-daily high tides—are the periods of the moon's maximum gravitational effects upon the atmospheric tides over Evanston; this same gravitational effect would produce high ocean tides if Evanston were a coastal city. Recently, from simultaneous studies of fiddler crabs collected from beaches with differing local tidal times, we have learned that these creatures are also able to reset their tidal rhythms of running activity to accord with lunar zenith and nadir, despite absence of any obvious cues as to these times. Obviously some subtle atmospheric fluctuation related to local lunar time is able to substitute for local ocean tides and reset the periods of maximum activity. The same factor must continuously signal the lunar periods.

Living things as different as fiddler crabs and potatoes continue indefinitely to display both solar-day and lunar-day rhythms in their metabolism while they are subject to constant conditions in a laboratory. These two rhythms co-operate to provide both species with a synodical monthly rhythm. Plainly, the artificially isolated organisms continue to derive a wealth of information about outdoor atmospheric rhythms. Some of the evidence available is quite fantastic.

The solar-day tides of the atmosphere are expressed in rhythms of barometric pressure. The atmospheric tide rises in the morning, reaching its highest point about ten o'clock, and then falls to its lowest in the afternoon. The daily rhythms of organisms, even when they are sealed off from such pressure changes, are somehow associated with these daily tides of the atmosphere and their regular modification by lunar influences.

Nature provided us with a ready means for discovering this relationship. The daily tides of the atmosphere in temperate latitudes are continuously distorted by large irregular, weather-associated pressure changes. We know that both potato plants and crabs follow some outside factor reflecting the daily atmospheric tides because the daily cycles in their rate of oxygen consumption continuously reflect significantly the unpredictable distortions in the daily pressure cycles. Since it is inconceivable that living things are provided with a detailed program of all the erratic weather changes which are to occur while they are sealed under conditions including unvarying light, temperature, humidity and pressure, we must conclude that information reaches them continuously.

All of numerous species of animals and plants which have been studied reflect, in their metabolic processes between five and seven a.m., the amount the barometric pressure changed between two and six o'clock that same morning. Their metabolism from five to seven p.m. reflects the amount the pressure changed between two and six o'clock that same afternoon. These times are highly specific; no comparable relationships are found at any other time of day.

In both winter and summer the atmospheric tide tends to rise in the morning; at the latitude of Chicago, the time of lowest tide occurs about two p.m. during the coldest months and about seven p.m. during the warmest months, and so the afternoon pressure tends to fall during summer and rise in winter. The metabolism of potato plants, even when they are sealed off from pressure changes, conforms to this annual pressure change.

A by-product of this study has been the astonishing discovery that the late-afternoon biological activity of nearly all living things, while only remotely related to mean daily barometric pressure of the same day, is intimately related to that of the second day thereafter. These organisms seem to be "predicting" the atmospheric-pressure trends. The biological explanation of the riddle is this: the afternoon pressure change which the organism's late-afternoon metabolism reflects is itself quite inexplicably tending to predict the barometric pressure trends two days in advance. Imagine the predicament of a meteorologist, sealed away like the potatoes, and faced with the problem of weather prediction.

Fluctuations in the numerous factors in the earth's atmosphere are variously interdependent. The discovery that the metabolism of living things, even under hermetic seal, reflects erratic changes in such rhythmic environmental factors as outdoor air temperature, cosmic radiation and general background radiation was, therefore, not surprising. Collectively, these relationships, continuing year after year, compel us to conclude that the organisms, even in so-called constant conditions, are not fully shielded from their rhythmic geophysical environment.

Within the past year my associates and I have implicated magnetism as one subtle factor related to the rhythms. Terrestrial magnetism is known to fluctuate rhythmically with the solar and lunar periods. Additionally, the earth's magnetic axis, at an angle with its polar axis, wobbles as the earth rotates and produces a movement of the magnetic field in relation to the polar axes. Snails, when oriented geographically, were found to display solar- and lunar-day rhythms in their tendency to veer from a true southward path, even while in presumably unchanging conditions. Experiments with magnets further proved the snails could perceive very weak magnetic fields. In addition, the snails' response to a bar magnet showed both solar and lunar rhythms.

The snails were able also to distinguish directions of magnetic fields and, therefore, they possess a magnetic compass. The snails' perceptive system for a magnetic field behaves like two rotating "directional antennae," the rotation of one is related to the sun, the other to the moon. For fields of equal magnetic strength, the field parallel with the snail's body was most effective when the sun or moon was above the horizon, while a field at right angles was most effective under other conditions. Hence, the magnetic receiver behaved like a living compass geared in with the living-clock system. This compass may serve as a navigational instrument.

These magnetic-field studies have introduced a subtle and pervasive geophysical factor with which biologists must now reckon. It seems highly probable that other animals will be found similarly armed with both a clock and a compass. We have, furthermore, experimental evidence suggesting that both flatworms and snails perceive changes in electrostatic fields, the fields surrounding electrically charged bodies. And, as with magnetic fields, the response seems to be regulated by the living-clock system.

The weight of all the evidence suggests that living clocks depend upon some universal-time, geophysical rhythm—one with simultaneous world-wide changes. Magnetic and electrostatic sensitivities support this theory, since these forces are known to fluctuate on a universal scale. If living things truly possess such a universal timer, they have always available what man terms Greenwich time and uses for purposes such as navigation and astronomy—a means for pinpointing their location on the earth's surface. Interestingly, studies of bee, bird and fish navigation have proved that these creatures are acutely aware of the heavens.

Experimental evidence suggests, therefore, that life, time and space, in the range of their terrestrial dimensions, are very intimately interrelated. It appears that the forces regulating the

187

life processes are dependently related to their counterparts of the outside physical environment. The living organism is a diminutive oscillating system with periods paralleling those of the physical environment.

What kind of timing system did nature fit into the microscopic dimensions of single cells—a timer which could reproduce so unerringly the long natural periods?

Evidence suggests the primary timing system to be the movements of the sun, moon and earth. Nature provided means by which this timer could simultaneously serve the rhythmicalities of both living organisms and their environment. Ingeniously the timing bridge to living systems was fashioned, not in terms of such variable and biologically potent forces as light and temperature (to which organisms must respond in specifically adaptive fashions), but in terms of more stable forces demanding little or no specific adaptive response and simultaneously so pervasive that no living thing would ever normally be deprived of their influence. Only with such provisions could living clocks become the loyal servant rather than the domineering master of life.

JOHN KENNETH GALBRAITH

[*Photograph by Philippe Halsman*]

John Kenneth Galbraith, now Ambassador to India, was born in Canada in 1909 and received his higher education at the Universities of Toronto and California and at Cambridge. After war service with United States Government agencies, Professor Galbraith served on Adlai Stevenson's 1952 and 1956 campaign staffs. Professor Galbraith's iconoclastic survey of American economic problems, The Affluent Society (Houghton Mifflin), was a best seller during much of 1958 and 1959.

Men and Capital

BY

JOHN KENNETH GALBRAITH

Those who guide our worries on large issues regularly ask us to ponder man's losing competition with the machine. On the assembly lines he is being replaced by automatic machinery which is regulated and instructed by electronic controls. If the resulting product is a consumer item, it has almost certainly been designed to minimize both the effort and intelligence required of its user. Not even the question of whether people will want it has been left entirely to judgment. This has been ascertained by market surveys and ensured by advertising, and both, perhaps, were analyzed with the aid of an electronic computer, sometimes too ambitiously called an electronic brain.

The tendency to dispense with men and intelligence is held to go far beyond the consumer gadgets. The unmanned missile is about to replace the old-fashioned hand-operated bomber. In the near future, according to enthusiasts, unmanned missiles will take flight to intercept other unmanned missiles which will prevent these from intercepting still other unmanned missiles. One gathers that the whole operation will be handled under contract by the manufacturers. If the globe were larger or the explosions smaller, the prospect would be attractive. The machines having taken over, men would all be noncombatants. The charm of war has always been greatest for those whose role was to observe it from a certain distance.

These visions of the triumph of the machine can be multiplied endlessly. We do not take them quite seriously, for we do not really believe that we are being replaced, and our instinct is sound. If there is a competition between man and machine, man is winning it—not for at least two centuries has his position been so important as compared with that of the apparatus with which he works.

The fact that this is the age of ascendant man, not triumphant machine, has practical consequences. If machines are the decisive thing, then the social arrangements by which we increase our physical plant and equipment will be of first importance. But if it is men that count, then our first concern must be with arrangements for conserving and developing personal talents, for it will be these on which progress will depend. Should it happen, moreover, that our society succeeded in supplying itself with machines and failed in providing itself with adequately trained manpower, there would be cause for concern. There is such cause; for that precisely is our situation.

But first, what is the evidence that men have been gaining on machines—that skill and intelligence have become more important in what we call economic progress than in capital plant and equipment?

The change is most prominently reflected in the position of the owner or supplier of physical capital. For a half century he has been a man of steadily declining prestige and importance. Once it was taken for granted that ownership of an industrial enterprise—the ownership of the capital assets or a substantial share of them—gave a man a decisive voice in its direction. So it was with Ford, Carnegie, the elder Rockefeller, Commodore Vanderbilt and John Jacob Astor. And to be a source of capital, as in the case of the elder Morgan, ensured an almost equal power over the enterprise. It also ensured the supplier a favored position in the community. Because the provision of capital conveyed such power, the system was called capitalism.

The ownership of capital, or the capacity to supply it, no longer accords such power. Few large corporations are now run by their owners: those like Du Pont, where for many generations a talented family has had a decisive influence on the enterprise it owns, are becoming a rarity. Typically, the power now lies with the professional managers. These managers make elaborate obeisance to the stockholders. But they select the board of directors, which the stockholders then dutifully elect, and the board then solemnly selects the management that selected the board. In some cases—of which the Standard Oil Company of New Jersey, once dominated by the first Rockefeller, is one—the board consists exclusively of members of the management group.

There are numbers of reasons for the rise of the professional manager, but by far the most important is that ownership of capital has come to count for much less than ownership of ability and brains. The man of ability could get the capital; the man who had capital and was devoid of other qualification was a hopeless case. So the relatively impecunious but better-trained, more intelligent, more determined or politically more adept managers have taken over. Once in office it is only rarely that the owners of capital can dislodge them.

Nor is this a misfortune for the companies in question. Some of the worst cases of corporate mismanagement in recent times have been those in which the owners of the capital have used their power to keep the professionals out. In the '30's and early '40's the elder Henry Ford used his power as the sole owner of the Ford Motor Company to remain in command. It is now freely acknowledged that the company suffered severely as a result. Following his death, the management was professionalized and much improved. The great merchandising house of Montgomery Ward provides a parallel example. Control and direction of a large company by a capitalist has become indeed a slightly risky affair.

But though it is most visible at the top, the shift of the comparative importance of men and capital is perceptible throughout the modern industrial enterprise. The procedures by which the large and successful enterprise raises funds for new plant and equipment are orderly and predictable. And, depending on circumstances, there is a considerable range of choice— earnings can be withheld, there can be resort to banks, or securities can be sold. A great deal of pompous ritual attends this process, but for the large and successful firm this signifies neither uncertainty nor difficulty, but only that we have considerable respect for money and expect large sums to be handled with decent ceremony. And the rites and ceremonials of high finance give those involved a harmless sense of their own importance.

There is no similar certainty in the procedures by which even the most successful concern supplies itself with talent. It must send its emissaries to participate in the annual talent hunt, and if the most pompous men still go to the money markets, the most eloquent go to the colleges. The bag is always uncertain and frequently inadequate. If a successful firm is contemplating a considerable expansion, it will almost certainly worry more about where to find the men than the money.

And the change is reflected in the fears and apprehensions of the community at large. We wonder whether we are investing as much as we should in physical capital; we hear that the Soviets, who in our time have largely replaced conscience as the stern small voice of duty, are doing much more. But there is a much more everyday concern about the state of our schools and colleges. Are they doing properly by our children? Where can we find the resources to enable them to do better? And increasingly we are wondering about the adequacy of our output of highly trained and educated people.

This has a very practical impact. Every family knows that the automobile industry is equipped to supply it with a new car almost on a moment's notice. Such is the admirable condition of our physical plant. But it cannot be at all sure there will be a place for the children in a good college. Such is the contrasting state of our facilities for human development.

The forces back of the change in the relative position of man as compared with capital are not new. Some of them, curiously enough, are those which at first glance seem to suggest the ascendancy of the machine.

The classical trinity of productive factors were land (including natural resources), labor (broadly defined to include both physical and intellectual effort), and capital. All production was seen as resulting from the combination of these factors in one form or another and in one proportion or another. Some economists have questioned whether there was much difference between land and capital goods—both support man's efforts to produce things. Many have insisted on adding, as a fourth factor of production, entrepreneurship, or the human effort which was devoted to organizing and managing the other three factors. Subject to these modifications and quibbles, the classical delineation of productive agents is still accepted and, indeed, is deeply imbedded in economic thought.

All production requires all three—or all four—factors, and in this sense all are equally vital. But the importance attached to the different factors has changed remarkably in the last 150 years. At the beginning of the last century—the formative years of modern economics—land seemed peculiarly important. Population was growing. Europe and Asia looked very crowded. The vast fertile spaces of the Americas, Australia and Africa were but slightly appreciated. The effect of modern agricultural techniques on production per acre was, of course, beyond view. Both Ricardo and Malthus, two of the towering figures in the history of economic ideas, concluded that man's fate would be decided largely by the relentless pressure of population on land. Labor being abundant, perhaps excessively so, it seemed far less important than land. Capital, though important, also lacked the life-and-death significance of the land supply.

As the nineteenth century passed, capital rapidly achieved a position of dominance in the trinity. The new world added enormously to the supply of land. The decisive question was its development, and for this ports, steamships, roads, railroads, farmsteads and farm equipment were needed. The land was there; the labor came almost automatically; but the more capital the greater the pace of progress.

This emphasis on capital was reinforced by the nature of industrial advance during the last century. It consisted not of the invention of a great number of new techniques but the spread of a relatively small number of spectacularly important ones. Thus, textile manufacture became a factory industry. Steam power was applied to manufacturing, transport and mining to replace power from men, animals, falling water or wind. Iron and steel became plentiful and cheap and thus available for many new uses.

These inventions resulted, so far as anyone could tell, from a combination of accident, inspiration and genius. Men like James Watt, Benjamin Franklin and Eli Whitney could not be cultivated, and while they could be protected by the patent office, that was about all that could be done to foster technological progress.

But if little could be done to stimulate inventions, much could be done about putting them to use. Saving could be encouraged by exhortations to thrift—and even more by a system of morality and religion which assured the diligent, abstemious and self-denying man esteem in this world and salvation in the next. Investment could be encouraged by stable government and laws which assured investors that profits would be theirs to enjoy. Economists came to measure progress by the proportion of the nation's income that each year was saved and invested.

Investment in physical capital is still a prime measure of progress, but it is an increasingly inadequate one. Progress is coming to depend more and more on the quality rather than the quantity of the capital equipment in use and on the intelligence and skill of those who use it.

There are reasonably good figures to guide us in making this judgment. Between the early '70's of the last century and the decade 1944–53, according to calculations made under the auspices of the National Bureau of Economic Research, the net output of the American economy increased by an average of 3.5 per cent a year. Less than half of this (1.7 per cent) is explained by increases in the supply of capital and labor. The rest was the result of improvements in capital equipment—technological advance—and improvements in the working force, including, of course, its leadership and direction. The share in the advance attributable to technological improvement and to the improved skill and ability of workers, technicians and managers has been increasing.

But both technological advance and improved skills and abilities are the product of personal development. Machines do not improve themselves; they are the product of improved men. And most technological advance is now the result, not of the accident of inspiration or genius, but of highly purposeful effort. Once we had to wait for the Edisons and Wrights. Now, through education and organization, we get something approaching the same results from much more common clay.

So it comes to this. We now get the larger part of our industrial growth not from more capital investment but from improvements in men and improvements brought about by improved men. And this process of technological advance has become fairly predictable. We get from men pretty much what we invest in them. So now in its turn, after land and after capital, labor—highly improved labor, to be sure—has come to the center of the stage. Investment in personal development is therefore at least as useful as an index of progress as investment in physical capital. This is the kind of change which solemn men of self-confessed soundness of judgment will continue to resist; the familiar is always defended with moral fervor just before it becomes foolish.

What practical accommodation are we making to this new urgency of investment in personal development?

At first glance our position would seem to be quite good. We have been reaping large gains from the application of trained intelligence to our economic life. This is the fruit of one of the world's pioneer experiments in public education. Surely our gains will continue.

We cannot be so optimistic. Until the last century learning and even literacy were the badges of privilege. They thus became symbols of achievement and equality—symbols that our grandparents were not disposed to overlook. Hence the free elementary schools, high schools, the land-grant college system, and the remarkable number and variety of other institutions of higher (and not excessively high) learning.

This system was adequate, even admirable, so long as education was a social service designed to ensure rough equality of opportunity. It has ceased to be sufficient as education has become a form of investment.

The test of what a community should spend on a social

service is what it can afford—what it believes it can spare from other forms of consumption. The test of investment, by contrast, is what will pay for itself. We apply the investment test as a matter of course to physical capital, and even the commonplace terminology reflects the different attitudes—while we "invest" in physical capital we "spend" for education.

The investment test is far the more generous of the two. It implies an aggressive canvass of all possible outlays to see what will pay off at a profit. To find new ways of investing at a profit is to prove one's enterprise. One of the most familiar theorems of accepted economics is that, subject to some lags and irregularities, investment in physical capital will occur whenever marginal return exceeds the marginal cost—that is, whenever the return to additional investment is sufficient to cover the added cost, including interest and some allowance for risk.

The test of what can be afforded, by contrast, invokes far more frugal attitudes. The outlay is vaguely self-indulgent. If we wish it, we must measure the cost in equally or more important alternatives. Virtue resides not in finding ways of investing more, but in finding ways of spending less. The community honors the man who is identified with economy. Yet, as we have seen, the outlays so economized now yield as large (perhaps a larger) return as those for physical capital.

Investment in personal development is also handicapped by the lack of a close relationship of outlay with the resulting benefit. A chemical company invests in a new plant because it knows it will get the higher earnings. If it invests in the education of a young chemist, it has no similar assurance that it will get a return from its outlay. The fellow may decide to become an artist or a farmer, or he may go faithlessly to work for a competitor.

To see what the same relationship of cost to benefit that exists for physical capital would do for investment in personal development, one need only imagine an arrangement by which promising youngsters, when halfway through high school, were indentured for life to a corporation. The latter would then be responsible for all further education and would be assured of their services for life. Performance of the companies tomorrow, it would soon be evident, would depend on the quality of the executives, scientists and other specialists being selected and trained today. The quality of this stable would become a matter of major concern. It would be under the eye of accomplished educators. Money would start flowing into it. Investment houses would seek information as to its quality. If one of the larger oil companies found that the schools and colleges available for training its oncoming geologists and engineers were inadequate, it would obviously have to take steps to remedy the situation— perhaps by establishing its own. Otherwise, in a few years it would be outclassed by the companies with better talent. And one can imagine bond issues to develop stronger technical echelons. The result would be a substantial and possibly an astronomical increase in outlays for personal development—all justified by the resulting profit. All this would be the result of giving the corporation a firm lien on the individual's services and thus on the return on the money it spends on him. It would be the result of making human beings as privileged, for pur- poses of investment, as are machines.

The final reason for thinking that our arrangements for in- vesting in personal development are deficient is that the Soviets have, technically speaking, superior ones. They begin with all resources under public control; hence there is no problem in transferring those to be devoted to personal development from private to public use. And outlays for physical capital and those for personal development are items in the same huge budget. The returns from one type of investment can be measured against the returns from the other. There is no inherent reason why physical capital should have a preference, as in our case. The result is that the U.S.S.R., by our standards still a poor country, treats its schools, research and training institutes, uni- versities, and adult education with a generosity which impresses all western visitors. These outlays, not old-fashioned expansion of physical capital, were decisive for launching the Sputnik and landing its successor on the moon.

We cannot solve the problem of personal investment by indenturing our youngsters at a tender age to a corporation. And we should not expect the kindly corporation to rise to the rescue with large voluntary grants for education. Time has already been wasted on this notion. The problem is far too serious to be left to the conscience of those with a particular willingness to spend the stockholders' money.

Most likely we will solve the problem by making fuller and better use of the familiar instruments of public finance. We must see outlays for personal development not as a cost but as an opportunity. Then we must make sure that we are taxing ourselves sufficiently to exploit this opportunity. That the Federal Government must play a role is elementary. It has access to fiscal resources inherently far greater than that of states and localities; now that education has become an investment rather than a social service these resources are indispensable. There is at least a likelihood that investment in personal development is a better guarantee of effective national position than many of our present military expenditures.

We need also to review our attitudes toward state and local taxation. In a poor country there are sound reasons for reluctance in taxing objects of everyday consumption in order to have more public services and amenities. But we are not a poor country, and personal development has become not a service but an investment. So states and localities should no longer hesitate to use sales and excise taxes to pay for schools and universities. And liberals, in particular, should control their indignation when this is proposed.

There is another possible way of putting provision for personal development on a par with that in physical capital. We assume that a corporation, either by withholding from earnings or by resort to the capital market, will assume responsibility for improving and expanding its physical plant. The pressure for voluntary contributions by corporations to education reflects a feeling that there is a similar responsibility for personal development. Corporations are the largest employers of trained talent. They reap the rewards from such people. Why shouldn't they pay part of the cost of training this talent?

Perhaps they should. And while voluntary contributions which many do not pay are inequitable as well as inadequate, a payroll tax for education and training would encounter no similar objection. As a percentage of total payroll the levy would be roughly proportioned to the quantity and quality of the people employed. Thus it would be related to benefit from past investment in personal development; and it would mean that the company was assuming its rough share of the cost of replacing with improved talent the skilled workers, technicians, scientists and executives whom it employs. Initially the tax would presumably be borne, in the form of higher prices, by the consumers of product. Ultimately the better talent would bring better methods, improved efficiency and lower prices.

Corporations are now at great pains to explain that their prices must include provision for earnings sufficient to replace and expand their physical capital. This, they regularly assure their public, means that production will continue and be more efficient in the future. But, as the National Bureau figures show, we have more to gain from improving the quality of people. So a levy for this purpose would be an even better bargain.

Maybe there are other ways of augmenting the flow of resources into personal development. Since the society is changing, we dare not assume that we have thought the last thoughts on the subject. For man has not retreated before the machine; rather the machine has become desperately dependent on the improvement of man. And our economy is better suited to supply machines than to improve men.

GEORGE W. CORNER

[Photograph by Philippe Halsman]

In 1958 Dr. George W. Corner won the Passano Award, established by the medical publishers, Williams and Wilkins, "in recognition of a long and distinguished career as investigator, educator, historian and philosopher of science, and for many contributions to knowledge of the physiology of reproduction, including the discovery of the hormone progesterone." Trained in medicine at Johns Hopkins University, Doctor Corner has been professor of anatomy at the University of Rochester, chairman of the National Research Council's Committee for Research in Problems of Sex, and director of the embryology department of the Carnegie Institution of Washington. Author of many articles and books on biological topics, he is now Executive Officer, The American Philosophical Society.

Science
and Sex Ethics

B Y

GEORGE W. CORNER

One June morning ten years ago in the Carnegie Institution of Washington's embryological laboratory, of which I was then director, some half dozen staff members stood about a microscope, watching a distinguished visitor from Harvard, the pathologist Dr. Arthur T. Hertig. For twelve years Hertig had been collaborating with us in the collection of human embryos at early stages of growth. He now emptied the contents of a small vial on a glass slide, adjusted the slide under the microscope lens and bade us each in turn look through the eyepiece. What we saw that morning nobody had ever seen before—a human embryo twenty-four hours after conception.

It was the climactic moment of a half century's research on both sides of the Atlantic. We could now observe every phase of human development from conception to birth. The specimen Hertig showed us, together with others obtained by him and his colleague, Dr. John Rock, clinical professor of gynecology at Harvard, also confirmed our understanding of the reproductive cycle. Behind the Hertig-Rock findings lay the arduous work of many researchers who had traced the sequence of events in the ovaries and fixed the time in the monthly cycle when the egg cell enters the oviduct.

The effect of all these discoveries upon the human birth rate has been profound. Innumerable couples the world over, for example, today use the "safe-period" method of birth control. As its originators, the gynecologists Kyusako Ogino of Japan and Herman Knaus of Austria, pointed out, the ovum is usually shed between the sixteenth and twelfth day following menstruation. Since the ovum remains fertilizable for only a day or two, the safe period spans the last week, if not a little more, of the normal twenty-eight-day menstrual cycle. This provides a statistically effective method of avoiding conception, even though not infallible in individual cases.

Much of our knowledge about the reproductive cycle has been learned through research on animals. Thirty years ago the National Research Council set up a Committee for Research on the Problems of Sex, under the leadership of the late Robert M. Yerkes. Among the resultant discoveries, and those of European laboratories, have been the two ovarian hormones, estrogen and progesterone, and the male sex hormones, the androgens. These have already passed from the laboratory into the pharmacy. In addition biologists have worked out the reproductive cycles of many animals, so that we can make fertility tests on female animals at selected stages or study embryos of known age. Thus, drugs thought promising for birth control can be tried out under precise experimental conditions.

Contraceptive materials are now widely available. By persistent research throughout the world, the day is approaching when simple, safe methods of birth control may be extended to whole populations and even to the most unsophisticated and illiterate. Such knowledge would place in the hands of mankind a power as unpredictable in its effects as nuclear energy—yet a power we must utilize, under proper control, if we are to avoid disastrous overpopulation.

There has also developed a still more radical kind of interference with human reproduction—artificial insemination. If a wife is childless though fertile, the gynecologist can often induce pregnancy by injecting the husband's seminal fluid, if he is fertile but impotent or, if the husband is sterile, that of an unseen donor. Another reason for artificial insemination may be that the husband is known to carry the genes of a constitutional defect. A dictator who wanted to improve his nation's human stock by breeding from superior males could now command the technique almost as easily as Hitler practiced genocide.

General scientific progress has further provided obstetricians with improved methods of asepsis and antibiotic drugs. Surgical abortion, once hazardous, is now so safe in competent hands that Russia, Japan and all the Scandinavian countries have legalized it for various social and medical reasons. Many Americans appear to agree, tacitly at least, with this judgment. The Institute for Sex Research at Indiana University recently reported on the rate of induced abortion in a population sample of urban American women of reputable social status and relatively high education. The conclusion of a demographer, Dr. Christopher Tietze, was that one fifth to one fourth of all pregnancies in a comparable sector of our population are terminated by abortion. Unhappily, thousands of women are impelled to this momentous decision by fear or despair and submit themselves to illegal abortion. In order to get this procedure into the hands of responsible physicians, many thoughtful people want the legal indications for abortion broadened to cover cases of serious social and economic distress.

Thus, the application of biological science to human reproduction raises large questions of right and wrong, not all of which can be settled by ethical principles developed in a prescientific age. Some of these problems, however, are as old as civilization. Our era is not the first in the history of human culture when the science of embryology has influenced philosophical and moral thinking. The Roman Catholic Church has always cherished the Judaeo-Christian concept of the soul as something distinct from the body and inhabiting the flesh only for a time, and it holds that an infant dead before baptism is forever denied access to the throne of grace. The early theologians, therefore, wished to know at what stage of gestation the fetus acquires a soul and, therefore, when the sacraments should be administered.

Some of the early Christian Fathers actually wrote embryological treatises upon this topic. The first to do so was Lactantius in the third century. In his *De Opificio Dei*, he took from Aristotle and Galen the statement, based on their scanty observations, that the human embryo passes through four stages— seed, vegetative organism, animal and finally, when all its parts are formed, human. At the human stage, believed to begin in the seventh or eighth week of embryonic life, the fetus receives its soul.

This bit of applied science was passed on by Saint Augustine and Saint Thomas Aquinas. Dante cites it in Canton xxv of the *Purgatorio*, and in the sixteenth century a London surgeon, Thomas Vicary, wrote:

> "Thus is the childe bred foorth in four degrees . . . the thirde degree is, when the principals be shapen, as the Hart, lyver, and Brayne: the fourth and laste, as when all the other members be perfectly shapen, then it receyveth the soule wyth life and breath; and then it beginneth to moue itselfe alone: so is there xlvj. dayes from the daye of conception unto the daye of ful perfection and receyving of the soule, as God best knoweth."

Vicary's calculation, by the way, agrees almost exactly with modern statements of the time when the embryo becomes an obviously recognizable human being. The late George L. Streeter, my predecessor at the Carnegie embryological laboratory, in his *Horizons of Human Development* placed the end of the embryonic period at about forty-seven days from conception.

We must remember that until almost a century after Vicary's time nobody had ever seen a human embryo, or an embryo of any other mammal, during its first three or four weeks. No one realized that the life of the embryo is physically continuous with that of its parents through an egg cell supplied by the mother and fertilized by a sperm cell from the father. Nor had anyone guessed better than Aristotle, who supposed that the embryo forms by a sort of coagulation of the male spermatic fluid deposited in the uterus. William Harvey, discoverer of the circulation of the blood, tried in the mid-seventeenth century to find embryos of deer during the first month and, having failed, decided that an embryo forms in the uterus much as an idea forms in the brain. Just as an artist can paint a landscape from memory, said Harvey, or a bird can sing in springtime the song it learned the summer before, so the uterus can produce an egg from no tangible substance.

In 1672 the young Netherlander Regnier de Graaf discovered rabbit embryos of the third day, and rightly assumed that they develop from egg cells in the organ we now call the ovary. Five years later, Anthony van Leeuwenhoek of Delft and his student Ham, equipped with crude microscopes, first saw the sperm cells in both human and animal semen. Leeuwenhoek leaped to the conclusion that each sperm cell is a rudimentary embryo, and thus started a scientific controversy that lasted for decades between the "spermatists" and the "ovulists," each party claiming for one of these cells the sole honor of giving rise to the embryo.

Some of Leeuwenhoek's followers carried his mistaken view that the sperm cell is a rudimentary embryo to absurd lengths. One of them sent the Royal Society of London a drawing of·a spermatozoon in which he said he had seen through his microscope a tiny but complete human figure. In strict logic, he noted, such a manikin must himself have testes containing sperm cells, and so on, ad infinitum. The philosopher Leibnitz applied this concept to the soul. The first man, he reasoned, must therefore have carried in his genital organs the whole race of man, the body and soul of each generation awaiting their turn to unfold. The fact, so obvious to us in the twentieth century, that the egg and sperm must unite to form a fertilized egg cell that can transform itself into an embryo, was not grasped until 1827 when the German, Karl Ernst von Baer, saw the actual mammalian egg cell, and two Frenchmen, J. B. Dumas and J. L. Prevost, proved that the spermatozoa are essential to the development of the egg into an embryo.

Having observed every stage of embryonic life, we came at last to understand that development of the human individual involves a building of the body anew, generation after generation, from its biochemical elements. It is a continuous process, proceeding from a tiny packet of unrealized potentialities to the child capable of independent existence. Theologians who regard the soul and body as two separable entities have, of course, not remained unaware of the embryological discoveries of the past three centuries. They know now that the embryo is a human organism long before the fortieth day. Although they differ among themselves to a degree that baffles a biologist who wants to state the position fairly in brief compass, most Roman Catholic theologians, Orthodox rabbis and some Protestants hold that the soul is infused into the body at the moment of fertilization. To the Roman Catholic, the loss of an embryo, even if too small to be seen without a microscope, of whose existence its own mother is not yet aware, means its soul must dwell forever in limbo, outside the gates of heaven. The Roman Catholic Church has ruled that physicians must always protect the life of the unborn infant, even at the risk of the mother's life.

Suppose, however, some modern Lactantius should ask today's biologists what they can now tell him about the schedule of human development in order to guide him in writing a new treatise on the embryology of the soul. He would find that most of us think of the body and the spirit as interdependent, their development and existence interwoven and inseparable. In the fertilized egg and the embryo, both, we are bound to suppose, are mere potentialities. What else can we say, we who have seen through our microscope the human being begin as a tiny sphere of mingled proteins and lipids, and have watched it slowly build its brain and its nerves, develop reflexes and voluntary motion, come to birth and at last begin to experience life and the consciousness of its own existence? Most biologists will agree that the spirit and the body develop together. When some untoward physical condition puts a woman's life in the balance against that of her unborn child, most of us think it no crime but rather a duty to protect the mother's body and spirit first, even at the loss of another, merely incipient living creature.

What, however, if not the mother's life but her emotional stability, or the economic welfare of her family, or her moral reputation is at stake? Are we to authorize abortion freely because it is relatively safe and might avert consequences often-times only less tragic than death?

The medical profession is divided as to the doctor's responsibility in such cases. Some high-minded physicians feel that if they were freed from the restraints of an outworn moral code and laws that forbid abortion for other than medical causes, they could help to reduce the desperation and danger that often attend unwanted pregnancy. The majority of American obstetricians are reluctant to perform an operation that involves a surgical risk, however slight, for any but medical reasons. Many physicians, as well, dreaded the results of yielding medical responsibility to nonmedical persons, who would have a voice in decisions made on social and economic grounds. Above all, they feel bound to consider the moral aspects of the problem. To make abortions easy to procure would inevitably tend to increase promiscuity.

Meanwhile, conscientious doctors solve individual cases as best they can by trying to persuade the unwilling mother to bear her child, arranging to have illegitimate babies adopted, reconciling shocked relatives. At the same time these doctors feel that birth control is the best long-term answer to the problem of undesirable pregnancy in and out of wedlock. It is as yet, however, far from effective; for in 1958, in New York City alone, 13,000 illegitimate babies were born.

Many moralists and theologians have objected to birth control, as I understand their position, for two related reasons. One is that intercourse which seeks to avoid conception is nothing more than self-indulgence. To be sure, few theologians today go so far as the seventeenth-century Pope Innocent XI, who ruled that those who eat, drink or copulate merely for the sake of pleasure are guilty of sin. The other reason given is that human mating is divinely intended for procreation. A Papal encyclical of 1930, however, accepted the morality in marriage of the safe-period method, because it makes use only of a natural rhythm inherent in God's creation.

Artificial contraception, on the other hand, clearly constitutes interference with physiological processes or natural law, as the theologians call it, and its moral justification they deny. The Anglican Church has recently devoted much thought to this problem. The authors of a report to the Archbishop of Canterbury in 1958, titled The Family in Contemporary Society, clarify the question of contraception in marriage by emphasizing that sexual intercourse has not only a generative function but also what they call a "relational" value. They regard this natural human act, with or without the immediate intention to produce offspring, as a constructive expression of love and trust between two human beings bound together in conjugal life. Far from being mere self-indulgence, they consider it a necessary and honorable element in domestic happiness. The archbishop's advisers concluded that there are strong grounds for holding the responsible use of contraceptives by married persons to be morally right. It is scarcely necessary to add that those scientists whose work on the physiology of reproduction deeply impresses them with the interdependence of body and mind in human sexual life warmly agree with the position of the Anglican commission.

But moral questions posed by contraception are far simpler than those raised by artificial insemination. Strict moralists contend that a woman who conceives a child by sperm mechanically transferred from a donor, even though unseen and unknown, and selected by her physician, commits adultery. Lawyers raise serious doubts about the legitimacy of a child thus produced and its rights of inheritance, unless the husband legally adopts it. Genealogists worry about a practice that makes a family tree misleading (though family trees have all too often acquired unacknowledged grafts in the ordinary way). Of genuine concern also is the psychological risk that the infertile husband may consciously or unconsciously come to resent the child he did not father. On the other hand, many instances are on record in which such a child has won full paternal affection from a husband grateful to medical science for saving his wife from frustration and his home from emptiness.

Conscientious physicians will not attempt artificial insemination unless both the husband and wife are ready for parenthood and fully agreed upon it, nor without complete anonymity of the donor, and careful selection of one suited by lineage and physical characteristics to substitute his genes for those of the sterile husband. They accept, in short, responsibility not only for the physical procedures but also for considering the emotional and psychological factors involved.

Having made contraception, therapeutic abortion and artificial insemination technically feasible, does science contribute anything to the principles upon which questions of morality and public policy must be decided? I believe it has, and in a deep, subtle way; for science accepts that these dilemmas involve both the spiritual and the physical nature of man. The biologist who has used rats and rabbits to help him understand the human cycle, who has shown how closely human embryonic development parallels that of other mammals, declares that no code of practical ethics or moral philosophy can ignore our animal structure and instincts. We may attempt to annul or direct their operation, as in birth control; we may give sympathetic heed to them as when we fulfill the yearning of a childless wife by artificial insemination. But we cannot disregard them in our philosophy of human conduct. In the light of this knowledge, the statesman concerned about population control, the theologian and the moral philosopher must all aim to reconcile the human necessities arising from our animal origin with the spiritual aspirations which distinguish men from beasts.

Embryology and the physiology of reproduction have brought us no new facts that of themselves demand alteration of our moral codes. There are no varieties of sexual conduct that have not long since been fully exploited. It is remarkable, for example, how little the discovery of the male and female sex-gland hormones has added to our knowledge of the sex urge. Their main function is to make and keep the reproductive organs responsive to erotic stimulation and ready for mating and gestation. Overt sexual behavior is largely determined by mental, not endocrine, processes. The observation thirty years ago that these chemical agents could restore both male and female patterns of sexual excitability to castrated animals led some students of behavior to assume that human homosexual activity results from an oversupply of the hormone of the opposite sex.

The studies of Kinsey and others, however, indicate that homosexuality is not generally accompanied by glandular abnormalities.

But even though scientific research has little to tell us about the subtler factors in the control of sexual behavior, it has nevertheless altered our outlook upon the problem in two ways. In the first place, birth control lessens the risk of undesired pregnancy, and the antibiotics diminish the risk of venereal disease. With sexual intercourse thus liberated to a great degree from the fear of consequences, only social prudence and morality are left to restrain us.

The other change in our outlook has come from comparative anthropological observations of sexual patterns in various societies. We have learned that people in general behave sexually in widely disparate ways, going far beyond the limits of the code we have set up on the basis of our Judaeo-Christian traditions. However strongly we hold to the moral code, however conservatively we advise our children, the fact remains that one rigid code will not fit all peoples everywhere, nor even everyone in our own society. In Sweden, for example, according to a recent census, about half the brides are already pregnant on their wedding day, which seems to indicate a scandalous breakdown of sexual morality. But as a Swedish physician pointed out to me, many of these premarital pregnancies when occurring in the country districts actually reflect a traditional emphasis on the need of heirs. Peasants want to keep their estates in the family. Premarital intercourse between affianced couples is, therefore, accepted as a practical test of fertility.

There are many signs that the public is beginning to modify some of its taboos because it understands better certain underlying biological and psychological factors. The furtive nineteenth-century sex manuals for boys, for example, with their bugaboo of "self-abuse" that frightened many sensitive lads almost to distraction, have gone out of print. Physicians, teachers and parents have come to understand that masturbation is a natural, practically universal outlet for nascent erotic impulses.

The Wolfenden Report presented to the British Parliament in 1957 by a committee on sex offenses provides another striking instance of changing attitudes. The members of that committee dealt with homosexuality as a behavioral anomaly, not as a crime, and concluded that the law should not regard as criminal, homosexual acts between consenting individuals in private. I would agree that homosexuality, or any other aberrant sexual behavior, should come under police jurisdiction only when it harms others or constitutes a public annoyance.

Basing its judgment on the balance of biological and social factors for good and evil, our modern society now openly admits what it long tacitly accepted: that extramarital intercourse is not necessarily unforgivable. What thoughtful person, not committed to a dogmatic code, would stigmatize as a mortal sin a sexual relation such as that depicted by Somerset Maugham in *Cakes and Ale*, which injured no one and calmed two troubled people; or that which Boris Pasternak depicts in *Doctor Zhivago*, between two high-minded and lonely exiles?

Alas, in real life human relationships are not often so simple. Even these fictional liaisons had their hurtful side, for the first was very largely physical and, therefore, not long satisfying; the second could only end in sorrow because it led to a deep attachment doomed to be thwarted. These imagined characters reveal what everybody must learn: that sexual experience alone does not yield permanent satisfaction. Enduring happiness in sexual relations depends upon the balance of physical activities with higher attributes of thought and feeling. As for right and wrong, biology and anthropology show us that, like animal species, human cultures exhibit many diverse forms of sexual relationship. Among the lower mammals the mating pattern ranges from lifelong monogamy to promiscuity. Among the Primates, our closest animal kin, the few species which have been closely studied, especially the chimpanzee and baboon, seem to organize family life in polygamous clans, each consisting of a dominant male with several mates. Some human societies have followed the way of these apes; others have worked out a variety of mating patterns, of which monogamy, prevailing at least as an ideal in our culture, is only one.

Yet amid this diversity the biologist recognizes certain facts basic to any code of sexual morality. In one characteristic, human breeding differs conspicuously from that of most animals. This is the prolonged period of infancy and adolescence, which society must protect if the race is to survive. From this necessity alone stems much of our social evolution toward conjugal stability, family affection, the love of comfort and beauty. An essential factor in this evolution, responsibility to wife and children, operates in many cuultures besides ours. No less a moralist than Albert Schweitzer has witnessed its benign effects in Africa under polygamy. Sexual promiscuity, however, is not compatible with such responsibility. Evolution has also made every man responsible to himself for the noblest use of his faculties—all that raises him above the beast, and carries him forward with love, hope and sacrifice. To this end he must discipline his natural instincts and appetites, and use the sexual urge as a creative force, not merely an indulgence. To involve another human being in the powerful emotional tensions of sex without regard for the other's welfare and lasting happiness is indeed immoral. The real sin is to indulge transient desires without concern for order, beauty and honor.

If now, after long experience as an investigator of sex and reproduction, I assume the role of a moralist, it is because I have seen nothing in my field of science to invalidate the age-old ideal of our culture—the permanent union of a man and woman in marriage; upon this ideal, with tolerance and understanding gained through the study of natural human needs, we can still base our sexual ethics.

Some will accuse me of casting away the safeguards that religion places upon tempestuous human instincts. Others will say that I am merely substituting a form of puritanism based on science for one based on dogma. Still others will remind me that people will go on forever disregarding any and every code of sexual ethics. To all I reply that we must have ideals, even if we do not always follow them. A lofty morality cannot be intolerant of human needs. Our principles of conduct must be based upon consideration of everything man can discover about his body, mind and spirit.

Further reading:

Corner, George W., and C. H. Heuser: "Embryology, Human," in the Encyclopaedia Britannica, Vol. VIII; 1951.

Sulloway, A. W.: Birth Control and Catholic Doctrine. Boston: Beacon Press; 1959.

Patten, B. M.: Human Embryology. New York: McGraw-Hill Book Company; 1953.

Keenan, Alan, and John Ryan: Marriage: A Sacramental and Medical Study. New York: Sheed & Ward; 1955.

Kinsey, Alfred C., and others: Sexual Behavior in the Human Female. Philadelphia: W. B. Saunders Co.; 1953.

Ford, Clellan S., and Frank A. Beach: Patterns of Sexual Behavior. New York: Harper & Brothers; 1951.

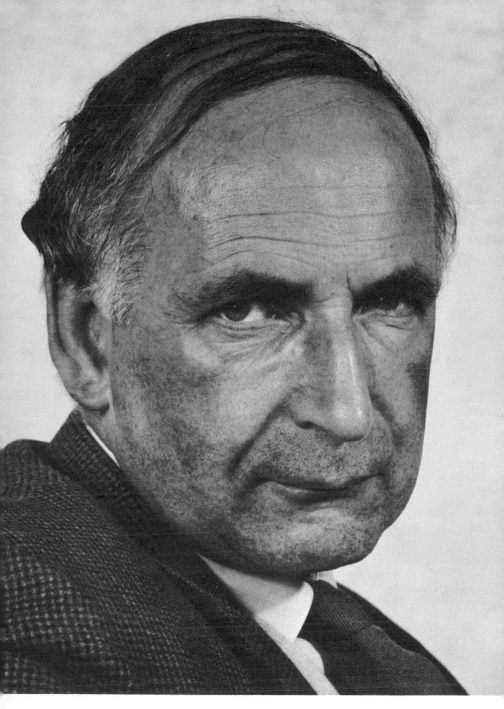

A. C. B. LOVELL

[*Photograph by Wolf Suschitzky*]

Sir Alfred Charles Bernard Lovell, physicist and professor of radio astronomy at the University of Manchester, England, is director of the Jodrell Bank Experimental Station, which operates the world's largest radiotelescope. Doctor Lovell began experimenting with the application of radar techniques to cosmic-ray research after wartime electronics work. Realizing the need for a large radio collecting mirror for detecting emissions from the Milky Way and other galaxies, he urged development of the spectacular 250-foot reflector he now supervises at Jodrell Bank. When Professor Lovell isn't tuning in on the stars, he enjoys such mundane diversions as gardening and playing the piano.

ｴｴｴｴｴｴｴｴｴｴｴｴｴｴｴｴｴｴｴｴｴｴｴｴｴ

Listening to the Universe

BY

A. C. B. LOVELL

Perhaps the greatest challenge to the intellect of man is the problem of the origin of the cosmos. Mathematicians and philosophers have attempted to reach solutions by the exercise of pure thought, and astronomers by exploring the depths of space with telescopes of ever-increasing size. None of these attempts has produced any conclusive answer. Now we have a new science—radio astronomy—which is man's latest hope to probe the mystery of the origin of the cosmos.

It is strange that the predominant instrument of this new science—the radiotelescope—can at one moment be used to explore the depths of intergalactic space, and the next to track earth satellites and space probes, or by radar to investigate the moon and planets in the solar system. Indeed, the radiotelescope, which is the newest instrument of the oldest science, is one of the most comprehensive scientific tools ever devised by man, with an observational reach which extends from a few hundred miles to beyond the present observable edge of the universe.

Though it is not uncommon for scientific discoveries to be made in unexpected circumstances, it would hardly be thought that the study of the static in a wireless set could have much in common with cosmological problems. An American radio engineer, Karl Jansky, was studying atmospheric interference in

221

radio about thirty years ago when he found that the residual noise in his equipment was maintained even in the absence of known terrestrial sources, such as thunderstorms. Jansky's crucial observation was that this residual noise varied throughout the day in a systematic manner, with a period of twenty-three hours, fifty-six minutes. This is the period of the earth's rotation with respect to the stars, and from this simple and elegant observation Jansky concluded that the noise resulted from radio waves reaching his equipment from outside the solar system. When Jansky was transferred to other research, interest in these extraterrestrial radio emissions was sustained for a decade through the efforts of Grote Reber, an American engineer and pioneer radio astronomer, who pursued his researches with home-built equipment in his spare time.

The work of Jansky and Reber, in effect, pulled aside the curtains from a second window through which man might look upon the universe. The first window, opening on the thin slice of the light spectrum available to the eye and the somewhat broader slice captured by the photographic film, is used by the optical telescopes. The new window provided by the pioneering work of Jansky and Reber allowed scientists to observe the energy emitted by the universe in the radio-wave part of the spectrum. Light waves and radio waves are fundamentally similar; they travel through empty space at a speed of 186,000 miles a second, but differ in their wave length. The wave length of light is so short that it is measured in millionths of an inch. The energy of a sodium lamp, for example, is concentrated on a wave length of about twenty-five millionths of an inch. The wave length of the radio waves which come to us from space is much longer. The hydrogen gas in the galaxy emits its energy in a concentrated spectral line at a wave length of eight and one quarter inches, and the radio waves from the depths of space can be picked up over a wide range of wave lengths from a few inches to several hundred inches.

The rapid development of radio techniques for military purposes during World War II reawakened interest in the radio waves from space and resulted in the development of a new science—radio astronomy. Radio astronomers soon realized that their instrumental problems were analogous to those facing the optical astronomers. Astronomers have striven to build optical telescopes of ever-increasing size for several reasons: first, because the large telescopes collect more light and so facilitate the investigation of fainter and more remote objects; secondly, because the resolution, or capacity of a telescope to separate images of discrete objects, increases with its size.

Similar reasons have dictated the construction of large radiotelescopes during the last decade. Here there is a difficulty because the capacity of the telescope to collect light or radio waves and its ability to resolve depends on the relation of the wave length to the physical size of the receiving instrument. Because of the long wave lengths used in radio astronomy, the radiotelescope must be of great physical size if it is to compete at all with quite small optical telecopes which deal with wave lengths of light which are measured in millionths of an inch. The steerable parabolic reflector (often called the Big Dish) at Jodrell Bank in England is 250 feet in diameter and weights 750 tons (2000 tons over-all). One of 600 feet in diameter is now being built at Sugar Grove, West Virginia.

These radiotelescopes are really gigantic versions of the common television aerial. The few rods on the antenna of the TV aerial give it a small amount of directivity or resolution to improve the signal strength from the transmitting station and at the same time reduce unwanted signals and interference from other directions. It would be quite possible to increase the size of this aerial by adding more rods, or even by using a dish-type antenna. Then the signal strength would be improved and so would the resolution, so that more care would have to be taken in pointing the aerial in the direction of the transmitting station. The purpose of this aerial is to pick up the radio waves from the TV transmitter, direct them into the receiving set and display them on the tube. The wave length of the TV transmissions is a few inches. This is also the wave length of radio signals from outer space. If the volume control of the TV set is turned up when no transmissions are in progress, a background hiss will be heard in the loud-speaker. Some of this is generated in the components in the receiver, and some will come from the electrical machinery in the neighborhood, but a good bit of it will be the noise of these radio signals coming from the depths of space.

The radiotelescope and the associated receiving and recording equipment is really a scaled-up version of this simple TV arrangement. The big dish acts as a reflector for the radio waves which it intercepts, and concentrates them on to the small TV-type antenna at the focus of the reflector, where they are taken by cable to the receiving set and the recording meter—which is often a simple pen-and-ink instrument. The TV set picks up the radio waves emitted by a transmitter at relatively short distances. The radiotelescope often deals with signals which have been traveling through space for trillions of miles. There is a well-known radio source at a distance of 700,000,000 light-years—4,200,000,000,000,000,000,000 miles. The strength of the signal from this source in an average TV set would be about 10^{-16} watts, or a ten-thousandth of a million millionth of a watt. The Big Dish at Jodrell Bank collects 5000 times more energy from this source. Although this amounts to only one half a trillionth of a watt (an ordinary light bulb may use sixty watts), the receiving and recording equipment is so sensitive that the signal causes a big deflection on the recording chart. The lower limit of the Jodrell radiotelescope is about 50 to 100 million trillionth of a watt, at which level the signals from space get confused and submerged in the random radio "noise" generated locally and in the apparatus.

When the radiotelescope is used to explore the galaxy and the remote depths of space, it is used, like the TV set, as a receiver for radio emissions which are generated elsewhere. The big-dish type of radiotelescope is an adaptable instrument, however, and can be used as a transmitter as well as a receiver. Generally there is a special "transmit-receive" device which enables the telescope to do both jobs simultaneously—and it transmits in the same narrow beam it uses for reception, so that the transmitted energy can be concentrated on the moon or a planet and the reflected wave observed as a signal on a cathode-ray tube connected to the receiver output.

The reflector at Jodrell Bank was used in this fashion to

track the carrier rockets of the Sputniks and to send the signal which separated the payload of solar-orbiting Pioneer V from its rocket. For months signals were sent out daily to switch on the transmitters in Pioneer V, millions of miles out in space. On May 8, 1960, a coded signal was sent for the first time to switch on Pioneer's powerful 150-watt transmitter. The probe was then 8,000,000 miles from the earth. The signal from the telescope, traveling through space at 186,000 miles a second, took forty-three seconds to reach the probe, and the response of the probe took the same time to come back to earth. Nearly a minute and a half to wait after sending the command—but this is almost instantaneous when compared with the multimillion year journeys of the signals from space.

An experiment which can be carried out with even a small radiotelescope is to make a record of the strength of the radio emissions coming from different parts of the sky. If this radio map of the heavens is compared with an astronomical map of the common visible stars, there appears to be a good correlation between the radio and visual star maps. The radio signals are most intense when the radiotelescope is directed to pick up the emissions from the densely populated parts of the Milky Way, and they decrease markedly in strength when the telescope is receiving signals from those regions of the sky which are thinly populated with common stars.

This would suggest that the ordinary visible stars are emitting radio waves as well as the light by which we see them. The possibility can be tested by focusing a radiotelescope on a prominent visible star such as Sirius or Capella. To do this it is necessary to use a large radiotelescope, because large instruments, like their optical counterparts, are more selective than small ones, and it is desirable to include as little as possible outside the region of sky containing the star. When this is done, however, no signals can be detected; in fact, no one has yet succeeded in recording radio waves from any of the ordinary stars—apart from the sun—in the Milky Way. We are not yet certain whether the sun really is an exception or whether we can pick up the radio signals from it because it is so close compared even with the next nearest star. Even if the next nearest star

(Alpha Centauri, 27,000,000,000,000 miles away) emitted radio waves with the same strength as the sun, it could scarcely be detected with instruments which we have today, because of the distance involved. Experiments are now being made to find out if other stars do emit radio waves like the sun, but even if this is proved to be the case their emission is so weak it has no part in the present story of the radio waves from space.

Two other neighbors of our solar system, Tau Ceti and Epsilon Eridani, are presently the subject of an experiment, known as Project Ozma, in which American astronomers are using a radiotelescope in an attempt to find out if any signals which are emitted could possibly be generated by intelligent beings. Modern theories of the evolution of the solar system indicate that similar planetary systems must be plentiful throughout the stars of the Milky Way. The search for intelligent signals is one of the long shots of the radiotelescope, but if Project Ozma should produce positive results it would indeed be the most dramatic discovery of all time.

This paradox of the superficial similarity of the radio and optical maps of the heavens is not yet fully resolved—indeed, as we shall see, it may well hold the key to one of the ultimate problems in cosmology. Nevertheless, ten years of probing the heavens with radiotelescopes of ever-increasing size and complexity has at least made it possible to give an indication of the various possible origins of radio waves from space. It is convenient to divide this summary into three categories: (1) the radio waves from our own galaxy, the Milky Way; (2) the extragalactic nebulae (that is, the millions of other "island universes") as radio sources; (3) the problem of the unidentified radio sources in space.

When early experiments revealed the similarity of the shape of the radio contours of the heavens to the density of common stars and yet failed to record any emissions from the individual stars, it was suggested that the radio waves were generated, not within stars, but in the interstellar gas of the Milky Way. This hypothesis is now accepted as explanation of at least a part of the radio-wave emissions generated in the Milky Way. The hydrogen gas which fills the space between the 100,-

ooo,ooo,ooo stars of the Milky Way exists in two forms. In the neighborhood of hot stars the hydrogen atom, a neutral element in its natural state, is torn apart by the intense stellar radiation so that the atom's constituent parts, the proton and electron, move as separate entities; gas formed of these freed, charged particles is ionized and has characteristic electrical properties. The ionized hydrogen gas emits radio waves over a wide range of wave lengths. This hydrogen gas closely follows the contours of the flattened disc of stars which forms our galaxy. It is prevalent in the plane of the galaxy, and it is the radio waves generated in this ionized gas which give rise to the marked increase in the strength of the radio waves recorded by a radio-telescope which scans the Milky Way.

The presence of neutral hydrogen in space is a different story. Although its presence was inferred, there was no means of detecting it until the Dutch astronomer Hendrik van de Hulst suggested during World War II that the interaction of the electron spin with the magnetic field of the nucleus of the hydrogen atom should give radio emission detectable on a specific wave length of twenty-one centimeters (eight and one quarter inches). The fact that this is a "line emisssion" in which all the radiation occurs at a single specific wave length means that any Doppler change arising from the relative motion of the hydrogen clouds of the galaxy and the solar system can be measured. Such measurements have been used to determine the spiral structure of the Milky Way system of stars—an achievement denied optical investigators by the opaque dust clouds which lie between us and the central regions of our galaxy.

The ionized and neutral hydrogen gas is but a part of the story of the radio emission from the Milky Way. The modern radiotelescope has revealed other exciting features of our "home" galaxy. Surrounding and enclosing the system of stars there is a vast halo, or corona, of radio emission extending far outside the recognized stellar confines of the Milky Way into regions of space where no matter can be seen in the optical telescopes. Our current belief is that this radio halo is generated by high-energy electrons moving in the magnetic field associated with the galaxy—by a process known as synchrotron radiation.

The other feature is the existence of powerful localized, or discrete, sources of radio emission lying among the stars of the Milky Way. These are often called radio stars, and for some time after their discovery the failure to associate them with any particular object seen in the 200-inch Palomar telescope caused considerable dismay. The most powerful radio source of this nature in the sky lies in the constellation of Cassiopeia and when its position had been measured with sufficient accuracy, the 200-inch telescope was able to photograph in that region an area of diffuse filamentary gas in rapid internal motion. Another strong radio source was identified with the Crab Nebula—the remnants of the supernova of A.D. 1054, the star whose explosion was recorded by the Chinese astronomers. There are two other unambiguous cases of supernovae in the Milky Way—those observed by Tycho Brahe in 1572 and by Johannes Kepler in 1604, and these are also associated with localized radio sources. In fact, the localized radio sources in the Milky Way seem to be regions of gas in violent motion, and the present tendency is to regard them all, including Cassiopeia, as the remnants of supernovae in various stages of antiquity.

The radio astronomer's view of the Milky Way is therefore a complex of radiations arising from the interstellar gas concentrated among the common stars of the system, in which are embedded the powerful localized sources, probably the gaseous remains of stellar cataclysms, the whole being surrounded by the galactic halo. Even when these various components are included it is evident that the radio map of the heavens cannot be explained by this Milky Way complex. There remain many thousands of localized sources of emission, or radio stars, which seem to be evenly distributed in space and which apparently lie outside the limits of our galaxy.

This raises the question of whether any of these sources are related to the extragalactic nebulae which populate the universe. Our nearest extragalactic neighbor, the spiral nebula M31, in Andromeda, is 2,000,000 light-years from the Milky Way, and in view of its general similarity to the Milky Way it might be expected to generate radio waves in a similar way. Indeed, this is found to be the case. The intensity of the radio waves from

M31 is just about that which would be expected on the basis of the integrated strength of the Milky Way radio emission. Unfortunately no radiotelescopes yet possess the resolving power necessary to detect any individual sources of radio emission in this galaxy 12 millions of millions of millions of miles away, but we do know that it is surrounded by an extensive halo of radio emission.

The large radiotelescopes of the northern and southern hemisphere have, between them, succeeded in associating about three dozen of these extragalactic nebulae with radio sources, and the existing evidence is that they behave as would be expected in the radio sense if the Milky Way and M31 are taken as typical. No radiotelescopes in use today are powerful enough to detect the radio emission from individual galaxies lying at distances greater than these three dozen or so of the brighter extragalactic objects. It has been evident for some years, moreover, that although the millions of extragalactic nebulae scattered throughout the universe may well be radio sources in their own right, we cannot account in this way for the several thousand localized radio sources which are detected by contemporary radiotelescopes.

Here we reach the third stage of our explanation of the picture of the heavens revealed by the radiotelescopes—an explanation which may involve ideas of ultimate cosmological significance. The second-strongest radio source in the sky lies in the constellation of Cygnus, and detailed inspection of the star map fails to reveal any visible object which might be responsible for the generation of these radio waves. A few years after the discovery of the Cygnus radio source, F. G. Smith of Cambridge, England, measured its position with sufficient accuracy to justify a detailed photographic survey of the region with the 200-inch Palomar telescope. In 1951, astronomers Walter Baade and Rudolph Minkowski, using an exposure time of many hours, succeeded in photographing the object which was responsible for the radio emission—a remarkable event in which two spiral galaxies were in a state of collision. Studies of the spectra showed that the interstellar gas of these galaxies was in a state of tremendous excitation and that their distance from us was 700,000,000 light-years. It is presumed that the violent interaction of the gas of the colliding galaxies is the source of these abnormally strong radio emissions.

This dramatic discovery has had important consequences in the subsequent developments of radio astronomy. It was realized immediately that such a radio source, though it was already on the limits of optical detection, had such an output of energy in the radio spectrum that it would be observable to radiotelescopes at ten times its present distance.

Further investigations since that discovery have revealed a few other cases of colliding or interacting galaxies which are relatively strong radio sources. It seems that when two galaxies are close enough to interact, the output of energy in the radio-wave region is vastly greater than that which is produced by the individual galaxies. This suggests that the majority of the radio sources may be colliding or interacting galaxies which lie beyond the 2,000,000,000 light-year limit at which the 200-inch Palomar telescope can resolve a recognizable *image* of the object.

This idea is of vast cosmological importance because it may imply that our radiotelescopes can explore the condition of the universe as it existed six or seven thousand million years ago. The signal from Pioneer V at 8 million miles took forty-three seconds to reach the radiotelescope, the light from the sun takes eight minutes on its journey of 93,000,000 miles, the radio waves from these distant galaxies take many thousands of millions of years to reach us. The information which they convey relate to a past epoch—our information is of time past, not of these distant objects as they are at this moment. If our assumptions are correct, we may now be able to test, by direct observation, the conflicting theories of the origin and evolution of the universe—theories discussed in preceding contributions to this series.

There are two striking features of the arrangement of the material of the universe as seen by the optical telescopes. There is an over-all large-scale uniformity in the spatial distribution of the galaxies, and these galaxies exhibit the Doppler red shift which is interpreted as indicating a recession of the galaxies—the expansion of the universe. The velocity of recession appears to increase with distance so that some of the most distant galaxies yet photographed, in Hydra, are receding with a speed of about 37,000 miles per second, which is one fifth of the velocity of light. By imagining these recessional processes to be reversed as we recede into the past, we are led to the conclusion that the primeval material from which the galaxies were formed must have been condensed into a very small superdense state about 10 thousand million years ago.

Such an interpretation is not inconsistent with the cosmology derived from Einstein's theory of general relativity. Unfortunately there is an undetermined constant in the equation— the cosmical constant, which permits various interpretations to be placed on an evolutionary universe of this type. If the constant is zero, the theory is consistent with a universe which began at this epoch with explosive violence, and the recession which we witness today is the result of the impetus of this initial explosion. On the other hand, the Belgian astrophysicist, the Abbé Lemaître, has considered in great detail the possibility of the cosmical constant being a positive quantity. He concludes that if this is the case the epoch of 10 thousand million years ago represents an intermediate stage in the evolution of the universe and that the beginning of the universe may have been 30 to 60 thousand million years ago. Ten thousand million years ago the impetus of the explosion was exhausted, and the universe began to settle down into a uniform distribution of hydrogen gas with a size of about a thousand million light-years. Then disturbances occurred which led to the beginnings of the condensation of the clusters of galaxies. The forces of cosmical repulsion associated with the positive cosmical constant came into play, overriding the forces of Newtonian attraction on the cosmical scale and leading to the recession of the galaxies which we now witness.

The difficulties of accepting any concept which implies a specific beginning for the universe, coupled with the conflict between the possible ages of the universe derived in this way stimulated new developments in cosmological thinking. One important result was a theory postulating continuous creation and steady-state conditions in the universe. According to the steady-state theory, matter was not created in a universal event

—hydrogen atoms are being continuously created at a rate sufficient to replenish space with the galaxies which are forever
receding from our field of view. This theory postulates that the
expansion of the universe arises from the pressure of the created
matter, not from an initial explosion or the operation of forces
of cosmical repulsion.

It might be thought that the optical telescopes would be
able to distinguish between these two theories with their differing pictures of the past. According to the steady-state theory,
the universe, when considered on the large scale, would appear
to be the same however far we recede into the past; according
to the evolutionary theories, the contents of the universe
would become increasingly closely packed as we move into
earlier epochs. Unfortunately the 200-inch telescope does not
give a decisive answer to this question because within the limits
of its penetration the two opposing theories do not predict
differences of any great significance in terms of the spatial concentration of galaxies. The new possibility that the radio telescopes may penetrate that much farther into space and into the
past, into regions of space and time where the theories differ in
their predictions, is therefore a matter of the greatest cosmological significance.

The initial attempts of the radio astronomers to answer this
question have led to a dispute about the interpretation of the
results which has paralleled the conflict between the cosmological theories. This is partially due to the lack of a distance scale
in radio astronomy. The optical astronomers have been able to
estimate a distance scale from the red-shift measurements obtained through spectroscopic analysis of the light waves they
study. No such possibility yet exists in radio astronomy; the
only distances established for the radio sources are those for
which optical identifications have been made.

The first approach to this problem of distance and, consequently, the recession of time by the radio astronomers has
been on a statistical basis. Measurements of the intensity of the
unidentified sources have been made to show the relation between the number of sources at various intensity levels. If it is
assumed that the sources are all of the same absolute intensity—

and that the measured differences in intensity arise because of their various distances—this relationship should give some information about the distribution of the sources in space. Calculations do show, in fact, that if there is a uniform distribution of the radio sources throughout space, there is a definite relationship between the number of the sources and their intensity.

If the basic assumption is correct—that the unidentified radio sources lie at cosmical distances beyond the range of the 200-inch telescope—experimental results which supported a direct relationship between number and intensity would favor the theory of continuous creation. If the evolutionary theories are correct, on the other hand, then the clusters of galaxies will be very much more concentrated in space at great distances (that is, in the remote past), collisions between galaxies will be more frequent and there will be a disproportionate number of faint radio sources.

One of the first attempts to deal with this question was made in Cambridge, England, a few years ago, by considering the intensity-number relationship for nearly 2000 unidentified radio sources measured by a radio telescope. The results seemed to favor an evolutionary universe. Simultaneously, radio astronomers in Sydney, Australia, carried out a similar experiment with another type of radio telescope. Their results did not specifically favor the evolutionary theory. All that can be said is that the statistical approach has not yet yielded a definite conclusion regarding the two cosmological theories.

In view of these difficulties another approach to the problem has been made at Jodrell Bank, where the radio telescope has been introducing a distance scale for individual radio sources by measuring their size as well as their intensity. First, it is established whether the intrinsic radio output of the source classifies it as a case of colliding or interacting galaxies. In such cases an estimate of distance can be made by measuring the apparent diameter of the source. If it is assumed that the sources are of the same absolute size, the angular diameter of any source will diminish with distance.

Some 300 sources have been studied in detail, and in about

10 per cent of the cases the evidence is that we are, indeed, dealing with events which may be cases of colliding galaxies at distances approximately ten times that of the Cygnus collision. Striking evidence has now been obtained in favor of this opinion, with the recent announcement that one of these sources has been identified, in a photograph of the spectrum of its radiant energy taken with the 200-inch Palomar telescope, as a system of galaxies 6,000,000,000 light-years distant, receding with a speed of about 90,000 miles per second—almost one half the velocity of light. This means that we may be studying events in the regions of time and space which may finally tell us how the universe evolved.

Further reading:
  Lovell, A. C. B.: THE INDIVIDUAL AND THE UNIVERSE. New York: Harper & Brothers; 1959.
  Hoyle, Fred: FRONTIERS OF ASTRONOMY. New York: The New American Library of World Literature, Inc.; 1957.
  Brown, Hanbury, and A. C. B. Lovell: THE EXPLORATION OF SPACE BY RADIO. New York: John Wiley & Sons, Inc.; 1960.
  Pawsey, J. L., and R. N. Bracewell: RADIO ASTRONOMY. New York: Oxford University Press; 1955.

FRANÇOIS MAURIAC

[*Photograph by Philippe Halsman*]

François Mauriac is perhaps the greatest living Catholic writer. Novelist (The Viper's Tangle, A Kiss for a Leper, The Frontenac Mystery), *playwright* (Asmodée, The Egoists), *and formerly chief editorialist for the renowned Paris newspaper,* Le Figaro, *he was elected one of the French Academy's "Forty Immortals" in 1933. In 1952 he won the Nobel Prize, and in 1959 an honorary membership in the American Academy of Arts and Letters. A jury of thirteen French novelists placed his* Thérèse Desqueyroux *among the thirteen best French novels since the turn of the century. This moving testament of faith forms the concluding chapter of Mauriac's most recent book,* The Son of Man, *issued by the World Publishing Company in January, 1961.*

The Final Answer

BY

FRANÇOIS MAURIAC

I f I were to give a human reason for my fidelity to Christ in this evening of my life, I would call it His quieting of the radical anguish that is in me. This anguish is not to be confused with the fear spoken of by Lucretius, that gives birth to gods; for anguish is not fear. My very singular anguish, which I did not learn from anyone, tormented me from the moment I began to grow aware of the tragedy implied in the fact of being a man; that is to say, a creature condemned to death and who lives under a stay of execution for an unknown length of time. This stay grows shorter each year, and my life resembles that "sorrowful flesh" which one of Balzac's heroes contemplated with horror as it shrank to the size of a coin in his trembling hand.

Anguish is so consubstantial to the human condition that it is already cruelly manifest in childhood. I still remember, to the point of reliving them, those early torments in my unlighted bedroom; I still hear those slow and heavy footsteps on the stairway; and I still bury my head beneath the blankets. I still feel the hot tears that coursed down my cheeks when, as a boarding-school student, I watched the flickering gas flame trace vacillating shadows on the walls of the dormitory. Perhaps I was a small, timid boy who felt himself less robust than the others in the playground filled with noise and quarrels.

Perhaps I was afraid of being called to the head of the room by a contemptuous teacher who was quite capable of making me appear ridiculous and idiotic before my classmates. Perhaps, too, I remember the room in my parents' home where someone had died some time before and where the shutters remained forever closed upon a horrible mystery. Each object in it seemed to have suffered death's somber magic—the glass of water, the arrested pendulum, the armchair still sagging near the fireplace where the fire would never again be lighted.

Yes, for many children anguish is a secret and permanent state. To keep from going insane, I needed the limitless love which my mother poured out on me, the touch of her hand upon my brow during those terrible nights, the comfort of her breath in my hair, and the sound of her voice softly complaining, "What's the matter, silly child? What are you afraid of? I am here; close your eyes and go to sleep."

What, indeed, was tormenting me? My memories help me acknowledge this fact: anguish does not come from without; it is in no way linked to the catastrophes of a given age. The anguished child that I was lived in a time when the war we were fighting concerned only the last king of Dahomey, Behanzin, and when the refrain which a blind man chanted in the courtyard of our home reminded me that the French flag had just been raised at Madagascar. There was much argument about us, apropos of a certain Dreyfus; but his misfortunes did not sadden me at all. In fact, almost all the famous people, people who would not have harmed a fly, had only one fear—that Dreyfus would not be convicted again.

My anguish of later years already existed in that child of a comfortable family in the Third Republic—bourgeois, powerful, rich, peaceful, although capable of aggression for a good cause.

Of course I do not pretend that the era of calamities which began in 1914—the first premonitions of which were evident much earlier—has not nourished the anguish of modern man or that there was no causal relationship between the unhappiness of the times and the existential anguish of "being in the world." But these events, however tragic they were, did not create my anguish, even though they obliged me to relate it to the vicissitudes of history. Let us say that we can no longer "distract" ourselves from them, in accordance with Pascal's use of that word. I believe that even in those ages when history confronted human nature with nothing that was singularly tragic, in the peaceful and happy ages—peaceful and happy at least for the privileged classes, because there is never a happy age for the working class—man was smitten by the unhappiness that comes of being a man who loves and is not loved; who is loved and does not love; who had a son and lost him; who was young and is so no longer; who was strong and healthy and who one day heard a doctor tell him, after a long examination, "We might try an operation . . ." and who hears the automobiles in the streets, a radio playing upstairs, a woman's laughter, but who knows that in six months he will be dead. But even if this trial is spared him there remains the adequate torture—as the historian Michelet called old age—of the gradual deterioration of strength, the decline of the mind, the slow and noiseless approach of ineluctable dissolution.

In this matter I disagree with Michelet and so many others and I exclaim with Lacordaire, an outstanding nineteenth-century Dominican preacher, "Gentlemen, I bring you happiness." I bring you the kind of happiness that a Christian begins to discover at my age. In the measure that I have grown old, anguish has loosened its grip on me. "The man who grows old becomes more aware of the eternal," says Romano Guardini, a contemporary Roman Catholic theologian. "He is less agitated, and the voices from beyond are better heard. The encroachment of eternity pales the reality of time." There is a prayer by Saint Gertrude, who must have been very old when she uttered it, in which she calls Christ "the love of the evening of my life" and in which she says, "O my Jesus of life's evening, let me fall asleep in you quietly. . . ." But all of this was already expressed at the dawn of the Christian Era when the aged Simeon pressed the infant God to his breast, "*Nunc dimittis servum tuum, Domine. . . .*"

Christ is not a defense which I have erected against anguish; on the contrary, anguish was a permanent state during the days of my stormy youth when I did not have recourse to Him, when

239

I dwelt apart from Him. No, my anguish did not create God. The quieting I now experience, the silence that falls upon my last days, permits me finally to be attentive to the answer which was unceasingly given during my tormented life, but to which I preferred my suffering because I preferred my sin. What more do I know today than I did as a despairing adolescent? The adolescent loved neither happiness nor peace. It took me a long time to learn to love God. I can say nothing on this subject that is not part of my life; as an adolescent I loved my anguish and I preferred it to God. Far from inciting me to imagine a God to deliver me, my anguish provided me with reasons and excuses to escape the presence, in me and about me, of a love to which I preferred an unhappiness born of covetousness.

It is not anguish which creates the Father in heaven whom Christ taught us to know and to love. It was rather my anguish, the somber delectation that lasted throughout my interminable youth—I say interminable because my heart remains young even though I am not—it was this delectation in anguish that inclined me to turn away from God and even deny that He existed. It furnished me with arguments and proofs against His goodness, against His love.

This is undoubtedly not true of all men. But it is true of those writers and poets who cherish in their anguish the very source of their inspiration, and more precisely in that form of anguish which is born of an attraction for a God who is rejected by flesh and blood. I have often applied to myself the image from Maurice de Guerin—a French poet of the nineteenth century—in which he compared his thought to a heavenly fire that burns on a horizon between two worlds. It is the torture of being incapable of choosing between the world and God that constitutes in effect the drama of many artists—a drama which both torments and delights them.

"If thou didst know the gift of God," Christ said to the Samaritan woman. And what is the gift of God? It is precisely the opposite of anguish. "Peace I leave with you; my peace I give to you," Christ repeated to His friends on the last night, before He entered into His agony. It is precisely this peace which we do not want; it appears redoubtable to us because we

do not love the hero of the story Chateaubriand interpolated in
The Genius of Christianity—peace. "Arise, desired tempests!"
was the cry of René, at the dawn of the Romantic Age; and
this cry reveals the vocation of so many young people to unhappiness. I went first of all to the damned poets, and they
attracted me to the prince of darkness and his eternal unhappiness. Was this literature? Yes, but it was a strange literature in which despair was so often, in surrealist circles, authenti-
cated by suicide. Saint John denounces this hatred of peace; he
tells us that light came into the world and that men refused it
because they preferred darkness. The creature seeks darkness to
obliterate himself. The victory of Christ in a life is summed up
in this difficult acceptance of peace in light.

I am aware of this objection: Christianity itself is anguish.
But it is not enough to say that there is a Christian anguish. All
those who revolted against Christianity in the nineteenth century accused it of being against nature, of having darkened the
world, of having calumniated life. It is true that the name of
Christianity masks many contradictory tendencies which set
Christians at odds with one another. Those who are called to
love one another have burned one another. There are many
mansions in the Father's house. And one of them, from Saint
Augustine through Calvin and Jansen, was erected under the
sign of fear and trembling—anguish in the strictest sense of the
word. But there is another anguish which is less harsh—that of
love which is totally contained in the regret for having offended
the loved one, in the fear of no longer being loved by him and of
no longer feeling ourselves capable of loving him. The love of
the creature for the Creator is no more exempt from what
Marcel Proust calls the intermittences of the heart than human
love. But this is not the anguish we refer to when we speak of
fear and trembling.

Monsieur de Saint-Cyran has always seemed to me to be the
worst kind of theologian. Let us say that in France, to speak
only of France, Port Royal is still the most illustrious source of
that anguish which is centered upon an obsession with personal
salvation. The Infinite Being refuses or gives His grace according to an unpredictable plan to a creature tainted from birth,

totally impotent except to do evil—for in what concerns evil, human nature has the power of a god. We are delivered naked, trembling, disarmed, to an arbitrary God. This is the root of Jansenist anguish.*

It is impossible to indicate in a few words the contents of the immense work reflecting Jansenism in which, over the centuries, a whole school of Christian thinkers has collaborated. I will simply allude to the permanent source of anguish, and even of despair, that such theologies, from Saint Augustine to Jansen, have premised upon a wounded heart. It has generated innumerable and lamentable progeny—progeny who are the terror of Catholic confessors—scrupulous souls obsessed by trifles, adorers of a niggling divinity with whom they must bargain craftily. André Gide referred to the "cramp of salvation." This cramp, as imposed by Augustinian theologies, is so painful that many young people who began by following Christ drew away from Him to escape the frightful obligation of rendering an account of their least desire, their least thought. They threw the whole Christian heritage overboard. "What is wonderful about Communism," a recent convert to Marxism told me one day, "is that my personal salvation no longer interests me."

What I propose as a defense against this form of anguish is another anguish which is generative of peace and joy. I propose a kind of spiritual homeopathy, that is a release from anguish through anguish. Obsession with our personal salvation will not be dominated and conquered in us unless it is transposed to the order of charity. It goes without saying that we should nourish the hope of salvation and that the whole of a Christian life ought to tend toward eternal life. But if it is clear that we ought to have a passionate desire for salvation, we should not be obsessed with it in the pathological sense of the word. In my youth I was frequently seduced by the words which Pascal put in Christ's

* *Editor's note.* Jansenism, a Catholic sect founded in the seventeenth century by Cornelius Jansen, bishop of Ypres, is characterized by rigorously pietistic dogma and a pessimistic view of man's fate. Pope Innocent X pronounced the basic Jansenist doctrines heretical. The abbot de Saint-Cyran was Jansen's close friend and collaborator; the convent of Port Royal, near Versailles, was a center of Jansenist activity. The sect has survived, and in America claims twenty churches and 2217 adherents.

mouth, "I thought of you in my agony. I lost so much blood for you." These words impress me less today because I discern in such a desire for redemptive blood the complacency of a creature resigned to the eternal damnation of most of the human race, and not agonized by the thought that he is set apart with a small flock of the elect.

Anguish transmuted into charity—anguish for another— delivers us from the terror felt by so many Christian souls before the mystery of predestination and liberates us from an obsession with personal salvation, not in respect to what is essential but in respect to what is morbid. Our anguish then becomes more than a matter of personal concern; it embraces mankind, or at least that part of mankind which is "the neighbor" for us, and can extend to a social class or to entire peoples. For a worker priest, the neighbor is the whole working class, as the Jews were for us during the Nazi persecution.

For Sartre, "Hell is other people"; but for us, others are Christ. He tells us Himself that the Son of Man is come to save what is lost—*all* that is lost, and not merely this one or that one for whom He would have consecrated a special, miserly drop of His blood.

The Christian life is first of all a personal relationship between each one of us and God. "You have not chosen me; but I have chosen you." It goes without saying that the extension of our anguish to embrace the suffering of men will not yield all of its fruits unless our apostolate is rooted in a life of close intimacy with Christ. I believe, I have always believed, that the Christian life is essentially a friendship, a love and, therefore, that which is most personal, most individual; that each one of us has been called by his name; and that at the beginning of every conversion there is this encounter at the turning of the road spoken of by Lacordaire—an adorable being, demanding, tenacious, whom nothing discourages, and to whom we prefer so many creatures whom we shortly forsake or who forsake us. But He is always there, never so close to us as when we believe Him to be absent, awaiting His hour which, in the case of many men, is unfortunately the last, when there is no longer any possibility of betrayal.

But what is the reality of this Christ whom all believers strive to imitate, unless it be that He took upon Himself human anguish? Therefore, we must also take upon ourselves the anguish of one another. The saints did so literally, to the point of identifying themselves with the Father's abandonment of His Son in the horror of the night. This secret of Christ's agony was profoundly understood by Bernanos, the French Catholic novelist, and this is what gives his fictional priests, particularly the country priest, their mysterious density. For us, as simple faithful, it is sufficient to unite ourselves with the anguish experienced by Christ, in our brothers.

Here, then, is the strange remedy for anguish which I propose: peace and joy are the fruits of anguish. "Peace I leave with you, my peace I give to you; not as the world gives do I give to you." We understand now the profound meaning of the last promise which the Son of Man made to us before entering into His agony—peace and joy in this plenitude of suffering which consists in espousing, each one according to his vocation, the suffering of the hungry, the persecuted, the imprisoned, the tortured, the exploited. This is the Christian paradox.

We know that there is a difference between human hope and spiritual hope. We may lose all hope for the temporal salvation of mankind and still await the Kingdom of God. In the very midst of the Atomic Age, we await it confidently. But it must not be concluded from this that our hope concerns only eternity; it also concerns the dark world of the living. For the crimes of the will to power, which sum up temporal history, do not prevent the leaven of which Christ speaks from working tirelessly in the human mass. The fire which He came to cast upon the earth is always smoldering, and the bloodiest years of history are nevertheless years of grace.

"Thy kingdom come," we pray in the Our Father. Millions and millions of human beings have prayed thus over the nearly two thousand years since this prayer was taught to us, and with the absolute certitude of being answered. Indeed the prayer is already answered; the Kingdom has already come; it is among us, within us in such a way that we are never defeated except in appearance. And as our anguish is the very condition of our peace, our defeat is the very condition of our victory. "Have confidence; I have overcome the world." He who challenged the world so boldly did so at the very hour when He was about to be betrayed, outraged, made a laughingstock, nailed to the cross of a murderer.

Saint Paul tells us that all of creation groans and suffers the pains of childbirth. Our anguish is indeed inspired by childbirth, and it seems interminable by our ephemeral standards. But those of us who have kept the faith know what the end will be. To those who succumb to anguish and who are about to lose heart, we can do no better than repeat what Saint Paul affirmed to the faithful of Rome, "Who then shall separate us from the love of Christ? Shall tribulation, or distress, or famine, or nakedness, or danger, or persecution, or the sword? . . . But in all these things we overcome because of Him who has loved us."

Further reading:

Guardini, Romano: Lord's Prayer. New York: Pantheon Books, Inc.; 1958.

Ricciotti, Giuseppe: Life of Christ. St. Paul: Bruce Publishing Co.; 1947.

Adam, Karl: Spirit of Catholicism. New York: Doubleday & Company, Inc.; 1959.

Berrigan, Daniel: The Bride, Essays in the Church. New York: The Macmillan Company; 1959.

Mauriac, François: Life of Jesus. New York: David McKay Co., Inc.; 1951.

BARBARA WARD

[*Photograph by Wolf Suschitzky*]

Barbara Ward (Lady Jackson), writer on international affairs and economics, was educated in England, France and Germany, being graduated from Oxford University with an honors degree in philosophy, politics and economics in 1935. A onetime governor of the British Broadcasting Corporation and a participant in its Brains Trust program, Miss Ward has been an editor of The Economist for twenty years. Miss Ward gives an annual course of lectures at Harvard and is also widely known as a journalist and a speaker on economic subjects. She is now working on a Carnegie fellowship in the field of economic-assistance programs. She is married to Sir Robert Jackson, Commissioner of Development in Ghana, and lives in Accra. Sir Robert and Lady Jackson have a three-year-old son.

‮ᒪᎧᒪᎧᒪᎧᒪᎧᒪᎧᒪᎧᒪᎧᒪᎧᒪᎧᒪᎧᒪᎧᒪᎧᒪᎧᒪᎧᒪᎧᒪᎧᒪᎧᒪᎧᒪᎧᒪ‬

The Economic
Revolution

B Y

BARBARA WARD

Three quarters of the human race today is involved in a vast movement of revolutionary economic upheaval. They are attempting to modernize their economies—to move from the old patterns of static agriculture and limited commerce which made up the general pattern of the human economy for millennia on to the new productive, dynamic economy of modern industry, technology and science. The change is not so much a matter of choice as of stark necessity. Everywhere among the emergent peoples, populations are doubling every generation or so. Resources must at least keep pace if even present standards are to be maintained—and these, incidentally, allow each person an average income of no more than $120 a year. If life is to be a little more secure and healthy, a little better nourished, housed and clothed, a trebling of resources would hardly be sufficient. But there is no possibility of such expansion under the old economic methods. Static agriculture has only one means of growth—to take in more land. But in most of Asia there is no more land. Unless economic methods are radically recast, the outcome in the next forty years must be deepening misery, anarchy and despair.

This world-wide revolution of economic modernization is one in which the wealthy West is fundamentally involved. It was in the Atlantic area that the revolution began. It was under western influence that the first impact of the new methods reached the other continents and determined decisively the conditions under which they in their turn would seek to modernize their economies. Thus to ignore or to be indifferent to the present world-wide movement of economic change would be the equivalent of canceling at least 300 years of western experience. Worse, it would entail withdrawal from the greatest contemporary human effort to remold society and remake the face of the earth. And it is a fact of history that those who seek to withdraw from its great experiments usually end by being overwhelmed in them.

We cannot fix a date for the origins of the modern economic revolution. A hundred different conditions, influences and decisions set it in motion, and the changes came cumulatively over several centuries. In part, it was rooted in medieval Europe's constitutional development which gave the merchant what he never had in the Orient—status, security and inducements to save. Calvinism played its part, teaching that hard work in pursuit of profit was blessed by God and that money so earned should be saved, not spent in luxury. The scientific temper of the eighteenth century encouraged progressive landowners and aspiring artisans to experiment with new methods of production. In Britain toward the end of the eighteenth century all these separate streams—of acquisitiveness, of work, of invention—had begun to flow together into that flood of economic and technological change which we loosely call the Industrial Revolution.

The men who made this revolution did not know what they were doing in any general sense. Each pursued his own interest and profit, and the sum of interests made up the working of the system. But with our hindsight we can disentangle the essential principles, the changes without which dynamic growth is impossible—the preconditions, therefore, of modernization anywhere else.

The two most important principles underlying the revolution of economic growth are productivity and saving. Productivity results from any method which helps men to produce more goods for the same output of effort and resources. The decisive changes in productivity in Britain's early industrial revolution were better agricultural methods and the application of a new form of power—steam from coal—to machines made by new processes of iron founding. The new machines began to flood the market with cheaper consumer goods—which incidentally wiped out handicrafts imported from Asia. Expanding trade created the need for better transport, bigger towns and harbors. New industrial techniques called for steadily increasing education.

These were the first steps. Since then invention has multiplied a thousandfold the effect of every instrument of growth. Above all, vast new sources of energy have been discovered—electricity, the atom. But the basic requirements of modernization have not changed. Now, as then, they are better farming, more education, "infrastructure"—roads, power, ports—and industrialization.

All these techniques of greater production depend upon saving—that is, upon the postponement of consumption. In the eighteenth century, Coke of Holkham postponed direct returns on his farms when he experimented with crop rotation. The fourfold increase in output paid him back handsomely and provided capital for further ventures. Similarly, when the duke of Bridgewater built the first canal to Lancashire, he took laborers and materials away from the immediate tasks of farming. When, as a result of the saving on transport, the price of coal in Manchester was halved, resources were available to recompense the duke and to provide for further experiment. John Wilkinson used his savings—and other people's—all his life to pioneer new methods of iron founding and new uses for cast iron. One result was the steam engine and the first fundamental revolution in energy, that greatest of all sources of productivity.

Even the most primitive economies save a little—putting aside seed corn for the next harvest. Perhaps 5 per cent of national income is saved in this way. Economists reckon that, as a general rule, when the level of productive saving has reached about 15 per cent of national income, the economy has reached

251

the point of "break-through" and can generate each year enough savings to insure the expansion of both savings and consumption in the future. This process—the process of self-sustaining growth —is the ultimate objective of all developing economies today.

One can see that it works in a cumulative way. The more techniques of progress there are—better methods, more powerful machines, more skilled labor—the easier it is to save. Yet there is always a period during which the original investments have to be made. Consumption is postponed for the first investment in better farming, for the first machines, for the first expansion in power. As a general rule, increases in capital at this stage have come from agriculture because in all preindustrial societies farming is the occupation of nearly 90 per cent of the people. And the chances are that the process will entail great hardships for them. Saving is, after all, not-consuming. Farming people in a static economy are not, in general, very rich. Their surpluses are small. If they are to consume less and send off their surplus to the towns, they are likely to be poorer, unless—as in America and later in Japan—farming is actually expanding at the time of the transfer.

Nor is this the end of the difficulties inherent in beginning to save. If in Britain after 1810 all the output of the new machines had been consumed at once by the thousands of workers herding into the new industrial cities, there would have been no margin for further expansion. The organizers of the new wealth —the rising industrialists, the bankers, the landowners—kept the surplus created by the machines and devoted it to increased investment. In Britain between 1820 and 1860, little of the new production directly benefited the bulk of the workers. It was not until the system was fully established and goods began to pour out from the new processes—and workers themselves were beginning to organize and bargain for better wages—that a general rise in living standards began.

Since then Britain's national income has increased on the average by more than 3 per cent a year; and this is the general figure for the industrial West. In recent decades the pace has even quickened a little owing to higher levels of investment, both public and private, and new methods in technology. Today, therefore, the harsh times of original saving are quite forgotten. America's 176,000,000 people enjoy a national income of nearly $500,000,000,000. For years now 15 per cent and more of this income has been set aside for further investment while the citizens' own consumption has steadily increased. But in free Asia, in Africa and Latin America more than 1,000,000,000 people have a total income of only $120,000,000,000. Take 15 per cent of this for investment, and every form of consumption has to be cut. Saving is as harsh a discipline as it was in Britain in the 1850's. In fact, it is harsher, for the pressure of population is greater and the task of cutting consumption correspondingly more drastic.

It is in the context of these early grinding days of forced saving that we can best grasp both the origins and the continued appeal of Communism. All Marx's thinking was conditioned by the grim conditions of early industry in Britain. His contemporaries, as we have seen, had no very clear picture of the forces molding the new economy—nor apparently had Marx. He saw that a vast release of productive forces was taking place and gave the industrialists credit for it. But his attention and energy were fixed on the appalling conditions of the workers, and he denounced, like an ancient Hebrew prophet, the ugly fact of exploitation.

In part, he was right. The organizers of the new wealth were undoubtedly rewarding themselves handsomely—as commissars were to do a century later. But he missed the other facet of their policy—that the saving sweated from the workers provided the necessary capital for extending the whole base of the economy. In fact, Marx did not grasp *how* in practical terms a modern industrial society had to be built. He assumed that the *bourgeoisie* would first look after that; then the workers would take over a functioning machine once their deepening misery had driven them to revolt. There are thus no blueprints in *Das Kapital* for a modern economy, and when in 1917 the Communists found themselves with the whole of Russia on their hands, it was to their own pragmatism, not to Communist theory, that they had to look for guidance.

Russia had some beginnings of modernization. But the

country was flattened by war and revolution. The first efforts of Communism—turning the factories over to the workers—made the confusion worse. In 1921 Lenin in fact decreed a modified acceptance of the market economy, hoping that peasants and traders would get the economy somehow back into motion. But by this time a fully integrated industrial society existed in the West which could be copied. The tremendous armaments built up by governments in the First World War showed what central direction could do to accelerate heavy industry and to mobilize the people's savings and work. It was Stalin's fateful achievement to use total state power to transpose to Russia the techniques of production evolved in the industrial West. The first Five Year Plan and its successors established the "infrastructure" and the heavy industry of a modern advanced economy by government fiat. At the same time it set in motion the vast schemes for education which would keep trained manpower in step with the machines. At first technicians and engineers were borrowed from abroad. But within a decade Russian development was self-sufficient. The break-through had been achieved —and at horrifying cost.

Communist Russia could not, any more than could capitalist Britain, avoid the iron necessity of beginning to save. There had to be capital—for the new sources of energy, the new factories, the new machines—and only the people at large could do the saving. But driven by his totalitarian daemon, Stalin pushed the percentage of national income devoted to saving far above the western figure. He compelled the Russians to save not 15 but 25 to 30 per cent of the fruits of their labors. Nor was this the end of the matter. Fearing an independent peasantry, he forced the farms to deliver their entire surplus to the government. They revolted, killed their animals and starved during the terrible imposition of collective farming. Far from agricultural techniques' improving, output actually fell. But relentlessly the saving went on. Conditions in Russian farms and Russian cities were more appalling than in Victorian slums. Consumption was less, the "trickle down" even slower. For a decade at least, the great foes of exploitation exploited their own people as no capitalist had ever done, and squeezed out of them the last kopeck of saving.

But this is only one side of the story. Russian modernization was accomplished at breakneck speed. It had advanced far enough by 1941 to withstand Hitler's invasion. It achieved prodigies of postwar reconstruction. It has driven expansion onward at a rate of some 7 per cent a year. In four decades it has come within sight of America's military and industrial power. Today, even consumption is at last improving. To the peoples in emergent lands the speed and vigor of the transformation, accomplished in so few decades, is a matter of hope as well as fear. The times of iron discipline and ruthless saving in Russia are receding. What is more in evidence today is the growth and power. Inevitably the Soviet achievement seems to present an alternative to the slower traditional western method of reaching the point of "economic break-through." Among the preindustrial societies of today, China has already chosen the Russian route. And few other governments can hope to escape indefinitely from the dilemma of this choice.

The western nations are more or less aware of how much they, too, have at stake in the decision. If a third of the human race despaired of the open society with its flexible experimental methods and mild disciplines, and chose instead the iron path of total Communist control, the balance of freedom in the world would be perilously upset. Not only would the emergent peoples lose their liberty. The West itself might suffer from that loss of nerve and breakdown in confidence which occurs when societies have the impression that their ways are not the ways of the future—that history is leaving them behind.

What is perhaps less clearly realized is the extent to which the West has influenced and, if it will, can still influence the outcome. The conditions today under which the emergent peoples are trying to modernize their economies have been brought about almost entirely by western policies and western influence. As late as 1939 most of the world was still controlled either by settlers of European stock—as in all of America—or by colonial rulers of the same origin. In Asia, it is true, the westerners came

out to trade, and it was only where local authority collapsed—
as in Java and India—that they took over political control. But
their economic influence undermined Manchu power in China,
and Japan could not have resisted them after 1850 if it had not
forcefully westernized itself. In short, western control or western
influence determined virtually the entire pattern of development in Asia from the seventeenth century to the end of the last
war. Africa in the last hundred years has similarly been under
total western domination.

The western contribution to the four levers of modernization proved uneven. Peasant agriculture remained static, and the
new plantations mainly benefited western interests. Modern education began—especially in India—but in 1936 there were still
only 516 university students among Java's 40,000,000 people. A
start was made on infrastructure, roads, railways, ports and
power—again, India led the rest—but industrialization lagged
far behind.

At this point we reach one of the consequences of the western impact which, though unintended, may have given a decisive setback to Asian development. Until the nineteenth century
China and India were exporters to Europe of manufactures—
hand-loom textiles, silks, pottery. In addition, peasant income all
through the vast countryside was supplemented by local handicrafts. In Britain such centers of artisan enterprise were often
the starting points of mechanized industry. In Japan after 1870,
they were to prove so again as thousands of small workshops
were moving to production with power and machines. But in
India and China as the nineteenth century developed, this widespread preindustrial system of manufacture was wiped out by
the flooding in of machine-made textiles and gadgets from the
West. Local centers were extinguished. Peasant income fell. Indigenous growth ceased. Later in the century, modern factory industry began; but often, as in China, it was overwhelmingly foreign. In India, given Britain's doctrines of free trade and *laissez
faire*, Indian enterprise did not secure full tariff protection until
after the First World War. Industrialization was thus slow in
spreading and would have been even slower if two world wars
had not hastened it a little.

The small extent to which modernization was encouraged by western colonial control can best be illustrated by the opposite experience of Japan, the one Asian country to exclude the westerners. After 1870, a policy of thoroughgoing modernization was carried through by the Japanese themselves. A land reform gave the peasant a stake in production; extension services helped him to increase output by 50 per cent between 1870 and 1910. Most of this surplus was transferred to the towns, where the state expanded roads and ports, railways and power, began a drive for universal literacy, sent young men overseas to train, established industries, sold back the big concerns to the clans—the Zaibatsu—and encouraged cottage industry to supplement them. Every lever of modernization was thus brought into service, and in a few decades the Japanese economy was within sight of self-sustaining growth, saving enough each year to increase the volume of savings thereafter—and this in spite of a population which was increasing as rapidly as any in Asia.

We cannot fairly assess the western impact without this background of population pressure. China already had a vast population and gross rural poverty when western economic influence became predominant after 1850. But in India and Java it was western control that helped the spurt. A hundred years of peace probably doubled India's population between 1800 and 1900. In Java the numbers grew from just over 3,000,000 in 1795 to nearly 30,000,000 by 1914. In the twentieth century, sanitation and medical services began to speed the rate of growth. Keeping pace with this increase would have required measures as vigorous as those of Japan to insure that economy and population grew together, each kind of growth stimulating the other as it did in the West. But under the impact of partial modernization—which best sums up Asia's western inheritance—population growth in most of the Asian countries began to accelerate before the economy had reached a position of self-sustaining growth. And this is perhaps the most fateful of all the legacies from the West.

Saving, it must be repeated, means not-consuming. The more mouths there are to feed in a static economy, the harder it is to postpone consumption. The only answer is to save more drastically and thus achieve growth. But how can this drastic saving be done when—after a century of rapid growth in population, combined with economic stagnancy—per-capita income has sunk to the margin? How can a government increase savings to 15 per cent of national income if—as in India—the citizen's average income is only sixty dollars? This is the dilemma which most of Asia has inherited from the West. And this is the dilemma which could lead—as it has done in China—to the choice of the Communist alternative. In Communist discipline, in Communist techniques of forced accumulation, in Communist readiness to wring the last ounce of saving from the countryside, there seems to be a possible escape from the Asian impasse.

Equally the dilemma of saving could give the key to an effective western policy. The broad aim over the next two or three decades should be to bring the flow of investment in the emergent lands up to the level needed for self-sustaining growth. Thereafter there would continue to be foreign investment on a normal business basis; but the period of emergency help, designed to overcome the obstacles created by partial modernization, would have to come to an end.

If the present position is taken as a starting point, one can broadly estimate that the emergent peoples in the free world—1,000,000,000 of them—with their annual income of about $120,000,000,000, manage to save the 5 per cent traditional in static economies. To this $6,000,000,000 is added each year about $3,000,000,000 of outside capital, public and private. These figures are roughly half of what is needed. But they cannot be doubled immediately because the local people lack the margins for tougher saving and because the ground is not yet prepared—in public utilities, in transportation, in technical training—to absorb a sudden startling increase from outside.

The process is essentially long term. But a reasonable aim might be to double the flow of capital from outside over the next two decades. If this extra injection of saving—of the order of $6,000,000,000 a year, both public and private—were used to increase local skills and infrastructure, domestic capacity to save would certainly increase, although a doubling of the level is perhaps too optimistic. But even if domestic savings increased by

50 per cent over the ten years, the next decade would open with total savings at least within sight of the goal of 15 per cent of national income. The second decade could complete the transformation of the local economies, and thereafter special assistance would taper off.

Such a scheme is, of course, no more than a statement of intent. The actual content of the program would vary from country to country and region to region, and would reflect the varying degrees of modernization achieved during the period of direct western control or influence.

Since the old colonial governments were not very active in the field of basic agriculture, most underdeveloped areas require at least a quintupling of expenditure on the land so that men and resources can be transferred from it to other sectors without imposing Stalinlike controls. Education, particularly in Africa, also needs really ambitious expansion. On the other hand, the colonial record of infrastructure is normally more lavish. Roads, railways, public utilities exist. It is usually a question not of starting from scratch, but of extending an existing system sufficiently to permit a frontal attack upon industrialization. Infrastructure is, incidentally, pre-eminently an area for public investment, since private enterprise is not attracted by the low returns over long periods which public services provide.

The sphere of private enterprise now as in the past is likely to be the development of raw materials for export and all the myriad forms of industry—processing plants, consumer goods—which expanding wealth can support.

Not all the emergent peoples are ready for all these policies at once, but where—as in India—much of the infrastructure in both men and services already exists, investment plans can be more immediate and ambitious, and outside assistance can be mobilized on a larger scale. In fact, India might well be made the model of a speedy, efficient, co-ordinated effort of internal investment and outside help. In spite of their desperate poverty, the Indians have increased their domestic savings by 50 per cent in the last decade and hope to have doubled the annual rate by 1966. Even so, it still falls below the 15 per cent needed for self-sustaining growth. If, however, outside capital from all sources—

public, private, international, national—could reach $1,000,000,-
000 a year during the third Five Year Plan, the point of break-
through would be in sight at the end of the period; and the largest free community in Asia, in which live 40 per cent of the free
world's emergent peoples, would have demonstrated that without totalitarian discipline, without the suppression of freedom
or the imposition of forced saving on a murderous scale, an underdeveloped land can achieve full modernization and the possibility of sustained growth.

There is one proviso to this hope. At some point in the next
decades there must be a check to the rate at which India's population is increasing—a need of which the Indian Government is
well aware. But, in fact, the connection between rapid economic
development and a more stable birth rate is exceedingly close.
In a desperately poor society the birth of many children is an insurance against tragic rates of infantile mortality and, in some
measure, an economic investment as well. It is only when parents, convinced of the chance of better health and rising standards, can hope to give their children surer prospects of survival
and nurture, that they will feel inclined to raise a smaller family.
It need hardly be stressed that in a free society, whatever measures are pursued by government, the decisive choice rests with
the parents. Thus—as in the West—a measure of economic advance and expectation is virtually a precondition of a slackening
in the population's rate of growth.

A target therefore may be set for the western nations of
$5,000,000,000 to $6,000,000,000 a year in investment of all
forms—public and private, from national and international
agencies—with an immediate plan to allot $1,000,000,000 of this
sum each year to India's crucial experiment in growth. That such
an aim is easily within the West's resources requires little demonstration. It is no more than 1 per cent of the combined national incomes of the western nations; and since the recent rate
of growth of these incomes is of the order of 4 per cent a year, to
allot 1 per cent to a world investment project requires no diversion of resources. It merely entails a slight postponement in the
rate at which consumption is actually increasing. To call this a
strain or a sacrifice is an abuse of language.

But the mere availability of resources will not determine the result. The fundamental political question has to be decided —whether or not the western powers accept the need for a sustained, long-term policy of world investment and world growth. The arguments from self-interest seem overwhelming. We are beginning—after a decade of uncertainty—to see that the direct political appeal of Communism is on the wane. Hungary and Tibet are reminders that Communism can be the stalking horse of a new form of imperial control. Communism's chief appeal is therefore social and economic—that it can throw out the landlords, revolutionize agriculture, build industries at breakneck speed and achieve modernization in a decade. To people caught in the impasse between saving and rising population, its techniques of forced accumulation can still appeal—unless there is an alternative, the alternative of western aid. Sustained world investment is thus a fundamental weapon in the struggle against Communist expansion.

But even if there were no Communists, the wealthy white western minority of the world could not hope to prosper if most of the rest of mankind were foundering in hopeless poverty. Islands of plenty in a vast ocean of misery never have been a good recipe for commercial success. As western industry and agriculture expand with rising investment and revolutionary changes in technology, wider markets, wider areas of consumption, greater sources of supply become a necessity. They cannot all be found round the North Atlantic. A developing world is now the precondition of prosperity for an expanding West.

It is not simply an economic interest. Times of misery and despair are also times of anarchy and war, as were the recurrent cycles of ancient China when population overtopped resources and the empire fell into a welter of civil war and destruction. The sterile expenditure on arms needed for security on a despairing planet would certainly far exceed any sums now proposed for world investment.

But more than economic profit or national security is at stake. In this century, owing to the work of historians and archivists, of archaeologists and explorers, we know more than men have ever known about the fate of civilizations. Our western forefathers could take their society for granted as the end product of a unique historical progress in which, little by little, the inventiveness and faith of free men had come to set up a world society under western influence and control. Today we know that progress is at best a fluctuating line; and that along the march of humanity many proud experiments in political organization, many essays in empire, many great and affluent societies have foundered by the way. We know, too, that again and again they failed not from any inherent lack of means and resources, but from something more subtle—a failure of the spirit, a loss of nerve or faith or inner control.

In the eighteenth century no society on earth seemed more splendid and self-confident than the Chinese Empire under the greatest of its Manchu emperors, Chien Lung. European philosophers admired it without stint. Voltaire exclaimed, "They have perfected moral science." And Leibnitz asked for Chinese missionaries to teach Europe "the aim and practice of natural theology." But the high confidence, the apparent wealth covered a flaw. The Chinese rulers dismissed the rest of the world as barbarians. No isolationism in the West has ever equaled their contemptuous dismissal of every foreign thing. Yet these same foreigners revolutionized their scientific and industrial techniques, and before a century had passed, China's pride and China's wealth alike were humbled. Westerners controlled its policy and its economic life. The ignored and neglected outside world poured in. Traditional China disappeared in the torrent.

The temptation facing the western world today is comparable. It is supremely wealthy and, on the whole, supremely confident. A deep instinct is to let the rest of the world go hang, ignoring Communist efforts to organize it and the Communists' steady drive to secure growth and power. Can we be certain that the fate of the Manchus does not await us if, like them, we rely on our affluence and superiority and leave the world at large to its present prospect of deepening crisis and Communist manipulation, with the ultimate possibility of total loss to the side of freedom?

But the temptation of indifference and superiority to which

China succumbed is not the end of the challenge to the human spirit in the West today. There is no greater defeat for a man or a society than to set a great experiment in motion and then to abandon it before it is half done. The modernization of the world is such an experiment. Casually, unconsciously, but with deadly effectiveness, western man all round the globe destroyed the traditional gods and the ancient societies with his commerce and his science. Now that the old world is dead, is he to make no special effort to bring the new world to life? He has plowed up the continents and scattered the seeds of new methods and hopes and ambitions. Is he indifferent to the harvest? Does it mean nothing to him if great areas of the world, where western influence has been predominant, emerge from this tutelage unable to return to the old life, yet unfitted for the new? It is hard to believe that the future could ever belong to men demonstrating irresponsibility on so vast a scale.

But the greatest challenge is also the simplest. The element above all others which western man has brought into history is the belief in its moral dimensions. When one considers the rise and fall of empires, the predatory imperialism, the violence, the irrational destructiveness which has marked so much of mankind's story, one is tempted to see in it only "sound and fury, signifying nothing." But in the Christian, rational and humane tradition of the West, the attempt has been made to rescue wider and wider areas of human existence from the tyranny of man's grasping, irrational and violent instincts—and a fundamental element in this search for moral order, of which Communism itself is a perverted by-product, is the belief that men should not prey on other men but that they are, in very truth, their brother's keeper.

In the past this principle has been limited by the few resources available in any society for active help. Private charity could lessen misery, but the levers of economic growth were not available for a frontal attack on poverty itself. The Industrial Revolution has removed this inhibition. Within western society the principle that the wealthier, luckier and healthier should assist the less privileged to acquire the education and well-being

needed to advance themselves—the principle of general welfare
—has brought about a wider and wider sharing of the new
wealth.

Today resources exist in such abundance that a world-wide
extension of the principle of welfare is physically possible. All
that is lacking is the political decision to do so. Is it possible that
a society which boasts of its humanity and its Christian inspiration should ignore the challenge? Is it conceivable that such a
society, having done so, should deserve to survive?

Further reading:
Ward, Barbara: INTERPLAY OF EAST AND WEST. New York:
W. W. Norton & Company, Inc.; 1957.
Ward, Barbara: FIVE IDEAS THAT CHANGE THE WORLD. New
York: W. W. Norton & Company, Inc.; 1959.
Rostow, W. W. and Max Millikan: A PROPOSAL: KEY TO AN
EFFECTIVE FOREIGN POLICY. New York: Harper & Brothers;
1957.
Zinkin, Maurice: DEVELOPMENT FOR FREE ASIA. New York:
Oxford University Press (Essential Books); 1956.
Stevenson, Adlai E.: CALL TO GREATNESS. New York: Har-
per & Brothers; 1955.

JESSE L. GREENSTEIN

Jesse L. Greenstein, professor of astrophysics at the California Institute of Technology and staff member of the Mount Wilson and Palomar observatories, is widely known for his studies of stellar evolution and composition. He is currently engaged in a study of the composition of our galaxy at the time and place where stars were born. Doctor Greenstein has discovered and studied so many strange types of dying stars that most of his friends call him a celestial undertaker.

Natural History
of a Star

BY

JESSE L. GREENSTEIN

T o the astrophysicist the universe is a machine in which the
stars are formed, produce energy and become extinct. To
understand these processes we use the rational methods of physics and mathematics. Nevertheless, both our comprehension and
our description of stellar activity are conditioned by the fact that
we are biological, psychological and spiritual entities; in consequence we tend to phrase our concepts in nonmechanical terms,
as though there were a biological struggle for existence in which
the stars are born, live and die. Actually the processes of cosmological evolution are much simpler than those of biological evo
lution, though they occur on an immensely grander scale.

The subject of stellar evolution is one of the central problems of modern science; we hope it may prove to be one of the
few natural processes which can be understood in its entirety. I
would like here to describe our recent progress toward this goal.

The sun is our nearest star, typical of the hundred billion
other stars in our galaxy. The sun is a ball of gas held together by
its own gravity. It is 330,000 times more massive than the earth.
From the cosmic point of view the sun is alive, if we may think

of energy production as life. The earth, the other planets, the moons, the asteroids—the debris of the solar system—are dead bodies. These orbiting slag heaps have no naturally self-sustaining energy sources, little mass and seem to have little cosmic significance. Our own earth, for instance, is composed largely of iron and silicon, which are nearly inert in nuclear reactions. The sun in contrast, contains about 70 per cent hydrogen, the ultimate nuclear fuel.

While hydrogen can be made into a dangerous nuclear explosive on earth, controlled hydrogen fusion processes occur in the sun—and the other stars—without explosion and provide the energy for sunlight and for our life. Nuclear fusion occurs in the sun mainly because of its high temperature and the density of its gases. Under such conditions, with temperatures reaching 25,-000,000 degrees, some hydrogen nuclei collide at distances of a thousand-billionth of an inch, with speeds of more than 1000 miles a second. As a result of these collisions some of the hydrogen nuclei fuse into heavy hydrogen. Further collisions convert the heavy hydrogen into isotopes of helium.

Such a fusion chain reaction ultimately converts the reactive, energy-rich hydrogen into stable helium. The probability that even a close nuclear collision results in a fusion reaction is amazingly low. At the center of the sun a million billion billion hydrogen atoms collide before one pair fuses into a heavy-hydrogen—deuterium—nucleus and releases its energy. Other reactions, such as deuterium and hydrogen, are much more probable; at the center of the sun a deuterium atom lasts only a few minutes, and is destroyed after a billion collisions.

The Atomic Energy Commission is supporting extensive research to produce, in the laboratory, temperatures higher than in the sun so as to initiate and maintain energy-producing deuterium fusion reactions for commercial power. During such processes 0.6 per cent of the original atomic mass is transformed into energy. Even this small fraction is enormously potent; when we compute the energy released from Einstein's famous formula relating energy and mass, $E = mc^2$, we find it to be five billion billion ergs, or energy units, per gram. The conversion, for example, of one ounce of hydrogen into 0.994 ounce of helium would release enough energy to supply the average family with electricity for 1000 years.

Hydrogen fusion, based on the use of heavy hydrogen found in sea water, if it can be put to controlled uses on earth, will be adequate for all of man's foreseeable energy needs. This treasure house, however, is not inexhaustible. Even the stars are working on a relatively limited budget. The sun, in converting its hydrogen into energy, is consuming 800,000,000 tons of hydrogen a second. This high rate of consumption, and the fact that the internal balance of the sun prevents complete use of all its hydrogen, suggests a total life of about ten billion years for our star neighbor. Since the sun and the earth are now but five billion years old, we have no immediate cause for concern. On an astronomical scale, however, even a billion years is a short interval of time. It is also well to remember that the earth receives only one two-billionth of the sun's energy radiation; the remainder—except for a similarly minute fraction intercepted by other solar bodies—is irreversibly converted into light and escapes into space, never to return.

Even when judged on the terrestrial time scale, some stars have surprisingly short life spans. The masses of the stars cover a wide range, from about 0.06 to about thirty times that of the sun. From observation and theory it is found that the luminous energy output of a star depends upon its mass. We know of some hot "supergiant" stars which weigh twenty-five times as much as the sun and are over 100,000 times as bright. Such objects have only 6,000,000 years before they begin to run out of energy. In a period of 10,000,000 years not much has happened on earth—the sun is the same, and the sea and the sky are unchanged. Man has come to be a dominant species, certain large mammals have disappeared, canyons in mountains have worn some feet deeper. But during this period an enormous star may have been born, have lived and died. If it had a planetary system, its planets, too, will have shared its fate—but probably without any life, because of the extremely slow pace of biological evolution.

If there are spendthrift stars, there are also energy-pinching, dull ones. The stars of small mass have luminosities as low as

269

one ten-thousandth that of the sun. In the life terms of such stars, called "red dwarfs," the whole history of sun and earth would seem infinitesimally short, since their future is assured for 10,000 billion years. Such faint stars are in fact the commonest species in the galaxy. While the myriads of red dwarfs add up to a large fraction of the mass of the galaxy, they give very little of the light, and few are visible to the naked eye.

While it is not unreasonable that stars should be born with different masses, it might seem strange that the rather small range of mass observed in stars results in such an enormous range of luminosity. The reason for the wide variation lies in the nature of the thermonuclear energy-producing processes involved. Very close and fast collisions are required to make atoms fuse. High temperatures produce the atomic velocities needed. The rate of the nuclear reactions involving two hydrogen atoms multiplies twenty times when the temperature is doubled, while another important nuclear reaction, involving hydrogen and carbon, increases a millionfold with the same rise in temperature.

Why are the more massive stars hotter stars? The weight of the outer layers of a massive star causes great pressure at the center. If the star is not to collapse, it must attain a high temperature, since only then can the gas pressure balance this weight. The higher temperature increases the energy production, which maintains the star against its own gravity—which would otherwise cause it to fall in upon itself. If such a star overheats, it expands. The expansion cools the center, and the energy-production rate decreases, again stabilizing the star. Thus a star is a stable, giant, thermonuclear furnace—a ball of gas held together by gravity and saved from collapse by the internal pressure of gas heated by the nuclear fuel.

Around us, in our own galaxy, are more than a hundred billion stars, some of potentially enormous age, some obviously very young. One inexplicable mystery faces us—that of the finite age of the galaxy itself. Man dates his age from his birth as an organism, but since we all carry some of the germ plasma of our ancestors, parts of us are in fact much older. Every one of our complex molecules is made of atoms, and most atoms are stable and might be thought to be eternal. The stars are made of the same kinds of atoms, and although we have said that the stars are from a few million to a few billion years old, we may ask whether their atoms are infinitely old. Are some stars, in fact, eternal?

The answer seems to be no. The atoms out of which man and the stars in our galaxy are made are almost certainly less than ten or fifteen billion years old. If they existed before that time, it was in another form, either as cold, pure hydrogen dispersed in space or as pure, high-energy radiation—but not in the present mixture of atoms of the different chemical elements. We know of no star in our galaxy which is more than ten billion years old. Likewise, the atoms of uranium and other radioactive elements on earth cannot be older than that, since they decay spontaneously into more stable forms in a few billion years. This suggests that the universe as we know it had a comparatively recent beginning, at least in its present state.

This startling fact, coupled with the one-way road by which matter is converted into light which escapes from the stars and into space, has suggested a dramatic event, a beginning of things. In this series of articles Fred Hoyle has discussed the scientific and philosophic background of this idea, the possible relationship between this beginning of things and the expansion of the universe, and the alternate suggestions which require the appearance of matter out of nowhere and its eventual expansion into nowhere (see "When Time Began," by Fred Hoyle, AD-VENTURES OF THE MIND, *The Saturday Evening Post*, February 21, 1959). But nothing Professor Hoyle implied, or that we know, suggests an infinite life for the particular atoms of which man and the stars in our galaxy are made.

I will discuss our own galaxy of stars, therefore, as if at some point in the past it was young, unformed and richer in nuclear fuel than it is now. I cannot suggest a picture of what, if anything, existed before this assumed starting point.

Scientists tend to believe that whatever existed at the beginning was in a completely disorganized but simple form, that in the beginning there was the simplest atom, hydrogen, in an enormous cloud, dispersed through space and containing the matter out of which all else has since been formed. The scale and dispersed form of this matter meant that large quantities of gravitational energy were available, and that when the dispersed material contracted into smaller aggregates, heat was released. How large were these aggregates—these first cosmic units? One possibility is that the first units were as large as whole clusters of galaxies—gas clouds weighing as much as a hundred thousand billion stars. These gas clouds then subdivided into smaller clouds, each as big as a galaxy. Finally, in these galactic clouds, stars began to form. In each of these evolutionary steps the gravitational energy of matter was available to heat the smaller units. These units—we will call them pseudo stars—evolved at different rates. The bigger pseudo stars, having more mass, contracted and heated rapidly in a few million years until their central temperatures reached 2,000,000 to 5,000,000 degrees. At such temperatures nuclear energy began to be released from the fusion of hydrogen, and the gas ball became a self-sustaining heat engine, a star. Once stabilized by the balance between gravity and energy production, a star lives as long as its nuclear energy permits, and then evolves to a final, dying stage.

It appears that perhaps one quarter of the gas in our own galactic cloud condensed into the oldest stars about ten billion years ago. Though at this stage the galaxy was nearly spherical, it gradually flattened as it rotated and became a flattened disk, which is the plane of our galaxy, or Milky Way. During these early stages of the evolution of our galaxy—a period lasting a few billion years—there remained some matter which was not condensed into stars. This residual gas continued to contract into stars, but more slowly, since there was less matter available. About halfway through this latter stage, about five billion years ago, the sun and its planets were born.

Stars are still being formed from this "interstellar gas cloud," which now contains less than 10 per cent of the mass of our galaxy. We can recognize this gas in photographs of our Milky Way, where it shines under the ultraviolet irradiation of nearby hot stars and also where, condensed into very small dust particles, it obscures the light of distant stars. Gas and dust clouds are found wherever there are new stars, and it is the existence of this reservoir of new, unused star dust that permits the continuous formation of new stars.

We have seen that there are bright, short-lived stars, with a maximum age of only a few ·million years. The existence of these very young objects, so different from the vast majority of stars, long puzzled astronomers. We now feel we have the answer to the puzzle—these are young stars recently formed out of the interstellar matter remaining from earlier periods of stellar evolution. The gas condenses into pseudo stars of all possible sizes; the massive objects become stars very rapidly, shine with very high luminosity for a brief span, and disappear. However, since this process is occurring fairly steadily throughout our Milky Way, we will have a supply of young stars of large mass and high luminosity as long as there is nuclear fuel in the interstellar gas. From such phenomena we can also draw another conclusion. Just as the existence of children proves that babies have recently been born, so the existence of these short-lived, young stars proves that stars are now being born.

While the late stages in the condensation process of a star can be observed, our knowledge of the early stages is hypothetical. We do know that many forces tend to keep the gas clouds from condensing—internal motion or rotation slow the growth of the pseudo star; magnetic fields and passing stars pull it apart. Under favorable conditions, however, in a giant dust-and-gas cloud weighing perhaps 100,000 times as much as the sun, a spurt of star condensation may occur and thousands of stars may be born. If the group is dense enough, it will remain as a cluster of stars, all having the same age and initial composition. (Much of our empirical knowledge of stellar evolution is obtained by studying such family groups to determine how stars change in size, brightness and temperature as they evolve.) From less stable groups new stars shoot into space like the sparks from the explosion of a skyrocket. These single stars merge with other stars in our Milky Way, which now contains a mixture of all types of old and young stars.

The rate of star formation in any galaxy depends on how much gas is left within the galaxy; some galaxies are enormously rich in gas and in young stars, others have exhausted all their gas and no longer contain young stars of high luminosity. Our own galaxy and one of its nearest neighbors in space, the Andromeda nebula, both have a dense central part, in which star formation has ended, and outer spiral arms, in which it is still continuing.

The interrelation between the stars and the interstellar gas may be even more complex. The sun, a relatively stable, normal star, has a steady outward flow of gas from its surface as well as many violent explosions such as prominences and flares. Particles blown out at 1000 miles a second strike the earth and cause auroral displays and disturbances of radio transmission, ring the earth with dangerous radiation and may affect the weather. Hotter, more massive stars produce even more violent effects; their rapid rotation expels rings, shells or pinwheels of gas weighing more than our whole solar system of planets.

Near the end of the stellar evolutionary process, evaporation or explosion takes place in nearly all stars. This cycling of matter between the stars and space is an important feature of new theories of the origin of the chemical elements. Hydrogen is transmuted into helium in a star; some of the helium is then ejected into space and mixed with free, unused hydrogen. The mixture of old and new may then condense into a new star. Thus some of the gas in space may once have been inside a shining star. This cycling of matter suggests that the more recently formed stars should be richer in helium and other products of stellar nuclear alchemy than the old stars. There is much observational evidence in favor of such an assumption. Unlike the products of biological evolution, however, the stellar species is not improved by such transmutations. Each stage uses up some of the precious nuclear fuel and each newer generation of stars contains more inert matter—heavier atoms which cannot react at stellar temperatures.

The atoms of elements with which we are most familiar on earth—carbon, oxygen, aluminum, silicon, and iron—cannot be made in the sun. They require much higher temperatures than the sun's interior. Probably they had their origin in long-dead stars and are much older than the sun. Massive stars, formed in the early history of the galaxy, exhausted their nuclear energy and evolved rapidly. Then, either by slow evaporation or cataclysmic explosion, they returned some of the heavy atoms which they had synthesized back to the interstellar gas out of which the sun was later born. Stars of large mass, which reach high central temperatures, can manufacture carbon and oxygen at 300,-000,000 degrees. At three to five billion degrees, nuclear fusion makes elements as heavy as iron, and results in the enormous explosion of a supernova. The sun, planets and living things are made of atoms which were once inside other stars.

Before we follow in detail the life history of a star, we should review some of the techniques and instruments which provide the necessary data. How can we know the distance, brightness, size and temperature of a star when even through the largest telescope the human eye sees the stars only as points of light? Unlike the physicist or biologist in their laboratories, we cannot experiment with the stars, but remain passive observers. Our understanding must come, therefore, from the detailed analysis and interpretation of the light received.

The telescope is a giant funnel, a light collector which focuses 500,000 times as much light as the unaided human eye. It feeds the light to a wide variety of auxiliary equipment. The astronomer takes photographs which, in a few minutes of exposure, record permanently and accurately more than the eye can ever see. Such photographs give positions, motions and distances as well as brightness and color.

The photographic method is being replaced by the photoelectric technique for brightness and color measurements. A photoelectric cell measures the brightness of a star much more accurately than a photograph, but can "look" at only one star at a time. Current development of "image-intensifier" tubes promises to give a brighter picture of a whole field of stars, by electronic amplification of the light received.

Theoretical and experimental laboratory physics provides laws which determine the temperature of a light source from its color or from the total light emitted. Hot stars are very blue and have great surface brightness, while cool stars are red. Thus the size of a star can be obtained from its brightness and color.

The most sophisticated and powerful single auxiliary to a telescope is the spectrograph. In this instrument the light is spread out into a band of different colors, which is then photographed in black and white. Each chemical element has its own sharply defined characteristic set of wave lengths—or colors—that it can emit, which are its spectral lines. These lines, like fingerprints, positively identify an element in the star. In addition, the strength of the lines changes with temperature, their width changes with pressure and their position with velocity. Again, modern atomic theory is used to interpret the photographs of these spectra. We can determine the composition of the atmosphere of a star with high accuracy, although we never will handle a sample of its atmosphere. I have obtained a spectrum for the analysis of a faint, dying star, only twenty-five light-years from the sun, on the same night as I photographed the spectrum of a brilliant, exploding supernova 25,000,000 light-years distant.

Once we have obtained all possible data on a wide variety of stars, we begin to see the over-all evolutionary pattern. Stellar evolution occurs so slowly that, except for rare catastrophes, we cannot expect to see a star change in the lifetime of a man. But, as in biology where individuals at different ages can be studied, the astronomer can see numbers of stars at different stages in their life cycles. With theoretical and mathematical insight, and imagination, we now begin to reconstruct their life story.

Let us follow the evolution of a star like the sun, remembering that many of the steps are hypothetical or controversial.

Some five billion years ago, in a quiet eddy of gas far out near the edge of our Milky Way, a cloud far more dense than the surrounding space formed in a region a few light-years across. (One light-year equals approximately 6000 billion miles.) The cloud, initially dense enough to hold together under its own gravity, survived several close approaches to other clouds or stars and gradually grew smaller and denser. Composed of gas and frozen dust grains at a temperature of about minus 300 degrees, the cloud warmed slowly as it compressed. The smaller and denser the cloud became, the more rapidly its temperature rose, until its interior reached 15,000 degrees. By this time the solids had evaporated and complex new phenomena occurred, since the molecules would have been split and hydrogen gas "ionized" into protons and electrons. On recombining they could begin to emit radiation.

The prestar's surface, however, was still frigid, and it remained a dark object. But now, as it condensed more and more rapidly, the prestar's temperature began to rise. While still 100 times its final size, the prestar's average temperature would be about 100,000 degrees, and its surface would glow at dull-red heat. At this stage violent convulsions occurred, during which excess gas and rotational and magnetic energy could be dissipated into space. (Some astronomers believe that during this stage stars can form a system of gaseous rings and whirlpools which are left behind to cool and build the planets.)

Some 100,000,000 years after its first appearance the gas ball would have contracted to approximately its final size. Heated to a few million degrees at the center, it would shine as a red star, somewhat brighter and larger than our present sun. At this stage the star's light would be variable, and it probably would be surrounded by clouds of gas and possibly by condensations of dust and rock which were growing into planets. During the entire first period of its life the light of the star would come from the gravitational energy released as the star shrank. Not until the temperature at the center exceeded 1,000,000 degrees would any nuclear-fusion reactions begin to occur. At a central temperature of 10,000,000 degrees the star would begin to tap its energy sources, readjusting its internal structure and temperature. At 20,000,000 degrees the star would reach its final state, with its present brightness, size and surface temperature.

This account of the first stages of the evolution of a typical star could be the early history of our sun. Since then, for the last five billion years, the sun has been converting its hydrogen into helium at an almost constant rate. For a billion years or more a fraction of the energy released by this process has been supporting biological life on earth.

What next? We expect another four to six billion years of the same sun and earth, far too long for any realistic prediction of the fate of the human species. But time runs only one way and the sun is not eternal. The details of the evolutionary stages may differ from star to star and the time scale may vary, but the general course of evolution is the same for all stars. From theory and observations of young and old clusters of stars, astronomers can predict the future of our solar system.

As it gradually runs out of nuclear fuel, the sun is slowly expanding, reddening and becoming brighter. Meanwhile, the earth will become warmer, at a rate of about ten degrees per billion years. After some six billion years the heating process will accelerate, and evolutionary changes will occur more rapidly. In the space of 100,000,000 years surface water will boil and oceans and air will evaporate into space as the earth's crust heats to 1000 degrees. Even the outer planets of the solar system will become hot. The sun will then be a giant red star about twenty-five times its present size. The stage is now set for the last act.

As its nuclear energy approaches a state of exhaustion, the bloated sun will gradually shrink and will probably lose a substantial portion of its mass to surrounding space. During this period the sun will retain its present brightness, but its surface temperature will rise to 100,000 degrees and it will shrink to a tenth of its present size. There will follow a period of further contraction at high temperature as the sun maintains its brightness by converting gravitational energy into heat. During this process some stars blow off rings of gas in minor explosions, others explode more violently as "novae," and a few blow themselves to bits in the most dramatic of all astronomical events, "supernovae." In such an explosion the star's remaining nuclear energy is released in a few seconds, the star becomes momentarily as bright as a billion suns and then disappears.

And so, peacefully or violently, within a few hundred million years our bloated red sun will have shrunk into a faint, hot, blue star. Having exhausted its nuclear fuel, it will enter the celestial graveyard.

Astronomers now understand many features of the strangest of all phases of stellar evolution, the "white dwarf" star. A small percentage of all living stars are already white dwarfs; ultimately most stars will reach this stage. White dwarfs, once much brighter than the sun, are stars which traversed the evolutionary stages more rapidly than average stars because of their initially greater mass and luminosity. The final white dwarf is extremely small for a star—hardly bigger than the earth. Since it has about half the mass of the sun, its mean density is nearly 1,000,000 times that of water. At its center matter is compressed to the unbelievable density of 100 tons per cubic inch. No solid can attain such densities; lead, the densest of the commonly known solids, weighs only a few ounces per cubic inch.

In a white dwarf, atoms are so compressed that they are stripped of their electrons, which enter a state of "degeneracy." Their freedom to move is limited, even though the star is still a gas. The star cannot contract any further, its nuclear energy is exhausted, and no known energy supply could possibly reverse the course of evolution and return matter to its former, low-density state. Since the star is hot, it must send light out into space, but at a steadily decreasing rate. The white dwarf's only energy source is its internal heat, so it must cool and become fainter and redder. From blue hot to white hot the fading takes a billion years, and down to red hot another ten billion years. Since such a star is already 10,000 times fainter than the sun, further cooling is an unimaginably long process. We doubt that our galaxy is old enough for any star to have cooled into invisibility, to become a "black dwarf." Since the star can never convert itself into an ordinary solid, the cooling black-dwarf stage is the ultimate one.

If the earth survives all astronomical accidents, what will the sky be like in ten billion years? The sun will be a yellowish point of light in a black sky—its disk too small to be seen without a telescope. It will be somewhat brighter than our present moon—bright enough to cast shadows on an airless, desiccated earth. The moon probably will not exist, but if it does, it will be only a faint ghost. The other planets will be invisible, since they are seen only by reflected sunlight. The sky at night will be nearly empty of stars. All the bright stars will have died; all the interstellar gas will have been consumed; only the faintest, red dwarfs, which are so cautious in their expenditure of nuclear energy, will still be alive. Although common in space, the red dwarfs are so faint that only accidental passages will bring a dim red star near enough to be visible from the earth.

The stars in the giant pinwheel of our galaxy rotate once about its center in 200,000,000 years. They will continue to do so, held together by gravitation, which we think is ageless. Our galaxy has made only fifty turns since its atoms were born. The sun will be dead in another twenty-five rotations. But the faintest red dwarfs will lead their dim lives for another 50,000 turns, the reward of parsimony! By that time our galaxy will have faded to a ghost, a hundredth of its present brightness, as will all the neighboring systems in space. Perhaps there still will be planets near other stars, with intelligence and spirit somewhere, but the gaudy part of the show will be over.

Further reading:
> Struve, Otto, and others: ELEMENTARY ASTRONOMY. New York: Oxford University Press; 1959.
> Payne-Gaposchkin, Cecilia: STARS IN THE MAKING. Cambridge: Harvard University Press; 1952.
> Gamow, George: BIRTH AND DEATH OF THE SUN. New York: New American Library of World Literature; 1945.
> Schwarzschild, Martin: STRUCTURE AND EVOLUTION OF THE STARS. Princeton: Princeton University Press; 1958.

GERALD W. JOHNSON

[*Photograph by Arnold Newman*]

Gerald White Johnson, one of America's most respected political journalists and historians, insists that his career can be summed up in the words the Duke of Gloucester wrote to Edward Gibbon after receiving the last volume of the Decline and Fall: *"Always scribble, scribble, scribble, eh, Mr. Gibbon?" "That's me," says Mr. Johnson, "thirty years in newspaper shops, fifteen as a free lance." The scribbling has produced a score of illuminating studies, among them* American Heroes and Hero-Worship; Woodrow Wilson; This American People, *and* The Lunatic Fringe. *His latest,* A History for Peter, *of which Morrow & Co. published the first of three volumes in 1959, is a history of American ideals in language he hopes his ten-year-old grandson will be able to understand.*

The U.S. Presidency

B Y

GERALD W. JOHNSON

The Presidency of the United States has come down from George Washington to Dwight D. Eisenhower in a succession uninterrupted for nearly 175 years by any exterior force save that of human mortality. The contingency of death was foreseen, and the succession provided for by law. Even when there was no clear election by the people, as in 1800 and 1824 when no candidate received an electoral majority, and in 1876 when the apparent majority was challenged, those crises were successfully met by legal devices without resort to force.

This gives the Presidency an appearance of great stability. It is probable that the typical American, if questioned, would confidently assert that no political office in the world is more solidly established, or has been less affected by the sweeping changes that have transformed almost everything else since the establishment of the republic. But the appearance is deceptive. The real characteristic of the office has been and is now a malleability that amounts almost to fluidity. Under no two men has the Presidency been exactly the same, and even its constitutional significance has altered until it is, in important respects, the opposite of what it was in Washington's time.

The impact of personality upon the office has been too conspicuous to pass unnoticed by the most superficial observer; but the changes forced by events are more important, although subtler and hard to perceive except in historical perspective. Everyone knows that the Presidency changed radically when Abraham Lincoln succeeded James Buchanan, and the facile explanation that Lincoln was a war President is inadequate. The country was at peace when Theodore Roosevelt succeeded William McKinley, yet the change in the Presidency in 1901 was, if anything, more spectacular than the change in 1861. Far more important than the effects of individual temperament, although less readily observed, are such changes as that between the time when Jefferson established the rule that the President receives, but makes no social calls, and the time when Eisenhower set out on his 1959 odyssey across the world.

Temperament has nothing to do with these changes. All men know that as far as his personal desires were concerned, the last thing Mr. Eisenhower wished was to undertake that physically and mentally arduous journey; he went because he deemed it his duty, not his pleasure, to go. It was the same motive that impelled President Washington to make his even more taxing trips through the country. The difference is that the first President could halt at the national boundary, while the thirty-fourth must cover the world. But nobody planned it so; it is the effect of the trend of events, not of human volition.

Washington did not expect this kind of development. The "Farewell Address" is full of foreboding, but the changes he foresaw and dreaded were to be effected by ambition, not by necessity. "In the most solemn manner" he warned us "against the baneful effects of the Spirit of Party . . . a fire not to be quenched; it demands a uniform vigilance to prevent its bursting into a flame, lest, instead of warming, it should consume." The Spirit of Party, he thought, must in the end "incline the minds of men to seek security and repose in the absolute power of an Individual; and sooner or later the chief of some prevailing faction, more able or more fortunate than his competitors, turns this disposition to the purposes of his own elevation, on the ruins of Public Liberty."

A dismal prospect indeed, but severely logical in view of the information available to Washington. The power of the presidential office has increased, not steadily, but by fits and starts, speeded up by strong Presidents, slowed down by weak ones, but never reversing its general trend; until today it vastly exceeds anything dreamed of at the beginning of the nineteenth century.

Yet the calamitous results foretold in the "Farewell Address" have not yet come upon us. They may be impending, for it would be fatuous to deny that the Presidency contains the seeds of dictatorship; but they are not here yet, and an inquiry into why the seeds have not sprouted, flourished and borne their deadly fruit ought to be suggestive, at least, of means by which we may hope to keep them latent indefinitely.

Washington's anxiety was based upon the assumption that any additional powers accruing to the Presidency must of necessity be subtracted from those of one or both of the other branches of government. It was his belief that the "system of checks and balances" in the Constitution had separated the powers of government and distributed them all; he and his contemporaries accepted the theory that the powers of Government consist of the legislative, the executive and the judicial, and that once these were lodged in different and independent hands, government would be completely organized. The problem thenceforth would be to keep anyone from encroaching on the authority of the others.

What the men of 1787 did not suspect—and is, indeed, but imperfectly realized by our own generation—is that there is a fourth power of government, difficult to define legally and not disposed of by the Constitution, yet as important in a democracy as the executive, legislative or judicial. This is the power of the initiative, which we commonly term leadership. The history of the Presidency is a story of the slow accretion of this power in the hands of the man in the White House.

To understand why this factor was overlooked by statesmen as far-sighted as those who dominated the Constitutional Convention, one must remember that they were theorists, guided by reason, not by experience. The only form of government under which any of them had lived was monarchial; parliamentary government was indeed taking shape in England, but it was not yet clearly defined, and parliament was far from being a representative democracy, such as our Constitution envisaged. Thus the Americans had no pattern to follow; for the direct, not representative, democracies of ancient times were horrible examples, rather than models, since all of them had failed. The Greek city-states, for example, where each man entered the assembly representing himself alone and, therefore, usually voted in his own interest alone, oscillated between tyranny and anarchy, never establishing an enduring balance of public and private interests. Nor were other democracies able long to escape either domestic autocracy or foreign domination.

But if the founding fathers lacked a reliable guide, they did have a stern warning. The centuries-old, not then terminated, struggle for power between the king and parliament had taught them that in such a contest the rights of the people are pretty sure to be trampled by both contestants; and the logical means of protection against that was the system of checks and balances.

Some of them—Hamilton, for a conspicuous example—did understand that such a system, if brought to perfection, would result in impotence, a government hung on dead center, unable to move in any direction. They had an example in the Polish monarchy of the seventeenth century, so effectively checked and balanced by the requirement of a unanimous vote of the nobles that it was brought to ruin by sheer inertia. But the highly practical Americans were aware that their own system was by no means so delicately adjusted, since even the veto of the President could be overridden, and they assumed correctly that its very imperfections would prevent a complete deadlock.

What they did not take into account, or did not give sufficient weight in their accounting, was the possibility that in making absolute power unattainable, they had checked ambition, especially in the legislative branch, severely enough to discourage the development of effective leadership there. This was a contingency extremely remote in a government of undivided powers. Leadership originally vested in the monarch, could not be wrested from him except by leadership developed elsewhere—in a court favorite, perhaps, or in the legislative or even in the judiciary. The complete disappearance of the fourth power of government was one danger against which the Americans did not prepare, presumably because they did not envisage it.

It can be plausibly argued, nevertheless, that this country has suffered more, very much more, from excessively static than from excessively dynamic government. The example customarily cited is the inertia of James Buchanan as the danger of secession was visibly mounting; but the monumental uselessness of Buchanan was merely a continuation of a condition that had afflicted the Presidency ever since the administration of James K. Polk. The Pennsylvanian's misfortune was merely that he happened to be in office at the time when the lack of effective leadership produced its logical result. Buchanan is its spectacular exemplar, but the condition has been characteristic of the Presidency more often than not.

Evidence to support this assertion is not far to seek. How many Americans can name offhand eighteen of the individuals who have held the office? Everyone remembers Washington, Jefferson, Jackson, Lincoln, Wilson and the second Roosevelt because great significance attaches to their names. Perhaps most of us recall also the first Roosevelt, John Adams, Monroe (on account of the Doctrine), possibly Cleveland; but beyond that the typical American grows vague. The reason is that none of the others exercised the power of the initiative in any memorable way. Hoover, Truman and Eisenhower are excluded from this account because all three are still living as these lines are written.

The half dozen first named, pretty generally regarded as the Big Six, are a remarkably varied assortment as regards their intellectual and cultural endowments, but they are alike in one respect—Washington established the Presidency and each of the other five added materially to its power. Each was, in Washington's words, "the chief of some prevailing faction," but that any turned the situation "to the purposes of his own elevation, on the ruins of Public Liberty," as the "Farewell Address" grimly predicted, will be asserted only of Franklin Roosevelt, and of him only by blind and bitter partisanship. To the vast majority of Americans they were great Presidents, the greatest in the list.

Here, then, is what at first glance seems to be a mystery, a cause not followed by its logical effect: the vast accretion of power that Washington apprehended has come to the Presidency, but the calamitous results that he feared have not followed. This odd circumstance can be explained only on the theory that the President has added to his power by occupation, but not by usurpation; that is to say, the addition to the Presidency has not been a subtraction from either of the other two branches. They retain unimpaired to this day all the powers delegated to them in 1789. If the Presidency has advanced relatively, it is by assuming the power of the initiative, never clearly envisaged by the Constitution makers, and, if it had been, probably incapable of legal definition.

Some years before he entered the White House Woodrow Wilson noted the fact. In *Constitutional Government*, published in 1908, he observed that "the President is at liberty, both in law and in conscience, to be as big a man as he can. His capacity will set the limit; and if Congress be overborne by him, it will be no fault of the makers of the Constitution—it will be from no lack of constitutional powers on its part, but only because the President has the nation behind him and Congress has not. He has no means of compelling Congress except through public opinion."

What a tremendous exception that is, probably Wilson did not fully realize in 1908, although he had the example of Theodore Roosevelt before his eyes. But Wilson himself demonstrated it during his first two years in the White House, and the overwhelming proof was furnished by the second Roosevelt in his first Hundred Days. A President who can seize the initiative at all is assured of some success; and one whose first few moves receive popular approbation is irresistible.

The recourse of Congress is to seize the initiative itself, and occasionally—as, for instance, in the case of Andrew Johnson— it has done so. Congress, too, is at liberty, both in law and in conscience, to be the biggest thing in the nation if it can. But the historical record of congressional efforts to assume leadership makes depressing reading. Certainly the most brilliant, and perhaps the most honorable, of those men who have seized leadership outside of the White House were Alexander Hamilton and Henry Clay; but Hamilton succeeded only in hobbling—and infuriating—John Adams, while Clay was a millstone hung around the neck of every President of his own party. In later days the Reconstruction policy imposed upon the country by Thaddeus Stevens brought upon his memory an odium that still persists; and if the almost equally powerful legislative leaders, Thomas B. Reed and Joseph G. Cannon, are remembered more favorably it is because of their more amiable personalities rather than for their triumphs of statecraft.

The member of Congress, senator or representative, is not in a favorable position to exercise national leadership. One of its essentials, and one that is increasingly important as government becomes more complex, is the capacity for swift and decisive action. In this respect the President enjoys an inestimable advantage in that his close associates are his subordinates, whereas those of a member of Congress are his equals. The President can order, where the congressman can only argue. For this reason a weak President can contend on better than equal terms with a legislator immeasurably his intellectual superior—a John Tyler can frustrate a Henry Clay.

The first genius to appreciate this situation to the full and to exploit it was Andrew Jackson. The magnitude of his achievement is evidenced by the fact that the tradition still persists that Old Hickory was a simple soul, rough, but transparent. In fact, Jefferson himself was not more complex and devious.

Jackson was the first to understand the implications, for the President, of the fact that the votes are cast by individuals, although the country does not consist exclusively of individuals. The country includes territory, wealth, land and water, forest and field, mountain and plain, ecological variations that are wide and highly important. Individuals are, however, one constant in this giant aggregate of variables. Since the President is the sole elected official chosen by the whole country—for who ever voted for or against a Vice President?—he alone can afford to neglect the variables and devote his whole attention to the constant.

A senator from Texas, for example, must represent the Texans, of course, but he must represent oil also, as a senator from

Montana must represent copper and one from Oregon, lumber. Not long ago the late Senator Neuberger acknowledged that publicly, and said that if any senator had failed to represent the dominant economic interest of his state, the fact has escaped Mr. Neuberger's notice.

Jackson's triumphant career was based on his success in convincing men and women that he represented people in a special way that no other official could. But he did more. He persuaded them that the President is, and of right ought to be, the people's man, speaking for them and for no local or nonhuman interest whatsoever. Jackson, more than any other President, established the claim of the Presidency to the power of the initiative. Incidentally, he also furnished at least one glaring illustration of its dangers. "John Marshall has made his decision; now let him enforce it," may not have been his exact words, but they certainly portray his attitude in the Indian lands case. By withholding the comity due from one branch of the government to another he, in effect, vacated a ruling of the Supreme Court—as clear a usurpation of the power of the judiciary as can be imagined. But there can be no shadow of doubt that it asserted the leadership of the Presidency in the nation at large, not merely in the executive branch.

Nearly a hundred years passed, however, before the claim was formalized by Wilson in his public announcement that he proposed to be head of his party, as well as head of the state. Even then the opposition professed to regard Wilson's statement as scandalous, although every strong President since Jackson had held leadership of the party; and to this day there is some dispute as to where the power of the initiative should lie.

Curiously enough, opposition to Wilson's position has included some of the Presidents themselves. Harding is the obvious example, but it may be argued that he was incapable of leadership in any circumstances; McKinley and Benjamin Harrison are better illustrations. Their distaste for the Wilsonian doctrine is understandable, if not particularly creditable, for it imposes upon the President formidable responsibility. If he is to lead the country successfully he must be resourceful, energetic and resolute, all to a high degree. This is hard labor, not to be undertaken willingly by a man who approaches the office in the spirit of the remark attributed, doubtfully, to Giovanni de'-Medici, "Since God has given us the Papacy, let us enjoy it."

But evidence is already abundant and increases daily that the Presidency is the right location for the power of initiative. Since 1914 the tempo of events has accelerated to such an extent that crises tread upon one another's heels, and capacity for rapid and decisive action may soon be, if it is not already, the price of national survival. The Korean affair is an instance still vividly in mind; President Truman's course may not have been the ideal one, but his action was swift; and in politics as in military operations it is better to do any intelligent thing than to lose time searching for the perfect move.

In a world as tense as that of the twentieth century, speed in seizing the initiative seems likely to increase, rather than to diminish in importance; which suggests that the dominance of the Presidency in that respect is more likely to be strengthened and extended than to be reduced. Hitler, being only human, could not always be wrong, and he hit upon a great truth in his assertion of "the leadership principle" as essential to successful government in the modern world. Certainly a huge democracy, such as the United States, stands in as grave danger from lack of leadership as from usurpation of power.

It is not that usurpation is inconceivable in this country. Jackson's case was not the only one. Lincoln in suspending the writ of habeas corpus where the courts were still open, unquestionably infringed the prerogative of the judiciary, and Theodore Roosevelt, in ordering the motto, "In God We Trust," left off the coins, invaded Congress' exclusive right to coin money. Jefferson was inclined to think that he usurped powers of both legislative and judiciary in making the Louisiana Purchase. But the usurpations thus far have been either pardonable, as conducing to the general welfare, or unsuccessful, or so trifling as to come under the rule *de minimis*. . . .

This is, however, no guarantee that they will retain that character; and a generation that has been appalled by such apparitions as Mussolini, Hitler and Stalin knows only too well what horrors may rise from a perversion of leadership. The Twenty-

second Amendment, forbidding any man to hold the Presidency
more than ten years, is evidence of our extreme sensitiveness to
the remotest possibility of the rise of dictatorship here. Our immediate peril, in fact, is probably much less the risk of submitting to tyranny than the risk of hobbling necessary leadership by
hysterical efforts to ward off tyranny.

At the same time every thoughtful American must regard the
development of the Presidency with something less than ebullient enthusiasm. It is clearly necessary to lodge the power of the
initiative somewhere, and the hands of the President seem to be
its logical repository, because he alone can exercise it effectively.
It is clearly necessary, also, to insist that he shall exercise it, and
to avoid electing any man incapable of doing so. In prudence
as well as in equity it is clearly necessary to support the President
strongly in the legitimate exercise of this power.

But it is not to be denied that this course, however necessary,
involves a calculated risk, and it is always possible to miscalcu-
late. This possibility must be taken into account in any extrapo-
lation of the historical development of the Presidency. The
tricky factor is the enormous potential of the force that we call
public opinion. Against it, neither legislature, executive, judiciary, nor even the Constitution itself can stand. It has hitherto
been the constructive power in erecting the political fabric of
the republic; but a power capable of so gigantic a feat obviously
could be terrifically destructive were it channeled in that direction.

To put this power absolutely in the hands of one man would
be suicidal. We have had a grisly demonstration of that in the
case of the German people, when the potent majority of them
committed their minds and consciences to Hitler and blindly
followed him to destruction.

That the American people will go to any such extreme seems
highly improbable. Our historical experience, our educational
methods, even to some extent our prejudices and superstitions
militate against it. Artemus Ward's complacement proclama-
tion, "I am not a politician, and my other habits are good," was
something more than a jape. It reflects a skepticism of Whitman's "elected persons" that is deeply embedded in the Ameri-

can character—a prejudice perhaps touched with superstition, but one that operates against any attempt at the deification of Caesar.

It would be unrealistic, however, to deny that there are forces in the modern world that operate in the other direction; nor are they confined to the ideologies of Marx, Lenin or Mao. We seem, indeed, relatively immune to ideologies; in no large country has the Communist Party had less success in recruiting the masses, and even the Socialists have never polled as many as 1,000,000 votes. But there are conditions, not theories, that are subjecting the traditional American system to a considerable strain.

Some of these conditions are technological, others political. Communication, for instance, has been perfected to the point at which one man may speak to the entire nation; and with the aid of television he may bring to bear upon an audience of many millions all the resources of dramaturgy—not rhetoric and euphony only, but gesture also, as well as "wanton Wiles, Nods and Becks and wreathèd Smiles," and if you think these are ineffective, remember that David Garrick, the actor, once said that he would give 100 guineas to be able to say "ah" as the Rev. George Whitefield, the evangelist, could say it.

The assistance of technology is available equally to statesmen and to demagogues. The statesman may employ it to inspire the nation to great deeds; but the demagogue may use it to foment all the evils inherent in herd psychology. Since demagogues as a rule outnumber statesmen, it is evident that the mass media of communication, especially the newer ones, radio and television, must subject the common sense of the American electorate to a severe test.

The political organization of the modern world also is a condition and not a theory. American military and economic power is now the chief defense of political liberty abroad as well as at home. When the Constitution assigned to the President the conduct of foreign relations, the work consisted almost exclusively of safeguarding American interests; its expansion to cover the whole free world obviously has put the President in a different position. His power has been greatly increased, but so has his vulnerability; the President in self-defense is being forced more and more to act as his own Secretary of State. Even Mr. Eisenhower, who disliked and distrusted this development, was finally forced to accept it.

A President of a different temperament, however, might find it very much to his taste. Think what Theodore Roosevelt, for example, might have done with the leadership of the free nations! That idea is in a sense a test of the division in American political philosophy—one school holding that so dynamic a character given Eisenhower's opportunity would have ruined us, the other holding that lack of dynamism in the Presidency is the cause of at least half our present difficulties.

The mocking devil of it is that both schools seem to be right. A generation that has witnessed the passing of Mussolini, Hitler and Stalin must shudder at the idea of leadership concentrated in an individual; at the same time, a generation numbed by fifteen years of cold war must be appalled by the possibility of a total paralysis of leadership.

The rather dismal conclusion of the whole matter would seem to be that the American who seeks to peer into the future, no matter what his philosophy, has reason to shudder.

But was it ever otherwise? Our Constitution, said Justice Holmes, is an experiment, but only, he added, as all life is an experiment. It is unrealistic to ignore the fact that it is dangerous to be free, but it is equally unrealistic to ignore the fact that this nation has lived dangerously yet has survived for nearly 200 years. In that period the Presidency has gradually acquired powers that would have staggered the writers of the Constitution, and the prospect, at least for the years immediately ahead, is that the welfare of the nation and the world will necessitate entrusting greater, not diminished, authority to the office.

This may be the road to dictatorship, but it is the road we have been following because we could find no other. And there are optimists who do not believe that it leads inevitably to tyranny. Unreasonably, perhaps, they see the history of the United States as the aged Jefferson described it in that famous letter to the still-older Adams: "Laboring always at the same oar, with

some wave ever ahead threatening to overwhelm us and yet passing harmless under our bark, we knew not how, we rode through
the storm with heart and hand, and made a happy port . . .
and so we have gone on, and so we shall go on, puzzled and pros-
pering beyond example in the history of man."

EARL A. EVANS, JR.

[*Photograph by Frank Ross*]

Earl A. Evans, Jr., chairman of the biochemistry depart-
ment at the University of Chicago, has for the past four-
teen years engaged in research on virus growth. The ideas
on the origin of life which he considers here are an out-
growth of this work. Professor Evans was educated at Johns
Hopkins and Columbia. In 1942 he won the Eli Lilly
medal of the American Chemical Society for the early use
of a radioactive isotope in biological experiments. After
wartime work on malaria, he served as chief scientific offi-
cer to the United States Embassy in London. His current
interest, the chemical approach to virus research, he finds
"fascinating because of its difficulties and implications."

ᒪᒧᒪᒧᒪᒧᒪᒧᒪᒧᒪᒧᒪᒧᒪᒧᒪᒧᒪᒧᒪᒧᒪᒧᒪᒧᒪᒧᒪᒧᒪ

How Life Began

BY

EARL A. EVANS, Jr.

At the recent Darwin Centennial celebrating the publication, in 1859, of the *Origin of the Species*, ten experimental scientists of various interests and backgrounds discussed the origin of life. They included Darwin's grandson, Sir Charles Galton Darwin, a physicist; two geneticists; a neurophysiologist; a general physiologist; an astronomer; two biochemists; and a microbiologist, G. F. Gause of the Institute of Antibiotics, Moscow, the only Russian present. The panel, sitting around a table covered with red cloth in the Gothic gloom of the University of Chicago's Mandel Hall, talked for three hours. To the audience the discussion was in part instructive, at times amusing, now and then trivial. One participant napped quietly when the talk moved beyond his interests. At the end a reporter asked the panelists what they thought of a prediction, made by one of the biochemists, Hans Gaffron of the University of Chicago, that life would be synthesized in the test tube within the next thousand years. They all agreed with Gaffron. Indeed one of the geneticists, Hermann Muller of Indiana University, asserted that such a synthesis had already been accomplished.

The panelists were not only unanimous, but all of them also reflected the general belief among contemporary biologists that life originated from nonliving matter. Specifically this means that during some earlier period in the history of our planet the

299

inanimate materials of the earth's cooling surface spontaneously interacted to form a series of increasingly complex systems, and that these systems culminated in a primitive type of living organism. The transition from nonliving to living was gradual; once it had occurred, the further development of living creatures followed the ramifications of the evolutionary process described by Darwin. However, it is the beginning that concerns us here, and what we can say of the conditions and mechanisms of chemical evolution.

The study of fossils shows the presence of primitive life some 1,000,000,000 years ago. The earth itself was then five times as old. As for the written records of human life, they cover only about 6000 years. The precision of these figures is less important to our study than their relative dimension—time-spans so vast that they are hard to conceive. The transition from the first primitive cell to the nerve cells in the human cerebrum required only a fourth of the time nature took to form life from nonlife. The proudest human pedigree in the Almanach de Gotha can be traced back no more than 100 generations, whereas a complete record would list more than 50,000,000 generations. Thus nature had ample time for the endless experimentation she required to create life. Like Darwinian evolution, the process of chemical evolution involved chance variation followed by selection and survival of forms able to exist in the environment of the moment.

The dependence of life on a suitable environment corresponds to our own experience in that we can survive only if our surroundings are neither too hot nor too cold, neither too wet nor too dry. However, an environment suitable for the survival of an advanced form of life, as we know it today, is not necessarily suitable for the transition from nonlife to life, a process that may still be going on. Our inability to observe this may be due to lack of sufficiently subtle methods. A more likely explanation derives from the drastic changes that have occurred in the earth's environment since life began—changes caused partly by living organisms.

Regarding the origin of the universe and of our earth, geochemists believe that the gradual cooling of the earth's original hot mass produced a thin crust of solid material supporting the warm waters of the primeval oceans. The chemical composition of this outer crust and its gaseous atmosphere differed enormously from our atmosphere today. The principal constituents of the primitive atmosphere were hydrogen, ammonia and methane—gases now present only in small amounts—and water. The most notable difference was the absence of free oxygen, without which the higher forms of life cannot exist. Solar ultraviolet rays act upon oxygen to form a peripheral layer of ozone which shields the surface of the earth from deadly ultraviolet radiation. Only with this protection, only after enough oxygen had accumulated to supply a source of the ozone layer that now exists some twenty miles above the earth's surface, could life move from the ocean to the land, and evolve to higher forms. All the evidence indicates that life originated in the absence of oxygen and that the addition of oxygen to our atmosphere was brought about by photosynthesizing organisms.

In the primitive world then, the oxygen-free atmosphere of the planet was exposed to the full force of the light and heat energy of the sun. In our world the ultimate source of energy for living things is that part of the visible light that can be absorbed by the photosynthetic apparatus of plants. But this mechanism evolved only after life itself, so that we are concerned with the effects upon the primitive atmosphere of such forms of energy as ultraviolet light, the electrical discharges that occurred in atmospheric storms, cosmic radiation from outer space and the radioactivity of the components of the earth's crust.

During the last ten years scientists have imitated in the laboratory these once-prevailing conditions. For example, at the University of Chicago the chemists Stanley Miller and Harold Urey exposed a mixture of hydrogen, methane, ammonia and water to the continuing action of an electrical discharge. The results were remarkable: some thirty-five or more organic, carbon-containing molecules, which are the smallest portions of a substance that retain their chemical identity, formed in quantities sufficient to be chemically separated and identified. It seems highly significant that these compounds are known to be the precursors of the typical molecules of living organisms, that is, substances from which life builds its characteristic fabric and organization. The organic chemist can put together in the laboratory many of the complicated molecules that occur in living organisms by using the proper materials and sources of energy. On the primitive earth the full impact of solar radiation on the simple components of the earth's crust would have resulted in a similar synthesis.

The implications of the Miller-Urey experiment for understanding the changes undergone by the primitive earth are twofold. First, the action of solar and other forms of radiant energy would result in the transformation of the primordial oceans to increasingly complex and concentrated solutions of organic molecules—what one investigator compared to the composition of "a hot, thin soup." Second, these small precursor molecules would inevitably react together to form the same large molecules seen in the living cell, if there were enough time.

This time element requires a digression into some aspects of modern biochemistry. For a hundred years biochemists have been tearing apart living cells to determine their chemical nature. Information as to the kinds of molecules present is almost complete, and we know a great deal about how these molecules interact in the living organism. They consist of familiar carbon-containing substances many of which can be synthesized in the laboratory. The same laws operating in inanimate nature determine the molecular interactions in living cells. Two of the molecular aspects of life are especially pertinent.

First, the chemical patterns underlying the most diverse forms of life are amazingly similar. The green chlorophyll of the photosynthesizing plant and the red hemoglobin of our blood are chemical cousins; the malaria parasite uses sugar for energy in the same fashion as mammalian muscles. This similarity indicates the common origin of all living organisms and provides valuable evidence—especially when we study variations—of the evolutionary process.

Second, we find in all living cells proteins, nucleic acids and an organized molecular structure that is unstable without a continuing supply of energy—the chemical energy of food in humans and the energy of sunlight in photosynthesizing plants.

The famous Hungarian biochemist, Albert Szent Györgyi, said that "whatever a cell does has to be paid for—and the currency of living systems, with which the cell has to pay, is energy." What we call "death" overtakes living cells when the energy to maintain their organization is no longer available, or when the mechanisms by which energy is used are defective or destroyed. In addition to these chemical and organizational qualities, living cells can both reproduce themselves and mutate, that is, they can occasionally form cells differing from the parent cell which, when they reproduce, transfer their altered characteristics to their progeny.

The nucleic acids, long, helical structures, constitute the genetic units of the cell and are responsible for maintaining the unique and heritable characteristics of a particular cell. Usually the gene is precisely reproduced when the cell divides, but on occasion the copying is inexact, and from such a failure arise mutant cells.

Proteins function chiefly as enzymes, or catalysts, for the reactions by which the cell uses energy to reproduce, move, and so on. It is important to realize that enzymes alter only the speed at which a reaction occurs, but that they cannot initiate the reaction. For example, we think of the cane sugar on our breakfast table as a stable substance. But the inherent tendency of sugar to react with oxygen and be converted into carbon dioxide and water is concealed by the extremely slow rate of conversion under ordinary circumstances. In muscle or liver, and in many living cells, the conversion is swift and complete, with the energy thus liberated used for other cellular activities. Actually, a long series of protein enzymes regulate the rate of many individual reactions making up the whole process. But these enzymes do not create the reactions; they only accelerate them.

Genes and enzymes being indispensable components of living cells, it is also important to understand how the cell manufactures them. The 1959 Nobel prize went to the biochemists Severo Ochoa of New York University and Arthur Kornberg of Stanford University Medical School for discovering enzymes which can be extracted from living cells and will synthesize nucleic acids from a mixture of the appropriate starting materials.

It was this discovery that prompted Muller to say that life had already been synthesized in the laboratory. We know less about the details of protein synthesis, but we do know that proteins are built up from simpler compounds, the amino acids, and that in some fashion the nucleic acids control the order and selection of the amino acid-building stones.

The significance of the Miller-Urey experiment becomes apparent with the observation that the small molecules they found are identical with those used by the living cell for its starting materials. The cell transforms these into its large molecules in an orderly and rapid fashion through its enzymes. But as we have seen, given the same starting materials and enough time, the same products would result.

Applying the Miller-Urey experiment to the conditions of the primeval earth and bearing in mind the millions of years that lay ahead, we conclude that the primeval ocean ultimately contained an enormous variety and number of the large molecules of nucleic acids and proteins present in living cells.

These molecules were still remote from any recognizable form of life, and we must invoke another process to explain later chemical evolution. Called autocatalysis, this process refers to the situation wherein a substance formed by a given chemical reaction serves as an accelerating agent for the reaction itself. By way of analogy, picture a group of men trying to climb over a high wall. If each man reaching the top can reach down and help the man behind up, obviously the rate at which the men get over the wall will grow faster. Similarly, the molecules produced by autocatalysis will, once formed, accelerate the formation of identical molecules.

What is the direct implication of autocatalysis in considering the primitive solution of proteins and nucleic acids? Imagine, for example, the formation—by random combination and after an enormous lapse of time—of a particular nucleic-acid molecule which can dictate the structure of a protein molecule. The protein would have the catalytic property of accelerating the further formation of that particular nucleic acid. Thus, instead of a passage of a million years for the spontaneous formation of the nucleic acid, the synthesis would occur very rapidly.

If at the same time the primitive ocean contained a second protein, with the ability to accelerate the formation of the first protein, then we would have the conditions for the beginning of a primitive form of life, a system in which particular nucleic acids and proteins could reproduce themselves. Further, the continued operation of the autocatalytic process would eventually replace the primeval mixture of molecules by one in which self-reproducing molecules would be the dominating species. This, we believe, was the process whereby the simple molecules of the primitive world evolved into the complex, self-reproducing molecules verging on life itself.

As to exactly what happened next, as to the nature of the first living organism, we can barely speculate. However, three aspects of the evolutionary process call for comment: the development of the membranes which confine the self-reproducing molecules within the cellular units; the development of the various steps by which the cell operates; the development of photosynthesizing organisms, that is, living cells able to use the visible wave lengths of sunlight as a source of energy.

Though we lack direct evidence, the confinement of several large, self-reproducing molecules within a membrane must certainly have occurred at an early stage in the evolution of life. In this connection Aleksandr Oparin, of the Bach Institute of Biochemistry at Moscow, has studied the formation of the bits of jellylike materials called coacervates, which separate spontaneously from solutions of organic molecules having opposing electrical charges. The precursors of the coacervates were also present in the primitive "soup," and their spontaneous separation may well represent the beginning of cellular structures from which a highly organized internal apparatus could proceed.

Concerning the steps of cellular operation, Norman Horowitz, of the California Institute of Technology, was the first to surmise that they probably developed in a reverse order. The first living things, he reasoned, had available to them in the primeval oceans all possible precursors and needed only to combine these to reproduce themselves. With the depletion of one essential precursor, survival would be possible only for the organism that had the enzymes to replace the shortage from the other remaining molecules. When these also disappeared, survival would then depend on the ability of the organism to convert still other available substances into the required component. In this fashion, the gradual depletion of precursors would run parallel to the evolution of longer and longer chains of synthesis—such as we now find in living organisms.

Photosynthesizing organs probably developed relatively late in the evolution of living cells. In the photosynthetic process the energy of sunlight acts to separate the hydrogen and oxygen of water molecules, the hydrogen combining with the carbon dioxide of the atmosphere to form sugar, the oxygen being liberated as free gas. The cellular machinery involved appears to have two distinct parts. One part uses the green chlorophyll of plants and the energy of visible light. The other part forms sugar from carbon dioxide and hydrogen, and requires no light. Significantly, the second part exists in many primitive organisms which do not contain chlorophyll and do not require light. The process can be duplicated in test tubes with a suitable mixture of enzymes, including some derived from mammals and other nonphotosynthesizing organisms. From this we deduce that the photosynthesizing mechanism with its use of light energy must have developed after living cells had learned to carry out the dark process.

The eventual appearance of photosynthesizing organisms had a most important consequence in the further development of living forms. Photosynthesis, as we have seen, leads to the formation of gaseous oxygen. Large quantities of gaseous oxygen would produce a layer of ozone shielding the earth from the sun's lethal ultraviolet radiation. Thus shielded, the synthesis of the organic molecules in the primitive ocean could no longer occur and they would gradually disappear as living organisms proliferated. Moreover, the ozone shield would permit the evolution of organisms incapable of withstanding the ultraviolet radiation. Many of these require oxygen, but there also exist intermediate types that can operate with or without oxygen as their environment may dictate. That the molecular machinery for using oxygen in the higher forms of life is closely related to the green chlorophyll in photosynthesizing plants exemplifies the way evolving life modifies a basic molecular structure to new functions and objectives.

The evolutionary sequence has the beauty of logic. It can be traced through succeeding eras of enormous duration: the oxygen-free, hydrogenous atmosphere of the primitive earth permitting the synthesis and accumulation of organic substances as the precursors of living organisms; the interaction of these to form self-duplicating systems leading to the depletion of the organic molecules in the ocean and to the appearance of photosynthesizing organisms; finally, the emergence of oxygen-requiring organisms—each step irreversible and essential for evolution.

Where does this evidence lead us, if we accept the argument that human life, with its intelligence, its moral sense and spiritual aspirations arose from nonliving materials; that life is a spontaneous, irrepressible manifestation of matter; that, given the right environment, the necessary sources of energy and the suitable building stones, life inevitably results? The question prompts yet another question. What is matter?

Our reluctance to conceive of our physical being as nothing more than the matter of the inanimate world stems primarily from our consciousness of individual existence. We feel we are more than science can analyze. Yet every attempt to separate the psyche from the physical body has failed. If we modify or destroy our molecular fabric, we modify or destroy its psychic properties. The scientist concludes that they are but different aspects of the whole human. That life is a manifestation of matter can be expressed in a variety of vocabularies. No model, no concrete image of the nature of matter exists, and its behavior can be predicted and explained only in terms of mathematical equations. To say that matter is energy, or electricity, or a warpage of space reveals no more than to call it spirit, nature or God. Before such problems, the scientist tends only to retain his faith in reason and rational investigation, and to look for the next approximation rather than the last analysis.

Further reading:

Oparin, A. I.: THE ORIGIN OF LIFE. New York: Dover Publications, Inc.; 1953.

Gamow, George: BIOGRAPHY OF THE EARTH. New York: Mentor Books of New American Library of World Literature, Inc.; 1948.

Shapley, Harlow: OF STARS AND MEN. Boston: Beacon Press; 1958.

Tax, Sol, and Charles Callender (eds.): EVOLUTION AFTER DARWIN, Vol. III. Chicago: University of Chicago Press; 1960.

OWEN BARFIELD

[*Photograph by Wolf Suschitzky*]

Arthur Owen Barfield, British author and attorney, has had a lifelong interest in the relation between science and religion, a subject on which he has written several books. One of them, Poetic Diction, *deals with poetic experience as a form of cognition. After being graduated from Oxford, Mr. Barfield frequently contributed to England's leading literary and political journals. He subsequently entered the law, from which he is now "very nearly retired." In 1949, the 200th anniversary of Goethe's birth, Mr. Barfield gave a B.B.C. talk on the poet's scientific writings, a topic central to the theme of this article.*

The Rediscovery
of Meaning

BY

OWEN BARFIELD

Amid all the menacing signs that surround us in the middle of this twentieth century, perhaps the one which fills thoughtful people with the greatest foreboding is the growing general sense of meaninglessness. It is this which underlies most of the other threats. How is it that the more able man becomes to manipulate the world to his advantage, the less he can perceive any meaning in it? This is a paradox which has often been noted and has sometimes been attributed to a fundamental perversity, a sort of "pure cussedness," in human nature. In fact, however, it arises from a clearly identifiable and comparatively recent bit of history.

Most people are well aware that, with the advent of the Scientific Revolution about 300 years ago, the mind of man began to relate itself to the world around it in an entirely new way. The habit then first arose of meticulously observing the facts of nature and systematically interpreting them in terms of physical cause and effect; and this habit has been growing ever since, with incalculable and largely beneficial results for the accumulation of practical knowledge, or knowledge enabling the manipulation of nature. What is less clearly realized is the precise nature and significance of a certain further step which was taken in the nineteenth century. It was then that this habitual practice in the pursuit of knowledge was formulated as a dogma under the name of the "positive" philosophy, or positivism.

Positivism is the philosophical name for the belief now more widely known as "materialism." It is the doctrine—propounded originally by Auguste Comte—that the above-mentioned method of interpreting the facts of nature is not merely a useful but the only possible one. Obviously a proposition that only one method of scientific investigation is possible cannot itself (except for devout believers) be based on scientific investigation by that method. The proposition is, therefore, in fact a dogmatic belief; although it has been so thoroughly absorbed into the thought stream of western humanity that it has come to be regarded, not as a dogma, but as a scientifically established fact.

Now there is usually little connection between the physical causes of a thing and its meaning. An important physical cause of what I am just now writing is the muscular pressure of my finger and thumb, but knowing this does not help anyone to grasp its meaning. Thus, in investigating the phenomena of nature, exclusive emphasis on physical causes and effects involves a corresponding inattention to their meaning. And it was just this exclusive emphasis which came into fashion about 300 years ago. What happened later, in the nineteenth century, was that a *habit* of inattention, which had become inveterate, was finally superseded by an *assumption* (sometimes explicit but more often implicit) that scientific attention to the meaning, as distinct from the causes, of phenomena, was impossible—even if (which was considered improbable) there was anything to attend to. The meaning of a process is the inner being which the process expresses. The denial of any such inner being to the processes of nature leads inevitably to the denial of it to man himself. For if physical objects and physical causes and effects are all that we can know, it follows that man himself can be known only to the extent that he is a physical object among physical objects. Thus, it is implicit in positivism that man can never really know anything about his specifically human self—his own inner being—any more than he can ever really know anything about the meaning of the world of nature by which he is surrounded.

Up to now even those who reject materialism as an ultimate philosophy have been content to accept the limitations which positivism seeks to impose on the sphere of knowledge. True, they say, the spiritual values which constitute the true meaning of life can be dimly felt and are, in fact, what lie behind the symbols of religion and the mysterious phenomena of art. But we can never hope to know anything about them. There are— and this is often suggested with a certain unction—two kinds of truth: the scientific kind which can be demonstrated experimentally and which is limited to the physical world and, on the other side, the "truths" of mystical intuition and revelation, which can be felt and suggested but never known or scientifically stated. And if these seem to be incompatible with the truths of science—well, perhaps that is all the better. "The heart has its reasons whereof reason knoweth not."

In this way for a number of years a precarious equilibrium may be said to have been established between a meaningless and mechanical world of physical events described by science and some kind of ulterior spiritual significance which that world might be supposed to conceal and with which it had little if anything to do. The idealist philosophies of the nineteenth century made it their business to maintain this equilibrium by rationalizing it as best they could.

It was a state of affairs that could not last, and its latent instability has been exposed by a certain further step which the doctrine of positivism has taken in our time. The older positivism proclaimed that man could never know anything except the physical world-mechanism accessible to his senses. The twentieth-century variety—variously known as "logical positivism," "linguistic analysis," "the philosophy of science," and so on—goes further and avers that nothing can even be *said* about anything else. Language is meaningful only in so far as it communicates, or at least purports to communicate, information about physical events, which observation and experiment can then confirm or disprove. The ground is cut away from beneath the feet of any idealist interpretation of the universe by a new dogma, not that such an interpretation is untrue but that it cannot even be advanced. The language in which it is couched is not really language at all (although it may obey the rules of grammar) because it has no meaning. Not only that, the ground is cut away from any sort of inner life at all. Moral judgments, for instance, have no factual reference. If we say "cruelty is wicked," all we really mean is that we don't like it. Words which purport to refer to anything beyond the reach of the senses do not in fact refer to anything at all. Our conviction that they do is merely a mistake we make about the possible ways of using language. When we combine such words into sentences, we imagine we are saying something, but in fact we are merely making noises, which express our feelings, as laughter and tears and grunts express our feelings. This, it is claimed, has always been the case, and all mythology and religion, together with practically all philosophy before the rise of positivism, are simply examples of these linguistic errors.

The upshot of all this was once well put by C. S. Lewis, when he pointed out that by and large, if the new positivism is right, the history of the human mind since the beginning of time has consisted in "almost nobody making linguistic mistakes about almost nothing." Even so, modern "analytical" philosophy is interesting and significant just because it forces the issue to its logical conclusion and brings into the open the mental predicament which acceptance of positivism has always really implied. Like a sort of scalpel, linguistic analysis lays bare that connection which we began by affirming between the rise of positivism and the general sense of meaninglessness in the West. At last the choice is plain. Either we must concede that 99 per cent of all we say and think (or imagine we think) is meaningless verbiage, or we must—however great the wrench—abandon positivism.

"Wrench" is not too strong a word; for positivism is subtly entangled with our thinking at all points on almost all subjects. A rather similar wrench was required of the western mind at the close of the Middle Ages. Those who have not studied medieval thought will hardly believe how stubborn and inveterate the assumption had become that it was impossible to go outside Aristotle. Originality, new discoveries, experiments were all very welcome—provided they remained within the encompassing framework of Aristotelian conceptions: for instance, that the earth is fixed in the center of the universe, that the heavenly bodies are weightless, that heat, or fire, is one of the elements. These were taken absolutely for granted and anything which seemed to throw doubt on their validity produced—above all in the acknowledged leaders of contemporary thought—a violent reaction, which made them condemn it as nonsense or even blasphemy. The study of the transition from medieval to modern thought is the study of the great and painful wrench with which this dogma was at last abandoned. Now if we substitute positivism for Aristotelianism, we may get some idea of what is in store for us when we first begin to cast doubts on it. For it is a mistake to suppose that we are more open-minded today; we are merely open-minded about different things.

We will, nevertheless, try the experiment and we will begin at the furthest point which positivism itself has reached, as we have seen, in its nihilistic advance; that is to say, at the primary vehicle which we possess for the understanding and expression of meaning; in other words, with language.

How did it come about that a very high proportion of the words in any modern language do refer to matters and events which are not part of the world accessible to our senses? To the historical student, language appears at first sight to consist of what has been well called "a tissue of faded metaphors." From the time of the nineteenth-century philosopher, Max Müller, onward this has been the common topic of innumerable books on words. Thus, as Ernest Weekley explained many years ago:

> Every expression that we employ, apart from those that are connected with the most rudimentary objects and actions, is a metaphor, though the original meaning is dulled by constant use.

And he went on to illustrate his meaning from the words used in that very sentence:

OWEN BARFIELD

Thus, in the above sentence, *expression* means "what is squeezed out," to *employ* is to "twine in" like a basket-maker, to *connect* is to "weave together," *rudimentary* means "in the rough state," and an *object* is "something thrown in our way."

Above all, we find that all words used to describe the "inside" of ourselves, whether it be a thought or feeling, can be clearly seen to have come down to us from an earlier period when they also had reference to the outside world. The further back you go in time, the more metaphorical you find language becoming; and some of the pioneers of etymology even anticipated the later positivism we have just described by claiming that mythology and religion were simply the result of the "mistake" which was made when, later on, the "metaphors" came to be taken literally.

Since their time, however, a great deal more thought has been given to the whole problem of meaning and symbolism. In particular it has been realized that symbolic significance is not the exclusive attribute of religion and art, but is an intrinsic element in language itself. How did it come about that the shapes and objects of the outside world could be employed, and were employed, by man to express the inner world of his thought? It is because he was able to use them, not merely as *signs* for drawing attention to his feelings and impulses, but as *symbols* for his concepts. A thing functions as a symbol when it not only announces, but *represents* something other than itself. We owe the existence of language to the fact that the mental images, into which memory converts the forms of the outer world, can function not only as signs and reminders of themselves but as symbols for concepts. If this were not so, they could never have given rise to words—which make abstract thought possible. If we reflect on this fact unprejudiced by any positivist assumptions, we must conclude that this symbolic significance is inherent in the forms of the outer world themselves. The first metaphors were not artificial but natural.

In other words, the positivists are right in their conclusion that *if* (they would say "because") nature is meaningless to the

316

human mind, most language is also meaningless. But the converse is equally true that, if language is "meaningful," then nature herself must also be meaningful. In fact, as Emerson pointed out long ago, "It is not only words that are emblematic; it is things which are emblematic." Man, he reminded his unheeding contemporaries "is placed in the center of beings and a ray of relation passes from every other being to him. And neither can man be understood without these objects, nor these objects without man." It is precisely in this "ray of relation," which positivism cannot admit and which has therefore come to be overlooked, that the secret of meaning resides.

I have reached the conclusion that the natural world can only be understood in depth as a series of images symbolizing concepts; further, that it was out of man's rich awareness of this meaningful relation between himself and nature that language originally came to birth. How is it, then, that early man possessed this rich awareness while we have lost it? In answering this question we already begin to feel the great wrench; for we find that the abandonment of positivism involves a drastic revision of our whole conception of prehistory.

Consider the conventional picture of the history of the earth and man. It shows us, first of all, a purely physical earth without life or consciousness; then the arrival on that earth of animals and men as physical objects moving about on it; finally the development by man, out of nothing, of a faculty of imagination and thought enabling him to mirror or copy inwardly an outer world which had existed solidly for millions of years before him. We see the inner world evolving at a comparatively late stage from the outer. For this picture we shall surely have to substitute the more difficult and less crude one of inner and outer worlds coming into being alongside one another. For the reciprocal relation between the two, which language reveals, will not allow of one's ever having existed without the other. It points back instead to a *common origin*. The distinction between inner and outer, which seems so fundamental to us, will be seen to have been brought about by man himself in the very process of exercising the symbolizing faculty which gave him his language.

Ernst Cassirer, dealing with language in his *Philosophy of Symbolic Forms,* showed how the history of human consciousness was not a progress from an initial condition of blank darkness toward wider and wider awareness of a pre-existent outer world, but the gradual extrication of a small, but a growing and an increasingly clear and self-determined focus of inner human experience from a dreamlike state of virtual identity with the life of the body and of its environment. Self-consciousness emerged from mere consciousness. It was only in the course of this process that the world of "objective" nature, which we now observe around us, came into being. Man did not start on his career as a self-conscious being in the form of a mindless or thoughtless unit, confronting a separate, unintelligible objective world very like our own, about which he then proceeded to invent all manner of myths. He was not an onlooker, learning to make a less and less hopelessly inaccurate mental copy. He has had to wrestle his subjectivity out of the world of his experience by polarizing that world gradually into a duality. And this is the duality of objective-subjective, or outer-inner, which now seems so fundamental because we have inherited it along with language. He did not *start* as an onlooker; the development of language enabled him to *become* one.

Let us digress for a moment and examine the other, the received view, that the history of human thought *is* the history of an onlooker learning to make a better and better mental copy of an independent outer world. All positivist science is based on mathematics and physics; and modern physics originally set out to investigate nature as something existing independently of the human mind. But this was a postulate which it had more and more to abandon as time went on. At a quite early stage a distinction was made between "primary" qualities, such as extension and mass, which were assumed to inhere in matter independently of the observer, and "secondary" qualities like color, which depend on the observer. Roughly speaking, physics has ended by having to conclude that *all* qualities are "secondary" in this sense, so that the whole world of nature as we actually experience it depends for its configuration on the mind and senses of man. It is what it is because we are what we are. Thus our common assumption that the main effort of human thinking has been to make a mental replica of a pre-existent outer world is incompatible even with the scientific approach to things out of which it arose. This assumption is indeed determined by science; but by a science of the day before yesterday.

Early man did not observe nature in our detached way. He participated mentally and physically in her inner and outer process. The evolution of man has signified not alone the steady expansion of consciousness (man getting to know more and more about more and more); there has also been a parallel process of contraction—which was also a process of awakening—a gradual focusing or pinpointing down from an earlier kind of knowledge, which could also be called participation. It was at once more universal and less clear. We still have something of this older relation to nature when we are asleep, and it throws up the suprarational wisdom which many psychoanalysts detect in dreams. Thus, it is rather true to say that we have come to know more and more about less and less.

"Man is the dwarf of himself," said Emerson. It is this fact which underlies the world-wide tradition of a fall from paradise; and it is this which still reverberates on in the nature-linked collective consciousness that we find expressed in myths, in older forms of language and in the totemic thinking and ritual participation of primitive tribes. It is from some such origins as these and not from an alert, blank stare of incomprehension that we have evolved the individual, sharpened, spatially determined consciousness of today.

It is a process which continued even back into our own era. We have only to go back as far as the period immediately before the Scientific Revolution in Europe, when the world picture still held sway of man as a microcosm within the macrocosm, and we shall find the felt severance between man's inner being and the world around him still noticeably less than it is today. There is not space to do more than casually allude to one or two examples; but anyone who studies medieval art and medieval thought a little will find that, for instance, the four elements, earth, water, air and fire (which were not conceived as merely physical substances) were assumed as a matter of course to be functioning not only in the outside world but also in the human temperament as its four "humours"—melancholic, phlegmatic, sanguine and choleric—while similar links between the planets and the metals and the dispositions of man were equally taken for granted. Of course, positivist thinking assumes that these were all erroneous speculations and had nothing to do with fact; but apart from that (and I have given some reasons for thinking that to be mistaken) it is clear from the whole course of history that they were in truth vestigial remains of the "common origin" of man's outer and his inner world.

It remains to be considered whether the future development of scientific man must inevitably continue in the same direction, so that he becomes more and more a mere onlooker, measuring with greater and greater precision and manipulating more and more cleverly an earth to which he grows spiritually more and more a stranger. His detachment has enabled him to describe, weigh and measure the processes of nature and to a large extent to control them; but the price he has paid has been the loss of his grasp of any meaning in either nature or himself. Penetration to the meaning of a thing or process, as distinct from the ability to describe it exactly, involves a participation by the knower in the known. The meaning of what I am writing is not the physical pressure of thumb and forefinger, or the size of the ink lines with which I form the letters; it is the concepts expressed in the words I am writing. But the only way of penetrating to these is to participate in them—to bring them to life in your own mind by thinking them. A Chinese looking at this page would indeed be limited to describing its outer appearance. We are mere onlookers at a language we do not understand. But confronted with a language we have learned to understand, we not merely observe the shapes of the letters—in the very act of observing these we "read" their meaning through them. In the same way, if we want to know the meaning of nature, we must learn to read as well as to observe and describe. Is there any possibility of scientific man's ever recovering the old power to "read," while still retaining his hard-won treasure of exact observation and manipulative control—for no one would advocate a mere relapse into the past? Signs are not altogether wanting that there is such a possibility, though they are at present rudimentary.

We have seen that man can only begin to "read" the meaning of nature, when instead of merely copying and describing what he senses, he begins to apprehend it as a series of images symbolizing concepts. Now the word "imagination" has come to mean, for most people, the faculty of inventing fictions, especially poetic fictions; but in its deeper sense it signifies that very faculty of apprehending the outward form as the image or symbol of an inner meaning, for which we are looking. It is therefore not surprising that the first stirrings of a movement of thought in this new direction should have occurred among those who interested themselves in the deeper significance of art, and especially of poetry. Thus, it was held by Coleridge that the human imagination, at its highest level, does indeed inherit and continue the divine creative activity of the Logos (the "Word" of the opening verses of St. John's Gospel), which was the common origin of human language and consciousness, as well as of the world which contains them. Out of the whole development of the Romantic Movement in Europe at the turn of the eighteenth century and in the nineteenth a conviction arose in these circles that man's creative imagination can be applied, not only in the creation and contemplation of works of art but also in the contemplation of nature herself. Through its exercise we begin once more to experience nature as image; and indeed an obscure recognition of images underlies that feeling for the beauty of nature which differentiates us so sharply from the eighteenth century. It may even lead, as in some of Wordsworth's childhood recollections or in our own time in the poetic vision of Kathleen Raine, to glimpses of the "common origin":

> Do you remember, when you were first a child,
> Nothing in the world seemed strange to you?
> You perceived, for the first time, shapes already familiar,
> And seeing, you knew that you have always known
> The lichen on the rock, fern-leaves, the flowers of thyme,
> As if the elements newly met in your body,

> Caught up into the momentary vortex of your living
> Still kept the knowledge of a former state. . . .

But all this does not amount to very much more than that vague "idealism"—a general intuition of some sort of meaning behind the totality of things—which, as we have seen, can peacefully coexist with the positivist dogma, at all events in the latter's earlier stages, before it begins to disintegrate language. It is much too subtle for the man in the street; but most contemporary enthusiasts for art and poetry accept some form of the doctrine of "two kinds of truth" to which we have already referred. They are content that the business of detailed investigation should be left to positivist science. In the book of nature the whole may mean something, but the details mean nothing; or if they do, we can never know it.

This however is not what we feel when we read an actual book. There the meaning of the whole is articulated from the meaning of each part—chapters from sentences and sentences from words—and stands before us in clear, sharp outlines. The vital question is whether science can ever discover how to read the book of nature in *this* way. It would not matter so much if its field were limited to mechanics and physics. But in fact man looks more and more to science for guidance on *all* subjects. As we rise in the scale of creation from the lifeless to the living and from the living to the psychic and human—from mechanics to sociology—the question of the *meaning* of what we are dealing with becomes ever more insistent. Must this always be ignored or can science ever learn to supplement its weighing, measuring and statistics with the systematic use of imagination? Of course, scientists already use imagination at a particular juncture in research—namely, the devising of hypotheses to explain new facts. But this would be something quite different; it would be the use of imagination at each point and in the very act of observation. Is such a development even conceivable?

It has not yet been very widely realized that the genius who was possibly Europe's greatest poet, but who was certainly the greatest figure in the Romantic Movement, actually devoted more of his time to scientific investigation than to poetry and at the end of his life attached more importance to this part of himself then he did to his world-famous poetry. Goethe was convinced that the scientific method which came into vogue with the Scientific Revolution was not the only possible one. In particular he held that for dealing with the phenomena of life and growth it was an inadequate method. For the whole process of "becoming" is one which eludes the categories of cause and effect. The method which he applied in his work on *The Metamorphosis of Plants*, and elsewhere, was based on the perception that nature has an "inside" which cannot be weighed and measured—or even (without training) observed—namely, the creative thoughts which underlie phenomenal manifestation. Before the Scientific Revolution, when some attention was still paid to such problems, they would have called it "potential," as distinct from "actual" nature. And, Goethe claimed that this side of nature, too, was perceptible, not indeed to the untrained senses, but to a perceptive faculty trained by systematic practice to participate in those creative thoughts.

By ordinary inductive science the unifying idea, or law, behind groups of related phenomena is treated as a generalization from particulars; it is an abstract notion, which can be inferred only from observations as their result; and it must be expressible in terms of measurable quantities. For Goethean science, on the other hand, this unifying idea is an objective reality, accessible to direct observation. In addition to measuring quantities, the scientist must train himself to perceive qualities. This he can do—as Goethe did when he saw the various parts of the plant as "metamorphoses" of the leaf—only by so sinking himself in contemplation of the outward form that his imagination penetrates to the activity which is producing it.

Goethe's morphological observations on plant and animal played a significant part in the development of the (then quite new) concept of evolution and are referred to by Darwin in the introduction to his *Origin of Species*. But, because their whole epistemological basis was undermined by, and submerged in, the rising flood of positivist assumptions, little attention has been paid to them. They have been looked at from time to time but almost always through the spectacles of positivism.

By detaching himself more and more from the world of nature—as he has been doing ever since the Scientific Revolution—man has gradually developed the exact quantitative approach which has given him, over such a wide area, his marvelous powers of manipulative control.

But in doing so he has necessarily lost for the time being that felt union with the inner origin of outward forms which constitutes perception of their meaning. He can begin to recover this only if he develops his science beyond its present positivist limitations; and it is just such a development to which the way has already been pointed by one of the greatest minds Europe has ever known. What is needed now is for someone to try the experiment of taking off his positivist spectacles and examining Goethe with the naked eye.

Further reading:
Barfield, Owen: SAVING THE APPEARANCES. New York: Hillary House; 1957.
Cassirer, Ernst: THE PHILOSOPHY OF SYMBOLIC FORMS. Vol. I, Language. New Haven: Yale University Press; 1953.
Langer, Susanne K.: PHILOSOPHY IN A NEW KEY. New York: The New American Library of World Literature, Inc.; 1948.
Lehrs, Ernest: MAN OR MATTER. New York: Harper & Brothers; 1958.

STANLEY HYMAN

[*Photograph by Philippe Halsman*]

Since 1940, when he was graduated from Syracuse University, Stanley Edgar Hyman has been a staff writer for The New Yorker and a contributor of critical reviews and articles to many other periodicals. His penetrating study of modern literary criticism, The Armed Vision, was widely acclaimed. At present he teaches literature at Bennington College. He is married to the distinguished short-story writer and novelist, Shirley Jackson. Their home in North Bennington, Vermont, contains four children, 12,000 books, a collection of blues records, and a cabinet of ancient Greek coins.

The Tragic Vision

BY

STANLEY HYMAN

A great financier sits in the Chicago courtroom, his face haggard. He is bankrupt, and worse, exposed to the world as a criminal. A short while ago he stepped out of his limousine like a king emerging from the royal coach, soon he will be doing all his stepping in the prison yard. In Hollywood, an old actor, the matinee idol and foremost lecher of his time, now hopelessly alcoholic, ends his days friendless in a shabby rooming house. A few blocks from Madison Square Garden in New York, a punch-drunk fighter, once the most arrogant of champions, begs from saloon to saloon.

These falls from great heights engage our emotions peculiarly. More than fifteen hundred years ago, Saint Augustine raised the question of that peculiarity. "What is the reason," he asks in his Confessions, "that a spectator desires to be made sad when he beholds doleful and tragical passages, which he himself could not suffer to endure?" That is still the important question about tragedy: Why do we enjoy the portrayal of suffering? Trying to answer it, we have to look back at the history of tragic drama, watch tragedy spread into other forms, then take note of whatever special sorts of tragedy we might have today, in a best-selling novel or a political downfall. Our values and literary styles are as far from those of ancient Athens and Elizabethan England as neckties are from Spanish ruffs, or atom bombs from Greek fire. Our tragedies, however, would be as understandable to them as their Oedipus and Hamlet are to us. There seems to be something about the tragic vision, some essential affirmation of the human spirit, that remains timeless and universal however much its superficial appearance changes.

The ancient Greeks might be said to have invented tragedy, as they invented so much of our culture, although there are anticipations of it in the earlier literature of the ancient Near East. The story of Saul and what the Lord calls "his bloody house" in the books of Samuel in the Bible looks very like tragic drama, as do the fates of David's descendants in the books of Kings. Even earlier, in the Babylonian epic of Gilgamesh, we hear the authentic voice of tragedy in Gilgamesh's awful mourning for his dead companion Enkidu—as moving in its way as the lament of David for Absalom. Behind that there are still earlier Sumerian and Akkadian related epics taking us almost back to the beginnings of history.

Nevertheless, the earliest tragic drama we have, whatever its sources, flowers suddenly in Athens in the fifth century B.C., in the marvelous plays of Aeschylus, Sophocles and Euripides. A century later Aristotle codified its principles in his Poetics, and that fragmentary treatise may still be the best insight we have into the art. Aristotle defined tragedy as the imitation or representation of an action serious, complete in itself, and of an adequate magnitude, written in embellished language. In that action a man like ourselves, neither wholly good nor wholly bad, is brought low through some shortcoming or tragic flaw in him. Its function is the arousing of pity for him and terror of his fate in the audience, and the purging of these emotions in the resolution.

Aristotle based his definitions principally on Sophocles' Oedipus the King, which he thought the greatest and most successful of Greek tragedies, as many others have since. Unfortunately, Aristotle's definitions do not fit other Athenian tragedies as neatly. The protagonist of Euripides' Medea is not a flawed man like ourselves, but a remorseless semidivine witch, and she is not brought low at the end, but appears in glory in the sky. The protagonist of Sophocles' Antigone does not bring on her tragic fate through any shortcoming, but because of her pious

328

determination to give her brother proper burial, although the tyrant Creon had forbidden it; and Orestes in the Oresteia of Aeschylus kills his mother not because he has a tragic flaw, but because the god Apollo had commanded him to avenge her murder of his father. We can only accept Medea as a tragedy in the later concepts of Longinus' treatise, On the Sublime, written in the third century A.D., which puts a new emphasis on such features of the tragic experience as "nobility," "grandeur," "transport," "inspired and vehement passion." Only in the nineteenth century, with Hegel's concept of tragedy as brought about through inability to obey two contradictory imperatives, does the tragic nature of the Antigone and Oresteia begin to make sense for us.

From the work of classical scholars, like Gilbert Murray at Oxford and Jane Harrison at Cambridge, we have learned that the form of Greek tragedy, which began as the sacrificial rites of the god Dionysus, preserves the stages of the annual sacrifice of the year-spirit: his contest with his enemy, his suffering, death, and tearing-apart; the lamentation for him, then the discovery of his body and its resurrection as the new year. These rites mimic and thus magically produce the annual cycle of vegetation: birth, growth, flourishing, decay, death, rebirth. Its culmination in nature is the joy of spring. The comparable affirmation in Greek drama heralds the Reliving Dionysus, who will spring up again from his dismembered fragments, and the final mood of Greek tragedy thus goes beyond pity and terror to exultation and joy.

The Greeks saw this tragic pattern, some higher and implicit in human suffering, not only on the stage but everywhere in their experience. Homeric epic is full of it. In the Iliad, Homer gets the whole of tragic acceptance into Achilles' fierce speech to the young Trojan Lycaon, who has begged him for mercy, just before he kills him. I quote from W. H. D. Rouse's translation:

> Come, my friend, die too; why do you cry like that? Patroclus died too, and he was a much better man than you. Don't you see me too, a fine big man? My father is a brave man,

my mother is a goddess; yet I too have death and fate fast upon me. The day shall come, morning or evening or midday, when someone shall take my life too in battle, with a thrust of the spear or an arrow from the bow.

In the Odyssey—perhaps the finest tragedy of all, and one of Longinus' examples of the "sublime"—is the disdainful silence of the ghost of Ajax when Odysseus meets him in Hades, still implacable over the wrong Odysseus did him in life. Here, in Ajax' simple gesture of turning away in bitter silence, we learn more powerfully than any words could tell us that the human spirit is stronger than death.

There is always a danger in quoting what Matthew Arnold called "touchstones" out of context, since the whole of a work is what produces its effect, not a moving scene, speech or line. The Iliad and the Odyssey are not tragic dramas, but the tragic vision —that man must go down into the depths of the human condition, that he must fall before he can rise, is strong within them. We find the same vision in Greek lyric poetry and philosophy, most dramatically in the death of Socrates in Plato's Phaedo. In Greek history, we have the Athenian historian Thucydides showing bitterly that when Athens, arrogant in its power, destroyed the weak and inoffensive little city of Melos, killing the men and enslaving the women and children, its subsequent fall was divine punishment for pride and transgression just like that of a tragic hero, and it could only arise again humbled and transformed. Some modern thinkers have even found the pattern of tragedy underlying the origin of scientific thought among the Greeks. Alfred North Whitehead says that the basic scientific assumption of an order of nature comes from Greek tragedy, so that "The laws of physics are the decrees of fate." In his brilliant book, Poetry and Mathematics, Scott Buchanan suggests that the experimental method itself, perhaps even the basic patterns of our thinking, come from the rites of contest, tearing-apart and apotheosis that underlie Greek tragedy.

Modern tragic drama begins with Christopher Marlowe's Doctor Faustus. In the last scene, as Lucifer and Mephistophilis come to get him, Faustus cries out:

Oh, I'll leap up to my God! Who pulls me down?
See, see where Christ's blood streams in the firmament!
One drop would save my soul—half a drop: ah, my Christ!

With this cry from the heart as damnation closes in on him, Faustus suddenly becomes not a cardboard necromancer but a man like ourselves, and the vigor of the emotion pulls apart Marlowe's singsong blank-verse line and makes Shakespearean tragedy possible. Marlowe himself, killed young in a tavern brawl, is a sacrificial figure like his Faustus, and out of his ashes arise the glories of the Elizabethan theater.

Shakespeare extends all of Marlowe's possibilities further—perhaps to their limits—and without knowing Aristotle's writing, succeeds in producing tragedies that fit the formula of the Poetics better than most Greek drama. Macbeth and Othello, Hamlet and Lear, are precisely men like ourselves, neither wholly good nor wholly bad, brought low by a tragic shortcoming: Macbeth's ambition, Othello's credulity, Hamlet's indecision, and Lear's blind inability to tell love from its counterfeit.

Shakespeare increases our ability to identify with the tragic action by weakening or discarding the supernatural motivation so strong in Doctor Faustus. The witches in Macbeth and the ghost in Hamlet are only trappings, the external forms of inner voices; and Othello and Lear battle not supernatural beings but malign human antagonists, Iago and the wicked daughters.

After Shakespeare, tragic drama in English runs downhill, turning into wilder and wilder bloody melodrama in the seventeenth century, becoming neoclassical and rather stiff in the joints in the eighteenth century, and leaving the theater entirely in the nineteenth century to become the unperformable closet dramas of poets. When tragedy is revived in our theater, the impetus comes from abroad, from Henrik Ibsen in Norway and Anton Chekhov in Russia. Here we have the new realistic tragedy of the middle class, with scenes in parlors rather than on battlements or blasted heaths. Again, as with the Greeks, we have no villains, only the protagonists' own crippling failures of insight, will, and love. Sometimes, in Chekhov, there is no crack of doom at all, only a fog of gloom and inertia settling over a household, as oxidation is sometimes the vivid flash of fire and sometimes the slow corruption of rust. Whatever rebirth is promised here will not spring up like Dionysus from the dismembered flesh, but will be a new growth, a better cherry orchard perhaps, out of decay.

With the Irish theater of John M. Synge and Sean O'Casey we are back to something like Greek drama, with destiny again working its remorseless ways. Now, however, instead of a Greek chorus we have two vulgar old women, a fruit peddler and a charlady, foretelling the fates in The Plough and the Stars; we must accept as "men like ourselves" not Prince Hamlet or King Lear but those sodden frauds "Joxer" Daly and Captain Boyle in Juno and the Paycock; and in Riders to the Sea, instead of proud Queen Hecuba of Troy, we have the peasant woman Maurya—whose name sounds so much like the Greek Moira, Fate—giving us the ultimate Greek tragic acceptance after her last son has been drowned: "No man at all can be living forever, and we must be satisfied."

In the tragic drama of our own time, the playwrights seem to be still consolidating the revolution of Ibsen, Chekhov and the Irish dramatists; reshaping the tragic vision to fit a world of new classes and values, a world with neither villains nor heroes, a world that has lost much of its faith and most of its hope. Perhaps least typical of our time is T. S. Eliot's Murder in the Cathedral, a frankly religious work written to be performed in church, yet a tragic drama all the same. Here, telling the story of the martyrdom of St. Thomas à Becket in the twelfth century, Eliot finds tragedy in the vision of man as a flawed agency of divine purpose.

Eugene O'Neill's The Iceman Cometh is a much more characteristic tragedy of our time in that it denies the existence of divine purpose, or any purpose, and shatters its characters, the derelicts of Harry Hope's saloon, with the discovery that all faith is a lying "pipe dream." Theodore Hickman, the salesman who sells them this discovery, is the Iceman of the title, a salesman of death, and when he is taken away by the police at the end, their shabby and pathetic hopes spring up again like some kind of unkillable life.

The Tragic Vision

Tennessee Williams' A Streetcar Named Desire takes a well-born lady with the passions of Queen Phaedra in Euripides' Hippolytus on that streetcar ride into the slums of New Orleans, and through them into disgrace and madness. Like the inhabitants of Harry Hope's saloon, Blanche DuBois has her pipe dreams—the plantation she grew up in is called *Belle Rêve*, beautiful dream. When she and her dreams are smashed at the end, in a scene of magnificent theatrical hokum, the hope may be for her sister's child by the coarse, animal Stanley Kowalski, growing up free of all such dreams.

If Blanche DuBois is like Queen Phaedra, driven by the arrows of the love-goddess Aphrodite to disgrace and madness, Willy Loman, the salesman of Arthur Miller's Death of a Salesman, is King Oedipus with a sample case, pursuing his own identity and responsibility—"Was it my fault?"—to his doom. Here, too, are the phony pipe dreams, but Willy has a true vision of a better sort of life, a life where "a man is not a piece of fruit" to be nibbled and thrown away. In his wife's big speech, the ultimate value of the human personality is passionately if somewhat inelegantly affirmed:

> I don't say he's a great man. Willy Loman never made a lot of money. His name was never in the paper. He's not the finest character that ever lived. But he's a human being, and a terrible thing is happening to him. So attention must be paid. He's not to be allowed to fall into his grave like an old dog. Attention, attention must be finally paid to such a person.

When they bury Willy at the end, that vision of human meaningfulness survives.

Beyond a slut Phaedra and a slob Oedipus, the end of the line would seem to be Samuel Beckett's Waiting for Godot, where the very bottom of the social order, two ragged and half-crazed bums, speak for us, and affirm the ultimate misery of the human condition, yet its deathless hope. Even Blanche DuBois tried to freshen up the Kowalskis' upholstery, and Willy Loman saw buyers long after they had stopped buying; but Beckett's characters do not act at all; they merely wait. What they wait

333

for, Godot, may not exist, and it may not matter if he does or does not. Francis Fergusson, in The Idea of a Theater, has phrased the tragic rhythm of action as, "From Purpose through Passion to Perception." Here is an authentic tragedy in which purpose, passion and perception all coalesce in one timeless, static "waiting." Vladimir, the more intellectual of the two bums, affirms their sad pride in waiting in words surprisingly reminiscent of Simonides' epitaph on the Spartan dead at Thermopylae:

> We have kept our appointment and that's an end to that. We are not saints, but we have kept our appointment. How many people can boast as much?

For us, as for the Greeks, tragedy has escaped the confines of drama, and we find it everywhere in our literature. One theme of lyric poetry that seems authentically tragic—as it was for Phaedra—is overpowering physical passion, fleshly love as tragic fate. It develops in Provençal poetry, and reaches its high point in Dante's Divine Comedy, when Francesca in Hell tells Dante, while Paolo, her lover, weeps, of the moment when she and he sinned. Modern poetry has made us thoroughly familiar with this tragic and devastating passion. Sometimes it is all implied, as in the marvelous economy of William Butler Yeats' six-line poem, A Deep-Sworn Vow:

> *Others because you did not keep*
> *That deep-sworn vow have been friends of mine;*
> *Yet always when I look death in the face,*
> *When I clamber to the heights of sleep,*
> *Or when I grow excited with wine,*
> *Suddenly I meet your face.*

At other times it is defined so physically that we are reminded of Dante, as in John Crowe Ransom's The Equilibrists, from which I quote a stanza that may take us even further back, to the Reliving Dionysus:

> *Great lovers lie in Hell, the stubborn ones*
> *Infatuate of the flesh upon the bones;*

334

Stuprate, they rend each other when they kiss,
The pieces kiss again, no end to this.

Some of the same tragic passion appears in Negro blues songs, understated in the words but overwhelming in the music, as when Jimmy Rushing, accompanied by Sam Price at the piano, sings How Long:

If I could holler like a mountain jack,
Go up on the mountain, and call my baby back.
Baby, how long? Baby, how long? Baby, how long?

In our fiction, we have the old tragic pattern of pride and fall, but with strange new varieties of prides and falls. Captain Ahab in Melville's Moby Dick is like the mad infatuate Shakespeare heroes, Lear or the later Othello. He has a new sort of heroic antagonist, however, no longer a malignant villain, but blind wild nature embodied in the great white whale. In Ahab's frenzied desire to "Strike through the mask!" and get at the ultimate evil of the universe, he is carried down to death lashed to the great whale. Only a transformed Ishmael, riding on a coffin, survives to tell the tale. The bitter intellectual protagonists of Dostoevski all in their different fashions believe that they are above or beyond society, like King Oedipus. Then like him they are smashed down below it, with some possibility of beginning their regeneration there.

In stories like Mann's Death in Venice and Kafka's The Judgment, we get a kind of Freudian tragedy of repression. It is, however, a species of tragedy that Euripides knew all about in The Bacchae, where puritanic King Pentheus represses his sensual nature until the god Dionysus, disguised as a handsome stranger, releases all that he has kept hidden and leads him to disgrace and death. Mann's Gustave Aschenbach similarly represses his sensual nature and presents an image of stiff rectitude to the world, until the appearance of the beautiful Polish boy, Tadzio, similarly breaks down his defenses and destroys him. Kafka's Georg Bendemann despised his old father in his dirty underwear, as Pentheus at first despised the effeminate stranger. Suddenly the old father, like Euripides' stranger, turns out to

335

conceal a divine omnipotence; he cries out, "I sentence you to death by drowning," and Georg dashes out and hurls himself off a bridge.

In other modern fiction the only transgression is the aspiration of the poor to rise to a degree of freedom and happiness. Perhaps the most tragic moment in James Joyce's Ulysses is the scene where Stephen Dedalus sees his ragged younger sister Dilly at a bookstall buying a coverless French primer for a penny, and realizes that she has the same aspirations he has, but that he can only save himself by letting her sink.

> She is drowning. Agenbite. Save her. Agenbite. All against us. She will drown me with her, eyes and hair. Lank coils of seaweed hair around me, my heart, my soul. Salt green death.
> We.
> Agenbite of inwit. Inwit's agenbite.
> Misery! Misery!

Suffering the "agenbite of inwit"—Joyce's Anglo-Saxon equivalent for "remorse of conscience"—in one tragic moment Stephen both accepts his common humanity and denies it out of desperate necessity.

Nor are the rich without their tragedies. In Shirley Jackson's The Sundial, a fantasy about the end of the world, the matriarch Mrs. Halloran brings on her death by donning a golden crown, precisely as King Agamemnon in the Oresteia of Aeschylus incurs the wrath of the gods and his own death by treading on the carpet of royal purple. In James Gould Cozzens' By Love Possessed, the upright and wealthy lawyer, Arthur Winner, is brought through suffering to feel something of the love and charity of the poor and dispossessed, a "winner" only of insight through humiliation.

The same tragic patterns confront us everywhere in our newspapers. We see the fated love of great princes in the British royal family—as though it existed to remind us of that lost Shakespearean world—first in the heartbreaking abdication broadcast of Edward VIII, then in the silent, smoldering tragedy of Princess Margaret. Our own tragic princes include the ruined financier, the fallen theatrical star, the washed-out sports champion with which we began this inquiry. The tragic movement is as visible in life as in art, since it comes into art from life. If Orson Welles' film, Citizen Kane, was tragic, so was the life of William Randolph Hearst that inspired it; if O'Neill's autobiographical plays and F. Scott Fitzgerald's autobiographical novels are tragic, so, visibly, were their lives. Below these famous figures there are the sordid tragedies and nameless sufferers of the tabloids: a daily creation of grimy Clytemnestras, Orestes, Electras and Phaedras.

When King Farouk of Egypt is driven from his throne we feel only the poetic justice that a wicked and dissolute wastrel has at last been humbled, a sense of relief and restoration of faith rather than any tragic exultation. But when Sherman Adams, a man like ourselves, neither wholly good nor wholly bad, an image of rectitude concealing a tragic shortcoming, is toppled from his high seat of power, we have true Aristotelian tragedy, and can feel pity and a kind of terror. When the people of Athens got bored with hearing the statesman Aristides called "the Just" and sentenced him to banishment, it was not simply spite and envy of an upright man. It was the same tragic sense they had of Pentheus and Hippolytus, and we of Adams, that too great a display of perfection challenges the gods, that pride goeth before a fall.

We return then, finally, to the mysterious satisfaction of tragedy, the question Saint Augustine raised so many centuries ago. For Aristotle, as we have seen, it lay in catharsis, the arousing and purging of pity and terror. For Hegel it was a sheer intellectual pleasure in the unfolding of the dialectic. Some, like Lucretius, have argued cynically that it is no more than a kind of sadistic pleasure we take in the sufferings of others. Schopenhauer believed with ultimate pessimism that the hero of tragedy atones for "the crime of existence itself." In Freud's view, the satisfaction of tragedy is that the lower impulses he calls Id find symbolic gratification in the hero's misdeeds, while the higher part of the personality he calls Superego finds *its* symbolic gratification in seeing the hero punished—and through him, the personality's own Id. Other psychological theory has talked similarly of our "empathy" or "projection" onto the protagonist's crime and punishment.

Kenneth Burke, in The Philosophy of Literary Form, has defined all art as the arousing and fulfilling of expectations. If we accept that basic conception of form, tragedy must always have a kind of inevitability. The Elizabethans seem sometimes to have conceived of it as merely a story that ended in death. There is similarly a tendency in our own time to see it as merely a sad ending, and perhaps to complain that there is so much misery in real life that art should be cheerful.

Not everything ending unhappily, however, is tragedy; it must satisfy the expectations it has aroused. An example of a work that sets out deliberately to violate these expectations is a remarkable French movie of a few years back called Forbidden Games. The audience is led to believe, by all sorts of suggestions, that the rustic Romeo-and-Juliet youths of two feuding families will marry, reconcile the families and bring happiness to a homeless child. The young people in fact do not marry, the families are not reconciled, and the child returns to misery. The audience is left at the end horribly wrenched and moved, but feeling only a terrible pathos, none of the inevitability, rightness and grandeur of tragedy.

The awful deaths of children in the news are pathetic in this fashion rather than tragic. The grisly kidnaping and murder of the Lindbergh baby bore no relationship to anything the poor infant had done, nor was the horrible Chicago parochial-school fire a moral judgment of any sort. These frightful accidents move us deeply, even to tears, but they are essentially meaningless and ugly, where tragic death is meaningful and even beautiful.

The best explanation I know of the nature of tragedy is Herbert Weisinger's Tragedy and the Paradox of the Fortunate Fall, a book to which my own understanding of the subject is considerably indebted. Weisinger insists that "the tragic protagonist must be made to achieve victory at the moment of his deepest despair." Tragedy, he reminds us, is "man's most vehement protest against meaninglessness"; it gives us "the sense of assurance, achieved through suffering, of rational order"; it proclaims that "man is free, but he is free within the limits set for us by his condition as man."

It is in terms of some such affirmations as these, I think, that the tragic vision is ultimately so rewarding. If it teaches us human limitation, it also teaches us human possibility. Hobbes reminds us that the life of man has been characteristically "solitary, poor, nasty, brutish, and short." Tragedy answers that it has frequently been all of that, but that it is never ludicrous or meaningless. How far this tragic vision of man is, despite its recognition of all the outer degradation and the inner evil, from views of man in some contemporary literature as "Angry" or "Beat." Tragedy reaffirms a nobility and grandeur in the human condition, even Longinus' sublimity. If it is man's fate to go down inevitably into suffering and death, some exultation nevertheless rises to the skies. Man may be crushed, but the human spirit is forever indestructible.

Further reading:

Hyman, Stanley Edgar: THE ARMED VISION. New York: Vintage Books, Inc.; 1955.

Hyman, Stanley Edgar (ed.): THE CRITICAL PERFORMANCE. New York: Vintage Books, Inc.; 1956.

Murray, Gilbert: THE CLASSICAL TRADITION IN POETRY. New York: Vintage Books, Inc.; 1957.

Burke, Kenneth: THE PHILOSOPHY OF LITERARY FORM. New York: Vintage Books, Inc.; 1957.

Fergusson, Francis: THE IDEA OF A THEATER. New York: Doubleday & Company, Inc. (Anchor); 1953.

Weisinger, Herbert: TRAGEDY AND THE PARADOX OF THE FORTUNATE FALL. East Lansing: Michigan State University Press; 1953.

J. D. WILLIAMS

[*Photograph by Sid Avery*]

John D. Williams is head of the mathematics division of the RAND Corporation, a private, nonprofit, government-supported research institution which studies space-age defense problems for the Air Force. Former astronomer and pool shark, wartime worker in the Office of Scientific Research and Development and currently a ranking administrator of RAND's many-faceted attacks on national problems, Mr. Williams sometimes likes to cross the security lines to ponder the common man's dilemma. THE SMALL WORLD *is such an excursion. Mr. Williams's book on the theory of games of strategy,* The Compleat Strategyst, *tells you how to win almost anything.*

The Small World

BY

J. D. WILLIAMS

The legend of the boy who cried "Wolf!" is used to teach our young that the fate of the liar is hard. It seems to me that the men of the community come off too well in this story of the foolish prank which turned to tragedy. For there really was a wolf and the boy gave clear warning. The men ignored the warning and lost their sheep—no trivial event in a community close to hunger.

I am about to point out some facts which form a modern equivalent of the wolf. These facts are not obvious, so I may be accused of crying "Wolf!"; but they form a sufficiently appalling apparition once you get them in focus. I am willing to associate myself with one of history's least successful pranksters in order to challenge the reader to avoid, if he can, imitating some of history's most futile men.

The problems of our age are massive. The Communist movement intensifies some of them, but the problems would exist even if the Communists did not. Thus our concern about Sputnik was somewhat shallow—as well as temporary—as we have had better cause than Sputnik to be deeply concerned for some time. If we do not become and remain deeply concerned, it appears that our history book is about finished. And it is a very short book.

Many of us are now old enough to sense that the life-span

343

of a man is short. When we were children the year seemed interminable, and even the month and the week were long. Now we look on the years which separate us from childhood as a brief period. Yet, if we are older than about thirty-six, we probably have lived the major portion of our lives—a fact difficult to grasp. If we grasp it well enough to wish we could lengthen the Biblical three-score and ten a little, then this becomes a unit of time with personal meaning. We will call seventy years the "life-span" and use it, and other units relevant to the biology of man, as tools with which to probe history.

We first observe that the recorded history of man almost vanishes if we look back only 100 life-spans. Most of what we know has been learned since the great days of Athens, which was not long ago. You could receive a message from Plato through the mouths of thirty-three men. For Jesus, twenty-eight men would do, and for Mohammed, nineteen. Even these somewhat startling calculations do not reflect adequately the explosive development of civilization and knowledge. You could get word from Gutenberg through a chain of eight men, and of Newton through four. About three life-spans ago the steam engine and two life-spans ago the modern lathe, keys to the industrial revolution, came into our hands, and the internal-combustion engine came one life-span ago. The rate of development during our lives has become fantastic, though we adapt to it easily; it took us about a couple of months to become blasé about man-made satellites. Thus most of what man knows and has accomplished is incredibly recent. We are living quite literally in the presence of an explosion of knowledge.

We are also living in the presence of a biological explosion, of which we see some evidence in our suburbs. To discuss its history involves some guesswork. Thoughtful guessers believe there were relatively few men on earth 100 life-spans ago, since there was little social organization or agriculture—enough, perhaps, to populate one of our large cities. Starting with, say, a population of 10,000,000 then, we could arrive at the number presently on earth by doubling the population approximately eight times, with such a doubling taking place every dozen life-spans. But it did not happen that way. The first doubling

344

point may have taken thirty to fifty life-spans, while the recent doubling points have occurred closer and closer together. For instance, the sixth and seventh doubling points were only two life-spans apart. The eighth doubling point was reached in one life-span. The world population at this moment is exploding at the rate of about two and one half times per life-span—and the rate is still increasing.

In the United States the native population is increasing at the rate of threefold per life-span, thanks to a medium birth rate and a low death rate. When immigration is included, our rate of population increase has been fourfold for some time— more than sixteenfold in two life-spans. Most of the ethnic groups in the world have birth rates which would result in fourfold to sevenfold increases if their death rates were reduced substantially. Such a reduction can be quickly accomplished; for example, Ceylon's death rate was cut almost in half in seven years simply through the use of DDT, and its population is now growing at the rate of fivefold per life-span. The natural limit of the explosion rate is supposed to be about sevenfold per life-span, when not substantially affected by things like food shortages, pestilence and social taboos—a rate realizable, for instance, when each woman bears four children (two daughters) by age twenty-five. Such a sevenfold rate, had it existed, could have produced our present world population from an Adam and Eve created less than 800 years ago—eleven men could span the period.

If our estimates had dealt only with people who have lived to be adults, the explosion rates would be increased—and it would be evident that the adults now alive constitute a noticeable fraction of all who have ever lived on this earth. Even so, we should look on ourselves as the forerunners of mankind, for the great masses of men are just now arriving. And they really are arriving—the net increase in humanity during the nine-month gestation period which ended today would populate the cities of New York, Chicago and Philadelphia, plus Los Angeles, Detroit and Baltimore, plus Cleveland, Saint Louis and Washington, plus Boston, San Francisco and Pittsburgh, plus Milwaukee, Houston and Buffalo, plus at least any other American city you choose. Such a mob is large enough, literally, to join hands around the earth. It is also a notably hungry, brutal and powerful mob—and it is likely to become more so as its numbers increase.

It is, of course, physically impossible for the population explosion to continue at this rate much longer. Either the births will be reduced or the dying will be expedited or both. The alternatives available are few and are not easy and pleasant. For instance, births may or may not be reduced by birth control—a practice difficult to establish and enforce. Furthermore, if the practice were widespread, the societies which did not conform might gain an advantage. On the other hand, the dying may or may not be increased by natural disasters and pestilence; but these events are rare and becoming rarer. War is becoming an increasingly efficient killer; it may solve the population problem, but we hope it doesn't.

If these factors don't stop population growth, famine will. For note that in less than a dozen life-spans—perhaps in as few as six—there would be 50,000 men for each one now alive if the present rate continues. There would then be one square yard of land—including the mountains, deserts and icecaps—for each person. If a citizen of that crowded world were lucky enough to have an arable piece of land, he might grow enough food in a year to sustain his body for an hour or so. If he wished to live, he would have to take title to an acre, which would involve eliminating about 5000 of his neighbors.

The present level of attainments of the men of the planet are remarkably varied. Some groups have barely managed to domesticate the dog, while others have developed the theory of relativity. Man is, however, remarkably nimble in this respect. It is perfectly feasible for a somewhat primitive group to advance as much during one life-span as the more advanced did in ten, because it is not necessary for the primitive group—or individual —to repeat the steps of those who preceded them. For instance, every child is now handed the powerful, modern symbolism of arithmetic, which took millennia to develop—a handful of life-spans ago, only superior minds could cope with problems of long division because of poor symbolism. Similarly a group which now wishes to develop electronic capabilities can exploit recent developments in solid-state physics, bypassing the intricate—and obsolescent—vacuum-tube technology. In fact, there are several large population groups which now have the vitality to surge beyond the United States in technological achievement during the next life-span, and they will almost certainly do so if we are content to enjoy the *status quo*.

The men of our planet are remarkably fierce. The head-hunters still outnumber the astronomers. Even the advanced and powerful nations have within our life-span demonstrated a capacity for cruelty and horror equal to any in history. This is not astonishing if you keep in mind that recorded history could be spanned by a chain of men you could accommodate for cocktails. At such a party, witnesses to the fate of Carthage, to Herod's massacre of babies and to the Inquisition could trade anecdotes, without shock, with guests familiar with the German gas chambers, the Russian slave camps and the cruelties of the Japanese during their conquests. In our own quiet society, perhaps one in each hundred able-bodied adult males is a policeman. It is an unpleasant fact that the hoodlum does not differ much from the norm among men—in manners, morals, values and goals. In view of this, if some new group captures world leadership, it may well obliterate us in the process. The quality of mercy is apparently an acquired taste.

Educated men have long known the earth to be round. Eratosthenes, some thirty-two life-spans ago, knew how to calculate its size and did so quite accurately. Despite this, most men have believed it to be flat—and this view would probably win today in an earth-wide plebiscite. The flat-earthers have not been troubled by their misconception because for practical purposes the earth has been flat. Men have generally lived and died in a small number of fixed groups in fixed places. Their principal contact with the rest of the world has been with the few groups in their immediate neighborhood. Such an existence can be carried on just as well on a flat earth as on any other kind.

As technical capabilities developed, some groups were able to extend their activity to such distances that the global properties of the earth became noticeable, though still not important.

Genghis Khan extended man's reach mightily eleven life-spans ago when his ponies carried the horde more than a quarter of the way round the earth. The time for conquest then was often measured in years. For the last six life-spans seafaring nations have sent war parties almost everywhere, exploring a largely empty world. The time for conquest was then measured in months. With the steam engine, the week became important. Within our life-span the airplane further shrank the time for conquest. The day became a significant unit and the fact that our world is a globe became important. We had little time to adjust to this situation before the time scale shrank closer to its ultimate limit—now. The global properties of the earth suddenly are profoundly important.

Since we found the "life-span" useful in discussing long periods, let us try the "breath of life" as a unit for short ones. From now until doomsday—which can be tomorrow—no man will ever be sure that he can breathe 1000 times before he dies by homicide. This statement could be false in a world with one government.

Now, a thousand breaths is less than an hour of living—and this applies only if one's destruction is set in train by the most distant man on earth, for it corresponds approximately to the flight time of a ballistic missile for a range of 12,500 miles. It would be more difficult to build one which would take longer because it would have to fly higher—so we should not expect an extension of the 1000 breaths. It would also be more difficult to build a quicker weapon because it would have to be sophisticated enough to avoid leaving the earth forever; but this one will, of course, be built.

If man survives long enough to develop weapons such as, say, lethal rays, which do not require the transport of mass, he may eventually manage to get himself killed from afar in a truly breathless fashion—in perhaps a hundredth of a breath. However, the 1000-breath weapon is as far as we have gone at present; and if we learn how to live with this weapon, we may have solved the problem of living with still more advanced ones. If we fail, we can leave the latter to some other race—of men?

Perhaps the most significant facts of life on a globe, in

contrast to life on a limitless flat world, stem from the circumstances that its surface is limited and danger may come from any quarter. On earth this peril is intensified by the smallness of the globe. The danger is swift. It is difficult to grasp this. To picture the situation more clearly, let us consider an analogy.

The earth is now equivalent, in important respects, to a partly flooded cellar—because of irregularities, one quarter of the floor is dry, but not necessarily habitable. If the cellar is twenty-five feet on each side, a calculation shows that the American enjoys the use of a six-by-two-foot plot on one of the dry areas—comfortable to live on, large enough to be buried on and with no wall to guard his back.

The American is one of sixteen occupants of the cellar. All are armed; most have knives, though several have hand grenades, and the rest would like to have them. The American's companions are a very mixed lot. He doesn't know them very well, and it isn't certain that a better acquaintance would make him fond of them. Actually he is scarcely aware of them. He has about half the food and other goodies which exist in the cellar and he has eyes mostly for these. His behavior is explainable but nonetheless idiotic. This attitude is based in part on his belief in the reality of geographic isolation—an illusion fostered by a life-span or two of good fortune in this matter. This sense of dissociation is fortified by the American's conditioning—almost every day of his life has been spent in an apparently benign world containing no visible threats, and he is confident that this will be true tomorrow. Though he does not realize it, his geographic isolation, after a term as a qualified fact, has vanished. This is not a matter of opinion or something his congressman might fix.

The other men in the cellar have less to occupy their attention. Five of them have the bulk of the remaining half of the goods, and the remaining ten are incredibly poor and hungry. The most popular activity in the cellar is the work of a club, now numbering some six or seven full members, which is dedicated to taking over the cellar. Unfortunately the elimination of the American is a major objective of the club, and members are required to forswear the rules of fair play.

The American knows about the club. It has spurred him

into a mild clublike activity of his own. His organization is a less formal, part-time affair, involving a few of his more affluent companions. It is the inverse of the other club. The American's club is not ambitious; it does not seek to undo the past successes of its rival. It seeks to maintain the *status quo*. This is obviously difficult, because it always requires the invention, instantaneously, of an inverse operation which will nullify any particular freely chosen move of the other club. Our man's mores, incidentally, stem from the sense of fair play, a fact which places constraints on his inventions.

The people of the earth in general, and of the United States in particular, are not aware that their world can be viewed as a twenty-five-foot cellar. They take it for granted that they are living on a flat earth of indefinite extent. It is difficult to see what, short of a cataclysm, will make them aware of the circumscription of their world. Mere availability of information seems to have little effect. If fact does not agree with personal experience, we tend to treat it as fiction.

The prospect at home is more pleasant than the larger view. We do have difficult and grave problems. Indeed, we may founder on them. But we also have many assets which, properly enough, we tend to enjoy. The hazards to life, liberty and property in this country are relatively low. Our society is rich in choices for the individual. It is also rich in its physical environment. It is remarkably rich in its organization of men and machines for the creation of various forms of wealth. This last, a vast and intricate system, has developed spontaneously and most of the time operates automatically. This is fortunate, for it is not clear that we understand the system well enough to fix it or to run it consciously. Since there is no guaranty, however, that it will continue to run well indefinitely, we persist in our efforts to understand it. Our economists feel they have important clues.

Many discoveries may rank with—or outrank—the steam engine and the lathe as key elements in the story of human technological development. Synthetic materials may have this importance. The nuclear chain reaction certainly does. Thanks to the confluence of the explosion of knowledge with our advanced technical position and our wealth, we are in a position to develop and exploit many of these keys. Unfortunately we cannot do so indefinitely without regard for the consequences. The nuclear chain reaction in a world of political anarchy will always be the textbook example. Another example is the case of the general-purpose antibiotics in the presence of a biological explosion. On the other hand, some developments will be essential. For example, it is time to stop talking about the weather and, instead, attend to it. Recent evidence suggests that the next ice age may be about to close in.

Another recent technological development of great significance is the feedback loop—the servomechanism—built largely of cheap, reliable electronic parts. This device permits a machine to engage in a limited way in self-criticism, to examine its own work and to make small improvements in its output. Significantly, machines may now become sophisticated at a moderate increase in cost. As a consequence it is now feasible to design machines, for example, to do some tasks which are repeated only ten thousand times, rather than tasks which are repeated millions of times.

We had scarcely begun to exploit the improved feedback loop when the electronic computer appeared. This new machine already reaches speeds of thousands of operations per second with high reliability and can carry within its memory the instructions needed for an almost endlessly long and complex sequence of operations. This computer can be used to control the behavior of another machine. Now, rather than use a costly special-purpose machine to perform some phase of a manufacturing process, we can use a more versatile machine, controlled by a computer, to perform more of it. And, by changing the instructions in the computer, we can use the same machine to make a different product. Elaborate as well as simple operations can be performed, and the machine can be used for quite short production runs. It can even construct prototypes. Thus the impetus toward mechanization has increased tremendously, presenting another complex and challenging set of problems with tantalizing potentialities.

The concept of an economic paradise-on-earth may be no

idle dream. It is possible that we could reach a stage where any given set of goods within our resources, from food to H-bombs, could be created with ease. The productive effort might involve a fraction of our labor force, or we might have our entire labor force work for a fraction of the time. But there are difficulties on both paths.

In order to operate with a fractional labor force, for instance, we must discover how to provide goods for those who do not toil. To employ the fractional-time labor force, on the other hand, we must as a people achieve a new level of intellectual competence; for the balance between manual and intellectual workers in a predominantly automated economy would doubtless be very different from the present balance. Yet we have recently placed most of our school system in the hands of people preoccupied with physical culture, togetherness and intellectually trivial curricula.

I have mentioned only the technical and economic feasibility of automation, from which one would infer that an explosive development is at hand. But any such development will undoubtedly encounter massive inertia from the vested interests of labor and capital—a resistance which will appreciably retard the process. It may, in fact, seem desirable to proceed slowly, to reduce the pains of adaptation. But this course also has its peculiar dangers. For example, more primitive populations, less cumbered by vested interests, may let the explosion run free and soon outdistance us technologically. That this would drive us out of the world's markets could be the least serious effect. It could also alienate those peoples who now think it well to stand with us because we are technologically strong. Almost certainly a technologically superior foe would sooner or later overwhelm us.

I have refrained from calling automation the final stage of this explosion. You see, the theory of machines which can reproduce themselves is already partially in hand—as well as machines which can themselves evolve new kinds of machines.

This brief survey of certain striking features of our times emphasizes the fact that we have a lot of thinking to do and not much time for it. Clearly, on both a global and national scale, we must make important, difficult and sometimes unpalatable decisions. We will be wise to make them deliberately while there are real alternatives, rather than make them by default when there are none. The prospects for just bumbling through are poor. Rome looked good to the ancient world for about ten life-spans, but, as we have seen, the pace of life has quickened frighteningly since then. Vitally significant changes can now occur in a tenth of a life-span. For instance, the United States was, between one and two tenths of a life-span ago, the most powerful nation in history, both absolutely and relatively. Today its relative power has so diminished that we do not know to what extent it can control its own future—and this despite our conscious desire not to bumble, despite our effort toward specific technical improvements in our strength and posture, despite our day-to-day amelioration of international crises.

This deterioration does not necessarily reflect on the magnitude and quality of our efforts, just as a patient's illness or death need not reflect on the doctor's efforts. The analogy between individuals and civilizations is uncomfortable, for their last battles have never been won. The patient always dies; the doctor may fight a brilliant delaying action and provide some comfort, but he never wins the last battle. Of course, we may be imputing to these defeats of individuals and civilizations an immutable characteristic which does not actually exist—that they must die. We can only prove that they tend toward death. But conceivably neither need die. Conceivably there may exist ways of controlling our environment and our capacities· of adaptation which would permit both individuals and civilizations to survive indefinitely.

At present the doctors of civilization seem too relaxed, too cheerful. Are they simply ignorant? Or are they already using drugs to make the end easier for us? One senses a euphoria in the social atmosphere scarcely compatible with the problems before us.

I doubt that the efforts now devoted to the major problems of civilization are either adequate or sensible.

NANCY HALE

Nancy Hale, novelist and short-story writer, is probably best known as the author of The Prodigal Women. Born and educated in Boston, she later served on the editorial staffs of Vogue and the old Vanity Fair and as a reporter on The New York Times. Miss Hale, who published her first novel, The Young Die Good, at the age of twenty-four, is married to Fredson Bowers, professor of English at the University of Virginia. Her most recent books are Dear Beast, a novel which appeared in 1959, and The Pattern of Perfection, a collection of short stories issued in 1960. THE TWO-WAY IMAGINATION originally appeared in The Saturday Evening Post as THE MAGIC OF CREATIVITY.

The Two-Way Imagination

BY

NANCY HALE

Years ago, when I was a young writer, I was planning a novel about the Paris of the '90's, where my father had been an art student. He used to tell me tales of his adventures there, and now they seemed to be taking a shape in my mind. But I had never been to Paris, and I asked my editor, Maxwell Perkins of Scribner's, if he would send me some books about the place and the period, so that I could bone up on it. He wrote back, sending me a couple of books, but urging me not to do too much reading. He warned me of the dangers of research to fiction. "You don't want to know too much about it," he said. "You want to make it up out of your head." He was quite right. The dead hand of research lies heavy on too many novels. The part most alive in them comes out of imagination.

But a few years after Perkins said that to me, while I was still young and foolish, I was foolish enough to say at a party, to a theologian and a sociologist, that my editor had told me not to know too much about what I was writing of. I'll never forget the looks on the faces of the sociologist and the clergyman. Having spent their entire lives trying to know as much as possible about what they were writing of, the clergyman looked at me as if I had blasphemed the Holy Ghost and the sociologist looked even more shocked. Yet both of them knew that I was a writer of fiction. And that is what fiction is: fiction, not fact.

I often encounter similarly reproachful looks, as though of betrayal, in the faces of friends who have had to realize that something they have read of mine was not true, never happened. A nice woman in the town where I live admired a story of mine which is written in the first person and called *The Empress's Ring*. But one day I told her that I had never, in real life, possessed a ring that belonged to an empress; and that the ring I did own never got lost, as the one in the story did. She has never felt quite the same about me since. Yet actually she had fair warning that the story was imaginary. It was labeled fiction in the book's blurb.

Maybe we are up against one of those things which today it is fashionable to call a dichotomy. On the one hand, society—the reader, that is to say—is continually being puzzled, upset and betrayed by what the fiction writers dream up. But at the same time, society expects fiction to persuade it into the willing—or even unwilling, the inadvertent—suspension of disbelief. The reader *wants* to believe in the novel, or else he wants his money back. He wants to identify with the characters. He wants to live in the pages of the novel. It is only when he closes its covers at the end that he is not resigned to the realization that none of it was true. He's like those radio soap-opera fans who used to send real wedding presents—and later real baby clothes when their favorite heroine is expecting a blessed radio event. He is like the little boy who wakes up from dreaming that his pockets were full of gold and, full of anticipation, hurries to the chair where he hung his pants the night before.

Imagination is a kind of blind spot in the average, nonwriting member of society. Because, of course, everybody has imagination. If you have the thought, "Everyone hates me"; or if you consider it a good idea to see what is the matter with the light fuse by poking your finger into the socket; or if you suppose that you can sail a boat because you have seen other people do it; or if you conclude that a friend has turned against you, when in fact her brusqueness was the result of not thinking about you at all; those are all examples of an undisciplined imagination. It is obvious how dangerous such imaginings can be.

Malicious gossip—which takes the place of creation in noncreative lives—of course draws heavily on the imagination. Fear and superstition have their roots in imagination. The fact is that imagination is antisocial in that it is not in any relation at all to everyday reality. Then what is imagination in relation to?

Probably because of such destructive phantasies as those I listed, imagination hasn't a terribly good reputation in our society. Of course, to say that so-and-so is lacking in imagination is understood as not a compliment. But if I call someone a dreamer; or remark that someone has a head full of fancies; or say to someone, "That's all your imagination"—those are not compliments either. It might be objected that such disparagements only apply to those who might be called the amateur dreamers; that a novelist, for instance, is expected to have a highly active imagination. Yet to say "She certainly has a *lively* imagination" isn't praise either. That old phrase "Nothing but imagination," is one of the commonest, one of the most damning, in use today. I would point out, however, that even the greatest novels are "nothing but" paper, ink, a certain amount of miscellaneous misinformation, and imagination.

The space age opening before our eyes is "nothing but" the end result, scientifically supported, worked out with infinite toil, of man's first mad, unreasonable image of himself flying. When it was first entertained, a good while before Daedalus, that image was about as adapted to reality as if I were to feel the urge to lie, like Ariel, in a cowslip's bell. Yet today we do fly. Science fiction once prophesied, in its apparently wild flights of fancy, many of the aerial feats that have come to pass. Are these the only phantasies which are allowed to come to pass? May not what science fiction calls teleportation also come to pass, along with the contents of that bottle in *Alice in Wonderland* marked DRINK ME, and may it not be possible for some woman in the future to become tiny and find herself curled inside that golden cup?

The principle embodied here is that what man can imagine he may one day achieve. We know the part that mathematics, physics, chemistry and mechanics play in such miracles. We know the role on the plane of human character that persistence, courage, dauntlessness and what is sometimes called cussedness play. Yet there is in addition, I believe, a third element in what makes possible the transformation of dreams into realities, in what turns man's stark-naked fancy into an entity irreproachably clothed: a fact. Perhaps we might look into how imagination works, to find what this element may be.

When man faces something knowable and real, whether it is an object, a dilemma or a historical event, he directs toward it the battery of his functions of knowing—sensation, which tells him something is there; thought, which reasons what it can be; feeling, which tells him what it means to him; and intuition, which sporadically informs him of the why, the whence and the whither of the object. These four functions go to produce a total judgment, as far as the man is able to utilize them. It is when he is faced with the unknown that man's imagination springs to the fore, like a fountain gushing up out of a rock. It presents him, not with information about the unknown as it really is, but with an image of what the unknown is *like*. Nobody, for instance, knows what imagination itself really is. But it is like a fountain gushing up out of the rock.

In a sense, then, the workings of imagination can be said to be the facing *of* the unknown *by* the unknown. Man cannot endure not knowing about things; he can endure it even less than knowing about them, which can be quite unendurable too. So, out of ignorance, up springs fancy with its pictures. Sometimes, as we have seen, making her private image of what she doesn't know can lead a lady to put her finger in a fuse socket, with results we may mournfully deduce. Or imagination can make a breach between friends, founded on nothing more malign than a moment's brusqueness. Or imagination can lead to the creation of the flying machine. Or to *War and Peace*—the novel, as well as the states of affairs; for, as John Knowles says in his novel, *A Separate Peace*, wars are made by something ignorant in the human heart. In any of these cases, original motive power was supplied, not by altruism, knowledge or virtue, but by fancy, idle or employed.

We might make, of the faculty of imagination in its relation to the *real* world, an image of the blind spot in the eye. Opposite to where the sightless optic nerve empties into the retina there is in the scenery a tiny blank area which is normally compensated for by the other eye. Some percentage of motor accidents is said to be caused by the blind spot. At such times, the other eye did not sufficiently hasten to explain that little unseen area, in terms of what, in all reason, it had to be.

Not in this way, but in something *like* this way, imagination attempts to explain to man what he doesn't know in terms of other things that he does know. "Like" is the key word. *Like a poultice comes silence*, writes Oliver Wendell Holmes, maybe because he was a doctor. *Like an eagle caged I pine*, writes Epes Sargent when he's feeling landlocked and forlorn ashore. *Forlorn —the very word is like a bell*. But Keats, a much better poet, seldom used the actual word "like." As Archibald MacLeish has pointed out, A poem should not mean but be. In other words, *like* the flying machine, the poem is an imagining that has completed itself, that has come true. In some way, while facing the unknown with the unknown, the mind of the imaginer has contrived to arrange, before its spot of blindness, a compensation which truly fits—which does not *mean*, but turns out *to be*. Only one person makes this image of the hitherto unknown; but other people—society, if you like—read the poem and, certainly in the case of Keats's image, society recognizes it as true. James Russell Lowell says that the story of any one man's real experience finds its startling parallel in every one of us.

Now, "universal" is one of those words people turn to when they can't explain why a piece of writing should be so good. I would prefer not to use it. But how are we to explain the affinity between Keats and a host of conventional readers who are nothing like unconventional Keats? How is it that on some level Keats and his readers become, not the artist versus society, but the artist and society?

Not only in the arts is the unseeing used to face the unseen and, by means of images, discern truth. In the field of chemistry, for instance, a long account by the nineteenth-century German chemist Kekulé describes his coming upon his famous benzine theory. "I was sitting engaged in writing my textbook," he writes, "but it wasn't going very well. I . . . sank into a doze. . . . Atoms flitted before my eyes" (as they had before, when "I saw that frequently two smaller atoms were coupled together, that larger ones seized the two smaller ones, and that all whirled around in a bewildering dance."). "Smaller groups now kept modestly in the background. My mind's eye, sharpened by repeated visions of a similar sort, now distinguished larger structures of varying forms. Long rows close together, all in movement, winding and turning like serpents! And see! What was that? One of the serpents seized its own tail, and the form whirled mockingly before my eyes. I came awake like a flash of lightning. I spent the night working out the consequences of the hypothesis. . . . If we learn to dream, gentlemen, then we shall, perhaps, find the truth. We must take care, however," the scientist adds, "not to publish our dreams before submitting them to proof by the waking mind." The point to note is that what turned out to fill the missing need, the unseen area, in the benzine theory was not anything primarily pertinent to chemistry, but a particularly subjective image.

Again, Anatole France, in one of his stories about historical church figures, tells of the Abbé Oegger, who was a dreamer much given to worrying, particularly about Judas. It worried the abbé incessantly that Judas—so the teachings of the Church declared—was condemned to eternal punishment. The abbé felt that Judas actually was doing God's work, that his betrayal of Christ was essential in enabling Christ to complete his work of redemption of mankind. For if it had not been for Judas's act, Christ could not have been crucified; hence, resurrected either. Therefore, Oegger felt, a merciful God could not possibly have damned Judas. But the abbé was tortured by doubts. One night he went into the church and prayed to God to send him a sign. Thereupon he felt a heavenly touch on his shoulder. Next day he went to the archbishop and told him he had made up his mind to go out into the world to preach the gospel of

God's infinite forgiveness toward sinners. Not long after going out into the world, Oegger left the Catholic Church and continued his preaching within the fold of Swedenborgianism.

The Swiss psychologist and psychiatrist, C. G. Jung, commenting on this account, points out an interesting angle to Oegger's obsession with the problem of Judas: "When he becomes a Swedenborgian, we can now understand his Judas phantasy. Oegger was himself the Judas who betrayed his Lord. Therefore he had first to assure himself of God's mercy, in order to play the role of Judas undisturbed. For him, Judas was the symbol of his own unconscious intention; and he made use of the symbol in order to reflect upon his own situation—the direct realization would have been too painful for him." By the analogy we have been using, we might say that Oegger was using an outside unknown to solve an inside blind spot; since at the time of his absorption with Judas, Oegger was quite blind to the plan that was forming itself deep in him. His worries about the archtraitor of Christendom fitted his own unacceptable intention. There was a sort of likeness between a part of him and Judas.

I have said I believe that there is an element in the transformation of dreams into realities, quite apart from scientific verification of hypotheses, and the application of elbow grease. This element is demonstrated in the two examples I just cited, where the solution to the problems involved was provided, not by conscious functioning, but by imagination itself. Not Kekulé's scientific knowledge—profound as that needed to be —but his drowsy fancy supplied the missing link in the benzine theory. It was not Oegger's reasoning about the morality of an intention he didn't even know he had that enabled him to prepare the ground for his defection from Catholicism. Instead, a long period of worrying about the fate of Judas culminated in a conviction that mercy would be shown a defector.

That element in imagination which leads out of dreamland into the world of facts, actions and reality is, I believe, its peculiar two-way functioning. Things that are unknown and terrible in the outside world are *like* known things in man's inner world. Conversely, unknown and terrible inner things can be compared to things that are visible abroad. The ocean, for example—in its violence, turbulence, immensity, calm and grandeur —is like an element that exists within man's mind. On this inner ocean he often feels himself to be sailing; or from the ocean, stepping ashore onto some desert island. Or he is being shipwrecked on it or stranded in a Sargasso Sea. Since man did, in a preliminary manifestation, crawl out of the ocean and is still composed largely of sea water, it is at least conceivable to think of him as bearing the sea within him, as a conch shell does. It would be hard to say which, then, comes first for man when he imagines—the outside or the inside sea.

Likewise, it may readily be seen that one of these two oceans has to be an image of the other. One is the reality; the other is the symbol. But which is which? It is easy to say that the outside sea is the real one. But when a woman is so abnormally fearful of the ocean that she won't go on it, even in fair weather with a light breeze; or if she looks into its green and wavering depths with horror and has no trust in a quite seaworthy vessel, isn't she making of the outside ocean merely an image of the kind of ocean she has inside her? The fact is that it is characteristic of imagination to move from the outer to the inner, and from the inner back to the outer, in a wavelike motion. In the world of the imagination, correspondences exist to everything. "My heart is like a singing bird." "A drowsy numbness pains my sense as though of hemlock I had drunk." "My Luve is like a red, red rose."

In the world of outer reality, of course, everything is unique. Each snowflake in a blizzard is a little different from every other snowflake. A poem, created by comparing things to other things, is, once out in the world, unique. As a completed poem, it "should not mean but be." A jet plane—the end result of some poor wretch in antiquity looking up at the sky with the feeling that part of him was like a bird and could fly—is not really like a bird. It is like nothing but a jet plane. Man still tends to feel that there is something in him like a bird. But now he sees that this isn't a plane at all. The feeling is still in him, unsatisfied by his ability to reach Paris in six and a half hours. One quality of the real world, in fact, would seem to be uniqueness.

The Two-Way Imagination

We can say that when a dream has been transformed into a reality, when a poem is successful, it is not like any other real thing. In the outside world it is only when a creation is unsuccessful, incomplete—as in the case of a derivative painting or when a person is living somebody else's life—that things are like other things.

It is in the world of the imagination that things are incomplete, identifiable only by being compared to other things. The comparison helps them to become complete and real. *My luve,* Burns says, *is like a red, red rose.* Does he mean a girl, when he says his love, or does he mean the love he has for the girl? Does he mean a rose in the garden or the rose his heart feels like? What does it matter? He has the world with him. Everybody knows how a rose feels and how a girl smells. Everybody knows how a feeling blooms and how red sings. Rose, girl, love and red make up a completed line of poetry that is not like any other.

This article might have been subtitled, "The Role of Society in the Writer." The reason I didn't call it that was that I felt sure, sooner or later, it would be misunderstood as what I don't want to write about and am not writing about—the role of the writer in society. Society, meaning the agglomeration of people standing for the social *status quo,* plays a symbolic part as large as any ocean in the writer—particularly in the novelist. Frank O'Connor has, in fact, defined the subject of any novel as almost invariably the relation of the individual to society. Since the novel is a work of the imagination, however, not only its characters are imaginary, but also the society to which they are set in relation. Sometimes the society in books is very imaginary indeed, like the various societies in *Gulliver's Travels,* or like the small, furry, talking animals that constitute the good society in Kenneth Grahame's *The Wind in the Willows.* Sometimes it is less imaginary, like Thackeray's heartless society in *Vanity Fair,* or Dickens's sadistic society in *Bleak House.* Or like Jane Austen's decorous society, for a society set in the England of the early nineteenth century which never converses on the burning topic of the Napoleonic Wars is imaginary indeed. Jane Austen's notably talkative characters never even refer to them. Society, as a matter of fact, is the real hero of Jane Austen's novels.

But times have changed. I can't imagine a novelist today who would make a hero out of society—although early nineteenth-century English society wasn't precisely Utopian either. Jack Kerouac is one of the modern novelists whose images of the social *status quo* seem "terrifying and like villainous." In *The Dharma Bums* there is a passage in which Rosie, who had once been "a real gone chick and friend of everyone of consequence," goes crazy and tries to cut her wrists. She insists there is going to be a big revolution of police. "The police are going to swoop down and arrest us all, and . . . we're going to be questioned for weeks . . . and maybe years, till they find out all the sins and crimes that have been committed, it's a network, it runs in every direction, finally they'll arrest everyone in North Beach and even Greenwich Village and then Paris, and then finally they'll have *everybody* in jail. . . . They're going to destroy you. I can see it . . . it's only begun. . . . Oh, the world will never be the same!"

Although this is said by a disturbed character, her speech is given a vital importance in the novel, motivating the protagonist, Ray, to leave town and hit the road once more. " 'Isn't this the time to start following what I know to be true?' " he asks himself. "I said good-by to Japhy and the others and hopped my freight back down the Coast to L.A. Poor Rosie, she had been absolutely *certain* that the world was real, and fear was real; and now what was real?" Kerouac here imagines the forces of society as punitive and disciplinary, symbolized by berserk police. On the other hand, it is important to note that an equally modern and rebellious novelist, Paul Bowles, can rail at today's society in exactly opposite terms, seeing it as slack, inert and overpermissive.

A successful work of art is, as we have seen, not like any other thing in the real world. But just as God created man in His own image, man does create his works of art—or his anything else; his chemical formula or his plans to defect—in the image of himself. The two-way functioning of the imagination thus holds good for one further step. What the writer creates is *like* something in its creator. One reason a society can get so angry at novelists like Thomas Wolfe and D. H. Lawrence is that society, too, has done some imagining. It has imagined that, by some feat of magic, writers can look into the secret lives of the people they take as models for their characters. This seems to many an infringement on privacy. But a case can be made for what I think is the fact: that no one really knows anything about anyone else, except by deduction and induction, intuition and empathy. Certainly not by magic. The rest is all imagination. Since the long-gone day of the Elizabethan poet, Sir Philip Sidney, *look in thy heart, and write* has meant just that. It does not mean *look in someone else's heart*, for that is impossible.

In the greatest novels—novels as different as *War and Peace* and E. M. Forster's *Howards End*—we do, however, see demonstrated something far more magical. This is the existence of a brotherhood of man, an underlying unity, demonstrated precisely because the recognitions that such novels awake are born not out of a shared experience, but out of a solitary one. A man alone makes images that turn out to be common to all. His characters spring not so much from observation as from imagination. That character in his novels which is society is much the same order of image that we all use when we imagine fearfully "What will people think?" or longingly "I wish I were like other people." But it should never be forgotten that, in all his projections, the novelist is expressing not the self he knows himself to be but a self of which he is, so far, unaware.

For just as it is hard for people who distrust imagination to accept living by the imagination, it is hard for the writer to accept that he is anything else but a writer. Statistically, however, the writer is a member of society as well, whether he wants to be or not. There is no such thing as not being a member of society. He can be a reluctant member if he chooses. He can be an irresponsible member, or a dissident member, or a useless member. But he is a member; he is a part of why society is whatever it is. There are writers of today—rejecting, or unaware of, the member of society in themselves—to be seen on every hand railing at society, at war with it. The English poet, George

Barker, even advocates the complete cutting loose of the artist from society, to go it alone on standards set solely by himself. In my view this is alarming not just because an artist, cut off from real society, would have nobody to communicate with except other artists. As the poet, W. H. Auden, says, "Those who have no interest in communication do not become artists; they become mystics or madmen." It is alarming because it means that the artist would be, all unconscious of what he was doing, splitting himself in two—the social side from the writer side —and following the profound schismatic tendency that has appeared, since Luther, in every activity that goes deep into man's psyche.

As we have seen, the society the writer puts into his work is not real society. It is merely his image of society. It is *like* society. It is something, in the common phrase, out of his own head. If he pictures society as hateful and vicious, he pictures something unrecognized in himself; some Judas to his Christ. Mr. Kerouac's police-state version of society, for instance, must needs compensate a conscious self much in want of discipline. And indeed is that not what we do find in the undoubtedly gifted Kerouac? The writer generally feels that, by living in his imagination, he is somehow unique. But we have seen that, actually, it is only in the real world that things are ever unique —complete poems, complete inventions, complete people. In the world of imagination, a thing can only be like something else. What the writer's self is like—the part his imagination reveals—is in the thing he writes.

Keats's beautiful and frightening *La Belle Dame Sans Merci* expresses, as few poems have, a particular doom. It is the fate of one who loiters on the inhuman, cold hillside of imagination, after the granary is full and the harvest's done. If only, armed by what he learned of the danger of living in imagination, in the dream of pale kings and princes, that knight could have fled a land where no birds sing! She who has him in thrall is both an image of the fairy queen who reigns over poetry and a clinical picture of the deathly radiant mother who, psychologically speaking, draws her love victims to her in the embrace of tuberculosis. To us with hindsight it is unendurable to realize what Keats understood about himself—and at the same time was blind to. The wavelike motion which we have seen imagination describe is, actually, itself an imitation of— it is *like*—the wavelike motion of real life. Real life flows in to the real self and out to the real world again.

There was once a monk who, in order to escape the temptations of the world, the flesh and the devil, went into the desert to live alone in a cave. But at night, in the shadows his solitary fire cast against the walls of his cave, he found himself haunted by the same voluptuous and carnal images he had run away from. Just so the writer, in order to write, is obliged to leave the world of society, at least for the hours in which he is writing. Solitude, James Russell Lowell said, is as needful to the imagination as society is wholesome for the character. Thus sequestered, the writer's imagination is freed to pursue its work of endless likening; of visualizing the unknown in terms of the known. Only shadows of the real world, of society, haunt his study's walls. He can fight the shadows, he can scream at them, he can put out his fire and say there are no shadows. Or he can recollect his self. He can know the shadows for his social self, which is always there, whether he likes it or not. So he begins to make his peace with the world and to build a bridge between imagination and reality.

What the imagination is, in relation to whatever exists, is unknown and latent within the *status quo*. Imagination's special function is to bring to light this hidden X, through a process of comparing it with what is already visible. *Status quo* and imagination thus cannot exist healthily apart. For the writer to reject society and the world is as tragic as when society denies, as it so often does, the imagination. Those who refuse to accept imagination, cutting it off in terms of "nothing but," reject their own future. They restrict life to what has already, up to date, been realized.

For imagination is new reality in the process of being created. It represents the part of the existing order that can still grow.

R. W. GERARD

Dr. R. W. (for Ralph Waldo) Gerard, physiologist, teacher and scientist-at-large, is best known for his extensive research on the metabolism, electrical activity, growth and organization of the human nervous system. Doctor Gerard has held professorships at five universities and has toured the world on teaching and research missions for private foundations and on government assignments. At the present time Doctor Gerard is directing an extensive research program on schizophrenia and psychopharmacology at the University of Michigan Mental Health Research Institute.

Your Brain
and Your Behavior

BY

R. W. GERARD

Modern science, winning its way into the mysteries of
nature, is now facing one of its sternest challenges.
Does man's psyche—mind and sentience, will and purpose—
lie beyond the scope of science? Or are the inimitable properties
of man, whence flow the magnificent achievements of humanity,
the outcome of comprehensible processes which can be explained through the disciplines of science? In search of an
answer, we must turn to the relationship between brain and
behavior.

A guided missile behaves as if it has purpose. It "seeks
its goal" or evades a hazard, even though the maneuvers required
twist its path like a pretzel. Such goal-seeking, self-regulating
devices are known to engineers as servomechanisms. Neurophysiologists today are wondering whether the nervous system
is no more than this.

Whether more or not, the human brain is at the least a
marvelously spun servomechanism that can outperform its own
inventions. The airman on a team of physicists and engineers
is right when he objects to the idea that airplanes are now so
automatically controlled that the pilot can practically be eliminated. "Before you throw out the pilot," he asks, "consider

373

where else can you get a highly modifiable, versatile servomechanism, weighing only one hundred and fifty pounds, produced so cheaply by completely unskilled labor?"

A submarine, too, acts like a single living thing. It seems to show unified purpose. It keeps to a course, it corrects its errors. Yet the submarine and its machinery and cargo are products of many men, just as its crew is composed of many individuals. The structures and the functions of the many coordinate to form a larger unity, with a character and personality of its own. Any component may change—engines may be replaced, superstructure remodeled, hull repaired, crew rotated, a new captain placed in command—without interrupting the life course of the whole.

A submarine is like a man, at a different level. For a man, too, is composed of many individuals and their products, forming a greater whole with its own individuality. When egg and sperm unite, the single resulting cell divides into two cells, each of which in turn divide into two, and so on for some forty cell generations. The total number of cells so formed in a single human is a thousand times greater than the world's population. Under proper conditions each cell can survive separately. Some manufacture nonliving products—horn, hair, bone, blood, tendon. As cells develop they specialize in forming different tissues and organs. Muscle cells differ vastly from skin cells. Liver cells and kidney cells, both concerned with chemical changes, are readily distinguishable under the microscope.

The cells in the nervous system especially concerned with behavior are called neurones. Most cells resemble packed spheres, like marshmallows pressed together in a bag. They may lie close together, or they may be separated by fluids or by strands of fibrous material. Whether close or separate, they have little more immediate relationship than strangers in a crowd. Neurones are different. Extensions from their roughly spherical cell bodies make contact with other neurones, often far distant, and carry messages to or from them. Think of a spider suspended from a roof by a long, slender strand, its several legs extending from its body. Reduced manyfold it somewhat resembles a neurone. The long strand suggests the axone,

374

as in man's sciatic nerve, a single, thin, protoplasmic thread that constitutes an unbroken expressway for zooming nerve messages; the legs suggest the dendrites, shorter receiving branches that convey messages to the cell body.

These neurone strands comprise set paths linked to other neurones within the nervous system and form the nerves connecting to outside structures. Nerves from the sense organs bring information to the brain; nerves to effectors, such as muscles and glands, carry instructions for action. Normally, our muscles contract only when aroused by nerve messages, and these must be sent from the appropriate neurones. In taking a simple step, for example, several dozen muscles must contract and relax at the proper moments and in the proper strengths, and the neurones that control them must send their signals in precise patterns of time and space. When many potential connections become effective simultaneously, as occurs under strychnine poisoning, any incoming nerve message—even one from a gentle stroking of the skin—can discharge into so many channels that practically all the muscles are activated at once, and convulsion results.

This plurality of connections is further revealed by microscopic examination. There are well over 10,000,000,000 neurones in the human brain, and a single neurone may receive axones from as many as 10,000 other neurones. These axones end on the dendrites and body of the neurone, often in small knobs so closely packed as to form a covering scale, and each junction, or synapse, might transmit a message.

Ordinarily, only a small fraction of the synapses is working at any one time. Some important crossings are always open; some only when the traffic is heavy; some stay closed, like ceremonial gates, except under very special circumstances. Which paths are open, and when, is determined by the flow of messages and the local situation. By producing tiny electric currents or specific chemical substances, neurones can also influence their close neighbors even without sending messages along connecting fibers.

Three decades ago, when the outlines of neuroanatomy were already sketched, but before modern neurophysiology

375

emerged, the problem of the organization of the brain could be presented to beginning students in some such terms as these: Imagine a modern city, with billions instead of millions of people and buildings, and the whole shrunk to the size of a softball. The problem then is to work out the complete wiring connections—phone, light, appliances, intercoms. Today, knowing more, we must ask for far more information. Which switches are open? What fuse loads can be handled? Where can wireless signals operate? In what patterns can messages flow? Fortunately, in some ways all this makes the story simpler, for patterns of activity replace patterns of structure; it is easier to follow the action of a crowd than the behavior of individuals in it. In fact, the synapse, or junction, has taken front stage center in present-day thought. Here is the decision point that controls the action of the nervous system, and what a synapse does is more important than which one does it.

In an axone the nerve message runs like a train rushing along its private track. From toe to spinal cord and back would require only a fiftieth of a second in an unbroken nerve fiber. Yet the actual time required to pull away from a painful jab —and this can be done by the lower part of the nervous system, the spinal cord, with no attention from the brain—may be much longer than this. Part of the lost time is spent crossing junctions within the spinal cord, where the effective speed may be only a slow crawl. Moreover, the messages leaving any neurone may have little direct relation to those reaching it. Many factors besides the arrival of a single message at a single synapse determine whether the neurone fires a message along its axone and, if it does fire, how often and when the impulses run. Yet synapses are everywhere in the nervous system, especially in the gray regions of brain and cord where neurone bodies are gathered, and where the most important events occur. Clearly, speed and precision in carrying messages are of less importance than the contribution made by synapses—the decision points of the brain.

The situation resembles that of a telephone system. Messages rush accurately over the wires; at central stations time drags in comparison, and many errors occur. But a central, whether human or automatic, makes the great system wieldy, permits any station to reach any other with facility, and generally controls performance.

The significant point, then, is that what emerges from a synapse is not wholly determined by what enters the synapse. Variability and novelty, learning and imagination depend on just this loose relation between input and output. This loose coupling of direct stimulus and immediate response, even at a single junction, clearly foreshadows the great problems of awareness and action at the level of the whole individual. The issues of determinism and freedom, of automatic and willed behavior, of sensation and memory and volition are thus raised. Before deciding on answers let us look at some further facts.

When one impulse in one axone reaches a neurone, this is usually not sufficient to make the neurone fire its own impulse. Often, series of impulses in one axone or simultaneous impulses in several axones are necessary. But conversely, an excess of ordinary incoming impulses may fail to activate a neurone and even make it less responsive. Further, certain types of nerve messages have an inhibiting effect upon neurones. Whether these reverse effects depend on special substances released at the axone ending or on the particular parts of a neurone to which the ending comes or on yet other mechanisms is still under vigorous study. (Extensive research on exciting and inhibiting transmitter substances has not yet firmly jelled. Acetylcholine, norepinephrine, serotonin, histamine, and gamma amino butyric acid are at present of great interest.) In effect, some totalizing of all arriving messages is achieved at the neurone—much as a pari-mutuel totalizer takes account of all bets to determine the odds in a race—and if the stimulating level is high enough, the neurone fires.

Just how high the stimulating level must be is a separate problem. A neurone that has been active recently or is bathed by depressant chemicals—whether formed in the body or given as drugs—or is in a low phase of its own spontaneous cycle of sensitivity or subjected to the feeble electric currents always flowing in the brain will be aroused to fire only at a relatively high level of stimulation. Other conditions of stimulation or of chemicals or currents reaching a neurone can make it more responsive.

Still, a good many specific predictions can now be made, and even more can be said about the direction of change in neurone firing that one or another change in conditions will bring about. But, with billions of neurones, each connected with thousands of others and subject to unlimited patterns of arriving messages, electric currents and ambient substances, it is almost impossible to say whether a given message in a given axone will fire a given neurone. What I wrote three decades ago on this point is still valid:

> And from this welter of influences . . . comes a single result: The cell fires messages along its own fiber to still other cells, or it does not fire. There is, to be sure, some gradation in number and frequency of impulses sent or in duration of inactivity and depth of inactivability, but essentially the balance is between action or no action. Just so the judge, depending on the state of his stomach or the temperature of the courtroom or the bombardment of arguments on each side of the case, renders a single decision for or against.

Fortunately, we can still work out a good deal without such detail, for considerable groups of neurones—thousands or millions of cells—are likely to work together. Then it is not as important to know whether given individual cells are active as to know what fraction of a group will respond. This can often be predicted with great precision. It is rather like a traffic survey. To predict or even to follow the path of each car is hopeless, but we can ascertain, and later predict, traffic loads on a road network under varied conditions. Thus, the integrated action of the nervous system is more understandable than the sum of all the actions of the separate neurones.

Is the action of each neurone, then, determined, while that of a collection of neurones—and so of an individual—is free? Is each unit neurone free, while the action of the whole brain is determined? Are both the unit and the whole determined? Or are both free? Perhaps a further look at the cell groups, or centers, will enlighten us.

Anatomists have charted the nervous system. The main neurone centers and the main fiber paths are well known. The anatomist can do more than describe the various nerve centers. By comparing them in different animals he can tell when they evolved and often can make shrewd guesses as to their function. The pathologist, comparing symptoms of disease with defects, also contributes to knowledge of the actions of particular neurone centers.

The physiologist developed his own methods of determining the function of each brain region. Originally there were two methods: A part of an animal's brain would be stimulated, mainly by electric shocks, or it would be destroyed. Such experiments are useless unless performed under conditions prevailing in human surgery. Movements in response to stimuli are the most easily observed, so that knowledge of where the nervous system receives sensations and how movements are controlled came early. Reflexes in the lower spinal cord, separated by surgery from the brain, for example, were found to be complex and precise. The foot will pull away from a pinch or will scratch at an irritant on the other leg, all unknown to the brain end of the animal. Today animals are led to gorge or to fast, to fight or cringe, mate or reject by local brain manipulation.

Recently many psychological tests for more complex behaviors have been developed, and the influence on these of under- and over-activity of many brain centers explored. Stimulant or depressive drugs are often injected directly into the brain. To study the problem of feeling, animals have been allowed access to a key that controls the administration of shocks by wires or of drugs by tubes reaching into particular brain centers. When a monkey presses the key several times a second, day and night, until exhausted, it seems reasonable to infer that the brain region so stimulated is associated with pleasurable experiences. So, too, humans report amorous feelings and sex arousal when electrical stimuli are sent through comparable portions of their brains.

Physiologists have long known that when a nerve fiber carries a message a tiny electric pulse accompanies it, that the brief current is, in fact, an essential part of the conducting mechanism. But only within recent decades have instruments been de-

379

veloped to exploit and extend this knowledge. Microelectrodes, ending in hollow tips less than 1/100,000th of an inch in diameter, are now thrust into single neurones without damaging them and measure electrical changes produced by natural and artificial activation or depression. The amplifiers must be powerful for this, and the cathode-ray tube used, similar to the TV picture tube, rapid, for the electric flicker may be as feeble as a few millionths of a volt—as in brain waves at the scalp—and last only a few ten-thousandths of a second. Currents can be passed through one set of microelectrodes to stimulate a single neurone or an axone uniting with it, and the neurone response can be measured by another set.

By such refined methods, the neurobiologist today can influence behavior almost at will by brain manipulation and, conversely, detect changes in the brain associated with all sorts of behavior. For example injecting a minute amount of strong salt solution into a certain region in the hypothalamus will cause the animal to drink itself to death if allowed enough water. Destroying or stimulating, say, a cat's amygdala—part of the older cortex—will arouse exaggerated sexual impulses, as will similar manipulation of different portions of the hypothalamus in a rat. Repeated shocks to the hippocampus of a monkey can make it submissive; other stimuli make it bolder. When a psychotic patient experiences hallucinations, a fine electrode harmlessly buried deep in the brain will disclose violent electrical activity, and a tranquilizer will abolish both the mental and electrical changes. Stimulation by the same electrode can produce the hallucination. Other regions, when stimulated, can set off other psychotic states even in normals, and still others bring back various past memories.

Such experiments indicate that unmanipulated human behavior is also related rather precisely to the grouped neurones. No amount of willing can keep the brain awake if deprived of oxygen and sugar. No amount of willing can stop the cold sweat of fear or the flush of anger, can allay anxiety or desire or sadness. Behavior depends on, and the brain acts in terms of, the responses of its myriad neurones.

So we return to the great questions about man's behavior.

Can he control that behavior? Does he have real volition and therefore responsibility for his acts? Is one neurone, or one group of neurones, the captain of the ship of life, the maker of ultimate decisions? Was Descartes right, in principle, when he conceived of a single brain structure—he guessed wrongly that it might be the pineal gland—as a center through which will controls action?

Something similar to Descartes' guess could be inferred from the fact that certain brain centers are now known which do control sleep and wakefulness. Yet it seems unlikely that any single neurone group could control the whole brain, let alone serve as a channel from mind to body. Almost any small part of the nervous system can be lost without destroying life, many different parts can each contribute to a particular major change in behavior, and damage to even a large area of the brain may cause only minor behavioral changes. Besides, even if we could establish the dominance of specific neurones, the problem would still remain—how could an act of the psyche affect those neurones? As we have seen, physical and chemical events activate or deactivate neurones. But a thought or a wish is no such event. Thoughts and wishes do surely accompany the activity of neurones, and willing an act might be the conscious counterpart of action by some master neurones. But this would still not explain how these neurones are aroused, if not through other neurones, chemicals or physical agents. Perhaps, then, freedom of action is something of a wholly different nature.

The most impressive attribute of man's behavior is its overt purposefulness, paralleled by an internal experience of purpose. So strong is the subjective feeling of free action that any sort of goal-directed behavior seems conscious and voluntary. When a torpedo tracks a zigzagging ship, we must sometimes remind ourselves that it is behaving as designed, that no consciousness or volition was built into it. The child or savage personifies the stone that tripped him and kicks back at it. An adult may become just as angry at a chess-playing machine that beats him, although he doesn't really believe it has personality. (In Portugal there is a chess-playing automaton that growls ominously when it loses and gloats when it wins.) Scientists combat harmful microorganisms without attributing hostility to them. These simple bodies, like the cells in our own bodies, merely perform the chemical functions their design permits, without motive or awareness, like the stone or the machine.

Our own bodies likewise perform all manner of "purposive" acts without our awareness. The endless balancing of blood chemistry, keeping each substance at a particular concentration, involves the on-and-off activities of liver, kidneys, digestive tube, endocrines and many other organs. Blood pressure is similarly balanced by the steady play of signals through the visceral nervous system. The eyes follow a moving object, the lenses focus, the pupils adjust for brightness just as well in a man with a cerebrum damaged to the point of blindness as in a normal man. A headless chicken can run around for a while. If a dog's brain is removed carefully, the dog can continue running for months or even years. In fact, decerebrated animals may prowl restlessly when starved, yet neglect the food offered to them. They must be handfed to survive.

In these various ways one sees fragments of purposeful behavior, which are yet mechanical. But, whereas no reason exists to attribute awareness to the stone, the engine or even the microbe, in some cases we are not so certain. It would be hard to say that the starved, prowling dog feels no hunger, even though its cerebrum is gone.

There is reason to believe that, in the course of organic evolution, consciousness evolved along with the nervous system. Simple awareness came first, with the swelling of the upper spinal cord. Then, as the core of the cerebrum appeared, feeling arose. Probably, painful sensations preceded pleasurable ones. Later, with the development of sight, sound, smell, touch—all associated with the growth of the cerebrum—came discrimination and conceptual thinking, came memory, reason and conscious purpose.

Certainly, behavior is wholly determined neither by a single external stimulus nor by the internal state. The entire past experience of the race and of the individual is also built into the neurone connections. The present state of health—physical and emotional—is coded in the condition of the synapses. Encouragement or rejection or neutral information from the outside world is brought by nerve messages converging upon the synapses. All together produce flickering patterns of neurone discharges that constitute both objective behavior and subjective experience.

The nervous system is indeed a superb servomechanism, but so infinitely more complex than any yet made by man that its resources of behavior partake of an entirely different order.

A distinguished scientist said we once thought that if we knew "one" we knew "two," since one and one are two; but we later found that we needed to know far more about "and." Neurobiologists know a great deal about the single neurone and synapse, and much about nerve centers. But at the higher levels of combination, vast areas remain to be explored. New properties and principles arise with increasing complexity. Even in mathematics the properties of a solid cannot all be found by extending the properties of a plane, nor those of a cubic algebraic equation from those of a square one. Theoretically, a machine, after reaching a sufficient level of complexity, can build a new machine more complex than itself. Certainly living organisms have steadily evolved into abler ones, and in the human brain the vast number of interacting neurones can give a practically limitless array of patterns of activity.

With half as many neurones in its cerebrum, the capacity of the cleverest ape is dramatically less than that of man. Among the properties of such magnificent machinery are self-consciousness, awareness of goals and the will to achieve them, symbolic communication and cumulative knowledge, altruistic co-operation and group aspiration.

Subjective awareness presumably has value or it would not have evolved. Yet it remains inconceivable in the light of our present knowledge that conscious experience can direct the material events in the brain. Rather, the active neurones and synapses seem to be responsible for both behavior and consciousness. All our knowledge of brain and behavior won in recent decades harmonizes with this view. Formerly, what happens in that soft, grayish mass, the brain, had to be inferred. Now, with tubes and wires, drugs and electric currents probing minutely the cells that compose it, the answer remains the same. Our increasing knowledge reveals no capacity of the brain that need be more than the action of a responding mechanism.

As recently as the turn of this century, "vital forces" were respectable crutches for our ignorance of life processes. Today, though much remains unexplained, no serious biologist doubts that these life processes can be explained through information-carrying patterns of matter and energy. Only three decades ago a sovereign state outlawed the teaching of evolution. Today the laws governing evolution are among the most precisely known in biology. Until yesterday, mind was beyond the reach of science. Today new tools for experiment and observation have breached this final wall.

But the capacities of mechanisms become richer with increasing complexity, and to a fantastic degree. The elements of earth and water, the atoms, built into intricate combinations in new molecules, gave rise to blobs of matter that replenished and reproduced themselves, and so were alive. The units of behavior, the neurones, embroidered into far more elaborate patterns, gave rise to individuals with directed and conscious behavior. The vastly enhanced repertoire of actions means an increased uncertainty as to which will actually occur. This unpredictability amounts to a sort of freedom, associated with a sense of purpose. We are satisfied that the organ of the brain plays the tunes of the mind; we are far from a full understanding of how it does so. And since each answer in science raises new questions, there will always be a penumbra of ignorance surrounding our zone of illumination. As Meredith said:

> The mastery of an event lasteth among men the space of one cycle of years, after that a fresh illusion ariseth to befool mankind. Doubtless other masters of the event will follow . . . and through the dispelling of illusion after illusion, mankind may ultimately encounter the ultimate residue, perhaps the ultimate of all illusions, which we optimistically designate as truth.

With understanding, even if partial, comes application. The life sciences have led to modern medicine and an almost un-

384

believable increase in physical well-being. The sciences of behavior will similarly lead to a great increase in the positive balance in mental and social health. Knowledge increases control, but even more it expands freedom. Language permits restrictive rules, but it also makes possible most of the riches of civilization. Bands of neurophysiologists, social psychologists, cultural anthropologists and other workers in the domain of behavioral science are moving across the open frontier to chart the great new continent stretching before them. Greater understanding will enlarge man's self-respect and enhance the dignity of mankind. Here also applies the motto of my alma mater, the University of Chicago: "Crescat scientia, vita excolatur"—"Let knowledge grow from more to more and thus be human life enriched."

Further reading:

Brazier, M. A. B.: THE ELECTRICAL ACTIVITY OF THE NERVOUS SYSTEM. New York: The Macmillan Company; 1951.

Fields, W. S. (ed.): BRAIN MECHANISMS AND DRUG ACTION. Springfield: Charles C Thomas, Publisher; 1957.

Herrick, C. J.: THE EVOLUTION OF HUMAN NATURE. Austin: University of Texas Press; 1956.

Pfeifer, John: THE HUMAN BRAIN. New York: Harper & Brothers; 1955.

Gerard, Ralph W.: THE BODY FUNCTIONS. New York: John Wiley & Sons, Inc.; 1941.

CHARLES L. BLACK, JR.

[*Photograph by Arnold Newman*]

Among lawyers Charles L. Black, Jr., enjoys a reputation as one of the profession's most cogent and eloquent expounders of legal philosophy. Born in Austin, Texas, in 1916, he took his law degree at Yale and practiced as an associate in a New York firm before he began to teach. He is at present professor of jurisprudence at Yale. With Grant Gilmore he wrote a treatise on The Law of Admiralty *in 1957, and in 1960 Macmillan published* The People and the Court, *Professor Black's study of the role of the Supreme Court in furthering democratic values.*

The Two Cities
of Law

BY

CHARLES L. BLACK, Jr.

On the ground of man's public life, two shapes of law may be discerned—sometimes in mutual complement, sometimes in contrast.

First, there is the law that prevails in society. Courts decide cases and give reasons for their decisions. Statutes are printed and read. Precedents are recorded and used as lawyers' ingenuity may devise. People enjoy legacies, lose cars to the finance company, get married, go to the penitentiary. And as a matter of psychological fact, there exists, in the minds of judges and lawyers, a conceptual framework to guide and explain all this activity. This structure of legal ideas is not exactly the same in any two minds, but there is enough agreement for law to do its work—and even the fact of disagreement is a fact about law as it exists. This law that palpably prevails in each nation may be called "positive law."

Second, as misty as a Chinese painter's mountain, but as insistently there as the Chinese painter makes his mountain seem, is another shape of law—the image of law as men in their time think law ought to be. This ideal law cannot be known, as positive law can be known, from the deeds and words of lawyers and judges at their professional tasks. Those who would persuade us of its requirements cannot point to the readable print of code or reported decision. All we can know from all these sources is the tenor of such law as exists and prevails— and that may be good law or bad law.

Yet we are compelled to seek the shape of right law. By taking up this quest, we may be transgressing the canons of scientific positivism, but if we do not take it up we strip ourselves of the insignia of humanity. And so from the earliest inscriptions in pyramid tombs down to the latest article in the *Yale Law Journal*, from the Cheyenne Indian before Custer to the man riding uptown on the Broadway Express, we try and always have tried not only to know the law as it is but also to discern, however dimly and uncertainly, what it may be that justice requires of law.

This search for light in law has taken many forms. Recurrently through western history, the name "natural law" has been given to the projected image of law as it ought to be. Aristotle and Cicero wrote of a law of nature, against which human positive law was to be measured. Aquinas brought the concept within his mighty synthesis. Grotius built it into the foundations of modern international law. John Locke made the idea a perdurable part of liberal thought in England, whence it crossed the Atlantic to enter our own Declaration of Independence, in that document's opening appeal to "the Laws of Nature and of Nature's God. . . ." "Natural-law" thought permeates the epochs of our intellectual tradition.

Natural law, as conceived by its proponents, bears none of the marks of positive law. It is not set up by the state; no court shapes it; no legislature establishes or changes it. Instead, its expounders have been philosophers and publicists, professors and ecclesiastics. Each proposition in each natural-law system can claim validity solely on the basis of arguments advanced by people who write books on the subject. Their reasoning starts with stated or assumed beliefs about the nature of man; from these beliefs are drawn conclusions as to what law ought to be. The end product, when fully developed, is a system of *ideal* law, which can be held up as a model for comparison with positive law.

390

Hugo Grotius, one of the greatest of the natural lawyers, shortly stated the underlying assumption:

> The law of nature is a dictate of right reason which points out that an act according as it is or is not in conformity with the social and rational nature of man has in it a quality of moral baseness or moral necessity, and that, in consequence, such an act is either forbidden or enjoined by the author of nature, God.

In the reach of historic time not one but many systems of natural law have been elaborated in this way. These have differed widely. But the root idea remains surprisingly constant; from it "natural law" thought takes its name. In age after age it has been maintained or assumed that there is a right law, a just law, inferrible by reason from the nature of man, and of his relations to his society and to the cosmic order.

It is implausible—though not impossible—that so richly accredited a tradition should turn out after all to be entirely worthless. It is therefore surprising that what may fairly be called the dominant view in British and American jurisprudence today rejects the concept of "natural law," and waves away the whole corpus of natural-law speculation. It is not that any single system of purportedly "natural law" is rejected, but rather that the value of natural-law reasoning as a whole is denied—expressly or by eloquent disregard.

This attitude can be explained on a number of grounds, not all of them necessarily applicable to the case of any one thinker. Most fundamental is the widespread modern view that only delusion beckons when we conceive of "justice" as having anything remotely like the objective reality which invests the positive institutions of law. We have no warrant, say the followers of this view, for supposing that there exists any "justice" which can be "discovered"; "justice" is merely a name for our own reactions. The difference between good law and bad law, between the just and the unjust, lies in the feelings of men; the goal, conceived as possessing shape and reality of its own, is a mere wishful imagination.

Others, without opening this ultimate issue, object to the

term "natural law," with its implication that the goals of law are themselves a kind of law. Nothing but confusion inheres, they say, in this willful blurring of what exists with what is desired. Nor, others would have it, can "natural" law really be inferred from man's "nature." Eskimo infanticide is as "natural" as our school-lunch funds; something beyond a knowledge of natural facts is required for our discriminating between these institutions.

Objection is also made to the lack of sharp, critical analysis in natural-law speculation. "A man," runs a recurrent natural-law precept, "is entitled to the fruits of his labor." "Property is to be protected," says another. Such formulas, to begin with, are largely if not entirely tautological; a man's "property" might well be defined as that which the law will protect or ought to protect for him. Insofar as they are not tautological they cannot be logically deduced from any validated generalizations about known human nature.

Of course, agreement with such vapid *sententiae* is easy to procure, regardless of logical gaps in their derivation. But such agreement means nothing, for the precepts themselves are too vague to solve real legal problems, and often tell with equal force on both sides of the same controversy. Is the recipient of a public old-age pension receiving the "fruits of his labor"? Or is the taxpayer who supports the pension being deprived of his? If you unknowingly buy a ring from a jeweler who unknowingly bought it from a thief, is it in justice your "property" or that of the man from whom it was stolen? The real problems of law involve not faithful obedience to beauteous maxims, but the mediation of competing claims, each with a measure of soundness.

And—the critics go on—even if we could, by speculation on the nature of man, reach warrantable and clear conclusions as to the goals of law, another formidable hurdle remains. The decision whether a law is good entails judgment not only on the desirability of its goal but also on its practical working. A father who will not be kind to his children, who shrugs off their problems, who willfully refuses to help them past the crises of growth, may be thought worse than a nonkilling bank robber;

the correction of his behavior may be a more appealing goal than the suppression of bank robbery. But would putting court injunctions on such men actually improve the relations of fathers with their children? What would be the social results of licensing off-track bookmakers? On the answering of such questions—questions about how a legal device will really work—altogether depends the sane evaluation of each rule and practice in law. They never can be answered more than tentatively; they cannot be answered at all by deduction from grand principles.

The schools of natural law, say the critics, are actually narrow and particularistic. Their splendid reasonings from the nature of man, universal as may be their phrasing, are fancy masks for the prejudices of a single time or sect or current of thought. Their "obvious" truths are obvious to the already convinced; their "deductions" seem compelling to those who have already accepted the conclusions. Truism and fallacy are the warp and woof of their loose, gaudy fabrics.

Each of these objections has great weight. Yet—as Lon Fuller and others have shown—there remains a value in the concept which the term "natural law" seeks to suggest. Let me try to get at this value by talking not in philosophic but in practical terms—in terms of what we actually find ourselves doing when we seriously ponder questions about law.

First, the impulse to shape the institutions of law toward more perfect justice is felt and obeyed by all kinds of men. It is surprisingly uncorrelated with philosophic views as to the objective validity to be imputed to "the good" or to "justice." Some of the people who, as philosophers, assure us that "justice" is merely a name for our own emotions, are tireless in advocacy for justice as they conceive it; their advocacy does not consist merely in exhibiting their emotions but also in giving reasons why other people ought to experience the same emotions. We need not ask here whether they thus contradict themselves; let us note instead the sheer fact that all people, everywhere, are given, when they consider law, to thinking and working and talking for law's betterment.

But before we can seek to improve our law, we must attain

some fairly clear conviction as to what goals are to be desired. The considerations and arguments with which we give shape to these goals may take many forms. But surely all sensible thought about the improvement of law must start with something like this assumption: *Good law is law that is good for man in his society and in the world.*

Of course, one cannot deduce any specific consequences from this formula. But the formula has nevertheless a certain clarifying power. For it reminds us that the quest for good law entails not only the forming of conviction about some abstract good but also the acquiring of knowledge about man—about the nature of man—and about the nature of his societies and of his world. Such knowledge alone may not tell us anything about justice, but it is an indispensable part of all thought about justice.

Finally, when we think deeply about shaping law toward justice, it always happens that we begin to think in some degree systematically. Problems of justice in law rarely present a single simple question. Many values are likely to be at stake. A measure of system is the alternative to chaos.

But a more or less systematic view of the requirements of justice, based in large and essential part on a more or less systematic view of the nature of man, begins to look like "natural law." One might almost say that it is the nature of legal man to think along natural-law lines. We do not have to construct all-inclusive systems of ideal law. We need not attribute to our partial and tentative conclusions the strutting, self-anointed pseudoinfallibility which has flawed much natural-law writing. We need not assume that knowledge about man's nature is enough; some value judgment, some act of sheer moral choice, must be added. But the route we must take, if we are to think to any purpose about the ends of law, goes in much the same direction as the path that natural-law thought has followed.

Whether we use the words "natural law" is a question of terminology. The essential thing is not to discard the good in natural-law thought, merely because we cannot accept all its past claims. Much natural-law speculation is pretentious, arrogant and absurd. Much of it consists in trivial juggling of high-sound-

394

ing expressions. But we could put up with all this, and with more, rather than reject the idea that human positive law ought to move toward a goal, however flickeringly and unsurely perceived, and that this movement cannot dispense with considerations—as soundly validated as may be and as clearly structured as the material honestly allows—about the nature of man, the maker and subject of law.

It is not surprising, therefore, that natural-law thought has had extensive and continual relations with the positive law of the United States. The relationship, to be sure, has been a peculiar and largely a disguised one. An American lawyer could live out his professional life at the bar and on the bench, without ever hearing the term "natural law." Our lawyers and our judges talk positive law—their reasonings concern precedents, statutes and constitutional provisions. Reference to the justice of the case, apart from positive law, is likely to be apologetic, and almost never purports to rely on systematic natural-law concepts. How then can it be said that natural-law thought has entered into the fabric of American legal culture?

To answer this question we must consider the separate senses in which American law has rejected and accepted natural-law thought. Let us begin with the rejection.

Early in our history the idea was put forward that natural law ought to be treated as a sort of law freely invocable in court and superior to other kinds of law. This would mean that, if the judge believed that a statute or constitutional provision outraged natural justice, his duty would be to disregard the positive law and to decide the case contrary to its command.

This notion was utterly and finally rejected; the judiciary dropped it like a hot potato. That the dogmas of any school of juristic philosophers should control and nullify the positive law of statute and Constitution, put in force by the people through their established organs of legality, was and is gratingly inconsonant with the theories of our political life. The suggestion was an insolent one; it was met with rebuke and slid into oblivion.

The result—and here we reach the acceptance—is that such force as natural-law thought may have in American law must operate not from outside but within and through positive law. So much of it is accepted as the people, through their representatives, are willing to accept—and no more.

Yet the acceptance has been large; judgments about right and justice, formed in part on the basis of beliefs as to the nature of man and society, permeate every level of our legal process. The most obvious illustration is that of formal legislation, including the Constitution and its amendments. The constitutional ban on the ex post facto law—the law punishing actions committed prior to its passage—implemented the belief that such laws contravened natural justice. The abolition of imprisonment for debt was motivated by convictions as to the rights of man. Our social-security laws rest on systematic thought about the nature of man's social relations. But any finite list of examples tends to minimize the connection between legislation and prevailing concepts of justice. Our laws on marriage, wills, taxation and criminal procedure—these and uncountably more—are determined in significant part by widely held views as to the requirements of justice, in the light of beliefs about man's nature.

It is less obvious, but clearly true, that in the decision of particular cases judges not only may but must fill out the incertitudes of positive law with something like natural-law considerations. This is an all-pervading part of our legal process; the aggregate effect is of major importance in the whole shaping of positive law. We have often thought of the judge as a kind of logic machine, deducing his result from precedents and statutes. Sometimes this is a substantially true picture; when the applicable precedents or statutes speak with a clear voice, the conscientious judge must normally obey, whatever he may think of the justice of the matter. But there are cases in infinite number in which this cannot be what happens—not because the judge is wayward, but because the law does not contain a single incontrovertible answer to the problem presented.

Our law is found in great part in precedents, in prior decided cases. But no two cases are ever entirely alike. The judge must often decide whether the difference is *enough* to justify a variation in result. This question cannot be answered by logical reasoning on the basis of precedent; it is a question that arises after such reasoning is completed.

The other major component of our law is statutory—the law of legislative acts. Very often the key terms used in a statute are quite vague; always there are borderlands of uncertain applicability. Sometimes it can be shown that vagueness was intended, that Congress or a state legislature deliberately left it up to the judges to make concrete the statute's generalities. But intended or not, the consequence is that the law does not unambiguously tell the judge what to do.

The judge, therefore, cannot always obey the command of precedent and statute, because the command often cannot be made out with clarity. This is nobody's fault; it is inherent in the nature of thought and language. Who would expect that something called "the law" could settle in advance every question posed by the infinite variety of life? It is both unsurprising and true that our legal system has large leeways, within which the narrowly technical materials do not speak clearly. This is not a defect, but the means by which law remains flexible and capable of growth.

But the judge must decide each case. If honest assessment of the "purely legal" materials does not produce decision, then what is to fill the gap? There are three possibilities; each of them plays a part, and in the particular case they may be complexly related.

First, the judge may try to make out the "principle" of the statute or of the lines of precedent, and then determine how this principle applies to the case. This principle, if discernible at all, must be, broadly speaking, a principle of justice, a judgment as to the requirements of good law. Such a principle cannot be understood without understanding the reasons for it. And these reasons, as we have seen, will commonly follow the lines of natural-law thought, in the generic sense which we have explored.

Secondly, the judge may have recourse to what he thinks to be communal feelings of justice. These, too, are often based on reasons grounded in popular apprehension of natural law; certain it is that ordinary people think and talk in terms of natural law and natural right.

Thirdly, where these more impersonal techniques fail to determine decision, the judge may be brought to his own views of the justice of the matter.

Now these three paths to decision are not really as categorically separable as might appear. Neither the "principle" of statute and case law nor the "sense of justice" of the community is at all easy to determine, and in every case these things actually take effect, in the process of decision, as they are registered in the mind of the judge. The underlying principle is the underlying principle as he discerns it; the communal feeling is the communal feeling as he senses it. But each of these three modes brings into the decisional process somebody's definition of justice and somebody's reasons—often of a "natural-law" kind —for proposing this definition; the judge must be able to handle and weigh such material.

And if he is any good at his job, he will not discharge this necessary part of it on a sporadic basis. He will have thought connectedly on the goals of law and on the good of man—to enable him both to clarify his own thoughts to the point of usability in his work and to understand the thoughts of others, where these must be brought to bear on decision. He will have thought, in other words, partly along natural-law lines, though by no means need he have done so in the oversystematized and dogmatic manner of some natural-law writers.

(I speak of judge rather than jury, because we assume that the jury deals with questions of fact rather than of law. But juries do sometimes decide on appraisal not only of fact but of felt equity. And the question formally of "fact" may contain a normative question; deciding whether a defendant was "negligent" entails deciding what constitutes negligence. In both ways the jury undoubtedly takes part in shaping law toward communal perceptions of justice.)

In its legislation, then, and in its judicial decisions, our positive law is suffused with natural-law thought in the general sense. There is here no question of an opposition between the two, much less of a radically antidemocratic suzerainty of natural law over positive law. Positive law, in a democratic society, admits just as much shaping toward ethical goals as the people desire. Their desire is expressed, as always, through their representatives. In this manner they have not only acted by legislation but also have left extensive and vital leeways in the technical framework of positive law, thus inevitably committing to their judicial representatives the task of filling the law out with such perceptions of justice as may be needful.

One level at which this process of suffusion operates is peculiar to our political system. Our Constitution, which controls other law, contains certain general provisions which stem from convictions as to the demands of justice: "due process of law," "equal protection of the laws," "freedom of speech," and others.

When a judge considers whether a certain procedural innovation offends against "due process of law," he may find—in historical documents, in past decisions, in other technical materials—a clear preponderance of evidence on one side of the question. If this happens, then he has no honest alternative to deciding the case accordingly. But if, as often occurs, the technical materials do not settle the question, then the judge must decide in obedience to his convictions as to the consonance of the new statute with the root principles of procedural fairness which he believes to be embodied in the words of the Constitution.

In this limited but important sense a component of what may be called "natural law" not only enters—as we have already seen—into the whole fabric of law at ordinary levels but also controls and even negates ordinary law. This happens not because "natural law" has any validity as law in itself. It happens because the American people in their basic juristic act—the putting and keeping in force of their Constitution—have chosen to embody in its words such principles as seemed good to them of what they have taken to be natural justice, leaving it to the courts to work out the application of these principles to concrete cases.

The American legal system, then, has rejected, as it should, the notion of a "natural law" standing outside positive law and dictating to the latter. But it has not for that reason fallen into the opposite error of proclaiming that mere legality is enough—that whatever is, is right. It has made a simple but most fruitful and creative synthesis. It has built into itself, as a positive-law system, abundant means of growth toward right law. The leeways are not ideally distributed; the controls are not perfect. Their effectiveness is altogether dependent on the qualities of mind and character of those who work in law. But I venture to say that no better solution has yet been devised to the problem of relating the positive law, the law that actually is, to the law of vision, the ideal law, the law that some have seen as implicit in the nature of man.

I want to conclude with a thought which—like the rest of this article—will doubtless be unsatisfactory or even objectionable both to those who hold natural law in scorn and to its earnest devotees. I will get at it by telling a true story. One afternoon last fall I was on my way to my class in Constitutional Law. I was going to lead a discussion of certain technicalities having to do with the application of the Fourteenth Amendment, as implemented by acts of Congress, to voting and other rights. My head was full of section numbers in the Federal Revised Statutes. I fear I was mumbling to myself, a practice I cannot recommend to those who hold reputation dear.

I happened to look up—all the way up, over the tops of the red stone buildings into the sky as the Indians of Connecticut must have seen it before the white settlers came, with its great autumnal castles of clouds as far as imagination could reach. And somehow, very suddenly, all this illimitable expansiveness and lofty freedom connected within me with the words I was tracing from the Fourteenth Amendment through the statute books—"privileges or immunities of citizens," "due process of law," "equal protection of the laws." And I was caught for a moment by the feeling of a Commonwealth in which these words had not the narrow, culture-bound, relative meaning we are able to give them in the "real" world, but were grown to the vastness that is germinal within them.

I went to my class with a different view toward the day's work. Not that I abandoned present technicalities and made a speech about alabaster cities. Far from it! The class was the most narrowly technical I had taught during the year. A musician who hears an unworldly music on his way to the concert hall must surely respond, if he is a musician, not by relying on his feelings when he gets up to play, but by being especially attentive to the accuracy of his tempo.

Nor did I go believing that, if only we all worked hard enough in law, that Commonwealth in the clouds would come down to earth. No, the Heavenly City is where it may be, and our earthly cities will always be dirty and full of noise.

But I walked toward my technicalities somehow sure that, though the work of law in society can never be lightened or its incertitudes smoothed away by the vision of perfect liberating justice, and though all the work we can do can never come within far galactic distance of bringing the vision to our life, still it is the vision that gives to the work the best value it possesses. I do not know exactly how this may be; the clearest thought I have about it is that all our work in law may be a ritual, celebrating the vision, assuring that while it can never be wholly found, it can never be wholly lost.

Law in latter days has gained much in realism, in hard-headedness, in disdain for orotundity and rhetorical glitter. This gain, like all gains, comes with its built-in peril—in this case the deadly peril of loss of the poetry of law. The poetry of law solves no legal problems; it was, in fact, brought into disrepute precisely by misbegotten attempts to make it solve legal problems—and herein all known schools of "natural law" have offended. The poetry of law is the motive for solving problems, the sacred stir toward justice, our priceless discontent at the remoteness of perfect law. The natural-law tradition, however irritating may have been its bumptious attempts to sell us its figmental street maps of the Heavenly City, has at least tried to keep the poetry of law alive.

Herein lies the clue, it seems to me, to our best utilization of the work that the natural-law thinkers, in all their schools, have done. We must first separate their poetry from their prose and then face the fact that the prose states no eternal, infallible truths, but only tentative conclusions, reasoned well or ill, about practical problems. There is no "anti-intellectualism" in believing that our minds are not made to ascertain beyond doubt the content of an immutable justice; one of the most precise and subtle uses of the intellect is in marking its own limits. Once through this realistic wringer, the prose component in each of the great natural-law constructions would surely have much to contribute, by way of fruitful insight and hypothesis, to the quest for justice.

The poetry, on the other hand, solves nothing, decides nothing, conveys no information, weighs nothing on the scale of argument. It is too precious for those uses. It may assure us, if we keep still and listen, that the whole business of decision, of argument, of long and disappointing search for information and solution, is after all worth while.

Further reading:

Curtis, *Charles P.*: LAW AS LARGE AS LIFE. New York: Simon and Schuster, Inc.; 1959.

Maritain, *Jacques*: THE RIGHTS OF MAN AND NATURAL LAW. New York: Charles Scribner's Sons; 1943.

Fuller, *Lon L.*: THE LAW IN QUEST OF ITSELF. New York: The Foundation Press, Inc.; 1940.

Cardozo, *Benjamin N.*: THE NATURE OF THE JUDICIAL PROCESS. New Haven: Yale University Press; 1921.

PHILIP MORRISON

Philip Morrison, professor of physics at Cornell University, born in 1916, is a physicist whose current interests are "the theory of cosmic-ray origins and the related behavior of the material in the solar surface and in interplanetary space." Doctor Morrison is a member of the Physical Science Study Committee which is developing the new physics curriculum for our high schools. Cause, Chance and Creation *won the first award in the AAAS-Westinghouse science writing awards contest for 1960.*

Cause,
Chance and Creation

B Y

PHILIP MORRISON

What you can read here has little to do with the head-lines that tell of applied science, like the space rockets, nor even with discoveries like new atomic particles. Here we discuss instead the very roots of physics, the sources of its strength and its fruit. They are at the same time its anchors. With them physics can sometimes take firmer hold on the real nature of man and universe than even the wisest of the seers and the philosophers can do without its aid.

How wide is the scope of physical law? Do life, thought, history fall within its orderly domain? Or does it describe only the inanimate, the remote and the very tiny? It is the claim of contemporary physics that its laws apply to all natural things, to atoms, stars and men. There are not two worlds: the cold, precise mechanical world of physics, and the surprising, dis-orderly and growing world of living things or of human existence. They are one.

This is no new claim. Since George Washington was a young man, there has been a view of the world based on Isaac Newton's physics. That view was mechanical; the world was a great clock rather like the newly understood motions of the planets. Feats like the prediction of the time of an eclipse of the sun, possible with high accuracy for a thousand years ahead, became the hallmark of a powerful science. Its proponents claimed that one day they could so explain everything. But there is a clear and common-sense retort. Life is not at all like solar eclipses; novelty and surprise, building a tangled complexity of events, are much more the essence of the world than is the serene dance of the planets, however intricately they weave.

So the physicist's view became first less plausible, then hardly more than absurd. Even in the last decades, the mechanical theory of the world is often taken to be the last word of physics. If this were so, I should make no wide claims for the implications of our science. For the world is patently not clockwork, not even clockwork with a few loose screws. In fact, what has happened is that physics has come nearer maturity; it can understand not only the neat and the mechanical but all the tangle of events in the everyday world in one and the same way, a richer way, a subtler way, than it first learned to chart for the motions of planets.

I will try to show how physics gained this new view and what it is. Along the path, we shall have seen as well something of how the isolated, rather technical bits of laboratory lore merge into a world view powerful enough to claim its share of the attention of everybody who thinks about the great questions of man and his place.

Let us begin by taking stock of the old philosophy of the physicists, the view that the world is only a great piece of clockwork. This point of view meant much to the history of our republic, which was founded by men who had been brought up in such a climate of thought. To say only that much is to prove that such a picture is not wholly tainted; the careful checks-and-balance mechanisms of our Constitution owe something to that philosophical view, however much they may owe to real political experience. Yet no one can fail to be repelled a little by the fatalism which this viewpoint implies.

It was Laplace, Napoleon's great official mathematical physicist, who expressed the mechanical philosophy in just the language we want. Said Laplace: "An intelligent being who, for a given instant," came to know all the forces of nature and all the positions of every particle, could predict every event to the end of days in one sure formula. "Nothing would be uncertain for him; the future, as well as the past, would be present to his eyes." Laplace saw in the astronomy of the day, with its predictions of planetary motion, its tables of eclipses from antiquity to the year 3000, a feeble foreshadowing of that state of total knowledge which he could view as the ultimate goal of science.

That sort of world is a hard world to breathe in; for clearly there is no use to make up your mind for good or for evil. It is all written in the orbits. Laplace's "intelligent being," if he is physically possible, mocks our hardest decisions with his complete book of all our future actions. It is a world without real novelty, without real change. Yet such a great Victorian as Thomas Huxley, the defender of Darwin, seemed to see the world so; he wrote once that even in the play of the spray on the waves in a stormy sea, all was predetermined to the last degree. Here is, I think, at least part of the reason why science and the humanities are so separate in our times, far more than they were in the eighteenth century. This cold doctrine became so difficult to hold during the wildly changing and difficult century which followed that educated men withdrew from science. They felt that science and its mechanical model of all things could say nothing plausible about the great choices of the time. If physics, as I believe, can now give indispensable guidance to any who wish to know the nature of man and his place in the world, it must have found a more reasonable way to explain a world bursting with novelty. It has. To trace the growth of this new view, and to try to see where it leads, is the object of these pages.

The physics of the twentieth century bears one signature writ very large: Albert Einstein. But Einstein's relativity, which shook the educated world far beyond the corridors of the laboratory, made no deep crisis for the clockwork picture of the world. Einstein showed—and we have found his every claim fully supported by experiment—that the notions of space and time held for two centuries were naïve. Neither distance in space nor passage of time could retain the simple meaning which we once thought part of "common sense." Space and time were curiously mixed together by his theory: what appeared to one watcher as a difference of a second in time between one flash of light and a succeeding flash might be measured by familiar, sound and sensible procedures perhaps as a half second, or as two seconds, by another observer who is moving rapidly past the first one. What value the moving man found for the *time* interval would depend on the distance *in space* between the two flashing lamps. Two flashes could be simultaneous to one observer, but successive to another. The concept of *simultaneous* is thus merely a relative one.

So much is well known. But nonphysicists seldom appreciate that Einstein's relativity, which plays so fast and loose with space and time, regards other familiar physical concepts as absolutes. What concerns us most here is that relativity insists that one relation must remain unchanged to every observer: every cause must always be separated by a minimum time from its effect. The order of flashes of light from two lamps may be relative, but the order of snapping the switch and seeing the light must be retained. The order of events *not* related as cause and effect *is* relative to the motion of the onlooker, but every cause remains distinct in time from its effects for every possible observer. In this sense the sequence of cause and effect is not relative but absolute.

The eternal web of cause and effect, then, is just as unbroken for Einstein as for Laplace's prophetic "being" and the Newtonian physics upon which Laplace rested his case. Yet, after Einstein's mighty shaking, two cracks appeared in the foundations of the older view. First, Einstein taught once and for all that even familiar and well-tested notions must be rethought and retested in every new domain of experience. The chain of cause and effect familiar from the eclipse predictions and nautical almanacs of Newton, Laplace and their successors was not in fact snapped by Einstein. But since what had once seemed the self-evident truth of the old ideas of space and time proved only approximate, one had learned not to be cocksure of anything. There is here the suggestion, which I think correct, that what we regard as "common sense" and the "self-evident" are only those matters which we have all early learned and which we were all well-taught. The physics student of today finds Einstein common-sensical enough; a generation back, only the few experts grasped what the theory meant.

Second, the idea of an instant of time became a little less simple. Laplace's all-knowing being, his prophetic demon, was to predict the whole of the future once he knew what was happening everywhere at one single instant. But Einstein showed that information could flow to any observer with a speed which at maximum was the speed of light. The imaginary being of Laplace could collect his data at his desk, to make his prediction, only after a great deal of time, enough time to bear the news from the far corners of the universe. Some part of his wonderful predictions become mere eyewitness accounts, for he cannot make them until the predicted event has already occurred. Predicting demon is thus both prophet and historian, for with Einstein the sharp differences between *now, the future and the past* have become blurred. He cannot hope to make observation and prediction simultaneous.

A still-greater blow to the universal clock was in the making for a generation before Einstein, and came to fruit in the generation after his great theory. Between the experiments of the early molecular physics, around 1870, and the maturity of atomic physics in the 1930's, we learned beyond doubt that the world is an atomic world. All matter, and even the seemingly smooth flow of light itself, is grainy, all made of tiny units of one sort or another whose myriad combinations and interrelations weave the fabric of events.

At first view, this seems agreeably Newtonian. Laplace spoke of "the positions of the entities composing nature" as just what his marvelous predicting observer had to know. Since indeed nature is built up of separate and distinct "entities"— atoms, electrons, light quanta and so on—this modern advance might appear only to confirm the Newtonians. But it is the very completeness of the atomic victory which makes trouble. The data which must be known and recorded if the world's future is to be predicted are prodigious in amount. Laplace, one fears, never examined just how much would have to be known by that Great Intelligence. The sheer bulk of the data he needs is itself no real criticism; for Laplace, while he had in mind no supernatural being, but one far more skilled than humans but "as finite as ourselves," was willing to allow him to be as well-equipped as necessary. The trouble is, the Observer and his note-books and his yardsticks and his stop watches and his very brain must all be made out of atomic matter or of grainy radiation. In preparing the data for his omniscient view of the universe, he must consume great amounts of material. If he wishes to economize on material, he can do it only by splurging on radia-tion, on energy. Try what we will, we cannot imagine him as the subtle, remote observer Laplace had in mind, but rather as the master of a great laboratory.

For knowledge itself must somehow be expressed, and there exists no more refined form of expression than embodiment in the grainy stuff of atoms or of radiation. As long as only human knowledge needs expression, the problem is not noticed. For atoms are so numerous that a human brain, for example, needs only a minute portion of its energy for the sheer material ex-pression of its knowledge. Almost all of the work of the human brain is a consequence of the particular living process by which it works. In principle, the energy or matter which is used for knowledge is an absolute necessity for the brain, but it is un-noticeably small compared to its own needs. But faced with the gigantic task of noting down every atom in the universe and its motion, the Predicting Being of Laplace turns out to become a major, even the dominant, portion of all the universe. With that enormous bulk his credibility disappears. For now it is possible to show that he cannot even know fully himself and his own laboratory, let alone all the rest of the universe. He is beaten by the atomic facts of life, the hard fact that no measurement can be made without the expenditure of some very small parcel of energy, no result recalled without the use of some atomic particle of minimum mass.

The eighteenth century was misled by its experience of sci-ence. For them, science was represented by the astronomer— at his telescope on the dark, quiet hill, with his pad and pencil and his tables of logarithms—plotting the paths of the undisturbed distant stars. Today the great humming machines of the nuclear laboratory, and its extravagant electric bill, serve the ends of the physicist who needs to study the heart of the atom by taking it apart. That contrast may make concrete what was described more abstractly in the preceding paragraph. Measurements of the numerous and tiny atoms require a more active intervention than mere distant rough observations of the great and remote.

Such intervention has, moreover, more important effects in the world of the small particles than it would have in the realm of the ponderous planets. A small delay in the first atomic event of a long chain may delay the whole chain, and thus a small cause, a part of the biography of one atom, may grow to have a giant effect. This amplification of causes is one of the characteristic features of the atomic world, and almost by itself would make foreseeing the future of a collection of atoms a calculation of probabilities, within the purview of statistics but not of the large-scale measurements of astronomy.

The world of the atoms is in fact far more predictable for us than for Laplace. He could not really understand the behavior of a single chemical substance, whereas, standing high on the shoulders of all those who have built science over three centuries, we are able to see far and wide in the world of matter. We are able to design new material of many kinds, building them up according to theoretical principles from commonplace atoms to serve many ends.

But the predictions we make are, without exception, for atoms in their crowds. They are not the individual predictions of the almanac, planet by planet, but rather the mass certainties of the actuary, who knows not when any one man will die, but who can set reliable expectations of life among very many. The most familiar example is that of radioactive decay. Here one may be sure that of 10,000,000 identical radioactive atoms, nearly 5,000,000 will disintegrate in the first week, say; 2,500,000 more the second week, and so on. But when only ten atoms remain, a week may see five more decays, or three, or even eight, following the well-known mathematics of random events. When only the last atom remains, though it has an average life expectancy exactly the same as all its fellows, it may by chance live for weeks, or it may expire in the next minute. No one can predict the moment of its demise. But if one takes a great many atoms of this kind, one may be certain that they will on the average live just one week.

This rise of statistical prediction, of probability, is perhaps the most characteristic of all the developments of twentieth-century science. It represents the realization that we cannot claim to know all the causes of things, for those causes are far too numerous. We have not measured enough, we have not recorded enough, we have not interfered in the past as much as we would have found necessary if we had tried to carry out the program of Laplace. But we have not lost our sense of the orderliness of the world; we have gained rather a sense of its complexity. And in that gain physics at one step found new and awesome powers. At last men could see how a world of novelty and surprise could yet be a world of scientific order.

There was one more step to go. That step was taken between the two World Wars, in the development of the modern quantum theory, during what was quite possibly the most fruitful generation of work in all the history of science since the Babylonian priests charted the morning star.

Quantum mechanics is subtle and versatile; by no means have all its difficulties been solved. But I think it is not too hard to try to give some sense of what this last and deepest revolution has meant.

We have already spoken of the world of atoms. A closer look at the atom is needed. Let two facts be recalled:

1. All the atoms of a given species—say all atoms of gold, are identical. This is evident even in common experience. A newly mined nugget from California and a worn Roman coin yield the same pure gold to the assayer. He may discard some dross, but the gold that remains is one and the same. But how different are the series of knocks and bangs the two samples have suffered! Yet even precise measurements do not reveal any differences between individual gold atoms, though they do show us that different mass samples of even pure gold differ

slightly, say in density. The near-identity in bulk depends upon the true identity of the atoms.

2. Yet the atom has a structure. If it were, as the Greeks thought, some indivisible—*a-tom* means *without cutting*—whole, we could understand the identity. Yet out of a gold atom we can pluck hundreds of electrons, protons and neutrons. It is a relatively complex structure made up of moving, interacting parts. If it were like the solar system, for example, we could not expect two atoms, which had suffered different series of knocks and bangs, to remain identical. Perhaps the hard knocks would break them apart, and we would simply no longer count them as gold. That indeed happens. But there must be many softer blows of fate in the lifetime of an atom, each of which ought to modify it a little, yet leave it still whole but distorted, as the solar system would be distorted by a passing distant star. On this view, which is surely the only one consistent with all we have so far said of physics, a sample of gold atoms might form a kind of population, rather similar as all peas are similar, or all pedigreed poodles, similar, and yet differing slightly one from another in more or less every property. The similarity of complex systems is never precise, in the old physics, but only approximate.

Thus do atomic identity and atomic structures conflict. Atoms are complex structures, yet they come in great armies of truly identical individuals. Only the quantum theory has explained this, in a fairly complete and certainly a deep and unexpected way. It is a way which contradicts flatly the old mechanics of Newton, and yet in a strange way bears it out.

In the modern mechanics of the atom, only certain definite patterns of internal motion can be long-lasting. These patterns differ from one another, not simply by gradual, almost imperceptible differences which shade smoothly one into another, as might the positions of the planets in a great number of similar solar systems, but by real gaps in energy, real differences in shape. Such distinct patterns are stable and self-maintaining against small disturbances.

If an outside disturbance—say, the shock of collision with

another atom—is sharp enough, it can throw the atom into a differing pattern. But if it does not become that serious, it makes no lasting effect at all on the atom, which remains in its original state after the collision. The pattern either heals completely, so to speak, or it dies and is replaced by another. There is no such thing as a mere wounding, ending in a scarred recovery, a little bent or distorted. Such behavior admirably explains the identity of the atoms.

But what of the atom's structure? How are the electrons moving in the atom? The answer is strange but quite definite. The electron motion is fixed by the whole pattern of the atom, but it is fixed only in a statistical way. Just as one cannot predict the day a given policyholder will die, so one cannot at all predict where the electron is in any given atom in its normal pattern. Nevertheless, if a great many of the identical atoms are inspected, to locate their moving electrons, a perfectly precise and definite pattern will be revealed in the statistics so compiled, just as the life tables give a regular change of mortality with aging or residence or occupation. The electron's every position is contained in the pattern of the atom. But it is contained only potentially: the pattern has the potential of showing up the electron now here, now there. What the very next result will be can be predicted only statistically. Yet statistically the precision is as complete as one could wish: every feature of the pattern is fully and precisely realized as the number of individual identical atoms inspected grows and grows.

The story can be told from the other side. It is possible to "prepare" a normal atom, confining it with electric forces, say, in such a way that one knows exactly where the electrons are. But then that atom has no long-lasting pattern; its electrons will move about in a way which depends upon every detail of the original preparation, as they would in the Newtonian physics. No sign of identity would remain. No two atoms would be sure to evolve in exactly the same way. Whenever atoms are found identical, then their electrons are not to be located except by stating their potential positions; as soon as the electrons are indeed located and tagged, then the development in

414

time becomes specific to the initial set-up, and the remarkable self-healing identity is lost.

There is no use trying to blink away that this dual behavior of atoms is a new state of affairs in physics. It has been studied and questioned in a thousand diverse contexts, and has so far withstood every test. The consequences turn out to apply to crystals or to fluids; to molecules, atoms, and their constituents; to light—to the whole range of phenomena in the universe. And the predictions that follow from it merge into the older physics, with a boundary between the two so smooth and neat that no joint can be seen.

For the possibility of true identity depends on the presence of the little gaps in energy between one persistent pattern and the next. If these gaps are larger than the energy transferred to the system in its encounters with the outside world, the structure will remain unchanged nearly always, and its pattern will heal. But if the gaps, the quantum jumps, are too small, then each external influence can make some lasting change in the system, and the whole complex will behave according to the old physics, showing the individual scars or distortions which it has acquired in its life. Then true identity will be absent.

Now, the size of the gaps depends on the massiveness of the system. Everything of atomic size will possess sizable gaps, and even hard knocks by similar atoms will generally be resisted. But anything so big as a dust grain will easily yield to disturbance and must then behave in the old way. Remarkably enough, even structures the size of gem crystals reveal their quantum gaps, and assume a structureless identity, whenever they can be sheltered from the ordinary atomic collisions. Such a quiet state is achieved at very low temperatures, near the "absolute zero" where molecular motion would, according to the old physics, cease.

The success of this new theory is the final attack upon the fatalism of Laplace. For we now see that the myriad particles which indeed do make up our universe form an unfolding pattern of events whose every *potential* future state may be predicted. But just what events are realized *in fact* can be foretold only in the statistician's sense, with a sureness that grows the greater the larger the piece of matter, or current of energy, with which the prediction is concerned. There is room to breathe in such a world. Yet it is no world of caprice or chaos. Chance and cause have been wonderfully married into a point of view in which precise pattern governs potential events, and yet in which the variety of the potentialities allows the full growth of that novelty which we know to govern the world we live in. Many have written of this richer theory of the physicists as based on the principle of uncertainty. *Uncertainty*, if you like; it seems a poor word to describe the richness of valid prediction which the science now possesses. It is becoming common sense.

True, some great questions still lie beyond the frontiers of our knowledge. One of them is part and parcel of the problem of atomic identity. For the building blocks of the atoms, the electrons and protons and neutrons and their like, are themselves marvelously identical. Yet in electron or proton the kind of inner structure is like nothing we have encountered before, if it is structure at all. For the parts we can take out of the proton, for example, are truly particles with mass and charge, yet can leave the proton unchanged. The proton can be made to yield up particle after particle and still remain the same, like the purse of the happy Fortunatus. Only energy need be supplied. This is no assembly like an atom or like the parts of a watch. Quantum theory alone gives us a start to understanding this, and even it has no full answer here.

By now we have surveyed most of the range of physics in our time; and the Laplacean clock that ticks away our lives by rote has not remained. In its place we have a few great new unexpected laws, which are in fact far more powerful, and yet somehow closer to common sense, than the simple and complacent physics of Napoleon's day. We might recall them in a terse list. The labels of time and space are not absolute, but cause and effect remain connected for all observers. Knowledge of the physical world is no mere passive, ethereal thing, but always is based upon action, measurement, and must be recorded or expressed in the only medium physics has, a grainy, atomic one. Cause and change are caught up together in the world of atomic scale: predictable pattern is found ruling the identical atoms, but their individual changes can be predicted only by the actuary's powerful schemes. Such is the subtle picture of the world which modern physics has drawn.

Now we come to temptation. Newton and Laplace built a picture of the universe which was based on their brilliant successes with clockwork and eclipses. We know now that the universe is not merely clockwork. Modern physics—Einstein, Boltzmann and Bohr will do as names of pathfinders—has a far grander picture, one that will one day beautifully explain atoms or stars, birds or bees, television cameras and antibiotics. But the universe is wider even than that. Every attempt to build upon the results of science a picture of the universe which will sustain the life and the values of men is risky. For science can never be complete, never without its insecure frontiers.

This is the essence of science. Notwithstanding, each generation must try. And I believe that in our times we have come to a scientific picture wide enough and supple enough to form a background for the philosophy of life of every man. Science cannot itself be such a philosophy, but it is the proving ground of every philosophy today. For the ideas of physics are no less invasive than the machines and the power lines which they have made possible. Just as the devices of modern technology press their way into ancient lands, so will the great ideas that lie behind them find their way, year by year and land by land, into the old ways of thought, into the long impregnable fortresses of belief and assumption everywhere. In the end, no view of the world can remain unchallenged by the physicists' findings: the future of every philosophy can be measured by the degree to which it can admit to the world of the mind the physical map of the atomic universe.

The aims and the values of men are not and will not be made by physicists. But if those values are to remain the basis of a way of life, they will need to come to terms with physics. Physics no longer sees its universe as a mere whirling automaton, but rather as a changing, chancy and yet an impersonally ordered and patterned place. In this place action and knowledge are not distinct; full certainty and complete hazard are equally unreal. Such a picture of the world admits the play of moral choice, yet it requires that even moral choice can be studied at least in part with the tools of science. We think often of the novelty of western science and technology as it sweeps violently across the old lands. But we do not see so clearly the ancientness of our own systems of values, standing as they do upon religions ten or twenty centuries old, or upon philosophical systems mainly older than modern science. The modernization of our own ideas may prove to hold as much of difficulty for us as the industrialization of the peasant ways has held and will yet demand of Asia or Africa. But like their hard trials, ours too may bring hope and the promise of a newer and a finer life of heart and mind.

Further reading:
Born, Max: RESTLESS UNIVERSE. New York: Dover Publications, Inc.; 1957.

Born, Max: NATURAL PHILOSOPHY OF CAUSE AND CHANCE. New York: Oxford University Press; 1949.

Heisenberg, Werner: PHYSICS AND PHILOSOPHY. New York: Harper & Brothers; 1958.

418

WILLIAM BARRETT

William Barrett, professor of philosophy at New York University, is one of the foremost American interpreters of European philosophy. His recent book, Irrational Man, is a definitive study of Existentialist philosophy for the general reader. A classical scholar with a training in Greek and medieval philosophy, Professor Barrett spent the five years which followed his war service as a literary journalist and as an editor of Partisan Review. This experience outside the academy prompted him, upon returning to teaching, to "relate philosophy to the real affairs of men in history."

CCCCCCCCCCCCCCCCCCCCCCCCCCCC

What Is Existentialism?

BY

WILLIAM BARRETT

What is Existentialism?
This question had a lively and journalistic, though somewhat superficial, ring at the end of World War II when we first heard news of this philosophic movement from France. Nowadays Americans are asking this question with a great deal more earnestness and seriousness. As Americans, of course, with our inherited prejudice for plain speech, we tend to be suspicious of any big "ism"; and the label "Existentialism" seemed to suggest something eccentric or exotic or both. Many of us, after all, had had our first news of this philosophy from some rather bizarre and Bohemian settings in Paris after the war. But these accidents of misunderstanding have now largely faded into the past; and in recent years Americans have begun to give serious attention to this new—and yet very old—philosophy.

There are many reasons for this change in attitude. For one thing, we have just learned here that in Europe for more than the past twenty years a well-developed movement in existential psychoanalysis has been going on; and, further, that this movement, far from being the creation of Bohemian intellectuals, is headed by practicing psychiatrists, directors of hospitals, sana-

421

toria and mental clinics. When healers of the mind have to go to a new philosophy for help in understanding human psychology, we, too, begin to feel that we may have more to learn from this philosophy than we might have supposed.

Another reason for this new and more serious interest is the continuing and mounting influence of modern art and literature. As we reflect more and more upon the strange and powerful art of the first fifty years of this century—upon the disturbing world of Kafka or Joyce or the early Faulkner, or upon the baffling image, or lack of image, of man in modern painting and sculpture; as we search for ourselves and our time in all this art, we begin to find our life today riddled with more questions than we had suspected. And we also see that Existentialism is the one philosophy of this period that has raised the themes that have obsessed modern art to the level of explicit intellectual questioning.

The immense vogue of such popular works of social analysis as Riesman's *The Lonely Crowd* and W. H. Whyte's *The Organization Man* has led people to reflect uneasily about what is taking place in modern society. These books have one central theme: that modern mass society, while it raises the material level of all, tends to swallow up the individual in its intricate machinery. Modern society becomes a kind of bureaucratically organized flight from the Self; a flight into which everybody can easily drift. These criticisms, however, do not originate with our own social analysts; more than a century ago Kierkegaard inveighed against the depersonalizing forces of modern society far more powerfully than do Riesman and Whyte. The same line of criticism has been developed with great subtlety by Ortega y Gasset, Jaspers, Marcel and Buber. Present-day sociologists have provided some admirable documentation of the way in which these depersonalizing forces work, but they have hardly attacked the philosophical root of the matter. For this we have to go to the Existentialists themselves.

Finally, a simpler and more direct reason for this keener interest in Existentialism is the increasing number of translations of the existentialist writings. As we get more English versions of the books of Martin Buber, Gabriel Marcel, Martin Heidegger,

Karl Jaspers, José Ortega y Gasset, the name of Jean-Paul Sartre no longer pre-empts the field; and we see that Existentialism is a basic movement among European thinkers, one that is neither peripheral nor faddist but central to our time. It becomes apparent that the body of the existentialist writings constitutes a commentary upon the human situation as rich and profound as any produced in our century, and that it would be folly for Americans to ignore it.

What, then, is Existentialism?

The question is relatively easy to answer; for the irony here is that, despite its portentous label, this philosophy derives from concrete and everyday human experience rather than from any abstract or specialized areas of knowledge. Existentialism is a philosophy that confronts the human situation *in its totality* to ask what the basic conditions of human existence are and how man can establish his own meaning out of these conditions. Its method is to begin with this human existence as a fact without any ready-made preconceptions about the *essence* of man. There is no prefabricated human nature that freezes human possibilities into a preordained mold; on the contrary, man exists first and makes himself what he is out of the conditions into which he is thrown. "Existence precedes essence," as the formula puts it.

Here philosophy itself—no longer a mere game for technicians or an obsolete discipline superseded by science—becomes a fundamental dimension of human existence. For man is the one animal who not only can, but must ask himself what his life means. We are all philosophers in this sense whenever we reach a point in life where total reflection upon ourselves is called for. Most of the time we try to avoid such occasions for total reflection by temporary expedients: we plug leaks in the ship without bothering to ask where it is heading. But if the problem is fundamental, expedients do not serve and we are faced with such questions as: What am I ultimately interested in? What is the point of it all? What meaning does my life have?

With these questions we become actively engaged with the problems of philosophy. The existential philosopher spends a lifetime asking these questions that assail the ordinary man only in unusual or extreme moments. One of the achievements of existential philosophers is that they have restored to the philosophical profession the true meaning of the latter word: a full-time vocation to which a man feels summoned or called. If the old saying that "Philosophy bakes no bread" has its point, it is also true that in the end we do not bake bread or in fact do anything else without a philosophy.

So much by way of a schematic answer to the question what Existentialism is. But Existentialism itself is opposed to schematic and abstract answers about human facts, which are always concrete, individual, situated in a definite place and time. Man is a historical being—that is his uniqueness among all other animals—and he can never be understood apart from his history. This is true of existential philosophy itself as a historical human fact. To understand it concretely we have to see where its roots lie in the history of modern thought and what urgencies of the modern spirit drive it onward.

The existential philosophers themselves have taught us to reread in a new and more profound way the whole history of modern thought. By showing us philosophy as an essentially human enterprise they have enabled us to see the whole history of philosophy for the momentous human drama it really is. Most of us tend to think of the history of philosophy as a succession of contradicting opinions held by rival philosophers or rival schools decade after decade or century after century. The dramatic parts of human history seem to be wars and battles, or great political decisions that change the external patterns of our lives. But for the Existentialist the history of philosophy is one of the most dramatic and fateful chapters in human history; the great philosophers, far from being mere airy speculators, are in fact the real prophets. Their thinking illuminates the problems that mankind as a whole, in its external and social history, will have to live out for generations.

Our modern epoch in philosophy—and with it our whole modern world—begins with the great French philosopher René Descartes (1596–1650). Descartes, who was also a mathematician and a physicist, wanted his philosophy to establish a basis for the then "new science" of mathematical physics. For this, the first step needed was to establish the solid objectivity of the world of physical things, and particularly those aspects of things that are quantitative and measurable and so can be expressed in mathematical laws. Hence Descartes declared that matter was essentially extension: that is, the real properties of any physical object are the quantitative ones. What about the qualities of things? They are declared to be merely subjective effects in the human mind. Here the world of the new science is no longer the ordinary human world in which we live. This qualitative world of our everyday life, with all the color, warmth and vibrancy of its texture, is thrust out of the real world and relegated to the human mind as a kind of shadowy specter. Such is the famous Cartesian dualism: the world of matter (objects) is split off from the human mind (subject). More significantly, it splits the human and the scientific worlds.

Today, we are still experiencing the consequences of this dualism. Descartes is a founder and a prophet of the historical era in which mathematical physics comes more and more to dominate the whole of human life. Today, when we tremble before the possibilities of atomic bombs and missiles, when the mathematical physicists and technicians are more important instruments of power than any military general, we need hardly be told that this Cartesian era of mathematical physics approaches its violent climax. But also, with all the human turmoil of our period, with its political unrest and individual rootlessness, we are aware of the skeleton that lurks in the Cartesian closet: our power to deal with the world of matter has multiplied out of all proportion to our wisdom in coping with the problems of our human and spiritual world.

Descartes could bear the consequences of his philosophy because in the rest of his person he was still a Catholic of the Middle Ages. Descartes the thinker was one thing; Descartes the man something else; although in Descartes' philosophy there was no place for the two to meet, in his life—for very practical human purposes—he had established a concordat between them by remaining a faithful son of the Church. When he discovered analytic geometry, he promptly made a pilgrimage of gratitude to the shrine of the Virgin of Loretto. So too in his philosophy: however much the prophet of the new science, he still retained the medieval conviction that human reason has its own luminous and direct access to the transcendent reality of God. So long as Descartes could prove to his own satisfaction that God exists, this omnipotent and benevolent God could heal the breach between man's physical and spiritual being.

But this comforting assurance of the Middle Ages receded more and more as "the new science" of Descartes and Newton made astounding progress through the next century. The trouble —and it is a trouble at the heart of our whole modern epoch— comes to the surface again with Immanuel Kant (1724–1804). Writing at the end of the great century of Rationalism in 1781 in his *Critique of Pure Reason*, Kant showed that the transcendent ideals of our traditionally Christian civilization—God, the human soul and its possible immortality, the freedom of man as a spiritual person—could not be known by human reason. Like everything human, reason has its history; and here, in the course of its evolution, it had at last become strictly scientific reason. Insofar as reason sought to be scientific and exact it had to exclude all references to the ultimate things that man had lived by in his ethical and spiritual life.

Had Kant been merely what is now called a "scientific philosopher," like the modern positivists, he would at this point simply have thrown out God and the human soul as "meaningless" and gone off in search of new values. Since he retained the vestiges of a pious Protestant upbringing, however, he chose to live by the values of traditional Christianity. Hence he went on to write a *Critique of Practical Reason* in which he argued that, though science could never deal with these ultimate things, man in the seriousness of his ethical striving is called upon to live as if he had an immortal soul, and as if there were a God who providentially guided the destinies of the world. Kant held that in our inner conscience we touch a reality more absolute than anything in science.

The human, or existential, import of Kant's whole philosophy comes then to this: what Kant the man lived by as an ethical and spiritual person, Kant the scientific thinker could not even bring into thought. The split between the scientific and the human world with which Descartes launched our modern epoch has here become more sharply drawn. Kant, like Descartes before him, had that naïveté which sometimes accompanies great genius, and hardly anticipated the explosive effects of his philosophy. When his first *Critique* dropped like a bombshell on intellectual Germany, Kant himself was most astonished that his contemporaries were shocked.

The idealist philosophers after Kant felt that he had dug a chasm between two parts of the human personality, and by one means or another they sought to restore the spiritual wholeness or integrity of man. One of the greatest of these was G. W. F. Hegel (1770–1831). Hegel's means of restoring the wholeness of man was an imperialism of reason so audacious that it eventually brought Existentialism into being as a necessary corrective. If there are ethical and spiritual realities that concern us ultimately as human beings, Hegel argued, then these must be accessible to reason. Reason takes in all areas of human experience; nothing can be denied to it. In making reason all-inclusive, however, Hegel also made it omnivorous: wishing to give it wings to soar, he also gave it the devouring beak of a vulture. Everything vital and individual is swallowed up in the maw of the Hegelian system. In Hegel's thought, religion—even a religion like Christianity in which the central faith revolves around the unique and unreasonable moment in history when God became man in order to save the human race —becomes merely a crude approximation, by parable and myth, of the absolute truth that reason can spin out of its own ideas.

Enter now Existentialism. The moment was perfectly timed in this great human drama of western thought—for the situation was ripe for revolt. The revolt came in the persons of Sören Kierkegaard (1813–55) and Friedrich Nietzsche (1844–1900), who are now accepted as the founding fathers of existential philosophy. Neither was an academic philosopher, though Nietzsche had earlier been a professor of classical philology; and perhaps just because they were outsiders to academic philosophy, they had sharper eyes for the real human root of the trouble. Sometimes an outsider coming into a family can see more clearly the source of its dissensions than can those blinded by their intramural quarrels.

Kierkegaard put an end to the totalitarian claims for reason made by philosophers like Hegel. If religion could be reduced to reason, said Kierkegaard, there would be no need for religion —least of all a religion like Christianity whose central belief in the God-Man is altogether paradoxical to reason. As a believing Christian, Kierkegaard insisted on the necessity of faith as a vital act beyond reason. But beyond this message as a Christian apologist, Kierkegaard brought to the attention of philosophers —and more recently to psychologists—the fact that human existence can never be totally enclosed in any system. To exist as an individual is to strive, change, develop, stand open to the future, be incomplete—while a system by its very nature is closed, complete, static, dead. The philosopher or scientist who thinks he can freeze our human existence into a system does so by substituting a pallid and abstract concept for the living and concrete reality. Life is lived forward and understood backward, says Kierkegaard. If we were ever to understand it completely, we would have to be already dead, without a future and with no untried and novel possibilities before us.

In one sense Kierkegaard returns us to the situation of Kant before Hegel: he gives a more urgent and powerful expression to the Kantian view that each of us, as individuals, touches reality inwardly in our moments of serious moral decision rather than in the detached speculations of reason. In another sense, however, Kierkegaard destroys the makeshift supports of Kantian ethics by calling attention to the fact that the values Kant espouses—and espouses in spite of scientific reason—live or die with the Christian faith. These values are not rooted in the eternal nature of the human conscience, but historically and existentially derive from the Christian religion; and the central crisis of the modern period is that this religion now stands on trial. Kant's values cannot be kept alive by mere rational reflection on the so-called "postulates of practical reason"; in the end they can be kept alive only by the energy of faith.

Nietzsche starts from this same historical insight, but attacks Kant from just the opposite direction. If, says Nietzsche, the development of human reason along the line of science has brought us to the point in human history where scientific reason rules out those transcendent ideals—God, the immortal soul, our essential freedom as moral agents—that Christians have lived by for centuries, then why persist in Kant's blind old prejudice for these concepts? Why not throw them on the dust heap of history? Besides, is not Christianity already dead or at least dying in our time when, though some people may give it lip service, it no longer rules the total life of man as it did in the earlier ages of faith?

Had Nietzsche stopped here, he would have been merely one among many nineteenth-century atheists; more brilliant and incisive in his language than the others, but hardly a founder of existential philosophy. Nietzsche was, however, a man of great imagination and perhaps even greater religious yearning. He could see that the abolishing of the transcendent world in which the human spirit had hitherto sought its home would not solve all problems, as some of the rationalists of his century thought, but would only bring into desperate relief the pathos of our human situation. For when God is at last dead for man, when the last gleam of light is extinguished and only the impenetrable darkness of a universe that exists for no purpose surrounds us, then at last man knows he is alone in a world where he has to create his own values. The disappearance of religion would be the greatest challenge in human history—perhaps the ultimate challenge—for man would then be fully and dreadfully responsible to himself and for himself. Moreover, the natural sciences that helped bring about this situation could not help here, for they can never explain to man what he really is. Man steps beyond the world of natural objects in the very act of asking what this world means, what he himself means, and in seeking to create this meaning for himself. The natural sciences are tools that man can use in the service of his own values, but these sciences will never create a guiding ideal for human life.

This slow, unfolding development of modern philosophy is like a great symphony which Descartes opens with the leading theme, andante; other philosophers enrich with variations and counterthemes, allegro; and Kierkegaard and Nietzsche bring to a furious and boiling presto. It might be tempting to hope that the existential philosophers of the twentieth century have at last brought us the grand finale; but unlike a symphony, the process of human thought admits no finale so long as man continues to be man, a being perpetually open to the future. The existentialists of this century are the heirs of Kierkegaard and Nietzsche, and their task has been, first, to save the great revolt of these two giants from being buried under the apathy of academic philosophers; and secondly and more importantly, to enrich and carry on the line of thought initiated in that revolt.

The very richness and diversity of existential thought in this century makes it difficult to fashion any easy summary of its conclusions. How sum up the philosophies of such men as Karl Jaspers and Martin Heidegger of Germany, Gabriel Marcel and Jean-Paul Sartre of France, Unamuno and Ortega y Gasset of Spain? Or the thought of such existential theologians as Nikolai Berdyaev and Paul Tillich? These men have different problems, attack the problems by different methods, and on a number of points are in disagreement. Hence some critics have declared that Existentialism is not a unified movement at all, with the implication that it may not even be a definite philosophy. On the contrary, a movement is alive and vital only when it is able to generate differences among its followers; when everybody agrees, we may be sure that it has declined into the stereotyped rigidity of death. Moreover, despite the differences among Existentialists, there is a common core to their thinking. Let us try now to see what some of the main points of this common core are.

If the modern era began with the way of thinking launched by Descartes, then we must, to save ourselves, recast our fundamental way of thinking. The world Descartes portrays—of material objects stripped of all qualities, extended in mathematical space of three dimensions, and with only quantitative and measurable properties—is not the world in which we live as human beings, but a high-level abstraction from the world that surrounds and involves us, exalts or enchants or terrifies us. We live in the human world, not in the world of science. And it is from the context of this human world that all the abstractions of science ultimately derive their meaning.

So, too, those fateful abstractions, the body and the mind. Man is not basically a body to which a mind is annexed in some incomprehensible way. Man is first and foremost a concrete involvement or enmeshment with the world, and within this concreteness of his being we distinguish the opposed poles of body and mind. We do not first exist inside our bodies and then proceed to infer a world existing beyond ourselves; on the contrary, in the very act of existing we are beyond ourselves and within the world. The verb "ex-ist" means, etymologically to stand outside or beyond oneself. It is this self-transcendence that makes man what he is and distinguishes him from all the other animals whose existence does not reach backward and forward in time and history, and which remain rooted in space to their own natural habitat.

Because he is this perpetually self-transcending animal, man cannot be understood in his totality by the natural sciences —physics, chemistry, biology, or purely behaviorist psychology —as materialists have held. Man has expressed the truth of his existence in art and religion as well as in science; we would get less than the truth about human life if we left out any of these expressions of truth. One great achievement of existential philosophy has been a new interpretation of the idea of truth in order to point out that there are different kinds of truth, where a rigid scientific rationalism had postulated but one kind: objective scientific truth.

Kierkegaard introduced this difference by his analysis of religious truth. The truth with which religion is ultimately concerned, said Kierkegaard, has nothing to do with questions of rational proof. We do not exclaim, "There is a genuinely religious person!" when we happen to encounter a man who is an expert in all the subtle dialectic of theology. If we have ever encountered a genuinely spiritual person, we know that the heart of the matter lies elsewhere: in the being of the total person, not in the cerebrations of reason. Religious truth is realized actively and inwardly in the life of the individual man; it is not something embodied in a system of concepts, like science. Hence the fact that seemed so catastrophic to Kant—that the existence of God could not be proved rationally—is perfectly acceptable. For God is never real in our lives when He is considered a mere object of scientific proof or disproof.

Similarly, Heidegger has elucidated the unique kind of truth found in art. Truth is that peculiar relation of man to the object in which he lets the object be seen for what it is. Science is truth in this sense, but so too is art, though its way of letting the thing be seen is distinctly different from that of science. What kind of truth would we have about the long life of man upon this planet without those great works of art that have appeared in the tortuous course of human history? Here Existentialism, a new philosophy, goes back to a tradition before Plato, who on purely intellectualist grounds condemned all art as illusion. The older tradition among the Greeks was that their great poets were seers who voiced the hidden wisdom of the race. The Greek people of that earlier age were wiser than Plato.

A contemporary poet, our own Robert Frost, seems to speak from this ancient wisdom. Though he can hardly be called an Existentialist, Frost, in a recent address on television, epitomized this central point of Existential philosophy with the simplicity and directness of insight that only a great poet can manage:

> This present of ours I hope will be found all right for what it was. That is, that it will have made its point in history.
>
> We're going to discriminate once and for all . . . what can be made a science of and can't be made a science of. And we're going to settle that. There's a whole half of our lives that can't be made a science of, can't ever be made a science of. And we're going to know more about that before we get through this period. That's what it will be remembered for.

If the poet is right in his prophecy for our age, if we really do discriminate what can and cannot be made a science of in human life, then this would be an achievement more significant for the future of mankind than the creation of jet planes, missiles or atomic bombs.

Because it denies the restrictions of scientific rationalism, Existentialism sometimes has been labeled a form of Irrationalism. This accusation is both glib and ungrounded. We do not cast all doubt upon an instrument by pointing out its functional limitations. A crowbar is not a key, and even if we wanted to pick the lock, we should do better with a hairpin. In making this observation we can hardly be called guilty of anticrowbarism.

Scientific reason is abstract and universal; life as we live it is individual and concrete. There are bridges between the two, but the former can never claim to supersede the latter without doing violence to it. You may use the crowbar to batter down the door, but then you will have to stand the expense of having the door repaired. We smile at the absurdity of the remark by the French mathematician Laplace after he had witnessed, without being moved, a performance of Racine's *Phèdre:* "What does it prove?" The mind of this great mathematician was geared to only one kind of truth. In considering Laplace's question absurd we are only using plain human judgment, not espousing a philosophic system of Irrationalism. When scientific rationalists raise the facile cry of "irrationalism," they are exposing their own mental blind spots. The danger to our civilization is that as this rigid rationalism attempts to embrace all areas of life we will not only profit from its vision but also be the victim of its blindness.

Reason, after all, is *human* reason and we should expect it, like everything human, to have its limitations. There is no positive without a correlated negative. Being always involves non-Being. As reason becomes more abstract, it seems to soar beyond the human conditions from which it took its initial leap; but it has perpetually to return to the solid earth of our human condition for refueling. What we need is neither a blind exaltation nor an empty rejection of reason, but a new concept of what Ortega y Gasset calls "vital reason"—a reason rooted in the fundamental conditions of human existence. The

433

man who exists and the man who thinks is in the end (as in the beginning) one and the same; and if as thinker he chooses to forget that he is a man, he will end, as Kierkegaard pointed out in rebutting Hegel, by becoming humanly absurd.

One final and central point common to the Existentialists is their emphasis upon time and history as fundamental dimensions of human existence. Among all the animals man stands in a unique relation to time because he stands open to a future in which the present conditions of life can be transformed. Standing open to this future, he orders his present and connects it with his past. Hence our lives become meaningful to the degree that we bind together tomorrow, today and yesterday in an active whole. Time is thus the fundamental condition of our human existence; without time there would be no human meaning. But time, real time, is never the abstract "once upon a time" of the fairy story; it is always time here and now, urgent and pressing upon us. We are temporal beings not because we reckon with abstract mathematical time sequences, but because we experience time in the historical pressure of our generation with its challenging and fateful tasks.

Here, clearly, Existentialism emerges as a philosophy that summons us to responsible social action. This is a far cry from the earlier impression among Americans that this philosophy merely expressed a mood of despair or nihilism or Bohemian eccentricity. To be sure, this summons to social action is subordinated by the Existentialists to the more basic human task of becoming an authentic individual in our own right: we cannot meaningfully go outward into the world unless we have also gone inward and downward into the Self. Nevertheless, the authentic Self (all Existentialists agree) is never found in some Platonic realm beyond time and history, but only within the world. All significant thinking points toward the future; the historical challenge that the existential philosophers call upon us to face during the second half of this twentieth century is nothing less than this: Are we, at long last, to decide whether this coming epoch shall be the Age of Man or the Age of Mathematical Physics?

Further reading:

Barrett, William: IRRATIONAL MAN: A Study in Existential Philosophy. New York: Doubleday & Company, Inc.; 1958.

Jaspers, Karl: MAN IN THE MODERN AGE. New York: Doubleday & Company, Inc. Anchor Books; 1957.

Buber, Martin: BETWEEN MAN AND MAN. Boston: Beacon Press; 1955.

Marcel, Gabriel: MAN AGAINST MASS SOCIETY. Chicago: Henry Regnery Co.; 1952.

Heidegger, Martin: AN INTRODUCTION TO METAPHYSICS. New Haven: Yale University Press; 1959.

STEFAN T. POSSONY

[*Photograph by Ollie Atkins*]

Stefan T. Possony, professor of international politics, Graduate School, Georgetown University, was born in Austria and studied philosophy at the University of Vienna, where he earned his doctorate. He came to the United States in 1940 and joined the Institute for Advanced Study in 1941. Doctor Possony later headed the German and Italian sections in the Psychological Warfare Branch of the Office of Naval Intelligence and served on the faculty of the National War College. Since 1955 he has been an Associate, Foreign Policy Research Institute, University of Pennsylvania and member, editorial board of Orbis, A Quarterly Journal of World Affairs. *His fields of interest include communism, geopolitics, political philosophy, and strategy and revolution in the twentieth century.*

᠌᠌᠌᠌᠌᠌᠌᠌᠌᠌᠌᠌᠌᠌᠌᠌᠌᠌᠌᠌᠌᠌᠌᠌᠌᠌᠌᠌

Words That
Divide the World

BY

STEFAN T. POSSONY

Nikita S. Khrushchev, prime minister of the Union of
Soviet Socialist Republics and first secretary of the
Communist Party of the Soviet Union, is communism's leading
traveling salesman. Even though he temporarily dropped the
pretense of reasonableness at the May 1960 summit meeting, he
has everywhere preached disarmament, negotiation, coexistence,
nonaggression and peace—all of them words sweet to our ears.
For example, on February 11, 1960, he told the Parliament in
India:

> It is our firm conviction that . . . all disputed interna-
> tional issues . . . [should be solved] through negotiations.
> . . . Lasting peace . . . would have a most beneficial ef-
> fect upon the life of all peoples of the world. . . . The
> realization of a program of general and complete disarma-
> ment would usher in a new era in the development of
> human society—a world without wars, without the nuclear
> missile race. . . . I profoundly trust that the forces of rea-
> son, the forces of peace will prevail in the long run over
> the forces of war and will ensure humanity a happy and

439

bright future under conditions of lasting peace and progress. . . .

But Khrushchev also has attacked "American warmongering" and he has expressed confidence that communism will "bury" capitalism. In this quote this same thought is presented in the form that "the forces of peace will prevail . . . over the forces of war."

What is Khrushchev saying? Is he talking peace or war? Why does he use a vocabulary which seems to lend itself to multiple interpretations and misinterpretations?

For the communists, language is not just a tool for communicating ideas or a means in the search for truth. They choose words not to clarify but to produce ambiguities and induce false thinking. Strongly impressed by the usefulness of cheap and powerful weapons, they have striven to become experts in verbal artfulness. They have created a special vocabulary to serve as the cutting edge of a technique of semantic deception. Like the winds and the seas which can hollow out the hardest rock, the weapon of semantics, more subtle and less immediately destructive than nuclear bombs, has the power of eroding society. Words can serve the same purpose as artillery barrages before an attack, preparing nations opposed to communism to accept with a minimum of protest the "decisive" or death-dealing blow. In brief, the communists have taught themselves to use language as an instrument of conquest.

Historically the communist vocabulary has consisted of two types of expressions—one set for communicating with one another, the other for communicating with the rest of the world. Their standard lexicon for internal use is replete with terms like "violence" and "class warfare." It is a language of combat designed to win the struggle for the world through force, revolution and war. By contrast, their Aesopian terminology—the words employed in external communications—is derived primarily from western political thinking and includes terms which evoke positive emotions. Communists are eager to create the impression that they are peace-loving and anxious to arrange for an international system of "live and let live." Thus, like the zebra, with its day and night barks, the communists use different languages to accommodate different audiences.

As communist semanticists attained virtuoso skills, they discovered that, in many instances, communications can be made to serve a dual purpose—to say one thing to communists while simultaneously conveying quite a different message to non-communists. To the party followers the usual communication is an instruction to revolutionary action. But this very same communication must present a soothing, attractive, pacifying and paralyzing idea to the outside world.

"This "double-think" or "double-talk" mission is accomplished by applying a practice developed more than sixty years ago by Lenin, who also coined the expression "Aesopian language." Aesop, the sixth century B.C. Greek fabulist, invented the technique of hiding moral and political points behind seemingly innocuous stories and originated such colloquialisms as "sour grapes," "the wolf in sheep's clothing," "the dog in the manger" and "belling the cat." In his time Lenin avoided tsarist censorship of his writings by masking "communists" as "strict Marxists" and substituting "*the* reform"—not to be confused with "reforms," which was an Aesopian term dear to moderate socialists—for the taboo word "revolution."

By now most of the original communist vocabulary has been given an Aesopian equivalent. "Dictatorship of the proletariat" grew into "democracy"; "expropriation" was transformed into "planning"; "revolution" was camouflaged as "liberation"; and "communism" itself was disguised as "anticolonialism," "anti-imperialism" or "antifascism."

The present leaders of the Soviet Union frequently reiterate their firm adherence to the principles of Marx, Engels and Lenin. This constant reassertion of allegiance to their "founding fathers" is more than a ritual profession of faith required by all true and pseudo religions. Far more significantly, it is a reminder to communist audiences that they must interpret all Soviet statements, even the most Aesopian, in the light of the original communist creed.

For example, while Khrushchev may use the term "peaceful coexistence" without qualification a few times, he soon takes pains to explain that he is talking about the "Leninist concept of coexistence." Communists know that this particular concept is quite different from what most westerners presume the word "coexistence" to mean.

Shakespeare asked: "What's in a name? That which we call a rose by any other name would smell as sweet." And that great master of the ruse, Stalin, laid down this rule: "Words must have no relation to action. . . . Words are one thing, actions another. Good words are a mask to conceal bad deeds."

The communist conflict doctrine is simple enough, and more or less self-evident. The goal—never rescinded and frequently reiterated—is to ensure the world victory of communism; that is, to seize power anywhere and ultimately everywhere.

The concept of how communists think they might be able to reach this goal can be summarized in three basic propositions.

ONE: There are three types of conquest techniques—the nonviolent, such as propaganda and economic warfare; the violent, such as terror, guerrilla operations and uprisings; and the military, such as civil and international, conventional and nuclear war. Communists must master all these types of conflict and be ready to employ each and any, singly or in combination, according to necessity or opportunity.

TWO: While much can be gained from propaganda and political warfare, strong opponents can be overthrown only by force and firepower. The world cannot be conquered for communism—or for anyone—without "frightful collisions" in the form of major wars.

THREE: Although war is inevitable, every effort should be made to weaken the opponents of communism before extreme risks are taken and decisive military battles are joined. Through careful preparation the military phases of the conflict should be rendered as cheap and easy as possible. If and when the communists achieve overpowering force superiority, the anticommunist nations may be prevailed upon to surrender rather than risk destruction.

The communists constantly update these simple concepts

to conform to changes in technology; yet basically these ideas have remained the guiding principles of communist behavior for half a century. They also are the key which deciphers the true meaning of Aesopian language. Let us apply this key and translate into plain English some of the catchy words which the Soviets are using to advance their fortunes. (In each case I give the nearest Russian equivalent for the English word or phrase.)

NEGOTIATION

ПЕРЕГОВОРЫ

The communists understand negotiation as a conflict technique facilitating conquest on the installment plan. It is a method of agitation and a tool for weakening the opponents of communism. But if genuine political issues are involved, it can never be a method for settling disputes with noncommunists. The true purpose of negotiation is to get and not to give.

The time consumed in a negotiation provides a breathing space; if a longer respite is required, an agreement may be signed. To be acceptable, agreements must have "revolutionary significance"; they must not, as Stalin put it, "hinder the Communist Party from conducting its independent, political and organizational work . . . and from preparing the conditions necessary for the hegemony of the proletariat." Once the agreement is signed, the respite achieved must be exploited "to secure future strategic advantages" (Stalin).

Agreements should be adhered to only so long as they are useful to the revolutionary cause. If agreements become onerous or impede the advance of communism, Lenin's rule applies, that communists should not tie their hands with "considerations of formality," and treaties and compacts may be broken —without warning and without renegotiation.

All international conflicts over relations between capitalism and communism as social systems—issues like unification of Germany, "lowering of tension," disarmament, armistices, peace treaties, and so on—involve political issues. When negotiations on such problems are held with the democratic nations, the communist intent is to gain concessions and time, and to convince the noncommunists that they must grant compromises which will lead to a "lasting" settlement of the problem. Yet no western concession can be final before ultimate surrender. If a problem is settled by negotiation now, another must be posed immediately, and then another, in an interminable sequence.

How does the "semantic misunderstanding" resulting from projecting our meaning of negotiations into communist statements affect international relations?

In 1958 Khrushchev declared, "We shall never settle controversial problems in relations between states by means of war. We shall endeavor to solve problems of this kind peacefully by negotiation." Like all other governments, communist states naturally find it useful to engage in negotiations of the customary type *if nonpolitical issues are involved.* In their language, "interstate" problems must not be confused with international problems. The latter are "political" and hence important, the former deal with technical matters. In this statement, then, Khrushchev meant that the really decisive questions could not be settled by negotiation. But superficial reading conveys the opposite impression. Actually, Khrushchev promised merely to "endeavor" settlement.

The record shows that the Soviets have an excellent chance to gain from negotiations with the West. Given their definition of the term, negotiation is a game that they cannot possibly lose. By adhering strictly to their understanding of what it means to negotiate, they are free to engage in endless talk and go home without agreeing to anything, or to sign an agreement "as a means of gaining strength" (Lenin), with every intention of breaking the agreement later, as soon as it ceases to have "revolutionary significance." Hence it is not surprising that in 1955 the Senate Judiciary Committee reported that within thirty-eight years, the Soviet Government had concluded nearly 1000 treaties and "broken its word to virtually every country to which it ever gave a signed promise." This finding is consistent with communist understanding of what the words "negotiation" and "agreement" mean. They acted exactly as their doctrine taught them to act.

PEACE AND PEACEFUL COEXISTENCE
МИР И МИРНОЕ СОСУЩЕСТВОВАНИЕ

The communists define peace as the nonmilitary phases of protracted conflict. To them, peace means: (a) an invitation to noncommunists never to resist efforts to expand the communist empire and to hasten the communization of the world; (b) the utilization of conflict methods short of war, such as propaganda, political warfare, uprising and guerrilla fighting; (c) the creation of optimum conditions for risking military battle; (d) the terminal point of communist world conquest; and (e), in the form of "lasting peace," the period after the consolidation of the classless society.

A "peace policy" is considered to be "merely another and —under given conditions—a more advantageous form of fighting capitalism." According to a Comintern resolution of 1928, "peace policy" provides "the best basis for taking advantage of the antagonisms among the imperialist states." The term does not imply that the communists intend reconciliation with capitalism: "struggle for world peace" is the Aesopian term for "cold war."

"Peaceful coexistence" is the current version of "peace policy." The term denotes a temporary situation in which there is an absence of violent struggle. During such a period careful and cautious tactics should be used while preparations are being made to resume the "advance of communism."

Khrushchev has defined coexistence in a most pedestrian way. He does not "want capitalism to exist . . . but cannot help but recognize that it does exist." Yet, he warned, "if you live among dogs, keep the stick with you."

Upon his return from the United States, a more orthodox Khrushchev explained peaceful coexistence by referring to Len-

445

in's "flexible" foreign policy in signing the peace treaty with Germany in 1918. Lenin himself frequently cited this particular treaty as an example of how communists could obtain a "breathing space" when they needed time. In 1925 Stalin defined "the essence of the question" as: "Who will defeat whom?" This definition applies to all conditions prior to communist victory—including "coexistence."

Whenever we transfer our American interpretations of peace and coexistence to communist statements on the subject, misunderstanding is sure to arise.

In May, 1959, Khrushchev met with a group of United States businessmen visiting the U.S.S.R. and remarked: "Do not be afraid . . . neither for yourselves nor for your children. You may sleep undisturbed, the U.S.S.R. will never use its forces to attack anyone." But by his own insistence Khrushchev is a good communist. He does not expect that communism can be established through democratic elections. "In the process of the proletarian world revolution, wars between proletarian and bourgeois states . . . will necessarily and inevitably arise" (Lenin). Khrushchev has promised the free world to bury it, and when he was in the United States he confirmed that he had used this expression. He explained that he did not mean to bury every American in a physical sense, a correction which he found hilarious. But he did mean, he said, that capitalism was historically doomed and that communism would prevail.

Khrushchev did not volunteer any particulars about the precise processes or procedures by which that abstraction, history, would bury the United States. In view of the hazards of nuclear war, Khrushchev probably prefers to prevail peacefully. But, so far, the communist dictionary has never said that the communists desire to coexist peacefully to the end of time: the book says clearly that coexistence is only for the time being.

In his farewell address to the American people on September 27, 1959, Khrushchev said: "In the Soviet Union everyone is in favor of living in peace." Of course, according to communist doctrine, "lasting peace and progress" can be attained only after the abolition of capitalist "property relationships." Thus, insofar as the communists are concerned, *lasting* coexistence envisages the peculiar relationship which the dog shares with the bone and the rope with the executed.

DISARMAMENT PROPOSALS

ПРЕДЛОЖЕНИЯ О РАЗОРУЖЕНИИ

The communists define disarmament proposals as efforts designed to divert attention from security problems, to weaken hostile military forces quantitatively and qualitatively, and to change the world balance of power in favor of communism. Since disarmament proposals may lead to negotiations, they are conceived as a device to "buy time."

Lenin maintained that a sincere demand by communists for disarmament is "reactionary," "illusionary" and "tantamount to the complete abandonment . . . of revolution." He taught that "every 'peace program' is . . . a piece of hypocrisy." Communists should make disarmament proposals "to recruit sympathizers . . . overthrow the *bourgeoisie*, and establish the proletarian dictatorship."

Obeying this injunction, the communists since 1922 have made seven radical disarmament proposals, and negotiations on the subject have dragged for a generation. Late in 1959 Khrushchev, asserting that the Soviets do not want to threaten or attack anybody, personally presented a "new" disarmament plan to the United Nations—a plan which Henry Cabot Lodge aptly described as a proposal for 100-per-cent disarmament and 10-per-cent inspection. Khrushchev's plan is inspired by the communist definition of "general and complete disarmament." This definition indicates that a "world without wars" would constitute "a new era in the development of human society"—meaning disarmament is possible only *after* the world revolution has been accomplished.

Similarly, according to the communist dictionary, international confidence can prevail *only* in a communist world. This being the case, communists "negotiate" about disarmament by arguing against control and inspection on the grounds that confidence must precede inspection. Hence, no inspection with-

447

out communism; but obviously in a world empire under communist monopoly rule, inspection would be redundant. Communist arguments about control exasperate United States negotiators; nevertheless they conform completely to communist understanding of the words involved.

In an attempt to prove the sincerity of his disarmament proposals, Khrushchev, in January 1960, announced to the Supreme Soviet that a "major reduction" of the Soviet armed forces would be carried out. In this case, "disarmament" simply meant disbandment of troops no longer needed. For in the same speech Khrushchev stated openly that "in reducing the number of men in the armed forces, we are not diminishing firepower. On the contrary, it has increased qualitatively several times." The communists are faithfully executing Lenin's directive to work toward "the arming of the proletariat . . . and the disarming [of] the *bourgeoisie*." They do desire disarmament; for by their own definition disarmament before the completion of the revolution means, first, the unilateral disarmament of their opponents and, second, the strengthening of their own forces. It would seem, then, that in this case the semantic divergence between communism and the free world is almost 180 degrees apart.

LIBERATION MOVEMENTS AND IMPERIALISM

ОСВОБОДИТЕЛЬНЫЕ ДВИЖЕНИЯ И ИМПЕРИАЛИЗМ

The term "liberation movement," if used by communists, differs from the western usage which became widespread during World War II and referred to indigenous forces operating against the Nazis and the Japanese in occupied countries.

Communists think of "liberation movements" as guerrilla or insurrectional forces fighting against "imperialists," "capitalist enslavers" and "national oppressors." Lenin asserted that "the liberation of the oppressed class [that is, the coming to power of the communists] is impossible . . . without a violent revolution." Liberation movements help to create the conditions for such a revolution.

"Liberators" may be democrats or nationalists, or even reactionaries and fascists, or they may be communists. As Stalin phrased it, so long as these movements "weaken imperialism and contribute to its overthrow," their own political orientation matters little to the Kremlin. Sometimes it is preferable for a liberation movement not to be communist, or to operate under an "anticommunist" label. As long as they create local unrest and disperse the forces of their opponents, movements which are potentially or actually useful to the communists are given the honorific title of "liberation." Yet the name changes quickly if and when activist political movements perform contrary to communist directives and interests. "Liberators" easily can be transformed into "lackeys" (of "imperialism" or "Wall Street"), and just as easily (often as the result of successful infiltration) may revert to the status of "freedom fighters."

In this context, what do the communists mean by "imperialism"? Originally they used the term to describe those capitalist powers which run colonial empires. Currently the term is used as a circumlocution for the United States, although occasionally it means any strong capitalist state.

Americans who pride themselves on being "anti-imperialists" should beware against falling into a semantic trap. The communist definition of "imperialism" involves the strongest hostility against the United States, hence espousal of "anti-imperialism" connotes anti-Americanism to communist ears.

WAR

ВОЙНА

The communists think of war as a creative force of social development, "the last word of social science on the eve of each general reconstruction of society" (Marx). Lenin voiced the opinion that "great historical questions can be solved only by violence." War is defined as the "locomotive of history" and is held to be inevitable so long as communism has not achieved its ultimate destiny.

Khrushchev has pointed out that "the forms of social revolution vary." The noncommunist ruling classes "will not surrender their power voluntarily," he admits. But the degree of violence required to force their surrender will differ with the strength which a given "ruling class" possesses. Weaker states may be impelled to surrender by revolution or insurrection. To effect the capitulation of stronger states ruled by strongly willed "classes," war is needed.

Yet war is not defined in purely military terms, but involves paramilitary and nonviolent operations. "Struggle," which is the generic term, requires employment of all and any conflict techniques which could be used to advantage. Political and nonmilitary operations of all types must precede, accompany and follow combat, to minimize risks and costs, and maximize the chances of military victory. War is merely a specific form of "struggle": it is both the most violent manifestation and the decisive event in each phase of the protracted struggle between communism and capitalism.

The communist definition of war distinguishes between "just" and "unjust" wars. "Just" wars are those which accelerate the global success of communism. "Justness" has no relation to the size or type of the war—it may be global, or it may be limited war, and it may be fought with any weapons, nuclear or conventional. "Any war . . . waged . . . with the object of strengthening and extending socialism . . . is legitimate and 'holy.' "

Communists define revolutionary wars as those in which communist forces participate directly; these wars are "more just" than other types of just wars. Liberation wars are undertaken by allegedly oppressed peoples against their noncommunist rulers. Liberation wars also are "just," and hence communists may lend covert or overt support to the side which wants to alter the status quo. Yet depending on changes in the international situation and in communist policy, the Who's Who of the "just" and the "unjust" may be reversed quite suddenly; and sometimes both sides are supported to keep the pot boiling. For war itself is the thing.

By contrast, the communists define any war fought by noncommunists as "unjust." Such wars may be imperialistic or predatory. Imperialistic wars are fought between strong noncommunist states; predatory wars are waged by strong capitalist states against weaker nations.

The question of who initiated the war has no bearing on the "justness" or "unjustness" of a conflict. This question is extremely important in western thinking, but according to Lenin's definition, wars fought by the communists are always "just." The respective "class character" of the belligerents—which is the decisive factor—is not changed by the formalities of initiation. The choice of an offensive or defensive strategy is a technical matter directed by necessity or opportunity and does not affect the moral character of the war.

The communist definition of aggression is closely related to their concept of "just" and "unjust" wars. According to their semantics, which bestow upon them, *a priori*, a blanket authorization for all their acts, communists never can be aggressors—even if they initiate war. Yet a capitalist state defending itself against a direct and unprovoked attack launched by the communists or by a "liberation movement" is necessarily an aggressor. According to this manipulation, the United States in future never can fight a just war except—perhaps—as an ally of the Soviet Union.

For about thirty years the communists have been advocating the signing of so-called "nonaggression pacts." This advocacy is perfectly compatible with preparation for what the West would call aggressive war, not only because deception must be part of an attack pattern but also because the U.S.S.R. by definition could not violate a nonaggression pact to which it is a signatory, even if it initiated attack upon a noncommunist cosignatory itself. Most of the states with whom such pacts were concluded are now behind the Iron Curtain.

When the communists talk about war, Americans frequently fail to comprehend the subtle points. For example, Khrushchev never tires of promising that the Soviet "armed forces will not be used . . . at any time for predatory purposes." He makes this promise in good faith, for according to communist semantics, it would be impossible for Soviet forces to fight predatory wars. Communists engage in armed conflict for one purpose only: to defend, "strengthen and extend socialism." Hence they simply cannot fight a predatory or an "unjust" war. The significant point is that Khrushchev never has forsworn the intention to use his military establishment for those kinds of war communists consider to be "just" in nature. Immediately after he left the United States, Khrushchev went to Peking, where he reassured a high-level party audience that while communists continue to condemn "predatory" wars, they still "recognize" just wars and wars of liberation.

In his frequent professions of undying love for peace, Khrushchev so far has refrained from taking issue with Stalin's assertion (1952) that to make war avoidable, "imperialism must be destroyed." Nor did he ever refute Mao Tse-tung's celebrated dictum that "political power grows out of the barrel of a gun."

On occasion Khrushchev has said that under the conditions prevailing in the contemporary world, wars no longer are "fatalistically inevitable." To the communists, looking for the easy solution, "the use or nonuse of violence in the transition to socialism" does not depend on the Soviet Union, but "on whether the exploiting classes resort to violence." Stressing that nuclear weapons and intercontinental ballistic missiles would cause tremendous destruction, Khrushchev claims—and perhaps believes—that unlike the capitalist nations, the communist camp could absorb such havoc and survive. According to him, "a third world war could only end in the collapse of capitalism." Obligingly the new-style communists have set themselves the task of persuading the "capitalists" that they should act like reasonable businessmen, liquidate their assets with the least loss, and not mess up the predestined revolution with nuclear bombs.

Yet, despite their hope that the specter of nuclear holocaust will frighten the free world into bloodless surrender, the communists continue to profess that as the final showdown draws near, the capitalists, in an attempt to preserve their system, may "lash out like a wounded beast." To guard against this eventuality, they have formulated a military doctrine of "pre-emption." This is not identical with the western concept of "preventive war," but is an attack to forestall an attack. Ostensibly a defensive concept like a parry in fencing, it could be used to justify plainly aggressive moves.

As will be remembered, even if the communists were to initiate war against the United States, they still would not hesitate to proclaim the "justness" of this adventure in tragedy. By their own definition, an all-out nuclear attack by the Soviet bloc to kill a huge part of the American people, an assault launched to cause the final collapse of capitalism, would usher in the *most just war of history*. Regardless of how devastating such war could be for the Soviet Union itself, this supreme and deadly struggle is considered by the communists to be both necessary and inevitable unless surrender can be induced. To the communist way of thinking such a war, however costly, would be the indispensable high road to that type of "lasting peace"—"without the nuclear missile race"—which the communist system alone is able to provide to "all peoples of the world."

These few examples show that to understand the communists, we must apply *their* definitions, not our own. Communist and noncommunist conceptions of the same terms differ. Not infrequently meanings are completely at variance.

The purpose of semantic warfare is to mislead the free world about the true objectives of communism and in particular to make believe that the communist movement—which plans to liquidate its opponents, to destroy democracy, and to abolish political, economic, intellectual, religious, cultural and personal freedoms—has humanitarian and progressive motivations.

The creation of illusions is an accepted part of politics. What is our defense against communist myth-making? The true doctrine of communism has remained an open book for more than a hundred years. Even Aesopian language can be freely interpreted, because Aesopian terms always retain some relationship to the concepts they are supposed to camouflage. Though the free world is sometimes deceived, more often the free world deceives itself with the wishful thought that communists have suddenly ceased to be communists.

If the communists really had changed, they would be eager to explain their new doctrine; they would find persuasive words to disclose the new outlook; and they would be compelled to explain the doctrinal changes in detail to the international movement and the rest of the world. Yet they reiterate frequently that they remain committed to the original writ.

Thus, Americans have no choice but to become familiar with the Aesopian technique. Communists rely upon a few dozen texts of key importance to motivate, condition and obligate the faithful and to explain the communist doctrine of protracted conflict. Protective semantic analysis involves asking questions such as these: Is a given communist statement consistent with basic communist doctrine? Are the communists employing expressions which amplify, modify or limit terms Americans are using in our own political conversation? Can we find the qualifications and modifications that apply to the communist usage of a given term? What are the original doctrinal Marxian terms which the Aesopian word replaces? Has the term previously been used to deceive? Is the particular line of argument addressed to *high* party audiences or to nonparty forums, or to both—and if so, what is the difference in the message?

The communists are trying to entrap us by the words we like best. They are attacking democracy where it is weakest: in its predilection for wishful thinking. In the words of Noel Coward, "It is discouraging to think how many people are shocked by honesty and how few by deceit." In order to fight the battle on even terms, we must become ever more skillful in translating communist double-talk. The free world must learn to face the totalitarian menace without illusion.

Further reading:
> Hunt, R. N. Carew: A GUIDE TO COMMUNIST JARGON. New York: The Macmillan Company; 1958.
> Labin, Suzanne: THE TECHNIQUE OF SOVIET PROPAGANDA. Washington: Government Printing Office; 1960.

454

Possony, Stefan T.: A CENTURY OF CONFLICT, COMMUNIST TECHNIQUES OF WORLD REVOLUTION. Chicago: Henry Regnery Co.; 1953.

Hunter, Edward: BRAIN-WASHING IN RED CHINA: THE CALCULATED DESTRUCTION OF MEN'S MINDS. New York: Vanguard Press; 1951.

Hodgkinson, Harry: THE LANGUAGE OF COMMUNISM. New York: Pitman Publishing Corp.; 1955.

C. DAY LEWIS

[*Photograph by Tom Blau*]

C. Day Lewis has been practicing the poet's craft since childhood. A minister's son, educated at Oxford, he was professor of poetry there from 1951 to 1956, and he has lectured in Cambridge. Under the pseudonym Nicholas Blake, Day Lewis also writes whodunits that have won a large following in both England and the United States. Although the financial exigencies of the poetic life originally caused him to try his hand at crime stories, he feels they have the additional benefit of "releasing the springs of cruelty," which, were he a country squire, might otherwise find its outlet in hunting. His autobiography, The Buried Day, was published in 1960 by Harper.

The Making of a Poem

B Y

C. DAY LEWIS

W hy is it that nowadays, when poetry brings in little prestige and less money, people are still found who devote their lives to the apparently unrewarding occupation of making poems? Is the poet a quaint anachronism in the modern world—a pathetic shadow of the primitive bard who, unable for some reason to take active part in the life of his tribe, won himself an honorable place in the community by singing of the exploits of hunters and warriors?

Certainly a poem is still a cry from solitude, an attempt the poet has made to break out of individual isolation and set down his experience in such a way that it can be shared by his fellow beings. And he still uses the power of incantation, of rhyme, rhythm and repetition, which the primitive bard employed to bind the social group together in a common emotion. But, while he is writing a poem, he is not aware of a need to communicate. He has two conscious motives: to create an object in words, and to explore reality and make sense of his own experience.

He wishes this object to be both self-contained and elegant —elegant in the sense that a mathematician will call an equation "elegant." The poem must stand up after the poet has got out

459

from underneath it; it must apply beyond the individual experience out of which it arose and carry meaning beyond the poet's own time and social environment.

This durability can only be achieved through a special way of using language. Deep thought and passionate feeling will not of themselves create poetry. Poets are not philosophers, and good poems can be composed—they usually are—from the commonplaces of human experience. The poet's instrument is language and, unlike those of the scientist, it is not an instrument of precision. He has to make something out of the words we all use—out of the vague, stale, wasteful language of common speech. He will do this, partly by the use of metaphor and image and partly by concentration of language—the packing of the greatest possible amount of meaning into the smallest possible space. When Marlowe's Faustus sees Helen, he cries out:

> Was this the face that launch'd a thousand ships,
> And burnt the topless towers of Ilium?

He is expressing the same emotion as the man who says, "That baby's got everything. I could go for her in a big way," but he is expressing it in an infinitely more concentrated, colourful and vital manner. Or again, when Robert Burns wrote

> Oh, wert thou in the cauld blast,
> On yonder lea, on yonder lea;
> My plaidie to the angry airt,
> I'd shelter thee, I'd shelter thee.

he made articulate, once and for all, through a simple picture given in the simplest words, the inarticulate tenderness of every lover wishing to protect his beloved.

The poet's medium is words, and his material is experience —his own states of mind or those of others into which he can sympathetically enter. He explores these states of mind, feeling his way with the sensitive instruments of his language. He may even, though he seldom consciously makes the poem for this purpose, change a state of mind by thus exploring and expressing it: a love lyric, an elegy, a satire will work out of his system, or at least temporarily assuage, the panks of unrequited love, the weight of grief for a dead friend, the nagging heartburn of hatred.

As a poet grows older, his states of mind are likely to become more complex. That is why lyric poems—which are single-minded, single-mooded, transparent and uncomplicated—have mostly been written by young men; and for a similar reason, in our own elaborate civilization, pure lyric poetry has yielded place to a poetry of irony and complexity. Time, too, has changed the way poets think about their craft. On the whole, the classical poet would have claimed no more—though he often *did* much more—than that his poetry was an "imitation" of life, that he was representing reality, and in such a way as to give instruction through pleasure. Since the great romantics, poets have come to think of their work not as an imitation of reality, but as a re-creation of it. They seek to interpret reality by creating an object of a different order of reality.

The common factor between the classical and the post-classical poet is the imparting of knowledge. "Knowledge?" you may say. "But isn't that the province of the scientist nowadays?" Yes and no. Both science and poetry stem from magic, man's earliest method of trying to gain knowledge of Nature and power over it. The scientist and the poet are still concerned with the exploring of reality to that end. The poet's descriptions, unlike the scientist's, are not capable of proof, only of assent; but this does not mean that they are not contributions to knowledge. Let us take two looks at the common wild daffodil; the first through the eyes of a botanist, the second through the eyes of Wordsworth.

Narcissus, pseudo-narcissus: flower stalk hollow, two-edged, bearing near its summit a membranous sheath and a single flower; nectary notched and curled at the margin, as long as the sepals and petals.

> *I wandered lonely as a cloud*
> *That floats on high, o'er vales and hills,*
> *When all at once I saw a crowd,*
> *A host of golden daffodils;*

Beside the lake, beneath the trees,
Fluttering and dancing in the breeze.

The botanist distinguishes, classifies and generalizes: his description is objective; and it can be proved, for all daffodils of this kind will be found to conform to it. Wordsworth's description is of a different order. His lines make us say, "Yes, that's what daffodils look like," or, "Yes, that's what it feels like to look at daffodils." The poet describes objects in the light of his own feeling about them. "But what's this to do with knowledge?" you may argue. I should reply, "Enlightenment about one's own feelings is as valuable as any other knowledge."

Though the poet differs from the scientist in the method and field of his work, both start from one basic assumption— that there is pattern, or law, in the cosmos. A poem is a microcosm in which the apparent chaos of life is made manageable, given order and pattern. Both scientist and poet, therefore, are deeply concerned with relationships—the scientist objectively and the poet in the light of his own feelings. The poet, like the scientist, must try to see things as they really are; but nothing "really is" in isolation, pure and self-sufficient: reality involves relationship; and as soon as you have relationship, you have—for human beings—feeling. The poet cannot see things as they really are, cannot be precise about them, *unless he is precise about the feelings which attach him to them.*

This precision he achieves through image, metaphor, analogy and his special way of using language. But scientists, too, unless they can employ the language of mathematics, must often work by analogy and do often use metaphorical language. The poet Burns says,

O, my Luve is like a red, red rose,
That's newly sprung in June;

or Gerard Manley Hopkins says,

O the mind, mind has mountains; cliffs of fall
Frightful, sheer, no-man-fathomed,

462

to describe accurately the feeling of love or the feeling of spiritual despair. "Let me compare my love to a June rose," Burns is
in effect saying, "and see what follows." The natural philosopher
Descartes did exactly the same. He proposed, "Let us compare
the universe with a clock, and see where we go from there." And
modern neurologists believe they may be able to learn from an
automatic brain something about the workings of the human
brain. This, too, is a method of analogy, an attempt to learn
about the unknown through the known. We know what a June
rose and a mountain precipice look like. So Burns and Hopkins
use them to convey to us an exaltation of love, an abyss of despair, which we may have experienced but cannot ourselves express or even perhaps fully *know* till the "no-man-fathomed" experience has clothed itself in rose or precipice. So the word is
made flesh.

The poet, then, like the experimental scientist, is an explorer. He needs to find things out for himself and record them.
For him, as a poet, all human experience—however common,
however trivial—is virgin soil; each poem is a fresh experiment
in the chemistry of the human soul. How does he set about these
experiments, these explorations which, like those of the land and
sea discoverers, are so often gropings in the dark toward an unknown destination? I can only speak authoritatively for one poet
—myself. But I believe many poets today would give a fairly
similar account of what is involved in the making of a poem.

First, I do not sit down at my desk to put into verse something that is already clear in my mind. If it were clear in my
mind, I should have no incentive or need to write about it, for I
am an explorer, not a journalist, a propagandist or a statistician. For me a poem begins with a vague feeling, part excitement, part apprehension, which I can sometimes localize in my
solar plexus. A feeling, it may be, comparable with that of a
woman just before her confinement begins.

My poetry phases—I tend to write a good deal of verse for
two years, and for the next year or so to write none and have
little desire to write any—are often preceded by some emotional
churning-up. But the poems I write during these periods are not

463

necessarily related to the cause of the disturbance. For instance, though I did write some "war poems" in 1939–45, the main effect upon me of the emotional disturbance of war was that, for the first time in my life, I was able to use in poetry my memories of childhood and adolescence. It was as though a seismic upheaval had thrown up to the surface of my mind strata of experience previously inaccessible to me as a poet.

During these creative phases I see the raw material of poems everywhere; everything, around me or in my memory, assumes a sort of poetic potency, and I feel an intermittent but confident exhilaration. This mood of vague, undirected excitement will often throw up a line of poetry, which seems to come out of the blue. I brood upon this line, trying to discover in what direction it is pointing, to what experience it refers, and to what sort of poem it is a clue. During the war, for example, a line came into my head—"the flags, the roundabouts, the gala day" —which turned out to be the germ of a sequence of nine sonnets about childhood and youth. This line, at the start, had the fascination of a riddle for me. Only gradually, meditating upon its quality of childish gusto and eager anticipation, did I realize what it was trying to tell me. Even a single word, "gala," helped. I had never heard this word used as an adjective except by my Irish relatives; and the sonnet in which that line was finally used contains also two key memories of my childhood days in Ireland.

Sometimes, of course, these clue lines or *données* emerge not quite out of the blue, but from some area of experience I am already preoccupied with. Recently, for instance, I had been thinking a lot about possessions—the way, in youth, some of us tend to be high-minded and haughty about our elders' love for acquiring objects, whereas when we ourselves grow older, our attitude changes and our material possessions become not merely status symbols but extensions and supports of our own personalities. These vague and far from original ruminations suddenly produced the phrase "streamlined whales and hulls." The phrase fairly rapidly developed into:

Think of streamlined whales and hulls
Accumulating barnacles

By moving long enough immersed
In their own element . . .

That original phrase directed my rather abstract thoughts about possessions into a marine allegory, *Travelling Light*. It also hinted at the right meter for the poem, just as "the flags, the roundabouts, the gala day" had suggested the normal sonnet meter.

If I am lucky enough to be given such a clue line—this *donnée*, together with the initial excitement of conceiving a poem, are all that I personally understand by the word "inspiration"—I use it as a bait. That is to say, I drop it back into the unconscious, and in a state of "wise passivity" wait for what it may catch. Other phrases, images, ideas and associations attach themselves to the bait, and I carefully reel them in. Thus, gradually, the potential subject matter of a poem is accumulated. But much of it will have to be discarded and will not figure in the finished poem. The selection of material—the deciding what is and what is not finally relevant—will be done partly, as we shall see, by the form of the poem (Paul Valéry said that we use strict form in a poem so as to prevent ourselves "saying everything" in it), but chiefly by the theme.

The theme of a poem is the meaning of its subject matter for me. When I have discovered the meaning *to me* of the various fragments of experience which are constellating in my mind, I have begun to make sense of such experience and to realize a pattern in it; and often I have gone some way with a poem before I am able to grasp the theme which lies hidden in the material that has accumulated.

There is a parallel here with scientific discovery. The scientist has at his disposal a mass of verified data. Out of the mass may emerge, through an imaginative leap of his mind, a hypothesis which relates all these data and makes sense of them. The scientist's hypothesis, if satisfactory, becomes a scientific "law." It is the equivalent of the poet's theme. At a certain crucial stage both poet and scientist are groping in the dark, hardly knowing—it may be—in what direction their data are tending, till a flash of imagination lights up the pattern for them. We have evidence, in the lives of the great scientific discoverers, how often this flash comes when the mind is asleep or occupied with other matters. But it would not have come, any more than a theme comes to the poet, without a great deal of preliminary work in the sifting and assessing of data and experience.

I would like to illustrate with a poem of mine called *The Gate*. It is one of several written in a state of creative exhilaration stimulated by my first visit to the United States a few years ago. I have chosen it partly because its data—which are all given in the first six lines of the poem—were apparently simple and straightforward and were already contained within a frame; for the poem arose out of a picture, painted by a friend of mine—a picture to which I responded with pleasure and excitement, but also with a sense that it held for me a special and mysterious meaning I must try to explore through poetry.

THE GATE

In the foreground, clots of cream-white flowers (meadowsweet?
Guelder? Cow parsley?): a patch of green: then a gate
Dividing the green from a brown field; and beyond,
By steps of mustard and sainfoin-pink, the distance
Climbs right-handed away
Up to an olive hilltop and the sky.

The gate it is, dead-centre, ghost-amethyst-hued,
Fastens the whole together like a brooch.
It is all arranged, all there, for the gate's sake
Or for what may come through the gate. But those white
* flowers,*
Craning their necks, putting their heads together,
Like a crowd that holds itself back from surging forward,
Have their own point of balance—poised, it seems,
On the airy brink of whatever it is they await.

And I, gazing over their heads from outside the picture,
Question what we are waiting for: not summer—
Summer is here in charlock, grass and sainfoin.
A human event? But there's no path to the gate,

Nor does it look as if it was meant to open.
The ghost of one who often came this way
When there was a path? I do not know. But I think,
If I could go deep into the heart of the picture

From the flowers' point of view, all I would ask is
Not that the gate should open, but that it should
Stay there, holding the coloured folds together.
We expect nothing (the flowers might add), we only
Await: this pure awaiting—
*It is the kind of worship we are taught.**

This poem was written more or less straight ahead. More often I compose a bit here, a bit there, like a painter. The first stanza objectively sets out the facts—the colour and detail of the pictured landscape. In the second stanza, the eye pans up to its dominant features—the flowers in the foreground and the gate in the center focusing the whole landscape together. At this point I still had no idea *why* the picture had such attractive mystery for me, or what it was trying to convey. However, in this second stanza I concentrated upon its main features subjectively —my sense that the whole picture was somehow there *for the sake of* the gate, the central mystery, and my sense that the foreground flowers stood in an attentive pose, waiting for something to happen.

But I still had not discovered the theme of the growing poem. So, in stanza three, I tried putting a number of questions to the picture. Just *what* are the flowers, and myself, the outside observer, waiting for? Several possible answers were given, and each of them in turn rejected; but the first seven lines of this stanza are constructed out of the several rejections, in such a way that their logical negatives create something emotionally positive. And then, at last, I saw what the landscape—and the poem—was saying to me. I saw it by moving from outside the picture and looking at the gate "from the flowers' point of view." In my tiny way I had done what Copernicus did when, with a superb imaginative leap, leaving the earth and placing

Note: Poems marked by asterisks on pages 467, 470, 471, and 472 are from the author's *Pegasus and Other Poems* (Harper).

himself in the sun, he found that the orbits of the planets looked simpler from that point of view.

What the picture was saying to me, I discovered, is first that the flowers expect nothing, their task being one of "pure awaiting," a kind of worship; and second, that they, and I, are not concerned with a divine revelation (the gate opening), but only that the gate should stay there—in other words, that we should retain the sense of some power at the center of things, holding them together. This idea had been foreshadowed (line eight) in purely visual or aesthetic terms. It was not till I reached the final stanza that I became aware of its deeper significance and realized that the poem was a religious poem. It is also obviously the poem of an agnostic—one who is, in a sense, "outside the picture"—but an agnostic whose upbringing was Christian. The "olive hilltop," with its echo of Mount Olivet, may conceivably have started the poem in the religious direction which, unforeseen by me, it was to take; and the "ghost-amethyst" colour of the gate certainly led me along to "The ghost of one who often came this way"—that is, the once-felt presence of deity in the human scene.

A few technical points: The poem has no end rhymes, but the two most important words in it rhyme and are repeated— "gate" six times and "wait" ("await," "awaiting") four times. The stanzas are carefully organized, the first corresponding metrically with the last, the second with the third. The pause between third and fourth stanza, which should be observed in reading the poem aloud, throws the greatest possible emphasis on "From the flowers' point of view," highlighting the change of position which is to reveal the theme. Finally, the rhythms are as flexible as I could make them, within a regular meter, so as to reflect the inquiring and tentative nature of the poem's thought process.

Talking about the poem in this detached way, I have given the impression perhaps that a poem "writes itself." Nothing could be further from the truth—in my case, at any rate. Certainly, in the first phase of composition, the "fishing" phase, the intellect is relatively inactive; one accepts, in a trancelike state, everything that comes up. But there follows a phase of the most arduous intellectual activity, when the gathered material has to be criticized in the light of the growing poem and of whatever inkling I may have about its theme. Since the two phases constantly overlap, it is almost impossible to give a blow-by-blow commentary on the making of a poem. All I can say is that my mind moves gradually over from passive to active, as it tries to perform the two functions of making and of exploring.

They are inseparable functions, because the technical patternmaking of the poem must go hand in hand and step by step with the search for a theme, the exploration of reality. What we aim at in pattern is a perfect consonance of image, rhythm and phrasing which will present the theme *whole*, with nothing irrelevant or superfluous, nothing diluted or scamped. A poem must indeed grow organically. I cannot tell *in advance* what shape it should take. But, once I have an idea of its shape, I must take great care in the shaping.

For this reason I find it particularly important to go slowly and tentatively in the early stages of composition, so as to avoid imposing the wrong shape on a poem—or, putting it another way, so as to keep open a number of avenues until I am fairly sure which is the right one for the poem to move along. Impatience, haste and glibness are great dangers to the poet who has acquired some technical facility, for they tempt him to let his poem take the easiest way—and this often turns out to be a blind alley. Just as an obstetrician may deliberately slow down a birth in the interests of the child, or a cook will keep a dish constantly stirred to prevent it "setting" too quickly, so I try to keep a poem in solution during the early stages. I have several expedients for this: composing the first draft in very small, faint pencil writing, for instance, and putting down a great number of alternative words, so that the whole thing looks tentative and provisional.

The dangers of haste, of letting a poem "set" too soon in a certain form, can be illustrated by *The New-Born*, which I wrote at the same period as *The Gate*. Excited by the birth of my son, I jotted down some notes, as follows:

baby—blank sheet (heat) but invisible writing
see here/original sin, eternal hope
naked as a nut/castaway
nine-month nonentity/this manikin.

Rashly and overconfidently I dashed on. The following lines, with a great many variations which I will not print, were produced:

This manikin who just now
Found his rough path into the world
And as a perfect miniature lies unshelled
From foot to brow

Was but an hour ago
A wish, a dread, a shape that we
Had felt through its nine-month non-
*   entity*
Quicken, and grow.

Heaved hither on mounting waves
Of agony, tossed up today
On earth, he lies limp as a castaway
And nothing craves
*But the long sleep birth ended . . .**

But there the poem stalled. It had been misfiring badly from the start—those stanzas are atrociously feeble—so there was nothing to do but get out, lift the hood and look for the cause of the trouble. I decided, eventually, that I had chosen the wrong form. I needed one which, because it was more elaborate, would help me to distance myself from my still raw paternal emotions. Perhaps if I replaced the four-line stanza with one of ten lines, in strict metrical form, would it do the trick? The first two stanzas now went much better:

This manikin who just now
Broke prison and stepped free
Into his own identity—
Hand, foot and brow

A finished work, a breathing miniature—
Was still, one night ago,
A hope, a dread, a mere shape we
Had lived with, only sure
Something would grow
Out of its coiled, nine-month nonentity.

Heaved hither on quickening throes,
Tossed up on earth today,
He sprawls limp as a castaway
And nothing knows
Beside the warm sleep of his origin.
Soon lips and hands shall grope
To try the world, this speck of clay
And spirit shall begin
To feed on hope,
*To learn how truth blows cold and loves betray.**

By using a form technically much more difficult than the original one, I had made it easier for myself to discover exactly what I wanted to say and to get deeper into the experience I was writing about. For example, the last two lines of the first draft are evidently much inferior to "And nothing knows/Beside the warm sleep of his origin," which concentrates two ideas in one phrase—that the baby knows nothing *except* his sleep in the womb, and that he knows nothing as he lies there *at the side of* his sleeping mother.

A third stanza, in which I extended the metaphor of the baby as a blank sheet written over with invisible ink "Which the day's heat/Will show," also ran well. But then, to my consternation, the poem stalled again. It took me a long time to find out what was wrong. But at last I perceived that, half-consciously, I had been edging the poem in the direction of that preliminary note, "original sin, eternal hope." And I do not believe in original sin—or not positively enough to make it a theme of a poem. In trying to do so, I had been insincere, and properly punished for it. So I restarted at the point where I had broken down, and two more stanzas were added, beginning:

This morsel of man I've held—
What potency it has,
Though strengthless still and naked as
A nut unshelled!

I have been discussing the kind of poems in which, as a maker, one is at full stretch. After finishing such a poem I feel exhausted, as if I had solved a diabolically difficult puzzle—usually, looking back at the poem later, I see that I failed to solve it. But there are other levels of poetry, more superficial, yet not valueless, at which the poet can work; and again, working upon a relatively "light" poem, I have occasionally found myself breaking through to a level of deeper significance. What is essential is to develop the sort of tact or flair which enables one to know how much weight of meaning and how dense a verbal texture each incipient poem will bear, so that one neither overloads it nor underplays it. Each poet must learn to recognize his limitations, yet be able to seize the rare chance of being possessed by a spirit that transcends them and makes him write better than he knows how.

Each new poem I begin is an attempt at making and exploring. Each finished one is, in effect, a way of praising life, a sacrifice in life's honor. I need devotion, discipline, sincerity, skill, and above all, patience, if the poem is to come to anything; but I also need something I cannot cultivate—call it luck. And when I see how rarely my own sacrifices are acceptable, I must say as I did in my poem, *Final Instructions:*

You are called only to make the sacrifice:
Whether or no he enters into it
Is the god's affair; and whatever the handbooks say,
You can neither command his presence nor explain it—
All you can do is to make it possible.
If the sacrifice catches fire of its own accord
On the altar, well and good. But do not
Flatter yourself that discipline and devotion
*Have wrought the miracle: they have only allowed it.**

Further reading:

Lewis, C. Day: ENJOYING POETRY. New York: Cambridge University Press; 1959.

Lewis, C. Day: POET'S TASK. New York: Oxford University Press; 1951.

Lewis, C. Day: PEGASUS AND OTHER POEMS. New York: Harper & Brothers; 1957.

Hopkins, Gerard Manley: SELECTED POEMS AND PROSE. Baltimore: Penguin Books, Inc.; 1959.

Burns, Robert: COMPLETE POEMS. New York: Thomas Nelson & Sons; 1943.

Wordsworth, William: SELECTED POETRY. New York: Modern Library, Inc.; 1950.

GARRETT HARDIN

Garrett Hardin, professor of biology at the University of California, spent ten years in microbiological research on protozoa and algae, photosynthesis and antibiotics before he undertook the task of interpreting current advances in the field of biology to the layman. Doctor Hardin's article is a portion of his most recent book, Nature and Man's Fate, *published in 1959 by Rinehart & Company. The book is an evaluation of the human implications of evolution.*

LIJLIJLIJLIJLIJLIJLIJLIJLIJLIJLIJLIJLIJLIJLIJL

In Praise of Waste

BY

GARRETT HARDIN

D arwin changed our views of the origin of living things,
but more important still, he changed our attitude toward
waste. Before Darwin, the adaptedness of species was explained
by William Paley as an example of "design in nature"—a design
that existed in the mind of a Creator Who then fashioned nature in accordance with His blueprint; only so, said Paley, could
such a marvelously adapted structure as the eye have been produced.

Not at all, said Darwin. It is not necessary that there exist
in some mind the idea of a beautifully adapted machine in order
that this machine may come into existence. It is enough if nature be permitted to try countless experiments—"mutations" we
now call them—among which a tiny percentage produces good
results. Each such successful experiment is saved by natural
selection and used as a base for further experimentation and
natural selection. Mutation occurs at random and entails enormous waste, but natural selection acts like a ratchet to preserve
each tiny element of progress; thus do nature's beautifully
adapted machines come into being. There need be no blueprint for design to emerge; trial and error suffice. Something of
this sort must have been meant by the poet William Blake who
said, "To be an error and to be cast out is a part of God's design."

Design can emerge from blind waste. How old is this

477

thought? Who can trace the earliest embryological stages of so tenuous an entity as an idea? Perhaps it is centuries old, but certainly its form was not unambiguously clear until Robert Malthus wrote his *Essay on Population* in 1798. This much-misunderstood work, yearly buried by liberal critics and yearly resurrected by its own vigor, has, entangled in its many errors, a correct view of stability achieved through waste—the Malthusian dynamic scheme of population. From the superabundant vitality of nature comes the ever-present threat of geometric increase, but this is opposed by the limitations set by the environment. The result is an equilibrium achieved through waste, an equilibrium that may, it is true, be subject to temporal shifts, but an equilibrium nonetheless. Forethought, planning and charity are either of secondary importance or are self-defeating in such a system.

This mode of thought met with immediate favor when it was put forward by Malthus, but within a very few years it was vigorously opposed by another idea of independent birth and apparently contradictory implications—the idea of cruelty, *i.e.*, the idea that cruelty is something to be abhorred rather than enjoyed. Strange as it may seem, this idea is a rather young idea as far as the bulk of mankind is concerned. In the distant past, the gentle Jesus was a conspicuous exception among men. It is only within comparatively recent times that many Christians have become Christian.

The Christianization of Christians was made possible by a change in perspective. In the Middle Ages it was common for the population of a city to be lowered as much as 10 per cent in a single year by disease or famine; even a 25 per cent loss was not unknown. In a world so filled with suffering not caused by humans, it would seem to some rather out of perspective to complain of a little human fun—like the Spanish Inquisition, say. As suffering and death from seemingly divinely caused diseases decreased—as it did even before Pasteur and bacteriology —man's view of his own cruelties changed, perhaps because they loomed proportionally larger. Cruel fate was becoming reformed; cruel man now looked crueler. Tender-minded poets and novelists were determined that he, too, should reform, and quickly.

Into this world of tender intentions burst Malthus, asserting that suffering was inevitable, simply because population had the capability of increasing more rapidly than the means of subsistence. A reasonable balance between population and subsistence—a decent scale of living for some—could be maintained only if others suffered from insufficient means of subsistence. Nor would it be a true solution for the haves to divide their means with the have-nots—this would merely encourage the production of more have-nots. Such a sentiment provoked a storm of protest from the literati, who were now making the cause of the poor and the unfortunate their cause. The wealthy Percy Shelley saw a great social threat in "sophisms like those of Mr. Malthus, calculated to lull the oppressors of mankind into a security of everlasting triumph." The poet's friend William Hazlitt asserted that "Mr. Malthus' gospel is preached only to the poor."

This is not the place to examine Malthus' thesis—or rather, his theses, for there were several. We need only point out that the early decades of the nineteenth century saw an establishment of sharp lines of battle between—shall we say—humanitarians and analysts; it is difficult to name the factions without arousing prejudice. It must not be supposed that men like Malthus were inhumane; in his personal relations with family and friends, Malthus was the kindest and most considerate of men. But in his public statements he insisted on the primacy of analysis in the attack on social problems, whereas his opponents insisted on the humanitarian treatment of all existing people—particularly the poor and unfortunate—in the hope, or belief, that future generations would present no problem. The here and now is much more real than the there and tomorrow. The humanitarians won the minds of common men—who are, in the nature of things, the majority.

What Malthus was trying to get at in his bumbling way, and all-unconscious of what he was doing, was what we now call the impotence principles of science and logic. The trisection of an angle with ruler and compass alone is impossible—this is an impotence principle. So also is the principle of the conservation of matter and mass, and the finite velocity of the speed of light. Impotence principles tell us what cannot be done and for that reason are inacceptable to immature minds. Angle trisectors, circle squarers, and inventors of perpetual-motion machines we will always have with us. What these men fail to realize is that impotence principles are not only restrictive but also permissive. Only if some things are impossible can other things be. The second law of thermodynamics not only tells us to stop looking for a perpetual-motion machine but also tells us how to improve the machines already invented.

One of the impotence principles of biology is this—waste is inevitable. Waste, in the Darwinian scheme, not only produces progress but also conserves the advances already made. There is no heredity without its tax of mutation; most mutations are bad; their production and elimination are a kind of waste. The sentimentalist who seeks to eliminate the waste in a species by preserving all mutants and breeding equally of all genetic types ultimately brings about the extinction of the entire species. It is a throwing of good money after bad. It is the saving of pawns and losing the game.

One of the most surprising things about science is the way it begins as common sense, and ends up with most uncommonsensical statements to which, nevertheless, common sense must give its assent once it has examined the evidence. The curvature of space is such an idea in astronomy. In biology we have the astonishing conclusion of the Haldane-Muller principle which says: In a state of nature, all bad mutations are, in their cumulative, ultimate effects, equally bad. How can this be true? To say that a gene that is only mildly harmful to the individual is just as harmful to the race as is one that is completely lethal to the individual seems to be flying in the face of reason. But it is true.

When we say, "Gene A is not as bad as gene B," what do we mean? How do we measure "badness" in nature? The only acceptable way, in an evolutionary sense, is by the gene's effect on success in leaving progeny. The "worse" the gene is,

the greater the diminution in progeny it causes in early generations; and consequently, the sooner the gene is completely eliminated. A gene that causes only slight damage in each generation does so for many generations. These two factors—damage
in one generation, and the number of generations sustaining
damage—bear a reciprocal relation to each other. As a result,
the total damage of a gene, over all generations, is a fixed quantity, the same for all deleterious genes.

The preceding discussion presupposes a species living "in
a state of nature." The meaning and the reason for the qualification should be fairly clear—the principle applies directly only
to organisms other than man, organisms that do not consciously
control their breeding. Man, if he controls his breeding, may
be said, in some sense, not to be living in a state of nature—
in which case the losses exacted by mutation need to be examined all over again. Can man alter these losses?

Certainly he can increase them. In fact, he is increasing
them now deliberately, though not intentionally, by increasing
the general radiation level through medical X rays, atomic
bombs and atomic-energy installations. How much he is increasing the mutational losses through his present actions we do not
yet know; nor do we know how much he will increase the general radiation level in the future. We play with atoms because
we believe there are benefits to be gained from our play. We
know there are losses. Ethics is not so well-developed a science
that it can tell us how to balance possible profits and certain
losses. At the present time, unavoidable mutations cause the
production of about 2,000,000 defective babies per year throughout the world. Suppose we increase radiation to such a level
that it brings about an ultimate increase in the number of defective babies produced each year by 200,000. Is this a trivial
addition or not? Is it small in comparison to the gains brought
by atomic energy? How can we say? It is a small wonder that
men of equal intelligence and Christianity come up with opposing answers.

Another of the impotence principles of biology, and of sociology, is this—competition is inescapable. The form of competition and the participants may change; but it is always with

us. A species that is not numerous competes principally against other species; as it increases in numbers, the situation changes. The "successful" species ends by becoming its own principal competitor. So it is with man, now. The world, in spite of comic-strip science, is a limited one. Man, freed of the population-controlling factors of predators and disease organisms, must—willy-nilly, like it or not—control his own numbers by competition with his own kind. By taking thought, he can elect the kind of competition he employs; but he cannot escape all kinds. This is not to imply that the election is a trivial matter. Surely there are few who would not prefer the endemic celibacy of the Irish to the ritual blood sacrifices of the Aztecs, who, at the dedication of the temple of Huitzilopochtli in 1486, slaughtered at least 20,000 victims—by the most conservative accounts —tearing the hearts out of the living bodies. There surely can be no serious question as to which behavior is preferable, but we should note that, though both practices have a religious "reason," both are, in the eyes of a biologist, competitive techniques associated with the threat of overpopulation, however unconscious of that threat the practitioners may be. The question is not whether competitive techniques shall be employed, but what techniques and by whom.

The game must go on; that is nature's command. But it is up to man to determine the ground rules and the teams. The determination of the rules is principally the responsibility of the specialist in ethics. The delineation of the teams—well, that is a task for which many disciplines are needed. It may be that no synthesis of all the relevant considerations is yet possible. But such a synthesis is one that we must work toward. The biologist, with the wisdom gained from a century's preoccupation with evolution, has some things to say about the choosing of the teams.

Any species that becomes one big melting pot of genes puts —to mix metaphors—all its eggs in one basket. If circumstances change rapidly, it may be unable to adapt, and so will perish. Conspicuous success in evolution, as in human affairs, is all too likely to be the prelude to extinction. That the dinosaurs should have become extinct at the end of the Mesozoic Era is no cause for wonder; what needs explaining is how such highly successful forms lasted so long.

It is not that the relatively unsuccessful have a better chance of survival because of their deficiencies. Rather, their advantage comes when their lack of success results in the species' being broken up into many separate breeding populations, among which there is very little interchange of genes. Under these conditions, there is a great increase in variety within the species, each isolated population necessarily differentiating into a different race; how different will depend on many factors, including the extent of environmental differences. With a greater variety of harmonious genotypes in existence, the species is better adapted to face a varying and unpredictable future. Not all of its breeding populations may survive a change; but the chance that at least some will is greater than the chance of survival of a single, large population. And those races that survive a change can then repopulate regions left vacant by those that have succumbed.

Such is the picture presented to us by a spelling out of the consequences of biological inheritance. But man is subject also to a kind of inheritance that we may call cultural. Will this alter the picture? We don't know. The Gregor Mendel of cultural inheritance has not yet appeared. But there are strong intuitive reasons for believing that the mechanism of cultural inheritance will, if anything, merely increase the contrast in the picture. The loss of adaptability of a species is the result of the inevitable tendency of a breeding population to become genetically uniform. Surely we have seen enough of social power to realize that the pressure toward uniformity is even greater in the cultural realm than in the biological.

To the biologist it is clear that the best chances for man's long-time survival depend on the fragmentation of the species into well-separated populations. But it would be foolhardy to say what form the separation should take. It might be a matter of nations, as we know them; or some sort of caste system that would permit genetic isolation with geographic unity; or—far more likely—some new kind of communities: neither nation nor caste nor anything yet conceived.

In postulating a new world are we adding but one more "utopia" to library shelves that are already too well stocked with these childish wish fulfillments? I think not, for what we have just suggested differs in significant ways from the classical utopias. These dream worlds, however much they vary, agree in two characteristics. The societies they sketch have a high degree of rigidity and finality; and they seek to eliminate all waste, which is variously conceived in terms of economic waste, human suffering or moral turpitude. The student of biological evolution cannot accept a utopia that embodies either of these features. Evolution is an unending process, in which waste plays an indispensable role. Until proof to the contrary is forthcoming, the evolutionist must assume that man is a part of nature. The biologist sees no end-state for man and his society, which must continue evolving until the day of his extinction. No one has conceived any substitute for the mechanism of evolution (whether biological or social) that does not necessarily involve variation and selection—that is to say, waste. Man, the slender reed that thinks, can alter the force and direction of natural forces somewhat, but only within limits. The wisdom of so doing is always questionable. Who is so wise as to descry the lineaments of man 1000 millenniums from now, using these visions as guides for consciously warping the course of human evolution? And as for waste, the more we try to eliminate it, the more we are impressed with its protean changeability and elusiveness. The time-study man who saves 1000 man-hours by altering work procedures, may be astonished to find himself faced with a sitdown strike that costs 1,000,000 man-hours. Reducing the waste of walking to work by inventing horseless carriages may ultimately double the time wasted in transportation by making possible the modern city and its congestion. And so it goes. We do not yet have a scientific theory of waste, but all men of experience recognize its ubiquity and its inevitability. We can often exchange one kind of waste for another; and we can sometimes—though not as often as we like —decrease it somewhat in amount. But always we must live with it. If we are wise, we even make waste work for us a bit.

But though we may never be able to get rid of waste entirely, it is only natural—or rather, human—that we should try to diminish it as much as possible. Spontaneous mutations entail waste; can we do anything about this? In one sense we cannot. The Haldane-Muller principle tells us that each gene mutation must be paid for by one gene elimination—"genetic death," Muller calls it. Genetic death—which is not really death —is a subdivisible quantity; it may occur by degrees and over many generations. A lethal gene kills at one fell stroke—this is death as we ordinarily conceive it. But a gene that has a selective worth of only 90 per cent (as compared with a normal gene) diminishes the reproductivity of every individual in which it shows by 10 per cent. If we multiply the fraction of the population that suffers this loss by the amount of loss each individual suffers, we come out with the number 1, no matter what the selective worth. This means that each new, bad mutation is ultimately eliminated completely, and that it "kills" a total of one individual, which it may do by "killing" fractions of several individuals. But it does not follow from this that there is nothing that can be done to diminish the loss to human beings. To say that nothing can be done is to assert that death is the only form of human waste, a thesis that surely few would hold. The sublethal gene does not merely diminish the reproductivity of its possessor, it also diminishes his vigor, his health, his *joie de vivre*. We would be little concerned if genetic death were the only consequence of Huntington's chorea, Mongolism, phenyl-ketonuria, pyloric stenosis, or fibrocystic disease of the pancreas. But these conditions cause other losses that we state in terms of human suffering. These losses can be reduced.

Until very recent times, the only method of attacking the problem of suffering was by medicine. Medicine is surely one of the glories of mankind, but we are now perceiving its limitations. For a disease in which it is accurate to say that the hereditary component is negligible—say, for smallpox—medicine has been an unalloyed blessing. But where the hereditary component is great—for instance, in hemophilia—we have our doubts. In such conditions recourse to somatic medicine only delays genetic death while increasing human suffering. Hemophiliacs are now kept alive by frequent, sometimes daily, blood transfusions.

We can, if we wish, encourage them to have children. Suppose we saw to it that hemophiliacs had, on the average, precisely as many children as normal people; what would be the result? Genetic death would thus be completely eliminated, but the cost in suffering would be established as a perpetual and continuing cost, a kind of overhead of misery. However small the cost might be per generation, it would increase without limit as time went on. Every bad mutation is a sort of fine levied against mankind. We can either pay the fine promptly or we can delay or avoid payment altogether—by paying in another way.

We are in the position of the traffic violator who either can pay a fifty-dollar fine once in court or can pay one-dollar hush money every week to a dishonest officer to keep from having the violation reported. In the long run, even the cheapest blackmail charge mounts up to more than the most expensive fine. In the long run, unobstructed genetic death is the cheapest way to pay for the unavoidable misfortune of mutation.

Mutation is a form of waste which, manage it though we will, we must in some sense accept. It is inevitable. It is the stuff from which are fashioned new adaptations to the world. In this realization we are brought back to an insight that is old, very old; much older than the theory of evolution. When we come to think of it, we realize that what we call charity owes its origin at least in part to a subconscious realization of the value of waste. Most interesting of early prescriptions for charity is the Jewish "law of the corner," which is given thus in Leviticus 19:9–10: "And when ye reap the harvest of your land, thou shalt not wholly reap the corners of thy field, neither shalt thou gather the gleanings of thy harvest. And thou shalt not glean thy vineyard, neither shalt thou gather every grape of thy vineyard; thou shalt leave them for the poor and stranger. . . ." Such a directive sprang, no doubt, in part from a tender heart; but it may also have indicated an embryonic recognition of the danger of an unmodified competition in human affairs—a recognition that if competition were pure and unbridled, the more efficient man (the landowner) would starve out him who was less so (the poor and the stranger). Coupled with this was a surmise that perhaps complete efficiency might not always be best or right.

In Deuteronomy 24:19, there is a further injunction: "When thou cuttest down thine harvest in thy field, and hast forgot a sheaf in the field, thou shalt not go again to fetch it: it shall be for the stranger, for the fatherless, and for the widow. . . ." Thus there came into being that curious entity of Jewish practice known as "that-which-is-left-through-forgetful-ness," which belongs to the poor. The devout were urged always to see to it that something was left through forgetfulness. It is certainly difficult to remember to forget. It is no wonder that the principle of the deliberate tithe—one tenth of one's income given to charity—later replaced so operationally difficult a procedure as deliberate forgetfulness.

Recent developments of the theory of evolution by Sewall Wright and R. A. Fisher have shown us that evolution also proceeds most effectively when the competitive process is somewhat interfered with. It is highly probable that the same principle applies to the social evolution of man. Countries that have been fully populated for long periods of time—for example, classical China—have produced a negligible amount of science. The reason is not difficult to find. Science—pure science—is, in its inception, pure waste. An item of information in pure science "pays off" in a practical way only after it has long been in existence and has been combined with other items of pure science. We are reminded of the new mutation, which is almost always bad, but which—if protected somewhat—may eventually be able to combine with other and similarly "wasteful" genes to produce a new and superior constellation of genes. Prosperity is the great protector of novel thought. A people whose nose is constantly to the grindstone of poverty cannot look up to see the world as it is; all that exists is the nose and the grindstone. A people living under completely Malthusian conditions cannot discover even so much as the Malthusian principle. Science is not produced by eternally busy, wretched people. The flowering of science in the western world in the last four centuries paralleled the increase in prosperity. Cause? Effect? Both. However the new science got started—prosperity was only a necessary condition, not a sufficient one—once started, it produced more prosperity as an effect which fed back into the system as a cause. Science and technology make a circular system that produces wealth and material progress.

Can this system go on forever? Who can say? It is not without its enemies, and among the most important of these today we must count the ever-increasing population of mankind and the "other-directed" men that crowding produces. An other-directed man—we use David Riesman's phrase—is an animal who tends to be intolerant of the independence of thought that is indispensable for the advancement of science. But other-directed men may be rational, and if rational, may be convinced of the necessity of cherishing those not of their own kind. The inner-directed man, he who is answerable only to his own conscience, is always a thorny tablemate, doubly so when nature's board is crowded. To ask that all men be inner-directed would be quixotic in the extreme; but it is not unreasonable to ask that other-directed men add the care and nurture of a small corps of inner-directed men to their tithing duties. It is not planning that is needed here, and certainly not organization. It is, rather, a systematic allowance for waste, for heterodoxy, for the unforeseeable. It is, perhaps, not even understanding that is demanded—that would be asking too much of other-directed man—but something in the nature of faith. Faith in the future, and faith in the fruitfulness of waste, properly allowed for.

Those who have painted pictures of an organized heaven have, implicitly or otherwise, appealed to the aesthetic sense in man to try to gain assent to their plans. We know now that a completely planned heaven is either impossible or unbearable. We know that it is not true that design can come only out of planning. Out of luxuriant waste, winnowed by selection, come designs more beautiful and in greater variety than ever man could plan. This is the lesson of nature that Darwin has spelled out for us. Man, now that he makes himself, cannot do better than to emulate nature's example in allowing for waste and encouraging novelty. There is grandeur in this view of life as a complex of adjustive systems that produce adaptedness without foresight, design without planning and progress without dictation. From the simplest means, man, now master of his own fate, may evolve societies of a variety and novelty—yes, and even of a beauty—that no man living can now foresee.

Further reading:

Hardin, Garrett: NATURE AND MAN'S FATE. New York: Holt, Rinehart & Winston; 1959.

Hardin, Garrett: BIOLOGY: ITS HUMAN IMPLICATIONS. San Francisco: W. H. Freeman & Co., Publishers; 1952.

Stern, Curt: PRINCIPLES OF HUMAN GENETICS. San Francisco: W. H. Freeman & Co., Publishers; 1960.

Darwin, Charles Galton: THE NEXT MILLION YEARS. New York: Doubleday & Company, Inc.; 1961.

Zirkle, Conway: EVOLUTION, MARXIAN BIOLOGY, AND THE SOCIAL SCENE. Philadelphia: University of Pennsylvania Press; 1959.

Huxley, Julian: EVOLUTION IN ACTION. New York: New American Library of World Literature, Inc.; 1957.

C. NORTHCOTE PARKINSON

Cyril Northcote Parkinson, famous English historian, author and journalist, recently resigned the Raffles Chair of History in the University of Malaya to fill visiting professorships in the United States at the universities of Illinois and California. Creator of Parkinson's First Law: in any administrative organization, subordinates will multiply in accordance with a known formula and without relation to the work (if any) expected of them. Also discovered Parkinson's Second Law: public expenditure rises to meet an income which is assumed to be limitless, a ceiling which is not there.

Can Democracy Survive?

BY

C. NORTHCOTE PARKINSON

An unexpected sequel to the American occupation of Japan has been the growth of Japanese influence in America. Those who set out to teach the Japanese something about democracy have ended by learning from the Japanese something about architecture. This is but one reason among many for wondering afresh whether that original idea of a crusade for democracy had the sanction of common sense. Are we now quite so certain that democracy must everywhere prevail as not only the best but the final achievement of human wisdom as applied to politics? Does history reveal nothing but a series of experiments, each failing in turn but each bringing mankind a step nearer this, its ultimate goal?

History, in fact, reveals nothing of the kind. We learn from it that various forms of rule have tended to succeed one another in what might seem to have been a significant sequence, democracy showing a tendency to collapse in a chaos from which dictatorship offers the only escape. There is little in history to show that democracy is much more stable than any other form of rule. What history does show is that people have always inclined to regard their own form of government as perfect, or

493

at any rate inevitable and eternal. Subjects of, say, a deified emperor have seldom supposed that any other form of rule was worth serious discussion. For most of them, at any period, talk of an alternative scheme would have seemed impracticable, blasphemous or merely crazy. Present advocates of democracy are apt in the same way to claim for that form of rule a universal validity which it would seem to derive neither from theory nor from fact. Representative democracy is a form of government which has a number of real advantages for some peoples at a certain stage in their development. To claim more than that, invoking some semireligious principle of human rights, is to assume just such an attitude as characterized the more pious inhabitants of dynastic Egypt. If we are to defend democracy in serious discussion, it must not be because it is sacred—few forms of rule have been anything else—but because it produces some demonstrably good result. If it is good, we should be able to explain why.

While a study of the past may warn us against accepting current beliefs merely because they are current, it throws only a doubtful light on the future. We can admittedly observe a sequence of political development in past civilizations; a recurring pattern in which monarchy has given place to aristocracy, aristocracy to democracy, and democracy to a dictatorship which has turned into monarchy again. Nor is there anything in the tempo of current history to suggest that what was once a phase in a recurring cycle should now be regarded as permanent. Were it possible to judge from political events considered in isolation, we might rather be tempted to assume that what happened before was likely to happen again. And indeed there is probably nothing in the present political scene— no movement, no investigation, no scandal or plot—for which past history affords no parallel. But the present age, which has so little to offer by way of political innovation, has much to offer in technical progress. The doubt is whether the political pattern can exactly repeat itself in an environment which has been so technically transformed. The argument from past experience may no longer hold good. Talk of technical achievement brings to mind the hydrogen bomb. But that is not so significant politically as other and less spectacular developments. Many of these might be instanced, and there are those who would maintain that a longer expectation of human life is the most important. But there are three other developments to which too little attention has been paid: developments respectively in psychology, communication and what is called "conventional" war.

To deal with psychology first, there was a time when the results of an election or plebiscite were given a sort of religious sanction. Victorian editors could announce that the people would oppose the Updrainville irrigation scheme, that the people had rightly demanded the construction of the Moose Canyon Bridge, or that the people had wisely chosen Mr. Clawhammer as governor. And while it may be doubted whether the will of the people had quite the force of revelation, there were many instances of the people proving right—the drainage scheme unworkable, the bridge vitally needed and Mr. Clawhammer a better man than his opponent. These side-whiskered men, leaning on their axes as they paused for thought, could arrive at the right decision. In a simply organized agricultural or pastoral society the relevant facts could be widely known. Today, in a more complex society, the mass psychologist has been able to dissect the voting process with disconcerting results. The will of the people breaks down under analysis, turning out to be ill-informed, emotional and liable to vary indeed from day to day; nor, incidentally, is there any close correlation between the views people express when approached individually and the views they express when collected in a group. Taken apart in this fashion, the will of the people turns out to be a myth. Voting is a more orderly process than rioting, but has only an even chance of producing the right answer. The Romans achieved the same result more cheaply by consulting the gods —whose guesses seem in general to have been no worse (or better) than their own. But the infallibility of the "general will" is a dogma that must remain where it belongs—in the last century; if not, indeed, in the last century but one.

As for communications, it must be remembered, first of all, that these have always determined the scale—and to some ex-

495

tent the nature—of political institutions. The earliest civilized states were each based on a river system as their means of communication, the length of the river determining the size of the state. Kingdoms based on the Nile, the Tigris or the Ganges could be relatively large; kingdoms based on the Tagus, the Mekong or the Scheldt had to be relatively small. The Romans and Chinese broke through these limits by building roads, but the river-system scale of political organization lingered on to a surprisingly recent period of history, determining the respective sizes of, say, Yorkshire, Virginia, Canada and Venezuela. A single government could stretch its authority only as far as it could reach, the amount of its influence being roughly proportionate to the distances involved.

Today the extent of a government's influence has been at once extended and intensified. Rail, road, telegraph, air and radio communications have made a distant supervision both effective and continuous. The river-system scale of political unit has become in some ways an anachronism; nor is there now the same need to establish a god-emperor (like Constantine or Stalin) whose shrine or effigy can represent him in places he will never visit. Today the Queen's voice, and even she herself, can come through the air; just as the President's personality can be projected by television or recorded on tape. Communication is no longer in the same sense a problem.

So, far from presenting any technical difficulty, communications now present the government, whatever its character, with almost limitless scope. By means of state-organized schools, newspapers, films, radio and television, a docile people can be taught practically anything—that all capitalists are wicked, that all Jews are criminals or that China does not exist. Techniques based on psychology and developed in advertising have already some remarkable achievements to their credit. Mass media of instruction would seem to have endless possibilities. So far the known results include the popular election, by enormous majorities, of both scoundrels and lunatics. There is nothing to prevent any government from building up for itself a dream world in which dramatized leaders with purely fictitious ability give the appearance of prosperity to lands of which the extent has been exaggerated, reporting triumphs over rival powers which have been invented for the purpose and boasting the success of improbable missions to other and imaginary planets. Past emperors of China built up such a dream world for themselves, but they lacked more than a fraction of the necessary equipment. The age of hallucination, of which Adolf Hitler was one of the earlier victims, has scarcely dawned. People will someday perhaps look back with wonder on a time when the camera was thought to matter less than the event it was supposed to record.

The world that has seen this revolution in the methods and speed of communication has also seen a transformation in the arts of war. From the time of the French Revolution to the time of the Russian Revolution land campaigns were mostly settled by massed infantry, national strength being roughly measured by the number of bayonets each nation could put in the field. It was also, and by no coincidence, the age in which the counting of votes had its greatest prestige. During World War II the massed-infantry attack went out of fashion, the strength of nations coming to be measured in quite other terms. Even if we ignore the possibilities of atomic warfare as something now probably obsolete, and even if we discount the possibilities of biological warfare, as something yet untried, the fact remains that numbers have come to matter less. The potential war strength of a country might be measured by the number of its scientists; it can no longer be measured by the mere number of its people. In general, democracy has best suited societies in which the equal value of votes has been reflected in the roughly equal value of the voters when armed for war. It has flourished less securely in societies where the decisive weapons—whether war chariots or cannon—have been in the hands of a few. For this reason it might be thought that the technical basis for democracy, in war as well as in peace, has by now been perceptibly weakened.

From facts such as these it would be natural to conclude that the days of democracy are over. The conclusion would be premature, however, for political systems do not evolve as rapidly as that. Where democracy exists, it may well survive for a further period; but there is good reason to question whether it is likely to take root in any soil to which it is new. With a less favorable climate, the transplanting becomes a less hopeful proposition and doubtfully worth the effort. What may flourish for a time in the atmosphere of the West has far more dubious prospects in the atmosphere of the East. For there the racial and religious background, the family, caste and clan relationships, the secret societies and fanaticisms, the prevailing illiteracy and ignorance make the voting process seem curiously irrelevant. There might be some point in the missionary effort if the technical progress of the age were moving in the same direction and at the same speed, but the East will feel the impact of improved communications long before it can absorb the lessons of nineteenth-century liberalism. If there was a time for that, the time is passing or has passed.

What, by contrast, are the prospects of democracy in the West? We have seen that it is there affected by technical developments which are mainly, if not entirely, adverse. Put in the simplest terms, it is now far easier for a government to tell the people what they are to believe than for the people to tell the government what it is to do. But that is not the whole story. In at least one important respect, democracy is being strengthened and it is important to see how this has come about—more especially in the United States.

The basic weakness of democracy has always been what the Greeks called "stasis," or class war. Given political equality, the lower classes, which have always in times past been the more numerous, have sooner or later used their votes to despoil the rich. They have voted, in effect, for economic equality—that is, for socialism. The effect of this has always been disastrous, and more immediately disastrous for democracy. In the stresses and strains brought about by the legalized plunder there are bound to develop all sorts of treasons, stratagems and spoils. From the conflicts which have ensued, one man, usually a leader of the winning side, has emerged as dictator. Whatever the result of the battle, freedom has always been the first casualty. In the struggle between capital and labor both sides are impelled by exactly the same material motive, and both sides are guilty

—as Gandhi pointed out—of exactly the same sin. Neither, of course, is concerned with the welfare of society as a whole.

In trying to transpose the Greek theory of class war into the terms of modern industry—which he very imperfectly understood—Karl Marx foretold a process by which the wealthy would become richer and fewer, the poor would become poorer and more numerous until the top-heavy absurdity of the situation would make revolution inevitable and irresistible. So would begin the rule of the proletariat, to last apparently forever; an odd conclusion for an admirer of Darwin to have reached. In the Marxist revolution the internal conflicts, as observable in the Greek and Roman city-states, have been neatly eliminated. There are only two classes, and the one had dwindled to a mere handful of people who can be hanged at leisure, after which event the unopposed remainder can live happily. Had Marx known anything about the working classes—a set of people with whom he had no social contact—he would have known that the problem is not quite so simple as that.

Quite apart, however, from any misconception that Marx may have had about the social equality existing between boiler riveters and bellhops, his account of the future has been completely falsified by events. There have been two Marxist revolutions on the large scale, both in countries almost entirely agricultural, while the industrial areas have developed, in the main, on lines of their own. Of this development the main feature has been the dwindling importance of the class which Marx expected to become supreme. His proletariat comprised for the most part the skilled workmen, the trade-unionists, of the mid-nineteenth century—the men who drove the locomotives or installed the plumbing, men who wore top hats on the way to church. That industrial society depended upon the skilled artisan was a truism of the period. The skilled artisan was the stanch supporter of Methodism and of labor politics—both anathemas to the gentry. He was a man who would do nothing for the really poor—insisting as he did upon the wage differential between himself and them—but the leader in all resistance to the capitalist. Trade-unionists of this type were so important in their day that few at first were to notice either their diminished status or their dwindling numbers. In twentieth-century industrialized societies it was not the proletariat that multiplied in growing poverty but a middle class that multiplied in growing wealth. The future lay not with the skilled artisan but with the qualified engineer on the one hand and the unskilled factory girl on the other. These were classes of people of whose existence Marx was only dimly aware. It is upon them, rather than upon the skilled artisan, that industry has come to rely.

A significant event in the development of western middle-class industrialism was the British General Strike of 1926. By all the accepted axioms of the day, a stoppage of railways—let alone all the other heavy industries—should have paralyzed the country. But the country was not paralyzed. It no longer depended upon railways. It also became suddenly apparent that the middle classes, which rallied against the trade-unions, were more numerous than the strikers. The strike failed and no subsequent labor victory at the polls could efface the impression that the middle classes had scored. The motorcar, which made them independent of the railways, was their symbol of victory. It was they, not the skilled artisans, who were to be the dominant group of the future. Marxism can appeal nowadays to such social groups in Australia as are psychologically still in the 1880's, but it long since died as a force in Britain; died with the discovery that the proletariat cannot be supreme and is not even particularly important.

The process by which the new urban middle class established itself in Britain was repeated, but with greater emphasis, in the United States. By a process of technical achievement, rehousing and education, the middle class came to outweigh the class above and outnumber the class below it. There are depressed classes in the United States, and there are people with a grievance against society; but they are swamped by the masses of people whose fear is that they will lose what they have—namely, a suburban home, garage, car, refrigerator, washing machine, television, telephone, supermarket and high school. That democracy in the United States should end in class war is now almost unthinkable, for the raw materials do not exist.

People are more likely to choke themselves, as in Los Angeles, with the fumes of their own exhaust pipes. It is true that the whole picture could be drastically altered by an industrial depression, but the story, whatever happened, would not conform either to Greek theory or Marxist prediction.

If American democracy is a middle-class affair, firmly based on the long-term interests of a strong majority, it should not end in socialism nor should it collapse in chaos. The fact remains, however, that it is vulnerable in other ways. We have seen already that the whole machinery of persuasion is in the hands of any government that cares to use it. How great is the danger that such an influence may, in fact, be used? In attempting to judge the possibilities we must note, first of all, that the effect of mass education is to expose people more, not less, to propaganda. In theory a university or high-school graduate should be skeptical about what he reads and hears. But do American graduates criticize or do they merely conform? The man least vulnerable to propaganda is the illiterate peasant who possesses no radio. His views may be narrow but they are at least his own. Most vulnerable of all are the people who listen and believe. Are people of that kind tending to multiply? There are some grounds for thinking that they are.

Against the dangers of intensive propaganda the accepted remedy lies in the party system. People forced to hear both sides of every question are compelled, we are told, to decide for themselves. Those considering the merits of any presidential candidate will hear as much against as for him. In this there is an element of truth. The theory breaks down, however, whenever the two parties become too much alike. In the days when British Tories alternated in office with their Liberal opponents, the electorate had to choose, it was said, which of two wealthy cousins should introduce the same bill. Is there no danger of that in the United States? The extent of the danger is to be measured by the proportion of voters who do not bother to vote. In general the nonvoting voter is unconvinced that it matters either way. A lack of public interest is normally the result of there being nothing to be interested in. If the crowd drifts away from the tennis match, it is usually taken as a comment upon the standard of play. There are those who believe that the great debate in the United States, at least as between the parties, is finished and that the voter's only concern is to defend his standard of living. For this theory there would seem to be some evidence. Some 62,027,000 valid votes were cast, for example, in the 1956 presidential election —a record figure but representing only 60.4 per cent of the theoretical maximum. To have had a few million less—to have had as few as 50 per cent of the voters participating—would have been a serious indictment of the whole system. With such a condemnation even remotely possible, the advocates of American democracy have cause to consider their case afresh.

One other weakness needs to be mentioned and it is this: there are too many people on the public payroll. This state of affairs could be denounced in the name of economy, but that is not to the present purpose. The question is how far this scheme for full employment is compatible with democracy. Let us take an extreme case and suppose that half the adult population were in public employment. This would mean that half the voters were employed under the direction of the party in power—dependent upon it for pay, security, privilege and promotion. Is that situation a proper basis for independent voting? Nor is the situation much improved if the roles were to be reversed, the voters blackmailing those by whom they are employed "Give us double overtime," they will say, "or we shall vote you out of office." Situations are seldom quite as simple as that, but the final result either way would be a one-party system with one party controlling or controlled by the civil-service vote and that party perpetually in power. To this it may be objected that those on the public payroll are not so numerous as this. It may also be urged that civil servants are persons of the highest character who would never use any improper influence in wage negotiations. Arguments such as these are not without weight, but neither are they conclusive. For one thing, an election can be decided by a bloc far smaller than the one described. Given anything like equal strength as between parties, a mere 10 per cent of the voters, acting together, could easily tip the scale. In Great Britain those in public employment, some 6,000,000 out of a total population of 51,500,000, form a far higher proportion than that. As regards the high character of the people concerned, it must suffice to remark that the character of some of the earliest voting civil servants—those of ancient Athens—would not seem to have been high enough. Nor were English politicians of the period very happy about all the excisemen employed by George III. The crime of enlisting the civil service in the cause of a particular party (his own) was the very thing that people held against him. It may be that the descendants of the Athenians, mingled under the American flag with the descendants of the excisemen, have now a loftier moral tone than their ancestors could boast. But it is not, surely, an issue upon which the betting would be much more than even. It lacks, as an assumption, the rocklike solidity upon which the enlightened lawgiver would care to build.

To give democracy in its American form not an eternal validity but a new lease of life, there would seem to be a case for reform. The system needs reinforcing at the points where it is weak. For the specific weaknesses to which attention has been drawn, three remedies suggest themselves: the vote should be restricted to those who have earned it; the legislator should be freed from improper influence; the public revenue should be limited under the Constitution to a stated proportion of the national income. To take these points in order, we may conclude first that the voter's negligent attitude toward the ballot box derives from the fact that his vote was given him. It was not merely given him but thrust on him. He was implored to take it and begged to use it. He is pursued with the vote and can be fined in some democracies for failing to exercise it; from all of which anxiety the natural inference is that the vote must be worthless. Were every American citizen presented with a university degree at birth—a measure of economy for which there is much to be said—few would trouble to put "A.B." after their names; just as few bother to claim the war medals to which nearly the whole of their generation are entitled. For a thing to be valued it has to be specially earned. On this principle the vote might well be conceded, with obvious reluctance, to those whose title to it derived from blood, sweat and tears. It might be restricted, for example, to people over thirty who had passed a certain educational standard, who had done public service, who had paid taxes above a certain minimum and who should apply in writing (with fee enclosed) for their names to be placed on the electoral roll. Girls who prefer to remain aged twenty-nine would be very properly ruled out as immature. Men without military service would be ruled out as unpatriotic. People who misspelled their letter of application would be ruled out as illiterate. The vote would thus be confined to those who have taken some trouble and shown some interest, and would be instantly lost again if not exercised.

For this last stipulation to be enforced, however, the voter must clearly be given the means of voting against all the candidates. If every voting paper had not only the names of the real candidates but the further name of a fictitious Colonel Bogey, each vote for him would suggest "that no election be made until an adequate candidate presents himself." The world's politicians have so far managed to exclude Colonel Bogey from democratic constitutions. Failing his candidature, however, the municipal voters of São Paulo in Brazil recently elected Cacareco, a female rhinoceros—weighing 2400 pounds—to their city council. The popular support for Cacareco seems to have been overwhelming; nor could there be any objection to her on the score of nationality, she being a citizen of Brazil by birth. Her disqualification was based, no doubt, on some legal quibble; connected perhaps with her age—she is four and a half. To have been born in the zoo is no bar, surely, to the exercise of democratic rights. But politicians may fairly expect to find themselves opposed by other candidates whose claims are broadly similar. Nor will it be possible to exclude them all on some trivial technicality. With the world's zoological gardens so well supplied with popular personalities, qualified for the legislature by residence and age, there can be no doubt that their fuller representation is to be expected. A few heavy majorities for such candidates—a tortoise here, a reptile there—would be no bad thing in the annals of political science.

To explain the second point of proposed reform it becomes

necessary to remind the reader that the English voter used to record his vote publicly on a "hustings" or platform set up for the purpose in the market place. He would sturdily march up the steps and audibly declare his choice amid the applause of his friends and the rotten eggs hurled by his opponents. It was for long defended, and with some reason, as an opportunity for the display of the manly virtues. It was certainly that, but there were drawbacks to set against its advantages. When the practice was finally abolished it was not because voters were being fatally injured—often as this may have happened. It was not even because some of them had to be carried up the steps, collapsing thereafter in a drunken stupor—as many in fact did. It was simply and solely to prevent corruption. The secret ballot ended individual bribery overnight. The voter might accept the bribe, but there was no means of knowing that he would earn it or that he had not been equally bribed by the other side. Since then bribery has had to be collective, which is not as much as to deny that it exists.

What few have remarked, however, is that the arguments for secret voting at the poll are at least as unanswerable as applied to the legislature. It can be urged against it that voters have a right to know how their representatives have voted. The point, however, is a doubtful one at best. After all, the representative is not a delegate. He should vote according to his conscience and knowledge, not according to the wishes of people who were not present at the debate. And the people who, in practice, watch the House divide are not the voters but the party bosses, financial backers and mere thugs; all who might be in a position to threaten or reward. Under secret voting, it might be objected, the representative might sell his vote without fear of exposure. To some representatives no idea could be more attractive. But there would be no one to buy it. Who will purchase goods of which the delivery is uncertain and of which it cannot be known whether they have been delivered or not? "On my word of honor," says the representative, "I shall vote as we have agreed." But who cares about his word of honor? He is a crook or he would not be accepting the bribe; nor do we know that it is the only bribe he has taken. In any representative body a secret and a public vote will produce quite different results. Which result gives the better indication of what men really think? To add to the authority of a legislature, more especially as against the executive, a system of secret voting in the House is a first and decisive step.

Last of all comes the question of the public payroll. That socialism, or anything like socialism, is incompatible in the long run with democracy is tolerably obvious. What the remedy is to be is appreciably less obvious. It would be simple to propose an amendment to the Constitution by which the number of persons publicly employed should be limited to a certain proportion of the voting public. That, however, would hardly achieve the end in view. For the line is not so easy to draw. Those employed by a private corporation which is wholly or even mostly engaged on government contract, are hardly to be distinguished, for this purpose, from those whose public employment is direct. To preserve democracy in anything like its present form—still more, to revive its energies—the need is not so much to restrict the numbers on the payroll as to limit the total cost of administration. The problem is too large for discussion here—it might almost be the subject for a book —but there are grounds, surely, for concluding that the governmental share of the national income has increased, is increasing, is likely to increase still more—and ought to be drastically diminished.

The price of democracy, it has been said, is eternal vigilance. Is that a price the American public is willing to pay? There are forces today which tend to preserve democracy, the disappearance of the proletariat being the chief of these. There are forces which tend to swamp it, of which public extravagance is perhaps the most dangerous. But this much is certain: that the democracy which merely drifts, swayed this way and that by technical development and cyclical trend, is no longer dynamic and no longer even alive. It cannot be sustained, still less can it be improved, without constant effort and constant care. A written constitution is a life belt to which the exhausted can cling; it is not, in itself, an aid to further progress. In most countries the traffic police are not unreasonably suspicious of motor vehicles manufactured much before 1930. They demand some test of their roadworthiness before admitting them into the stream of modern traffic. For a machinery of government perfected in 1789 a test at least as stringent might well be devised; and it would be odd indeed if no overhaul was ever found to be advisable. It is one thing to say that what has lasted for 170 years must have been soundly designed in the first place. It is quite another to conclude that what has lasted so long with such trifling repair, can last, unadjusted, forever.

Further reading:

> *Parkinson, C. Northcote:* THE EVOLUTION OF POLITICAL THOUGHT. Boston: Houghton Mifflin Company; 1958.
>
> *Parkinson, C. Northcote:* THE LAW AND THE PROFITS. Boston: Houghton Mifflin Company; 1960.
>
> *Barzun, Jacques:* THE HOUSE OF INTELLECT. New York: Harper & Brothers; 1959.
>
> *Kelley, Stanley, Jr.:* PROFESSIONAL PUBLIC RELATIONS AND POLITICAL POWER. Baltimore: The Johns Hopkins Press; 1956.

GERALD HOLTON

[*Photograph by Arnold Newman*]

Gerald Holton, professor of physics at Harvard University, is active in three fields—physics, teaching and scholarly editing. Doctor Holton pursues experimental research on the properties of materials under high pressures; he teaches and writes in the fields of physics and the history and philosophy of science; and he is also editor-in-chief of Daedalus, the journal of the American Academy of Arts and Sciences. Doctor Holton was born of Austrian parents in 1923.

ꝶꝶꝶꝶꝶꝶꝶꝶꝶꝶꝶꝶꝶꝶꝶꝶꝶꝶꝶꝶꝶꝶꝶꝶꝶꝶꝶ

The False Images
of Science

B Y

GERALD HOLTON

O f the influences that shape man's actions, none is more
powerful than the images we carry in our heads. Every
subject is apt to invoke in our minds a specific image, made
up of concrete information, misinformation, folklore, desire
and prejudice. Thus, how people see themselves as a nation
determines to a large extent how they will respond to any new
challenge. The roles we play in our family life, particularly with
respect to our children, depend greatly on what roles we assign
ourselves in the society around us.

In the same way, our images of science vastly affect the
relationship between science and society. Practically, these
images determine the level and the sources of financial support,
the quality and quantity of instruction offered, and the development of new scientists. The effects on professional morale
and the goals scientists set for themselves—in short, on the
scientists' image of their own work—are also considerable. But
even more important is the role images play in deciding this
urgent question: Can scientific activity be an integrated part
of our culture, or will it be forced to develop independently?

Right or wrong, ideas are powerful. Therein lies the chief

danger of false images. Like bad grammar, bad images become dominant when they gain wide currency, and so undermine communication among thoughtful people. It is high time, therefore, to consider the prevailing public images of the role of science, using the most straightforward language possible.

PURE THOUGHT AND PRACTICAL POWER

Each person's image of science is different from the next, but all are composed of seven main elements. The first goes back to Plato and portrays science as a tonic with double benefits—science as pure thought helps the mind find truth, and science as power provides the tools for effective action. The main flaw in this image is that it omits a third vital aspect. Pure science allows us to understand the physical world and, through its applications, allows us to control and change that world. But science also has a mythopoeic function; that is, it generates an important part of our symbolic vocabulary and provides some of the metaphysical bases and philosophical orientations of our ideology.

As a consequence, the methods of argument of science, its conceptions and its models, permeate first the intellectual life of the time, then the tenets and usages of everyday life. Our language of ideas, for example, owes a debt to the sciences of statics and hydraulics and the model of the solar system. These have furnished powerful analogies in many fields of study. Guiding ideas—such as conditions of equilibrium, centrifugal forces, conservation laws and the balance of energy or power, feedback, invariance or complementarity—enrich the general arsenal of imaginative tools of thought. All philosophies share with science the need to work with concepts such as space, time, quantity, matter, order, law, causality, verification, reality.

A sound image of science must, therefore, embrace this third function, in addition to those referring to pure understanding and to practical applications. However, more usually, only one of the three is recognized. For example, folklore sometimes depicts the life of the scientist as lonely, isolated, divorced from life and beneficent action in the larger sense.

ICONOCLASM

A second image of long standing is that of the scientist as iconoclast. Indeed, almost every major scientific advance, from the Copernican theory to the postulation of universal gravitation, from the discovery of the circulation of blood to the perfection of anesthesia and vaccination, has been interpreted as a blow against religion.

To some extent science was pushed into this position by the ancient but dangerous tendency of some philosophers to prove the existence of God by pointing to problems which science could not solve at the time. Newton himself, who was deeply interested in theology, wrote, "It is not to be conceived that mere mechanical causes could give birth to so many regular motions [in the solar systems]. . . . This most beautiful system of the sun, planets and comets could only proceed from the counsel and dominion of an intelligent and powerful Being."

The same attitude governed thought concerning the earth's formation before the theory of geological evolution, the descent of man before the theory of biological evolution, and the origin of our galaxy before modern cosmology.

This aspect of the conflict between science and religion results largely from a misunderstanding of both science and religion. To base one's religious belief on an estimate of what science can *not* do is as foolhardy as it is blasphemous. The reverse, the deification of the discoveries of science, is equally precarious, for scientific knowledge continually grows, superseding its older formulations. The only secure foundation for religious belief, as all great religious leaders have taught, is neither the capacity nor the failure of man's imaginative mind, neither the powers nor the limits of his science—but faith.

Today political overtones make a wider understanding of this problem both more urgent and more difficult. "Religious propaganda," a recent dispatch in Iron Curtain countries advised, must be counteracted by "scientific atheistic propaganda" distributed by local societies "for the dissemination of political and scientific knowledge."

The iconoclastic image of science has, however, other components not ascribable to an elementary misunderstanding of its functions. For example, the historian Arnold Toynbee charges science and technology with usurping the place of Christianity as the main source of our new symbols. Neo-orthodox theologians call science the "self-estrangement" of man because it leads him into realms where no ultimate—that is, religious—concerns prevail.

But this image fails to recognize the multitude of influences that shape a culture—or a person. Neither to Christianity nor to science can one properly assign more than a limited part in the interplay between man's psychological and biological factors on one hand, and the opportunities and accidents of his history on the other. Moreover, to set science and religion at odds, to view them as nonintersecting paths, is to neglect the valuable possibilities of synthesis. As Alfred North Whitehead wrote in *Science and the Modern World*, these are "the two strongest general forces, apart from the mere impulses of the various senses, which influence man. . . . [On their relationship] depends the future course of history." Whitehead held that "the force of our religious intuitions, and the force of our impulse to accurate observation and deduction," are complementary rather than conflicting. The way many scientists and theologians state the issue today makes it seem as if we must choose between two normal and powerful drives. This is like forcing a child to choose between his father and his mother because they disagree on some matters.

ETHICAL PERVERSION

The next image of science sees it as a force which can invade, possess, pervert and destroy man. The stereotype is Anthime in André Gide's novel, *Lafcadio's Adventures*, the naturalist turned unbeliever. Anthime snarls at his niece who dares speak to him piously of religion, and retires angrily to his laboratory, where he weighs a group of starved rats, half of them partly blinded, the rest fully blinded, to find out which are dying faster.

In the current version, the soulless, evil scientist is the mad

514

researcher of science fiction, or the nuclear destroyer—immoral if he develops the weapons he is asked to develop, traitorous if he refuses. According to this view, scientific morality is inherently negative. It causes the arts to languish, it blights culture and, when applied to human affairs, leads to regimentation and to the impoverishment of life. In short, science is the serpent seducing us into eating the fruit of the tree of knowledge—thereby dooming us.

The fear behind this attitude is genuine, but not confined to science. It is also directed against writers, artists, philosophers, theologians—in fact, against all thinkers and innovators. Plato condemned the work of Homer for conducing to impiety and immorality, and the same charge still greets many an original work. Society has always found it hard to deal with creativity, innovation and new knowledge. And since science assures a particularly rapid, and therefore particularly disturbing, turn-over of ideas, it remains a prime target of suspicion.

Factors peculiar to our time intensify this suspicion. Progress in basic scientific knowledge, being confined to a minority of specialists, cannot by itself directly disturb society. But the discoveries of "pure" science now readily lend themselves to widespread exploitation through technology. Applications spread swiftly and widely. Thus we are in an inescapable dilemma—irresistibly tempted to reach for the fruits of science, yet deep inside aware that our biological and psychological metabolism may not be able to cope with this ever-increasing appetite.

Probably the dilemma can no longer be resolved, and this increases the anxiety and confusion concerning science. A current symptom is the popular identification of science with the technology of super-weapons. The missile is taking the place of the microscope as a symbol of modern science. All efforts to convince people that science itself can only give man knowledge about himself and his environment, and occasionally a choice of actions, have been unavailing. The scientist *as scientist* can take little credit or responsibility either for the facts he discovers—for he did not create them—or for the uses made of his discoveries, for he generally is neither permitted nor specially fitted to make these decisions. They are controlled by considerations of ethics, economics, or politics, and therefore shaped by the values, fears and historical circumstances of the whole society.

THE SORCERER'S APPRENTICE

The last two views held that man is inherently good and science evil. Now we come to an image based on the opposite assumption; it expresses the fear that man cannot be trusted with scientific knowledge. He has survived despite his wickedness only because he lacked sufficiently destructive weapons; now he can immolate his world. Science, indirectly responsible for this new power, is here considered ethically neutral. But, like the sorcerer's apprentice, man can neither understand this tool nor control it. Unavoidably he will bring upon himself catastrophe, partly through his natural sinfulness and partly through his lust for power, of which the pursuit of knowledge is a manifestation. The fear inspired by this image also motivates the repeated demand for a moratorium on the pursuit of science. The most famous formulation was that of the Bishop of Ripon at a meeting of the British Association for the Advancement of Science. We should all be better off, he contended, if every physical and chemical laboratory were closed for ten years, and the energy now directing them were turned to establishing the brotherhood of man.

This suggestion is based on two misunderstandings. First, science is not an occupation that one can pursue or change at short notice, like working on an assembly line. The creative scientist does not have a free choice of action. He does not advance toward his new knowledge; rather knowledge advances toward him and overwhelms him. Even a superficial glance at the work of a Kepler, a Darwin or a Pasteur shows that the driving power of creativity is as strong and as sacred for the scientist as for the artist.

Secondly, salvation cannot be considered a reward for ignorance. To survive and progress, man cannot know too much about his environment. The real price of new knowledge is the obligation knowledge imposes on all of us to assume responsibility for ourselves.

It may yet turn out, paradoxically, that science will help to compel us at last to curb the aggressions that in the past were condoned and even glorified. Organized warfare and genocide are practices as old as recorded history. The exploitation of science now has so sharpened the knife edge on which civilization has always balanced that the main antagonists themselves recognize the enormity of the threat. Never before have even the war lords on both sides openly expressed fear of war.

If man is inherently evil, Judgment Day is surely near. But if good exists in him, one can be more optimistic. The alternatives are so extreme and so obvious as to allow hope that the instinct of self-preservation will reinforce good sense and moral strength. Mankind has come to its *experimentum crucis*.

ECOLOGICAL DISASTER

A change in the average temperature of a pond or in the salinity of an ocean may cause a large number of plants and animals to die. One calls this a change in the ecological balance. The fifth prevalent image of science similarly holds that while neither science nor man may be inherently evil, the rise of science happened, as if by accident, to initiate an ecological change that now corrodes the only conceivable basis for a stable society. In the words of theologian Jacques Maritain, the "deadly disease" science set off in society is "the denial of eternal truth and absolute values."

How did this change come about? The main steps are usually presented in this way. Before modern science, man thought of himself as the ultimate purpose and the earth as the center of creation. Then science showed our planetary system to be heliocentric, and man toppled from his throne. Science replaced purposive creation with blind evolution, and discovered that such absolutes as space, time and certainty are meaningless. All a priori axioms, like those of Euclidean geometry, were discovered one by one to be convenient but arbitrary. Modern psychology and anthropology have led to an acceptance of cultural relativism. Truth itself seems to have dissolved into probabilistic and indeterministic statements.

The abandonment of absolutes, so goes the argument, has affected all areas of life, particularly ethical values. Drawing largely upon analogy with the sciences, liberal philosophers have become increasingly relativistic, denying either the necessity or the possibility of postulating immutable verities, and so have undermined the old foundations of moral and social authority. For though doubt and skepticism may be useful as stimulants to scientific investigation, society cannot thrive in an atmosphere of change for its own sake.

Worst of all, the argument concludes, though science cannot help us distinguish between good and evil, it nevertheless claims to be the only reliable guide for making decisions and solving problems of all kinds. Having destroyed absolute standards, it puts nothing in their place. In short, although science has exploded some fallacious traditional beliefs and increased our material comforts, it has also cut us adrift from our only secure moorings.

It should be noted in passing that most applications of scientific concepts outside science merely reveal ignorance about science. For example, relativism in nonscientific fields is based on farfetched analogies. As Crane Brinton put it in *The Shaping of the Modern Mind,* "For the general public, Einstein was not merely the tribal magician of our time; he was the man who stood for relativity; for the notion that things looked different to observers at different places at different times, that truth depends on the point of view of the seeker of truth, that a man moving at one rate of speed sees everything quite differently from a man moving at another rate, that, in short, there is no absolute Truth, but only relative truths."

This is precisely how the general public understand Einsteinian relativity. But physics did not find that everything is relative. On the contrary, relativity theory reformulated the laws of physics so that they would hold good for every observer, no matter how he moves or where he stands. Not everything depends on one's point of view; rather, the most valued truths are wholly independent of the point of view.

Ignorance of science is also the only excuse for adopting rapid changes within science as models for antitraditional attitudes outside science. In reality, no field of thought is more conservative than science; each change necessarily encompasses previous knowledge. Science grows like a tree, ring by ring. Einstein did not prove the work of Newton wrong; he provided a larger setting within which some contradictions and discontinuities of the older physics disappeared.

But the image of science as an ecological disaster can be subjected to a more severe critique. Regardless of science's part in the corrosion of absolute values, have those values really given us a safe anchor? A priori absolutes abound all over the globe in completely contradictory varieties. Most of the horrors of history have been carried out under the banner of some absolutistic philosophy, from the Aztec mass sacrifices to the auto-da-fé of the Spanish Inquisition, from the massacre of the Huguenots to the Nazi gas chambers. It is at best an optical illusion which makes the fourteenth century look so serene and desirable to modern critics of the recent, "scientific" periods, just as the life of the "noble savage," so esteemed by eighteenth-century philosophers, has been exposed by modern anthropologists to be based largely on dread and misery.

If, therefore, some of the new philosophies, inspired rightly or wrongly by science, reject earlier bases of authority as faulty— as the founders of this nation did—if they point out that "absolutes" change and contradict one another, science cannot be blamed. The faults were there all the time.

In looking for a new and sounder basis on which to build a stable world, we shall find science indispensable. We can hope to match the resources and structure of society to the needs and potentialities of people only if we know more about the inner workings of man. Already science has much to say that is valuable and important about human relationships and problems. One must not be obsessed with the picture of bombs and missiles; from psychiatry to dietetics, from immunology to meteorology, from city planning to agricultural research, by far the largest part of our total scientific and technical effort today is concerned with man, his needs, relationships, health and comforts. Those who argue that the pursuit of science is necessarily the road to suicide have forgotten about this aspect of science. They do not believe, as I do, that man has been given his mind in order that he may find out where he is, what he is, and who he is.

SCIENTISM

The last four images implied a revulsion from science. We might describe the next one as addiction to science. Scientism divides all thought into two categories—up-to-date scientific knowledge, and nonsense. Some scientists subscribe to this view, but most of its adherents are outside the laboratories. Among the social studies, for example, there are some victims of the seductive idea that the mathematical sciences offer the only permissible models for successfully employing the mind.

A far more significant symptom of scientism is the growing identification of science with technology, to which I referred earlier. This trend is not difficult to understand. Nearly half of all the men and women trained as scientists are now working in industry or Government laboratories. Even in universities, applied research and development constitute about half of all scientific work. Of the huge sums spent annually on science and technology—about $10,000,000,000 in 1960 in the United States—less than 8 per cent is devoted to really basic research.

Not long ago the typical scientist worked alone or with a few students and colleagues and built his own equipment with "love, string and sealing wax." Today he usually belongs to a group working under a contract with a sizable annual budget. In the research institute of one university more than 1500 scientists and technicians are grouped around a set of multimillion-dollar machines; the money comes from Government agencies whose ultimate aim is national defense.

Everywhere the overlapping interests of university science, industry and the military establishment have been merged in a way satisfactory to all three. Science has thereby become a large-scale operation with a potential for immediate and world-wide effects. It is not frivolous to call physics the liveliest political science today. If for some reason all physicists in the United States heeded a call for a moratorium, nobody would be more deeply disturbed than would the Congress and the State Department.

These are merely indications that we are passing through a revolutionary change in the nature of science. The effective cause was the perfection and dissemination of the methods of basic research by teams of specialists with widely different training and interests. The result is a splendid increase in scientific knowledge, but the side effects are analogous to those of sudden and rapid urbanization—a strain on communication facilities, the rise of an administrative bureaucracy, the depersonalization of some human relationships. To a large degree, all this is unavoidable. The new scientific revolution will justify itself by the flow of results and the material benefits that will no doubt follow. The danger, the point where scientism enters, is that the fascination with the *mechanism* of scientific research may change society and the scientist himself.

The new science requires a new kind of scientist. The unorthodox, withdrawn individualist, on whom most great scientific advances have depended in the past, does not fit well into the new system. We must keep a special place for him and protect him—if only to symbolize our commitment to science itself rather than to the new machinery. Society, on the other hand, will also have to hold out against the seductive urge of scientism to adopt generally the pattern of organization of the new science; this pattern can only be justified by the quality of creative results in a specialized profession.

MAGIC

Few nonscientists would be likely to suspect a hoax if it were suddenly announced that a stable chemical element lighter than hydrogen had been synthesized, or that the United States had beaten Russia in a secret race to establish a manned observation platform at the surface of the sun. Apparently anything can happen these days; science has no inherent limitations. Thus, the seventh image depicts science as magic, the scientist as a wizard. Depending on our orientation, we tend either to fear him or to accept his opinions about everything.

Like the other false images of science, this one is partly an educational problem. All our voracious consumption of technical devices, all our talk about science, and all the money spent on engineering developments cannot hide that most of us are content to remain completely ignorant of science. In a recent nationwide survey, nearly 40 per cent of those who had attended college confessed they took not a single course in physical or biological science. Those who did devoted generally less than 10 per cent of their courses to these sciences. Moreover, in science class they miss all too often the kind of teacher who can impart to the average student a wider appreciation of both the inherent powers and the inherent limitations of science, who can show how to distinguish challenging from trivial problems, how to detect the inconspicuous hind leg of the solution by which to drag it forth.

THE ROOT OF THE FAILURE

To expose the falsity of the current images of science is not enough, any more than is treating symptoms rather than the disease itself. The inadequate scientific education the general student receives at all levels helps to explain the distortions, but only in part. When we try to understand why people hold these views and why they are satisfied with too little knowledge about science, we discover that the major share of the blame does not lie with the ordinary citizen. In this matter he is only taking his cue from the intellectuals—the writers, scholars, lawyers, politicians, scientists and all others who deal professionally in ideas. Among the scientists themselves, busy with exciting work, the majority feel no strong responsibility for taking part in the necessary educational efforts; many have forgotten that, especially at a time of rapid expansion of knowledge, they have an extra obligation to the general public, if only because it must foot the bill and furnish the next crop of young scientists.

Among the rest of the intellectuals the case is worse. The wrong images, which they share with the common man, prevail because they are anchored in two kinds of ignorance. One kind is basic and factual—what biology says about life, what chemistry and physics say about matter, what astronomy says about the structure of our galaxy. The nonscientist realizes that the old common-sense ways of understanding nature have become obsolete. The ground trembles under his feet; gone are the simple interpretations of solidity, permanence, reality; he flounders among four-dimensional continua, probability amplitudes, undecidable identities, indeterminacies. About the basic concepts of modern science that define the physical part of reality, he knows only that he cannot grasp them and never will.

On the second level of ignorance, the contemporary intellectual fails to understand how the different sciences fit together with one another and with the humanities as different aspects of one cosmos. He has left behind those great syntheses which once comprised our intellectual and moral home—the cosmic view of the book of Genesis, Homer, Dante, Milton, Goethe—and now finds himself blindfolded in a maze without exit. The brutal fact is that, by losing contact with even the elementary facts of modern science, our intellectuals, for the first time in history, are losing their hold on understanding the world. Of all the evils arising from the separation of culture and scientific knowledge, this bewilderment and homelessness is the most terrifying.

Indeed, it is amazing to me that the intellectuals have not attacked science, the source of the apparent threats to their common-sense sanity, much more fiercely, that the dissociation has not produced an even graver cultural psychosis. This, I am convinced, is likely to occur, for there is at present no mechanism at work in our society for dealing effectively with the situation.

What remedies suggest themselves? At the least, science must again be made a natural part of every intelligent man's common literacy—not because science is more important than other fields, but because it is an important part of the whole jigsaw puzzle of knowledge. This would require sound, thorough work at every level of education—for example, a good part of a person's college work, as used to be the rule in good colleges fifty years ago. It would demand imaginative new curricula, strength-

523

ened standards of achievement, more recognition of excellence whether exhibited by instructors or by students. Adult education, including the presentation of the factual and cultural aspects of science through mass media, is another obvious measure meriting the support and participation of our best minds.

Here and there, to be sure, some efforts are being made in the right direction, but the total is pitifully small. Virtually nobody has been courageous enough to face the magnitude of the problem squarely, so large is the range and amount of knowledge needed before one can "know science" in any real sense. The converse need—namely, the humanistic education of scientists—is also urgent; but at least in principle it can be served with existing methods of instruction. The tools of humanistic study are still in touch with our sensibilities. This, unhappily, is no longer so in science.

Every great age has been shaped by intellectuals such as Jefferson and Franklin, who would have been horrified by the idea of cultivated men and women turning their backs on science. That tradition has been broken. Few intellectuals are now equipped to act as informed mediators. And meanwhile science advances faster and faster every day, widening the rift between science and culture.

To restore them to some kind of reciprocal contact within the concerns of most men—to bring science into an orbit about us instead of letting it escape from the field of our common culture—that is the great challenge before intellectuals today. And nothing better illustrates the urgency and difficulty of this task than the false images prevailing about science.

Further reading:
Holton, Gerald: INTRODUCTION TO CONCEPTS AND THEORIES IN PHYSICAL SCIENCE. Reading, Mass.: Addison-Wesley Publishing Company, Inc.; 1952.

Holton, Gerald (ed.): SCIENCE AND THE MODERN MIND. Boston: Beacon Press; 1958.

Frankel, Charles: THE CASE FOR MODERN MAN. Boston: Beacon Press; 1956.

Bronowski, Jacob: THE COMMON SENSE OF SCIENCE. Cambridge: Harvard University Press; 1953.

Blanshard, Paul (ed.): EDUCATION IN THE AGE OF SCIENCE. New York: Basic Books, Inc.; 1959.

ROBERTSON DAVIES

[*Photograph by Karsh*]

Robertson Davies describes himself as ". . . a Canadian, born in 1913 in the cusp of Leo and Virgo with Mercury in the ascendant; it has been suggested that this accounts for a deplorable streak of frivolity in my nature."

Despite his astrological handicap, Davies is a playwright, drama and literary critic, syndicated book reviewer and novelist. He also edits the daily newspaper in Peterborough, Ontario. "I think such work good for an author; it keeps him from developing fanciful theories about people." The book from which material for this article was drawn was published in 1960 by Alfred A. Knopf under the title A Voice from the Attic.

Battle Cry
for Book Lovers

BY

ROBERTSON DAVIES

"Layman" is a word which has gained a new and disquieting currency in our language. For much of the 500 years or so that it has been in use it meant simply one who worshiped, as opposed to a priest, who had knowledge of the sacred mysteries. Then, by extension, it came to mean the client or the patient, in his relation to the lawyer and the physician. But nowadays the word is used loosely for anybody who does not happen to know something, however trivial, which somebody else knows, or thinks he knows. The meat eater is a layman to the butcher, and the seeker for illumination is a layman to the candlestick maker. Most reprehensibly the word is used among people who should meet as equals in education and general knowledge, within wide bounds. The layman is the nonexpert, the outsider; the implication is still that the layman's opposite has not merely special knowledge, but a secret and priestlike vocation.

It is particularly displeasing to hear professional critics using the term "layman" to describe people who are amateurs and patrons of those arts with which they are themselves professionally concerned. The fact that the critic gets money for knowing something and giving public expression to his opinion does not entitle him to consider the amateur, who may be as well informed and as sensitive as himself, an outsider. Admitting that there are triflers hanging to the skirts of the arts, it is generally true that we are all, critics and amateurs alike, members of a group which meets on a reasonably equal footing. The critics have their special tastes and firm opinions and are, in some cases, more experienced and sensitive than any but the most devoted of amateurs. But they should never assume that it is so; they, of all people, should know the humility which art imposes and avoid the harlotry of a cheap professionalism.

That is why I address this essay, which is about reading and writing, to the clerisy.

Who are the clerisy? They are people who like to read books.

Are they trained in universities? Not necessarily so, for the day has long passed when a university degree was a guaranty of experience in the humanities, or of literacy beyond its barest meaning of being able, after a fashion, to read and write.

Are the clerisy critics and scholars, professionally engaged in judging the merit of books? By no means, for there are critics and scholars who are untouched by books, except as raw material for their own purposes.

Then does the clerisy mean all of the great body of people who read? No; the name can only be applied with justice to those within that body who read for pleasure and with some pretension to taste.

The use of a word so unusual, so out of fashion, can only be excused on the ground that it has no familiar synonym. The word is little known because what it describes has disappeared, though I do not believe that it has gone forever. The clerisy are those who read for pleasure, but not for idleness; who read for pastime, but not to kill time; who love books, but do not live by books.

As lately as a century ago the clerisy had the power to decide the success or failure of a book, and it could do so now. But the clerisy has been persuaded to abdicate its power by several groups, not themselves malign or consciously unfriendly to literature, which are part of the social and business organization of our time. These groups, though entrenched, are not impregnable; if the clerisy would arouse itself, it could regain its sovereignty in the world of letters. For it is to the clerisy, even yet, that the authors, the publishers and the booksellers make their principal appeal.

Has this group any sense of unity? It had, once, and this is written in the hope that it may regain it. This is a call to the clerisy to wake up and assert itself.

Let us consider the actual business of reading—the interpretative act of getting the words off the page and into your head in the most effective way. It is not the quickest way of reading, and for those who think that speed is the greatest good, there are plenty of manuals on how to read a book which profess to tell how to strip off the husk and guzzle the milk, like a chimp attacking a coconut. Who among the clerisy would whisk through a poem, eyes aflicker, and say that he had read it? The answer to that last question must unfortunately be: far too many. For reading is not respected as the art it is.

Perhaps it would be more just to say that most people, the clerisy included, are impatient of any pace of reading except their fastest, and have small faith in their interpretative powers. They do not think of themselves as artists. But unless they make some effort to match their interpretative powers to the quality of what they would read, they are abusing their faculty of appreciation. And if they do not mean to make the most of their faculty of appreciation, why are they reading? To kill time? But it is not time they are killing; it is themselves.

Doubtless there are philosophical terms for the attitude of mind of which hasty reading is one manifestation, but here let us call it "end-gaining," for its victims put *ends* before *means*; they value not reading, but having read. In this, as in so many things, the end-gainers make mischief and spoil all they do; end-gaining is one of the curses of our nervously tense, intellectually flabby civilization. In reading, as in all arts, it is the means, and not the end, which gives delight and brings the true reward. Not straining forward toward the completion, but the pleasure of every page as it comes, is the secret of reading. We must desire *to read* a book, rather than *to have read* it. This change in attitude, so simple to describe, is by no means simple to achieve, if one lives the life of an end-gainer.

One of the advantages of reading is that it can be done in short spurts and under imperfect conditions. But how often do we read in conditions which are merely decent, not to speak of perfection? How often do we give a book a fair chance to make its effect with us?

Some magazine editors say that the public no longer enjoys fiction; it demands "informative" articles. But informative writing requires less effort to assimilate than does fiction, because good fiction asks the reader to feel.

The clerisy at least want to feel. They have reached that point of maturity where they know that thought and reason, unless matched by feeling, are empty, delusive things. Foolish people laugh at those readers of a century ago who wept over the novels of Dickens. Is it a sign of superior intellect to read anything and everything unmoved, in a gray, unfeeling Limbo? Happy Victorians! Perhaps their tears flowed too readily. But some of Dickens' critics—by no means men of trivial intellect— wept. If this should meet the eye of any modern critic, let me ask him: When did you, sir, last weep over a book? When did you last give a book a fair chance to make you do so?

Feeling is a condition of appreciation, and there can never have been a time when people were so anxious as they now are to have emotional experiences, or sought them so consciously. On the North American continent today sensual experience is frankly acknowledged as one of the good things of life. The popularity of "mood music" shows how eagerly we seek to deepen the quality of our experience. Everywhere there is evidence of this anxiety that no shade of sensual enjoyment should be missed; the emphasis indeed is on nursing sensual enjoyment to its uttermost power, and advertising of all sorts reveals it. Do great numbers of people feel that they are missing some of the joy of life? Who can doubt it?

Like all anxiety, this is end-gaining and carries the seeds of its own failure. Not ends, but means, must be the concern of those who seek satisfaction in the pleasures as well as the obligations of life. Take care of the means, and the ends will take care of themselves.

Let us consider the means of satisfactory reading. It is a truism that we shall find nothing in books which has no existence in ourselves. But we all have slumbering realms of sensibility which can be coaxed into wakefulness by books. Aldous Huxley tells us that "writers influence their readers, preachers their auditors, but always, at bottom, to be more themselves."

But do they know what they themselves are? Is not that what they are reading books to find out?

The best of novels are only scenarios, to be completed by the reader's own experience. They do not give us feeling; they draw out such feeling as we have. If fiction is going out of fashion—which is said from time to time, but which I do not believe—it is not because fiction is any worse than it was; the general level of it is probably better. But great numbers of people find fault with fiction because they do not give themselves a chance to respond to it.

It is the way they read which is at fault. The great success of Emlyn Williams in reading Dickens and Dylan Thomas to large audiences shows us where the trouble lies. I have see Mr. Williams hold a large audience spellbound as he read, in two and a half hours, an abridgment of Dickens' *Bleak House*. He had their undivided attention, and he read with all the resources of a consummate actor. He and his hearers were, for the evening, giving the best of themselves to *Bleak House*; his audience was moved to curiosity, to laughter, to horror, to tears, as audiences are not often moved by plays.

Ah, you may say, but this is a performance by an actor. Yes, and if you want the best from reading, you must learn to give the best performances of which you are capable, sitting soundless in your chair, with your book before you. The gifts demanded of a good reader are less those of the critic than of the actor. You must bestir yourself, and above all certainly you must cultivate the inward ear.

We live in an age when the eye is feasted, and the ear,

if not starved, is kept on short rations. Special merit is accorded to the cartoon which makes its effect without a caption. In the theater we expect a higher standard of scenic design, aided by elaborate lighting, than playgoers have ever known. It is not uncommon for a stage setting, at the rise of the curtain, to be greeted with a round of applause.

But how long is it since you heard an actor applauded because he had delivered a fine speech particularly well? This calls attention to our comparative indifference to fine speech; it is not altogether lacking, but we do not insist upon it as we insist on the gratification of the eye. But how do the books you read reach your consciousness? By words which you hear, or pictures which you see? Unless you have a visualizing type of mind, by words. And how do those words reach you?

In the Middle Ages readers spoke aloud the words they read, and a temporary hoarseness or loss of voice was a sufficient reason for a scholar to suspend his studies. In universities a principal means of instruction was the lecture—literally "a reading aloud"—in which the master read to the undergraduates from a work of his own composition. Holy Writ was read aloud in churches, and a point which was greatly emphasized during the Reformation was that it should be read in a language known to all the hearers and not only to the clerisy. The reason for all this vocalizing of what was read was that it might strike inward not only through the eye but also through the ear; even the most learned did not trust to the eye alone, simply because they could read.

Certainly it is not my purpose to suggest that we should return to all this reading aloud, creating in every library a hubbub like that which one hears when walking through the corridors of a conservatory of music. But are we not foolish to give up that inward voice in which books can speak to us? Not *ends*, but *means*, bring delight and fulfillment to the reader, and his means of reading is listening to the inward, reading voice.

What is that voice like? Its quality depends on your ear. If you have a good ear and some talent for mimicry, you can read to yourself in any voice, or as many voices as you please.

You have seen Sir Laurence Olivier's film of *Richard III?* Very well, can you hear him again when you read the play? If you can, and if you are a playgoer and a filmgoer, you should be able to find voices for all the characters in the books you read.

This is a game, and a very good game, but it asks for a good ear and makes heavy imaginative demands upon the reader. You may not be able to play it; perhaps you have no desire to do so; it is not for all temperaments. Your taste may be more austere. Besides, it only works with novels and plays. What about reading history or poetry?

The inner voice is of your own choosing, of your own development. It may differ greatly from the voice in which you speak. To read Trollope in the tones of Kansas, or Joyce in the cadences of Alabama, is as barbarous as to read *Huckleberry Finn* with a Yorkshire accent or Edith Wharton in the voice of Glasgow. One of the most dismaying experiences of my college days was to hear the whole of *Hamlet* read by a professor whose voice was strongly nasal and whose vocal range was well within one octave. Did he, I wondered, read to himself in that voice? Or did he hear, inside himself, a full, rich, copious, nobly modulated sound unlike the dispirited drone which came out of his mouth? There are, one presumes, utterly tone-deaf readers.

To talk of the rhythms of prose may alarm some readers who have trouble enough with the rhythms of poetry. But poetic rhythm is the rhythm of song, whereas prose rhythm is the rhythm of speech. Not always the speech of the streets or of conversation, but speech rising to nobility, to prophecy, to denunciation. It was Thomas Mann who contrasted the rhythms of verse with "the finer and much less obvious rhythmical laws of prose." Less obvious, but still to be captured by the attentive inward ear, and when so captured, to give a new and splendid dimension to the pleasure of reading.

To some of my readers it may seem that I am advising them to conjure up within themselves a host of dialect comedians and that I want them to read with the embarrassing vehemence of old-fashioned elocutionists. Nothing could be farther from my intention, and I know that many readers are happiest with a low-keyed and antitheatrical approach to their pleasure. But I do seek to urge them to approach reading in a less passive and more interpretative spirit. This cannot be done if the reader hears what he reads declaimed at the speed and in the tones of a tobacco auctioneer.

We would not dream of judging a piece of music which we heard performed on an untuned and neglected piano by a player not up to the work, long out of practice and ill-taught. But we treat a piece of literature, too often, in a comparable fashion. Good reading is the only test of good writing. Can you read this at high speed, without inward vocalizing, and make anything of it?

> Rest not in an Ovation, but a Triumph over thy Passions. Let Anger walk hanging down the head; Let Malice go Manicled, and Envy fetter'd after thee. Behold within thee the long train of thy Trophies not without thee. Make the quarreling Lapithytes sleep, and Centaurs within lye quiet. Chain up the unruly Legion of thy breast. Lead thine own captivity captive, and be *Caesar* within thyself.

You have no desire to read Sir Thomas Browne, and do not care what he has to say? Well, what about Mark Twain?

> It was a real bully circus. It was the splendidest sight that ever was when they all come riding in, two and two, and gentleman and lady, side by side, the men just in their drawers and undershirts, and no shoes nor stirrups, and resting their hands on their thighs easy and comfortable— there must 'a' been twenty of them—and every lady with a lovely complexion, and perfectly beautiful, and looking just like a gang of real sure-enough queens, and dressed in clothes that cost millions of dollars, and just littered with diamonds. It was a powerful fine sight; I never see anything so lovely. And then one by one they got up and stood, and went aweaving around the ring so gentle and wavy and graceful, the men looking ever so tall and airy and straight, with their heads bobbing and skimming along, away up there under the tent roof, and every lady's rose-leafy dress flapping soft and silky around her hips, and she looked like the most loveliest parasol.

The second of these passages is undoubtedly easier than the first, but neither can be taken at a gallop. The difficult Browne yields his secret, and his exquisite savor, when his pace and tone have been discovered; so does Huck Finn. The reader who has cultivated his appreciation of pace and tone has at his command one of the most powerful of critical instruments, and he will not be content with "those hopelessly banal and enormous novels which are typed out by the thumbs of tense mediocrities and called 'powerful' and 'stark' by the reviewing hack"—to quote Vladimir Nabokov, a modern novelist himself remarkable for the individuality of his pace and tone. Attentive, appreciative reading quickly sorts good writing from bad; to the book gobbler no such discrimination is possible, for he reads so quickly that he has no time in which to discover what is not worth reading.

This is not another evangelistic plea, officiously seeking to insure the literary salvation of its readers by exhorting them to read nothing save "the best." The best, as every true reader knows, is not always what one wants; there are times when one does not feel equal to the demands of the best. Indeed, one may without shame confess that for the time being one is tired of the best. Very often one wants no more than "a good read," to shut out the world while those bruises heal which the world has given. But there are degrees in all things, and degree is vastly more important in those realms which are not quite first-rate than on the level of "the best."

Nor is the exercise of judgment in reading to be confused with the attitude of the journalistic or academic critic. His special heresy is that his trade makes him an explainer, rather than an experiencer, of literature. In this heresy he is followed by many of those intellectuals who are not quite intellectual enough, and who would rather be modish than individual in their taste. All too often, to this type of mind, explaining a thing robs it of value. Having discovered what makes the clock go, it is no longer a matter of interest to them that the clock can tell time.

Most English-speaking people today can read and write. But although they can read, millions of these heirs of eighteenth-century idealism do not read. We need not despair because so many people, having been taught—with what staggering cost in time and money, with what wholesale creation of teachers and building of schools!—to read, read nothing at all, or read trash. The experiment of universal literacy is perhaps the most revolutionary in the history of mankind and, far from being done, it is hardly begun. We have reached the point where English-speaking adults can all read, after a fashion; that is a cause for triumph. Only mad romantics can ever have expected them all to read in the same fashion.

There is no democracy in the world of intellect, and no democracy of taste. Great efforts have been made to pretend that this is not so, but they have failed. The spread of literacy has emphasized what was apparent before. Teach everybody to read, and they will read what appeals to them, what accords with their experience and ideal of life. Their wealth or poverty has little to do with the matter; the man of means who reads rubbish and the poor man who exhausts the classics in his public library are still among us. But in the latter throes of the great experiment the clerisy, as an entity to be reckoned with in the population, has disappeared. It is due for revival, because it is needed if the future stages of the great experiment are to go in the right direction.

Not all readers are prepared, at all times, to make independent judgments. But the failure of modern education to equip them to do so, even when they have the inclination, creates a serious gap in modern culture. The enormously increased production of books and the appearance of an academic and journalistic junta of criticism have robbed the reading public of most of its ability to form its own opinions.

This robbery is not the result of a plot. No cabal of professors and reviewers, meeting in secret, have vowed to cheat the reading public of its rights. The reading public has itself connived at the deprivation, and has helped to shove the junta into power. The temper of the time is unfriendly to independent literary judgment. Readers lack leisure, for we tend to work longer hours than any but the nonreaders of the past. We lack standards of comparison also, for the classical education of a century ago is no longer general, and the literary taste founded on an intimate knowledge of the Bible is equally a thing of the past. To quote the Bible to a modern audience is to invite the same blank stare as greets an allusion to something in Homer. Long toil, a maimed education and small leisure are part of the heavy price we pay for our North American standard of living. It is reputed to be the highest in the world, and so it should be, for it is bought at an inordinate price.

Part of that price has been the resignation of literary taste, by the intelligent reading public, into the hands of professionals, of experts, of an intelligentsia. I have no complaint against the existence of an intelligentsia; on the contrary, I favor it. But I do not favor a small, professional intelligentsia, because the very nature of an intelligentsia is that it should be nonprofessional; belonging to it is not something at which anybody works.

Nevertheless, we have a professional intelligentsia now, and it has lost touch with most of the public. Not that determinedly anti-intellectual public which decries one presidential candidate because he is unmistakably literate, and worries about the chances of another because he has a modest skill in playing the piano. The anti-intellectual pose is one of the unforeseen results of our great experiment in complete literacy. Everybody can be made to read and write, but not everybody is going to like it. No, the public with which the intelligentsia has so unhappily lost touch is itself composed of intelligent humanists— a humanist being, by E. M. Forster's definition, a person possessed of curiosity, a free mind, a belief in good taste and a belief in the human race. The intelligentsia has lost touch with the clerisy.

What is to be done? My proposal is a revival of the clerisy. And surely those who have read thus far will know by now of what the clerisy consists.

If it is to become a more vocal and coherent body on the North American continent the people who comprise it must do a very difficult thing—a thing from which they now shrink. They must accept the fact of their clerisy, and be ready to assert it and defend it with good manners when the need arises. This will expose them to some measure of dislike, and probably a good deal of ridicule. They will find among their ranks many people in whose company they can take no joy—the contentious, the cranks, the ax grinders, the meanly ambitious—those pests who turn up in all large groups, and who seem determined to bring shame upon the cause they espouse. The clerisy must expect to be called "intellectuals," a word which has been given both a comic and a sinister connotation of late years.

Why are so many people ashamed of having intelligence and using it? There is nothing democratic about such an attitude. To pretend to be less intelligent than one is deceives nobody and begets dislike, for intelligence cannot be hidden; like a cough, it will out, stifle it how you may. No man has ever won commendation for standing at less than his full height, either physically, morally or intellectually. If you are an intellectual, your best course is to relax and enjoy it.

Obviously a revived, or awakened, clerisy is not going to be the one which fell asleep in the middle of the nineteenth century. We are the spiritual great-great-grandchildren of those people. Their world is not ours, nor have we their classical education or their Biblical culture; we do not live in a society so frankly class conscious as theirs, but in the dwarf's world of the status seekers. Where they had one new book to read, we have a thousand. Where they had a splendid certainty of their own taste and learning—one recalls the Victorian clergyman who replied to a young lady who observed that his pronunciation of a particular word did not agree with the dictionary: "My dear, dictionaries exist to record the pronunciations of people of education, like myself"—we defer to the opinions of journalistic critics who are, in their turn, reflections of academic critics.

We live in a world where bulk is often equated with quality, and though we know that the best seller is not therefore the best book, we can be awed by impressive sales. Nevertheless, we of the clerisy exist; we are not fools; we can make our existence felt by authors, publishers and critics simply by recognizing that we exist as a class which cuts across all classes and by making our opinions better known, verbally, in public, by correspondence and by the other means which present them-

540

selves in the course of daily life. We are people to be reckoned with.

Courteously but firmly we must refuse the outsider role, the layman label, which we have allowed the world of publishers and critics to foist upon us. By our own sheepishness we incurred this loss of our right; by our intelligence we shall reclaim it. We are not ashamed to reverse the words of Sir Nathaniel in *Love's Labour's Lost:* We *have* fed of the dainties that are bred in a book; we *have* eat paper and drunk ink; our intellect is replenished.

Further reading:

Cecil, *David:* THE FINE ART OF READING. New York: The Bobbs-Merrill Company, Inc.; 1956.

Lucas, F. L.: STYLE. New York: The Macmillan Company; 1955.

D. E. HARDING

[*Photograph by Tom Blau*]

Douglas Edison Harding, British architect, author and lecturer, was raised in the Plymouth Brethren, an ultrafundamentalist and puritanical religious sect. As a result of his subsequent apostasy from the Brethren, when he was a student at University College, London, Harding has devoted much of his life to a subject remote from his profession—the reconciliation of science and religion. A practicing architect since 1931, Harding has successfully combined his career with the pursuit of this philosophical quest. In 1952 he published the fruits of his speculations in The Hierarchy of Heaven and Earth. *"My hope," he says, "is that out of this unusual history has come an equally unusual point of view; of interest to those unable to live in a universe without religion and so without meaning."*

The Universe
Revalued

B Y

D. E. HARDING

Every age has its world-picture, its taken-for-granted view
of the universe and man's place in it. Ours is *supposed*
to be based on science, and no longer on religion or superstition.
But is it really the growth of science which has made a cosmology like Plato's or Shakespeare's incredible, and our own the
only possible one? Is our modern, educated layman's estimate
of the universe really founded on facts, or on prejudice?

It is certainly unlike the old estimate. Men once used to
think of the universe as full of life, of the sun and stars and
even the earth as visible deities, and of the blue sky as the country of the blessed. Priests and astronomers pointed up to the
same encircling heavens, to celestial realms whose divinity was
proportional to their distance from man at their center. Physical
height matched spiritual status.

All of this has now, we imagine, been finally disproved. Instead of a universe of concentric spheres, we have a centerless
one, a cosmic potato instead of a cosmic onion. Instead of an
aristocratic universe, we have a leveled-down one, whose prin-
cipalities and powers have long ago lost all their influence. Instead of awesome star gods looking down on us, we have so

545

many celestial firecrackers or blast furnaces blazing away in the night sky. Instead of a tremendously alive universe, we have an inanimate one in which sentient beings, lost like the finest of needles in the vastest of haystacks, manage to scrape a brief living. Instead of a meaningful creation—a proper place for man—we have a vast expanse of mindless space in which living things are the rarest accidents, or anomalies. And, in the last resort, even they are accidental collocations of particles.

Such, more or less, is the new world-myth. Roughly speaking, this is how most of us educated nonscientists regard the universe. And we are under the impression that science makes any other view impossible. Does it, in fact?

First let us note that, truly speaking, there is nothing about the universe which forbids our taking this earth—or the sun, or any other convenient spot—as its center. On the contrary, we have only to use our eyes to see that the universe is always arranged as a nest of concentric regions—occupied by such things as pipe bowls and spectacle rims, hands and feet, men and animals, clouds and aircraft, moon and sun and stars—around the ever-central observer. To discount altogether this eminently verifiable fact, in favor of some theory—however useful—of uniform space, is unrealistic. In practice, the dead and centerless cosmic potato is found to be a cosmic onion, whose observer-core is the very focus of life and mind.

Nor are the outer layers of this onionlike universe necessarily without life. True, we have direct evidence of only one inhabited heavenly body—our own. Nevertheless, according to recent scientific theories, a significant proportion of the stars are likely to have developed into solar systems resembling ours, and again a significant proportion of these systems are likely to contain planets which are suitable homes for the living. And where the right conditions arise—the right ingredients and temperatures—there, scientists assure us, life will follow. Consequently, the number and variety of inhabited worlds may well beggar imagination.

At any rate, then, we have better reason than Shakespeare for feeling, on starlit nights, that we are looking up into heavens well-sprinkled with life, some of it far surpassing our own.

And the chances are that, to find the more superhuman of these inhabited worlds, we should need to probe farther and farther afield from our earth-center. For the realm of the nine planets plainly holds less promise than the remoter realm of the stars—the hundreds of millions of stars of our own Galaxy—containing who knows how many earth-encircled suns. Nor is this realm a millionth part so rich in celestial possibilities as the still remoter realm of the galaxies, with its unthinkably great star population.

Thus science itself not only hints at the existence of the superhuman but links it with distance from ourselves. We are warned that the more exalted of the worlds above could be influencing us all the while in unsuspected ways—say by telepathy: the laboratory evidence for this faculty is impressive and, apparently, distance is no bar to its operation. In short, we are already back to something like the ancient world-picture, which science was supposed to have destroyed once and for all!

Clearly, then, we laymen can hardly claim the support of science for our pseudoscientific world-picture. But consistency is not our strong point. For instance, we talk as if it were somehow to our discredit that our universe home is on so splendid a scale, and as if we had lost and not found ourselves in it. We think of ourselves as mere pin points in the universe, as if our inability to weigh more than one or two hundred pounds apiece were somehow more significant than our scientists' ability to weigh the stars. Again, we speak of this vast expanse of mindless space as if it were anything but our life's source, saturated with and saturating our own mind if no other. We are urged to fight nature, as if we packed a secret supernatural weapon. As for the human self-portrait as an "accidental collocation of particles," and one moreover that walks around blandly describing itself as such—now there's a delightful spectacle! If this is a sample of what our idiotic universe can throw off *accidentally* chance (whatever that can mean), think of what it could do if ever it got around, by some particularly happy accident, to doing it *intentionally!* And, in fact, we don't have to go far to find intention in what it does. It does *us*, who are full of intention. At any rate, a certain part of the universe called "I" intends itself, and a good deal besides. And so, presumably, does every other star dweller who is not on the point of suicide. How this universe can be so steeped in intention, yet remain merely accidental, we do not explain.

Evidently we science-invoking moderns think of "living matter" as if it were somehow freakish, irrelevant to the nature of the universe. Yet science says that the physical basis of inert objects like heavenly bodies is the same as that of the creatures which come to life in them, formed of their substance. The difference does not lie in the raw material, but its organization. Thus the lowliest particles everywhere are capable of assuming the highest living forms. Potentially, all the stuff of all the stars is alive, purposeful and, indeed, superhuman. And even if such exalted functions could actually emerge only for a moment in only one spot, they would still reveal for all time the hidden nature of all matter. One small flower is enough to identify the biggest plant. It follows that there is no sense whatever in our description of the universe as lifeless and mindless.

The scale of this immense thing is what tricks us. We are not deceived when we consider a creature of handy size; for then we take its whole life history into account, and especially the more developed stages. Thus the plant is a *flowering* plant, even as a seedling; and the caterpillar is no mere worm, but a moth in the making, even if it should never come out in its true colors. *Flower* seeds, *mosquito* larvae, *human* embryos: the higher functions are always the most significant for us—provided our specimen weighs no more than a few hundred tons and survives no more than a few hundred years! Our unhappy cosmos lacks both qualifications. Its scale is wrong; therefore its higher functions tell us nothing important about it; we see it as defunct, and only *infested* with life! No matter what myriads of living worlds and species and individuals our universe-tree may sport, no matter how luxuriant its blossoms of mind and values (all arising naturally, science assures us), we still reckon it a flowerless tree! Worse, it is no tree at all; it is not even a branching vase in which we, mere cut flowers, are tastefully displayed, but merely their indifferent or threatening background! Thus, idiotically, do we human flowers deny the life of our cosmic plant because it is not *all* flower, but enormous leaves and stem and root, also!

The analogy is a false one. It does not go half far enough. A rose plucked from the bush is still a rose, but a man plucked from the universe is an absurdity. Yet this absurdity is the very core of our modern myth, which sees man as the clue to what the universe is *not* like!

To say the least, then, the ancient notion of a living cosmos is neither ridiculous nor inconsistent with science. But whatever we think of the universe as a whole, we feel quite sure that its bigger parts are not alive. The bulkiest organisms we recognize are the big trees of California and Oregon and the blue whale.

This is rather odd. For we have, extending from ultimate particles through atoms and molecules and cells up to man who includes them all, a well-filled scale or hierarchy of unitary beings; and then, immeasurably above man, the living whole. Why this cosmic gap? If the vast interval between man and his minutest particles is filled by a series of increasingly sub-human parts, surely the principle of nature's continuity suggests that the equally vast interval between man and the totality may be filled by a series of increasingly superhuman wholes. If these have so far escaped our notice, could that be because we have eyes only for our equals in the cosmic hierarchy?

Have we ever looked for our superiors? Would we recognize them if we saw them? It is notoriously difficult to find a thing one has no idea of. Therefore let us assume that this gap in the natural order is not empty. Let us posit a creature who outbulks a man as a man outbulks a cell, and ask how such a giant would have to differ from ourselves in order to live at all.

Apparently there are limits to the size of a terrestrial organism. If it is too big it is unlikely to survive. In that case, we can only assume that our giant takes flight from his parent heavenly body and sets up as a heavenly body on his own account. Then he not only can be very massive, but *needs* to be; otherwise, he can neither incorporate his own atmosphere and water supply, nor keep a firm gravitational hold upon them; and without water and oxygen, and atmosphere shells to shield him from meteorites and dangerous radiation and extreme temperatures, he cannot make the heavens his home. And once there, he cannot just wander at will, but must attach himself to some star for warmth and energy, keeping a safe distance and turning continually to avoid freezing behind and roasting in front. And he is certainly a lucky giant. As soon as he starts spinning and circling round his star, the laws of gravity and inertia see that he goes on doing so without effort or deviation.

As for his physique, what would he want with legs or arms, hands or feet, or even wings? Nose and tongue and ears, a mouth and rows of teeth, a stomach and bowels and an anus—anything like these would surely be an encumbrance and a laughingstock in the heavens. We are left, apparently, with some vast rounded body, its whole surface drinking in solar energy.

And supposing there were no convenient star to feed on? Well, if he cannot *find* what he needs, he must *be* it. Our starless sky dweller must himself incorporate a starlike source of energy—a great blazing heart to sustain the smaller and cooler peripheral body we have described.

To sum up: If we greatly enlarge the creatures we know, adjusting their physique and behavior to suit their size, we get creatures that are indistinguishable from planets and stars. If they exist, they are probably a familiar sight. Many a star shining in the sky could in fact be a living thing, a fit inhabitant of heaven. And so the scale of creatures does not necessarily end with us. The seeming gap could arise from a defect of vision instead of a defect in the universe.

A celestial detective story with no solution! Perhaps it is time we came down to earth again, to the life we know.

But *do* we know it? A living thing (scientists tell us) is an organization of nonliving ones. The salts of our blood, the acid of our stomachs, and the calcium phosphate of our bones are clearly not alive; but neither are the atoms comprising all our living cells. What is physics or chemistry at one observational level is a man at another, and at once alive and not alive. All depends on whether this thing is taken to pieces or not.

But if the pieces (as pieces) are lifeless, where shall we set the boundaries of the living whole? If by the whole man we mean one who is independent and self-contained, we can hardly leave out the air in his lungs and the saliva in his mouth and the chyme in his guts—at least, nobody has pointed out where these cease to be environment and become organism. And if *they* are caught up in the living whole of him, why not the tools without which he would starve to death and the clothes without which he would freeze to death? After all, he is far more dependent upon his shoes than his toenails, and upon his good false teeth than his bad real ones. They have become part of his life.

That is how he describes them, and that is what they feel like. He identifies himself with his possessions and is not himself without them. He may be more vain of his facade than his face, and more hurt by the loss of a few tiles than many hairs. Until he feels so all-of-a-piece with the clothes he wears, and the horse he rides, and the financial or political power he wields, that they no longer seem outside him, he has still to learn their use. The expert is one who, having incorporated his tools, is unaware of them. They have temporarily vanished into his physique. He doesn't sit on the seat of his pants, or even on a seat in a boat that sails on the sea. *He* sails, *he* is at sea. He doesn't grasp a handle that holds a blade that cuts bread. *He* cuts bread. That is how a man speaks because that is what he is—an endlessly elastic organization of "dead" parts, mostly outside his skin. Thanks to them, he can drink at the lake and browse in the field while attending a concert on the far side of the world—all without setting foot outside his own porch. Instead of going out to these places, he grows out to them.

Nor do these artificial but vital extensions complete his physique. To cut man off from the other creatures is homicidal, for species neither occur nor survive nor develop as things apart, but in great interlocking patterns of mutual dependence. Just as our muscle cells make no sense without our blood cells, so the bee's tongue makes no sense without the flower's nectary; and so on indefinitely—the more you study one bit of life the more you must take the others into account, so that really to know one would be to know the lot. If, then, we seek the living whole—and life, we have seen, is a question of wholeness—nothing short of the entire network of terrestrial organisms, growing up as one living thing from the start, really deserves such a title. And even this vast spherical organization is not yet a complete organism. This living earth-skin is still far from being self-contained—for without rock and water and topsoil and air it is as dead as the least of its parts.

In short, nothing less than the whole Earth is genuinely alive! Here indeed is a visible god or goddess. The giant we were seeking in the heavens was down here all the while!

Whose life is in doubt? Hers, or ours which is hers or nothing? The only *complete* living thing of which we have inside knowledge turns out to be a heavenly body—our Earth. And the *only* heavenly body of which we have inside knowledge turns out to be a living thing—again, our Earth. In fact, it is not *living* heavenly bodies which call for proof, so much as *dead* ones!

The behavior and build of such a creature are so odd that we need a new word for this high-level vitality, this superlife which is at least planetary. Oddity, however, must be expected here. The living cell is a very different story from one of its molecules, and man from one of his cells. It would be strange if the living Earth were not, in turn, unlike her animal and subanimal parts.

All the same, the Earth is no foreign body, living some mysterious life apart from ours. Admittedly her life-preserving maneuvers in the sky are less varied than ours in her; but if to act deliberately is to know with scientific precision what you do and why (its causes and effects in the past, present and future) then her behavior is much more deliberate than any man's. Admittedly her beginnings were unconscious and unpromising, but so were ours; and now who can match her adult complexity—all her own unfolding and no invasion? For parent, she has the sun; for anxiously awaited offspring, manned spaceships and satellites; for eyes, observatories whose binocular vision (like the merely human) enables her to place her nearer neighbors; for special sense organs, receptors tuned in to cosmic influences; for intellectual exercise, our science of the heavens. We hang her portrait on our walls, and the close-up of her face is familiar to every radio-equipped aviator as a luminous and noisy and ever-changing network and patchwork.

This is indeed no alien godling. She is the full extent, the filled-out body-mind of each of her creatures. For there is nowhere to live but heaven, and no way to live there but hers.

But, of course, even she is not really suited to the hard climate of the skies. The smallest complete creature fit for this universe is no sunless planet, but a star—a fully developed sun, a solar system whose "living" planet is a mere organ. And even such a star is not independent of its fellows in our Galaxy, and of the universe of galaxies itself. Only the whole is a genuine whole, and therefore altogether alive.

It is no surprise to find in the superhuman just such a hierarchy of wholes and parts as we found in the subhuman. Isn't this exactly what we wanted to fill the gap above man, and balance the orders below him—this ascending scale of beings—planetary, sidereal and galactic, but all finite—in which higher rank means more independence achieved, and more "dead" material raised to life? And isn't the life of man the indivisible life of the entire hierarchy—the upper half that he is in as well as the lower half that is in him—or nothing at all?

Is this view of man too speculative? Then let us imitate the scientist, whose business is unprejudiced observation (with a view to economical description and prediction or control). Let us try observing man. What precisely are you, when examined without prejudice?

What we make of you depends upon range. At ten feet, we see a human body; a little closer, a head. But the superficial view is not enough. Our instruments take us nearer and nearer, to places where we observe tissues, cell groups, a cell in detail, giant molecules and so on.

So much for the near view. Let us now move away from you. This time we find, in turn, a house, a city, a country, a planet, a star (our solar system) and a galaxy.

You may say that these are nothing like "you." But which appearance is less like "you," your particles or your planet, your cells or your city? If the first is "you" observed, why not the second? But we don't yet know what "you" are. We can only take what we find—namely, the whole scale of creatures from particles to heavenly bodies. And this confirms our conclusion that you are incomplete, not yourself, till you are celestially constituted.

You may reasonably protest that the distant view includes so much that isn't you, provided you add that the near view excludes so much that is you, and that the middle view is altogether too superficial. But all three objections beg the question: What are you? Surely the best hope of an answer is to ignore no view of this object, whatever the range. Only unprejudiced observation could reveal the astonishing totality, with all its metamorphoses.

You might reply that this merging and emerging, this cosmic elasticity, however true of your bodily or outer aspect, is untrue of your "real self."

To find out the truth, first listen to your self. You talk of *this* organ, *this* body, *this* house, city, country, planet and star. Clearly, what is felt as *here* varies from this aching tooth to this star, and what is felt as *there* varies from all the other teeth in your head to all the other stars in the sky. "Now" and "then," "fast" and "slow," "present" and "absent"—these little words are always giving you away. Anyone who can seriously talk of near galaxies yet the far side of the room, of old men in a new world, of giant atoms in a dwarf star, is either altogether elastic or beside himself.

Far from deceiving us, language is only underlining the facts. A diseased mind may so identify itself with one bodily organ that the rest are treated as alien or hostile. And evidently a man may so identify himself with his family, or country, or race, or planet (in the event of interplanetary war), or God, that he thinks for them, and is hurt when they are injured, and makes their good his good, and lives and dies for them without thought of his private welfare. In fact, anyone who lacked all such expansive feelings would be an intellectual and moral imbecile, incapable of objectivity or responsibility. The idea of the self as constant, as a unique, permanent, separate, immiscible something, will not bear examination. The facts make nonsense of it—they include the evidence of multiple personality, religious conversion, amnesia and parapsychology, not to mention the great problem of biological individuality. Nor does this nonsensical idea work. Quite the contrary, it is madness. To the extent that we cut ourselves off from anybody and everybody we are out of our minds and dispirited.

The truth is that this illusion of a separate self and the illusion of a dead universe are halves of a whole, segments of one vicious circle. The universe seems dead because I seem out of it. I seem out of it because the universe seems dead. Till the total mind in man rejoins its own total body, the universe, he is self-alienated and the universe appears corpselike.

Short of that goal, his elastic mind matches his elastic body; *here* and *there* grow and shrink together; subject takes on the rank of object; you and I are roughly equals. It is a man who greets a man, a ship that hails a ship, a planet that signals a planet. And just as it is not this eye (or even this head) that sees you, but this man (from top to toe) who does so, so it is not this man who studies Mars, but Earth that does so. She is our only astronomer—no mere man being equal to or equipped for the task—so that, in fact, there is the world of difference between the "I" in "I see a man" and in "I see Mars." Again, when the general (note the noun) says he will smash the enemy, it is the army that does so. And when the atomic physicist (note the adjective) says he will smash the uranium nucleus, it is neutrons that do so. Yet he does not feel small, any more than the general or the astronomer feel bloated. It comes so naturally to us to be almost everything, and the next moment almost nothing, that we never notice the transformation.

We have every right, then, to announce Earth's life. It is an aspect of our own infinitely elastic life. But this makes her peculiarly vulnerable. A word is enough to kill this great but sensitive creature.

For we have only to decide, in the teeth of all the evidence, that she shall be a "lifeless" planet, and then no matter what limb she flourishes, or eye she opens, or *Song of the Earth* she sings—nothing she can ever do or say will prove her alive: because it is all, by definition, not hers! It is living, and therefore alien or parasitic! Never shall the life *on* Earth be the life *of* Earth. Treat a man thus, and he is little more than a cell-infested skeleton. Examine the world's liveliest organism till you know it inside out, and you will find nothing but cell-populated terrain. The only way for us to rejoin Earth, to rank as geological specimens instead of antigeological ones, is to stop geologizing, and thinking, and living, and get ourselves buried and petrified. Then we are dead enough to belong again!

And, of course, our sun—now come to life as our solar system—gets the same raw deal. We have only to hand over the whole of his natural history to physics and astronomy (as if his men and beasts were unnatural and his flowers artificial) to reduce this star god to star dust.

A solar myth as curious as this does not spring up overnight. It, too, has a natural history.

To our early ancestors the sun was simply alive, as you or I, only brighter and more divine. But gradually the animating spirit was distinguished and divided from the gross body, which became a mere fireball steered by an independent god or angel. Then science reduced particular star spirits to general laws of nature, tendencies and forces. And eventually, coming down to our own day, even these ghostly remnants are seen as man-made or subjective, and so exorcised. The stars are no longer impelled or guided in their courses. They only take the line of least resistance. And while the solar life and mind are thus being wiped out, the body itself is being quietly disposed of. The sun's sensible qualities—his color, brightness, warmth—are drawn in from the object there to the subject here, to the eye of the perceiver. Even his apparent motion across the sky is really ours. Finally, and just in case any miserable residue of our victim should remain, physics dissolves his substance into space, dotted with inscrutable particles.

Here is the murder story of all time—nothing less than "cosmicide" committed over millenniums, and still going practically undetected. Fortunately, however, it is only a tale, a piece of solar crime fiction. For we could *get rid* of the solar life by absorbing it into our heads only if they were lethal receptacles, or else made off with their solar contents to some other star. In fact, the life of our solar system has suffered an internal shift; it has not vanished. Rather the reverse. Doubtless it is only by thus shamming dead that a planet-ringed sun can wake in the end to a fully self-conscious life. After all, our pseudoscientific myth of a dead sun must be seen as a solar, rather than a merely human myth, as an indispensable chapter in the natural history of our solar system, rather than a mere aberration. Only don't let us mistake this brief and somewhat crazy chapter for the whole story.

And don't let us mistake indifference to this story for real neutrality. The universe which is not seen as living is treated as dead. There is no halfway. Even if we could avoid taking sides, rejection of the ancient world-view amounts in practice to acceptance of the modern, with its immense consequences for religion and art and politics, to say nothing of science itself.

To sum up: We have found our modern myth, this life-abhorring world-picture that we laymen thought was scientific, to be nothing of the sort. Instead, we have found science pointing in the opposite direction, toward something like the old cosmic hierarchy culminating in the divine.

The outcome for you and me is as far-reaching as we care to make it. Already we have seen that, once we breach the artificial wall dividing our little selves from the hierarchy of our greater selves, the walls are apt to go on falling, till in the end we glimpse the one self of all. It is the first step that counts. Once we admit any life and mind above the merely human, we are apt to find ourselves admitting more and more, till we come to the highest life, our total mind, where we are safe home at last and outside nothing. That is where, say the world's great spiritual teachers, we could even now lose ourselves for good, in a deathless world whose divisions and opacity have finally vanished, and where everything is indescribably open, weightless and brilliant.

To some of us, this is danger signal enough. Our separate egos will defend themselves to the death. To others, here is a renewed invitation to the toughest adventure of all, whose end is variously called enlightenment, liberation, the Kingdom of Heaven and the mystical union. Several roads lead toward that goal; and the road whose first stages this article has sketched is certainly not everybody's. To the thoroughly Westernized mind, however, whose preoccupation has for two centuries been the "conquest" of nature, this approach may have more than intellectual interest. Nature, the "enemy," can now show us her kinder face. She can lead us further than ever before toward the one unchanging reality of which she is the manifold and fleeting appearance.

In any case, there exists for none of us, not even the most "spiritual," a merely human or personal liberation which leaves nature out, and which does not involve the liberation of every creature on the Earth and in the skies, however grotesque or seemingly unlovable. How could we *begin* to disentangle ourselves from any part of the One, in whom we all live and move and have our being? Englightenment is cosmic or nothing.

Further reading:

Harding, Douglas E.: THE HIERARCHY OF HEAVEN AND EARTH. New York: Harper & Brothers; 1953.

Lowrie, Walter (ed. and translator of selections from Gustav T. Fechner): RELIGION OF A SCIENTIST. New York: Pantheon Books, Inc.; 1946.

James, William: Vol. I of WORKS, ed. by Ralph B. Perry, ESSAY IN RADICAL EMPIRICISM, and PLURALISTIC UNIVERSE. New York: Longmans, Green & Co., Inc.; 1943.

Boodin, John E.: GOD AND CREATION, in two vols. New York: The Macmillan Company; 1935.

Tillyard, W. M. W.: THE ELIZABETHAN WORLD PICTURE. New York: Modern Library, Inc.; 1959.

JAMES BONNER

[Photograph by Sid Avery]

James Bonner, professor of biology at the California Institute of Technology, is engaged in research in the biochemistry and physiology of plants, enzyme synthesis, and the nuclear-cytoplasmic structure of the cell. The author of several books on these subjects, Professor Bonner also is interested in the future of plant-animal relationships as they bear on the problem of supplying food for the earth's expanding population. No book-bound scholar, Professor Bonner spends many of his winter weekends in the California mountains serving as a ski patrolman for the National Ski Patrol System.

The Messages of Life

BY

JAMES BONNER

Biology is today on the edge of understanding how living
things live. This almost-successful search for the principle,
the logic, of life may someday enable us to control the step-by-
step development of the human organism, to cultivate replace-
ment organs and perhaps even to initiate life in isolated cells. A
whole new world of medicine also awaits us across this thresh-
old of understanding; among the most urgent problems which
may yield to the new knowledge are the control of virus diseases
and of cancer.

This new biology—for it is a new branching of an old discipline—is largely concerned with the molecular facts of life.
One of the most complicated mysteries of nature is the way the
tens of thousands of chemical compounds that compose a living
creature work together to cause that creature to breathe, digest
and leave descendants. But this mystery is being unraveled.
Every day now brings new excitement as research biologists
draw close to its final solution. For they have discovered that
each cell of each individual contains a blueprint, an instruction
manual, which gives the cell detailed instructions on what kind
of chemicals to make from the available food, on how the cell
shall divide or replicate itself, on the size and shape of the
systems it shall form (that is, elephant or mouse)—in short,

561

how the cell should become a part of a particular kind of a living thing.

This cellular instruction manual, which biologists call "genetic material," possesses the extraordinary power of being able to print copies of itself. These copies are then passed on to the next generation. In this way living things leave their descendants directions on how to look, how to behave, how to be. The new biology seeks to read this genetic book and to find out what kinds of instructions it transmits, how the genetic information multiplies itself, how it acts, how it enforces its decrees.

The gateway to this new understanding of the basic life pattern has been found in the study of the living cell. All creatures consist of cells and have in common cells which are very much alike. All cells are made of various standardized types of components. Living creatures may, in fact, be looked upon as a series of models made of a kind of tinkertoy, with standard interchangeable parts. For example, the largest and most spectacular part of every proper cell is a nucleus. This nucleus contains the genetic material, the chromosomes, each made up of many genes. The genes are made of a special gene substance found nowhere else—deoxyribonucleic acid, known to biologists as DNA. The DNA of the nucleus contains, in coded form, all the information required to assemble the individual cell—and indeed, to assemble all the cells comprising an entire organism.

That DNA contains—and transmits—genetic information, was first shown by O. T. Avery at the Rockefeller Institute more than fifteen years ago. His experiment consisted of the transplantation of genetic information from one type of bacterial cell to another. The laboratory transplantation of such genetic information requires only that a portion of the DNA of the donor cell be placed in solution, together with some of the receptor cells. The receptor cells, in a fraction of cases, incorporate the alien DNA into their own genetic complement so that it becomes a permanent part of their genetic information. In this way genes for resistance or susceptibility to an antibiotic, or for ability or inability to cause disease—such as pneumonia, with which Avery worked—may be transferred from one strain of bacteria to another.

DNA has two characteristics which suit it uniquely to its role of information bearer. The first is a structure so arranged that it can carry information. The DNA molecule is a long chain, made up of four kinds of links, or building blocks, whose chemical names we can symbolize by the four letters, A, T, G and C. The four links may succeed one another in any of many permutations and combinations to produce many different words, all written in a four-letter alphabet, the alphabet of A, T, G and C. The DNA molecule is thus a sort of telegram, written in DNA language, which carries messages indicating how a cell shall develop and proliferate. We might call DNA a do-it-yourself book of instructions to its host cell.

The second unique property of DNA is its ability to produce exact copies of itself. DNA can so replicate because it is a twin molecule with two long strands, each composed of the building blocks A, T, G and C. These two strands are wound around each other to form a helix, a molecular barber pole. And it is a basic law of living matter that the sequence of the letters A, T, G and C in the one strand determines the sequence of letters in the companion strand. A in the one strand must be paired with T in the second, G with C, T with A, and C with G. The two strands are, as biologists say, complementary. We believe that when the DNA replicates itself, the two strands first separate, and that each then assembles upon itself its complement, using the chemical building blocks available in the cell. When the replication has been accomplished, we have two new double strands, each indistinguishable from the original, but bearing the same coded information as the original.

The double-stranded complementary structure of DNA, first recognized by James Watson of Harvard University and Francis Crick of Cambridge University, is a concept of great significance. It suggests the basic operation by which a living organism reproduces itself. And it appears that of all the substances in the organism, only DNA possesses this power of replication. All other substances are directly or indirectly made by the DNA. The DNA might be likened to a queen bee, hatching out workers who cannot leave descendants. Only the queen bee can proliferate—only the queen can produce the infertile workers and, from time to time, a new queen bee.

The DNA is then a set of self-replicating instructions, constituting the genetic material within the nucleus of the cell. But whence do the instructions come? How are they carried out? To answer these questions, the biologist leaves the central nucleus and he prospects in the surrounding cytoplasm of the cell.

A cell contains of course a multitude of parts. In addition to its nucleus, for instance, a plant cell possesses chloroplasts. These contain not only the chlorophyll which makes plants green but also the machinery for photosynthesis, which converts carbon dioxide and the energy of light into the plant material all of us nonplants use for food. All cells also contain units of a smaller order called mitochondria—the cellular powerhouses which burn the food and supply the energy for our muscular work, the operation of our nervous system and the process of chemical synthesis within the body.

All these cellular units are small, but they are large enough to be seen through a microscope, and biologists have been observing them for a generation or more. To find the direct linkage between the units in the cellular chain of command, biologists have had to descend into a still smaller world—a world observable only after the introduction of the electron microscope in the 1940's. On this minute stage—an area where the common unit of measurement is the angstrom, or the fractional part of one hundred millionth of an inch—the most interesting objects are the cellular enzymes and the microsomes.

One of the triumphs of modern biology has been the demonstration that each of the cell's chemical reactions is speeded on its course by a specific kind of enzyme with the sole duty of hastening that particular reaction. And since the cell carries on several thousand kinds of chemical reactions, it contains several thousand kinds of enzyme molecules. We know that the enzymes a cell produces are genetically controlled— that for each enzyme there is a gene in the nucleus which orders the cell to make that particular enzyme. Since there are about 10,000 kinds of enzyme molecules in a typical cell, there must be at least an equal number of genes in the nucleus of the same cell.

A striking example of this one-for-one relationship is an enzyme found in victims of the hereditary disease called sickle cell anemia, characterized by abnormal hemoglobin of red blood cells. We now recognize the cause of this enzymatic abnormality as a hemoglobin-determining gene different from the normal.

Among the many things we know about enzymes is that each consists of a unique chemical material. All enzymes are protein, that complex material which forms so large a part of all living matter, and all are made up of the same twenty kinds of amino-acid building blocks. An enzyme molecule consists of several hundred of these building blocks linked together in a long chain. What makes a particular kind of enzyme a unique material is the sequence of the building blocks. We may say, therefore, that an enzyme molecule is, like DNA, a message, but a message written in a twenty-letter alphabet—the alphabet of the twenty naturally occurring amino acids.

The cellular enzymes perform various essential tasks in the transformation of food into cell substance. But before an enzyme molecule can perform its task, it must first be assembled by the cell from the amino-acid building blocks. One of the exciting discoveries of the new biology is how the cell makes its enzyme molecules. It is a most logical arrangement. The cell contains superenzymes, called microsomes, for making ordinary enzymes. Though the microsome is about 100 times larger than the enzyme molecule, it is still so small that we can see it only with the electron microscope.

The functioning of a microsome depends upon a full set of built-in instructions. To make one particular enzyme—the hemoglobin molecule, for example—600 building blocks of twenty different kinds must be properly stapled together in the correct sequence. The building instructions are written in the microsome in coded form. The essential portion of the microsome is thus a coded directive about what kind of enzyme to make and how to make it. The building blocks of which the microsome is made are much like those of DNA, with the addition of a single chemical group essential to enzyme synthesis. The nucleic acid of the microsome, ribonucleic acid, or RNA, is more specific than the DNA of the genetic material in one respect—RNA can make enzymes; DNA cannot. On the other hand, DNA can replicate itself, but RNA cannot.

Microsomes, then, make enzyme molecules. But we also know that the DNA of the genetic material is the original source of the cell's information about what kinds of enzyme molecules to make. Clearly the genes somehow determine the kind of information contained in the microsome. Microsomes, in fact, are apparently made in the nucleus and then distributed throughout the rest of the cell. Further, it appears that the formation of microsomal RNA in the nucleus takes place only in the presence of the DNA, for if the DNA is removed, the cell loses its power to make microsomal RNA.

We do not know exactly how the genetic DNA makes the microsomal RNA. Obviously the next great step is to find out. We could, for example, put some DNA in a test tube and ascertain what else has to be added to cause RNA to be made. For the present we can say that the genetic material has two functions—(a) it can replicate itself or (b) it can synthesize RNA. This RNA is packaged as microsomes which go out into the cell and make enzymes.

The amount of information contained in the RNA of a single microsome is quite small compared to that contained in all of the DNA of the nucleus. We think, in fact, that it just about equals the information contained in a single gene. If this is true, a single microsome probably contains the message of but a single gene. One gene, therefore, would contain the information necessary to make one kind of enzyme. To get this information acted upon, the gene produces its special kind of microsome within the nucleus; the microsome then sifts through the nuclear membrane and out into the cell, where it manufactures the specified enzyme. Since the genetic material of the cell consists of several thousand genes, it follows that the cell contains several thousand kinds of needed enzymes.

The success of any organism is measured by the number of descendants it leaves. This is the principle of natural selection. The cell that leaves the most descendants wins out and populates the earth. But the division of cells to make more cells requires the multiplication of the genetic material, the replication of the DNA. Each unit of genetic information, each gene, each chromosome, must double before cell division can take place. The two daughter cells, products of the cell division, each contain the genetic information characteristic of the original parent cell —characteristic both in amount and kind.

In terms of the cell, multiplication is the goal of life, and multiplication means replication of DNA. And now we can sense the logic which requires the presence in the cell of the varied things which it contains. The genetic material of the nucleus contains information. This information is somehow transferred to microsomes. The microsomes go out into the cell and use this information to make enzymes. Some of these enzymes make building blocks for making more enzymes. Others make building blocks for making more RNA to make more microsomes. But—and most importantly—a portion of the enzymes are those which make building blocks for DNA, so that the genetic material may multiply, so that, in turn, the cell may produce more cells. A cell is a device arranged by the DNA to provide for its own welfare, to provide it with conditions suitable for its own replication. We might even say the same thing for the whole living creature.

In the logic of the living cell, then, the RNA and the enzyme molecules all originate with DNA. The DNA originates from itself, using its own body as a model. Where did the first DNA come from? The question of the origin of DNA thus becomes the question of the origin of life.

No one has yet synthesized life. It should, however, be possible. One would have to make some DNA and then put it in a soup containing the A, T, G and C building blocks that DNA needs to reproduce itself. The DNA should then be able to reproduce and make more DNA. Ultimately the replicating DNA would use up one or another of the ingredients—say, A—and replication would cease. Thenceforth only the occasional DNA molecule which had acquired information on how to make A from some other available precursor would be able to reproduce.

This acquisition of new information by a DNA molecule is known as mutation. Geneticists believe that mutation consists of little errors which occur from time to time in the replication of the DNA. Possibly a G is inserted where an A should be, or one letter is left out entirely, or an extra letter is put in. Once made, the error is ruthlessly replicated during the course of DNA multiplication—just as a printing press replicates all of the errors of the typesetter.

In any mutation, the altered DNA molecule will contain information slightly different from that of its parent. Often this new and randomly acquired information will serve no purpose. Occasionally, useful new information will be acquired. The properly mutated molecule will have a selective advantage over its nonmutated mates—it would be able, in our first example, to make A building blocks from some appropriate precursor and continue the production of the slightly different kind of DNA. This is natural selection at work. In time the system will run out of something else, such as the precursor of A. Only those DNA molecules will survive which have, by mutation, acquired the capacity of making the precursor of A from still another precursor.

Thus we can imagine that, as the DNA molecule reproduces and mutates in a soup containing all imaginable substances, mutation and selection will gradually enrich the soup with those DNA molecules which possess more and more sophisticated synthetic ability.

This is the kind of model most biologists today believe to be a reasonable one for the origin of life on our earth. (See "How Life Began," by Earl A. Evans, Jr., on pages 299–308 of this volume.) They conceive that aeons ago the oceans were a sort of primordial soup, containing an almost infinite variety of organic compounds which persisted because there were no creatures to feed upon them. The first living creature to appear in this soup must have been a simple organism, no more than a molecule constructed by random organic chemistry, yet a molecule capable of replication and mutation, so that it could adjust to changing circumstances. It must have been a molecule of DNA. And, over the ages, this aboriginal DNA molecule gained the ability, by mutation and selection, to house itself within membranes and to produce cells. And from cells arose, likewise by mutation and selection, the whole wonderful array of living things.

A single cell is, of course, just the beginning of a complex creature such as man. Each of us, however, does develop from a single cell—the fertilized egg. The fertilized egg cell divides into two cells. Each of these divides into two, and so on. As the process continues, individual cells begin to differentiate into different types of cells—structural cells, glandular cells, secretory cells, reproductive cells, nerve cells. We know such differentiation consists basically of differentiation in enzymatic constitution—different kinds of cells containing different kinds of enzymes that, in turn, produce different structures and functions.

But this leads to a paradox. Each enzyme is apparently produced by a particular kind of microsome, derived from the DNA—quite possibly the DNA of a single gene. We know that all cells of a creature have the same total complement of DNA and thus have all of the genes characteristic of that creature. Accordingly we should expect all cells to contain the same enzymes and therefore the same characteristics. How is it that the cells of a single creature develop into many different types?

The inescapable conclusion is that all genes do not always make their characteristic microsomes, their characteristic RNA. As an extreme example, take the cells which produce hemoglobin. In these cells all genes except those concerned with the production of microsomes for the synthesis of hemoglobin are inert; they are inoperative. Conversely, in the adult organism the gene for making hemoglobin is inoperative in all of the cells except those in the bone marrow which are concerned with the making of red blood cells.

It would appear, then, that part of the cellular system controls the activity of the genes within the nucleus, determining whether a given gene may produce its characteristic microsomes. We do not yet understand the nature of this control. Perhaps certain genes are responsible for it. Perhaps part of the information in the DNA directs the use of the rest of the information. Perhaps a portion of the DNA sends out signals informing each gene when it should be operative and when inoperative.

If biologists can learn how to turn the genes off and on, they will have taken the first step toward controlling the development of the fertilized egg into an adult organism. With such knowledge we could remedy defects as they appear in the developing child, replace worn-out organs and perhaps even initiate embryonic development in cells removed from the adult body.

Many current medical problems will yield to our increasing knowledge of cellular activity. We already know that some kinds of viruses are essentially pieces of DNA which can enter a cell and there replicate, foraging on the host cell for nutrients as they make more viruses. This is true of the bacteriophages, the viruses which attack bacteria. Other kinds of viruses, including those of influenza and polio, are more complex and consist essentially of small portions of RNA.

Though we do not yet know how these viruses multiply, we do know how to attack the problem. We must find out whether the host cell's DNA is necessary for the production of the RNA of the virus—as it is for the production of microsomal RNA—or whether the virus RNA, unlike the microsomal RNA, can multiply itself, Such knowledge might help us arrest the growth of disease viruses without harming the host cells.

As for cancer, though we can now describe the various forms of this disease and though we know there are many different agents, viruses and irritants which induce cancers, we still do not understand the basic mechanism which transforms a normal cell into a cancerous one. Possibly a cancerous cell is one in which a large number of genes are operative, genes which would remain inert in the normal course of development. Some part of the carcinogenic process may cause the cancerous cell to start producing microsomes for producing enzymes which that cell does not ordinarily produce. Perhaps, to use an exaggeration, a cancerous cell is a cell in which all the genes are operative. Here again we do not yet know the answer—but we expect to find it.

The new biology I have described is largely concerned with the molecular facts of life. Our progress has enabled us to make more clearly the boundary between molecular biology and the biology of even more complex matters—human behavior, for example. A fertilized egg cell develops into a creature—a human being, for instance—in response to instructions contained in the genetic material. Written down in the DNA is a vast amount of information—instructions on how to make all the cells and tissues and arrangements needed to assemble a man. Part of the instructions contained in the DNA of a human being direct the construction of a vast network of nerve cells, the brain and its associated sense organs.

Once assembled, this neural network is capable of receiving, through the sense organs, information about the outside world. It is also capable of storing, processing, sorting and acting on the information it receives. Though DNA contains instructions on how to make a human brain, it does not put information into this brain. The brain starts off with a clean slate. Each of us gathers his own information and acts upon it in accordance with what we learn and feel. Neurobiology, the biology of the neural network, is supramolecular biology. Its study is a challenge for the biologists of the future.

But the biology of today is molecular biology—life seen as the ballet of the big molecules, the dance of the DNA. The new biology promises much for human welfare; it has already provided much understanding. Through it we have learned that each living creature is, biologically, a cellular instruction manual written in symbolic genetic language, the language of the DNA. The DNA makes the RNA; the RNA makes the enzymes; the enzymes make the building blocks for making all three. The molecular logic of the animate world rests on this tricycle of life.

Further reading:
    Swanson, Carl P.: THE CELL: Foundations of Modern Biology
    Series. Englewood Cliffs: Prentice-Hall, Inc.; 1960.
    Gerard, Ralph W.: UNRESTING CELLS. New York: Harper &
    Brothers; 1949.
    Hutchings, Edward, Jr. (*ed.*); FRONTIERS IN SCIENCE. New
    York: Basic Books; 1958.
    Butler, John A. V.: INSIDE THE LIVING CELL. New York: Basic
    Books; 1959.
    The Physics and Chemistry of Life. By the editors of SCIEN-
    TIFIC AMERICAN. New York: Simon and Schuster; 1956.

JOHN CIARDI

[*Photograph by Philippe Halsman*]

John Ciardi, born in 1916, is a poet, poetry editor and critic (Saturday Review), *lecturer and professor of English at Rutgers University. He has expressed a personal belief that "poetry is itself a religion; it gives meaning to life." Boston-born-and-bred, educated at Bates, Tufts and the University of Michigan, Mr. Ciardi has published eight books of poems and won six important literary prizes; the last one being the* Prix de Rome *in 1956.*

The Act of Language

BY

JOHN CIARDI

At the beginning of *The Divine Comedy*, Dante finds himself in a Dark Wood, lost from the light of God. It was no single, specific evil act that led Dante into that darkness but, rather, the sin of omission. Its name is Acedia, the fourth of the Seven Deadly Sins, and by us generally translated "Sloth."

In American-English, however, Sloth may seem to imply mere physical laziness and untidiness. The torpor of Acedia, it must be understood, is spiritual rather than physical. It is to know the good, but to be lax in its pursuit.

Whether one thinks of it as a sin or as a behavioral failure, Acedia is also the one fault for which no artist can be forgiven. Time, as W. H. Auden wrote in his poem titled *In Memory of W. B. Yeats:*

> *Worships language and forgives*
> *Everyone by whom it lives;*
> *Pardons cowardice, conceit,*
> *Lays its honor at their feet.*

In place of cowardice and conceit, Auden might have cited any catalogue of pride, envy, wrath, avarice, gluttony or carnality, and he could still have said that time forgives. The poet may cheat anything else and still win honor from time, but he may not cheat the poem and live.

For a man is finally defined by what he does with his attention. It was Simone Weil who said, "Absolute attention is absolute prayer." I do not, of course, know what an absolute attention is, except as an absolutely unattainable goal. But certainly to seek that increasing purity and concentration of one's attention that will lead to more and more meaningful perception, is not only possible but is the basic human exercise of any art. It must be added, however, that *in art it does not matter what one pays attention to; the quality of the attention is what counts.*

I have just made a dangerous statement; one that will probably breed protest, that will be difficult to explain, and that will turn out in the end to be only partly true. It is still necessary to make the statement first, and then to go the long way round to explaining why it is necessary, and in what way it is true.

The need to go the long way round brings matters back to another parable of poetry that one may read in Dante's opening situation. The language of parables is always likely to be apt to the discussion of poetry.

As soon as Dante realizes that he is in darkness, he looks up and sees the first light of the dawn shawling the shoulders of a little hill. (In Dante, the Sun is always a symbol of God as Divine Illumination.) The allegory should be clear enough: The very realization that one is lost is the beginning of finding oneself.

What happens next is the heart of the matter. His goal in sight, Dante tries to race straight up the hill—to reach the light, as it were, by direct assault. Note that common sense would certainly be on Dante's side. There is the light and there is the hill: Go to it. Nothing could be simpler. Nor, as Dante discovers, could anything be more false. Almost immediately his way is blocked by three beasts. These beasts—a Leopard, a Lion and a She-wolf—represent all the sins of the world. They represent, therefore, the world's total becloudment of any man's best attention, for all that has ever lured any man away from his own good is contained within them.

The three beasts drive Dante back into the darkness. There Dante comes on the soul of Virgil, who symbolizes Human Reason. In that role Virgil explains that a man may reach the light only by going the long way round. Dante must risk the dangerous descent into Hell—to the recognition of sin. And he must make the arduous ascent of Purgatory—to the renunciation of sin. Only then may he enter, bit by bit, the final presence of the light, which is to say, Heaven.

The point of the parable is that in art as in theology—as in all things that concern a man in his profoundest being—the long way round is the only way home. Short cuts are useful only in mechanics. The man who seeks mortal understanding must go the long, encompassing way of his deepest involvement.

Americans, susceptible as they are to the legend of mechanical know-how and get-it-done, may especially need to be told that there is no easy digest of understanding and no gift package of insight. May they learn, too, that "common sense," useful as it can be in its own sphere, cannot lead a man as deeply into himself as he must be led if he is to enter a meaningful experience of art or of life. Every man who looks long enough at the stars must come to feel their other-reality engulfing his mortal state, and nothing from the world's efficiencies and practicalities is specific to that awareness in him.

Poetry is written of that man under the stars in trouble and in joy, and the truth of poetry cannot be spoken meaningfully in simple common-sense assertions. In poetry, as in all our deepest emotions, many feelings and many thoughts and half-thoughts happen at once. Often these feelings and thoughts are in conflict:

We love and hate the same thing, desire it and dread it, need it and are destroyed by it. Always, too, there are more thoughts and feelings in a profound experience than we can put a finger on. What has common sense to say to such states of man? Common sense tends always to the easier assumption that only one thing is "really" happening in a man at one time, and that a simple, straightforward course of action will take care of it.

Such an assumption can only blind one to poetry. To read a poem with no thought in mind but to paraphrase it into a single, simple, and usually high-minded, prose statement is the destruction of poetry. Nor does it make much difference that one can quote poetry, and good poetry, in defense of such destruction. At the end of *Ode on a Grecian Urn*, John Keats wrote:

> *"Beauty is truth, truth beauty,"—that is all*
> *Ye know on earth, and all ye need to know.*

Heaven knows how many enthusiasts have used these lines as evidence that poetry is somehow an act of inspiration not to be measured by any criteria but an undefined devotion to "beauty," "truth" and "inspiring message."

But if beauty and truth are all that Grecian urns and men need know on earth, Keats makes evident by his own practice that a poet also needs to know a great deal about his trade, and that he must be passionately concerned for its basic elements.

Those basic elements are not beauty and truth but *rhythm, diction, image* and *form*. Certainly Keats cared about beauty and truth. Any sensitive man must care. No matter that one must forever fumble at the definition of such ideas; they are still matters of ultimate concern. But so was Dante's yearning for the light, and he discovered at once that it can be reached only by the long way round.

The poet's way round is by way of rhythm, diction, image and form. It is the right, the duty and the joy of his trade to be passionate about these things. To be passionate about them in the minutest and even the most frivolous detail. To be passionate about them, if need be, to the exclusion of what is generally understood by "sincerity" and "meaning." To be more passionate about them than he is about the cold war, the Gunpowder Plot, the next election, abolition, the H-bomb, the Inquisition, juvenile delinquency, the Spanish Armada, or his own survival.

The good poets have not generally sneered at the world of affairs. Some have, but many others have functioned well within that world. Yet the need and the right of all poets to detach themselves from the things of the world in order to pursue the things of the poetic trade have always been inseparable from their success as poets.

The poet must be passionate about the four elements of his trade for the most fundamental of reasons. He must be so because those passions are both a joy and an addiction within him. Because they are the life of the poem, without which nothing of value can happen either in the poem or to the reader. Because writing a poem is a more sentient way of living than not writing it, because no poem can be written well except as these passions inform it, and because only when the poem is so written can the beauty and truth of that more sentient way of living be brought to mortal consequence.

The act of poetry may seem to have very simple surfaces, but it is always compounded of many things at once. As Robert Frost wrote in *Two Tramps in Mud Time:*

> *Only where love and need are one,*
> *And the work is play for mortal stakes,*
> *Is the deed ever really done*
> *For Heaven and the future's sakes.*

The voice of common sense rises immediately in protest. "Mystification!" it cries. "A poem still has to *mean* something. What does it *mean?*" And the poet must answer, "Never what you think. Not when you ask the question in that way."

But how shall the question be asked? Let the questioner listen first to a kind of statement he has probably passed over without enough attention. He can find one such in Walter Pater's essay on Winckelman. "Let us understand by poetry," wrote Pater, "all literary production which attains the power of giving pleasure by its form as distinct from its matter."

He can find another in a book titled *The Fire and the Fountain* by the English poet and critic John Press. "The essence of the poet," wrote Press, "is to be found less in his opinions than in his idiom." He may even find one in a textbook titled *Reading Poems,* in which Wright Thomas says, "The *subject* is a very poor indication of what the *poem* is"— to which I should add only that it is no indication whatever.

But if the meaning is not in the subject, what then does a poem mean? It means always and above all else the poet's deep involvement in the four basic elements of his trade. It means not the subject but the way the poetic involvement transfigures the subject. It means, that is to say, the very act of language by which it comes into existence. The poem may purport to be about anything from pussy willows to battleships, but the meaning of any good poem is its act of language.

Because it is an act of language, a good poem is deeply connected with everything men are and do. For language is certainly one of the most fundamental activities in which human beings engage. Take away a man's language, and you take most of his ability to think and to experience. Enrich his language, and you cannot fail to enrich his experience. Any man who has let great language into his head is the richer for it.

He is not made richer by what is being said. It is the language itself that brings his enrichment. Could poetry be meaningful aside from its act of language, it would have no reason for being, and the whole history of poetry could be reduced to a series of simple paraphrases.

Consider as simple a passage as the beginning of Herrick's *Upon Julia's Clothes:*

> *Whenas in silks my Julia goes,*
> *Then, then, methinks, how sweetly flows*
> *The liquefaction of her clothes.*

Who can read those lines without a thrill of pleasure? But now consider the paraphrase: "I like the rustle of Julia's silks when she walks." The poetry and the paraphrase are certainly about equal in subject matter. The difference is that the poetry is a full and rich act of language, whereas the paraphrase, though faultless, lacks, among other things, measure, pause, stress, rhyme and the pleasure of lingering over the word "liquefaction."

"But what is Julia doing there?" cries that voice of common sense. "She must have something to do with the poem or she wouldn't be in it!"

The owner of that voice would do well to ponder the relation between a good portrait and its subject. The subject is there, to be sure—at least in most cases. But the instant the painter puts one brush stroke on the canvas and then another, the two brush strokes take on a relation to each other and to the space around them. The two then take on a relation to the third, and it to them. And so forth. The painting immediately begins to exert its own demands upon the painter, its own way of going. Immediately the subject begins to disappear.

All too soon, for that matter, the subject will have changed with age or will have died. After a while no living person will have any recollection of what the subject looked like. All that will remain then is a portrait head which must be either self-validating or worthless. Because the subject cannot validate the painting, he or she will have become irrelevant. All that can finally validate the portrait is the way in which the painter engaged the act of painting.

And one more thing—the good artist always thinks in long terms. He knows, even at the moment of the painting, that both he and the subject will disappear. Any good painter will be painting for the painting—for the time when the subject will have blown away into time.

So with poetry. The one final and enduring meaning of any poem lies not in what it seems to have set out to say, but in its act of language.

The only test of that act of language is the memory of the race. Bad poetry is by nature forgettable; it is, therefore, soon forgotten. But good poetry, like any good act of language, hooks onto human memory and stays there. Write well, and there will always be someone somewhere who carries in his mind what you have written. It will stay in memory because man is the language animal, and because his need of language is from the roots of his consciousness. That need in him is not a need for meaning. Rather, good language in him takes possession of meaning; it fills him with a resonance that the best of men understand only dimly, but without which no man is entirely alive. Poetry is that presence and that resonance. As Archibald MacLeish put it in his much-discussed *Ars Poetica*:

> *A poem should not mean*
> *But be.*

If the reader truly wishes to engage poetry, let him forget meaning. Let him think rather: "I shall summon great language to mind. I shall summon language so fully, so resonantly

and so precisely used that it will bring all my meanings to me."
Then let him turn to poetry, and let him listen to the passions
of the poet's trade.

Listen to great rhythms. Here is the opening stanza of
John Donne's *The Anniversarie*:

> *All Kings, and all their favorites,*
> *All glory of honours, beauties, wits,*
> *The Sun it selfe, which makes times as they passe,*
> *Is elder by a yeare, now, than it was*
> *When thou and I first one another saw:*
> *All other things, to their destruction draw,*
> *Only our love hath no decay;*
> *This, no to morrow hath, nor yesterday.*
> *Running, it never runs from us away,*
> *But truly keeps his first, last, everlasting day.*

Wordly things pass away, but true love is constant, says the
subject matter. All true enough and tried enough. But listen
to the rhythm enforce itself upon the saying, especially in the
last four lines. For present purposes, let the voice ignore the
lesser accents. Let it stress only those syllables printed in capital
letters below, while observing the pauses as indicated by the
slash marks. And forget the meaning. Read for the voice emphasis and the voice pauses:

> *Only* OUR LOVE *hath no de*CAY ||
> THIS || *no to* MOrrow *hath* || *nor* YESterday ||
> RUNning || *it never runs from us a*WAY ||
> *But truly keeps his* FIRST || LAST || EVerlasting DAY.

Not all rhythms are so percussive, so measured out by
pauses, and so metrically irregular. Listen to this smoother
rhythm from Poe's *Israfel*:

> *If I could dwell*
> *Where Israfel*
> *Hath dwelt, and he where I,*
> *He might not sing so wildly well*
> *A mortal melody,*
> *While a bolder note than his might swell*
> *From my lyre within the sky.*

Or the rhythm may be percussive, but without substantial pauses, as in the last line of this passage from the end of Gerard Manley Hopkins' *Felix Randal*, an elegy for a black-smith:

How far from then forethought of, all thy more boisterous years,
When thou at the random grim forge, powerful amidst peers,
Didst fettle for the great gray drayhorse his bright and battering
  sandal.

Listen to the hammerfall of that last line: "Didst FEttle for the GREAT GRAY DRAYhorse his BRIGHT and BAttering SANdal."

Or listen to the spacing of the "ah" sounds as a rhythmic emphasis in the last line of this final passage from Meredith's *Lucifer in Starlight*:

> *Around the ancient track marched, rank on rank,*
> *The ARmy of unALterable LAW.*

Percussive, smooth, flowing or studded with pauses—there is no end to the variety and delight of great language rhythms. For the poet, his rhythms are forever more than a matter of making a "meaningful" statement; they are a joy in their own right. No poet hates meaning. But the poet's passion is for the triumph of language. No reader can come to real contact with a poem until he comes to it through the joy of that rhythmic act of language.

As for rhythm, so for diction. The poet goes to language— or it comes to him and he receives it—for his joy in the precision of great word choices. Give him such a line as Whitman's "I witness the corpse with the dabbled hair," and he will register the corpse, to be sure, but it will be "dabbled" he seizes upon with the joy of a botanist coming on a rare specimen. So when Keats speaks of Ruth amid "the alien corn" or when Theodore Roethke speaks of sheep "strewn" on a field, the good reader will certainly care about the dramatic situation of the poem, but he cannot fail to answer with a special joy to "alien" and to "strewn."

What, after all, is the subject as compared to his joy in such rich precision? Thousands of English poems have described the passing of winter and the coming of spring. Certainly there is little in that subject as a subject to attract him. But listen to the pure flutefall of the word choices I have italicized in the following passage from Stanley Kunitz's *Deciduous Bough*, and note how the self-delight in language makes everything immediate and new again:

> Winter that *coils* in the thicket now
> Will *glide* from the field, the *swinging* rain
> Be *knotted* with flowers, on every bough
> A bird will *meditate* again.

"Poetry," said Coleridge, "is the best words in the best order." How can anyone reading the Kunitz passage escape a sense that the language is being ultimately and unimprovably selected? The delight one feels in coming on such language is not only in the experience of perfection but also in the fact that perfection has been made to seem not only effortless but inevitable.

And let this much more be added to the idea of poetic meaning: Nothing in a good poem happens by accident; every word, every comma, every variant spelling must enter as an act of the poet's choice. A poem is a machine for making choices. The mark of the good poet is his refusal to make easy or cheap choices. The better the poet, the greater the demands he makes upon himself, and the higher he sets his level of choice. Thus, a good poem is not only an act of mind but an act of devotion to mind. The poet who chooses cheaply or lazily is guilty of aesthetic acedia, and he is lost thereby. The poet who spares himself nothing in his search for the most demanding choices is shaping a human attention that offers itself as a high and joyful example to all men of mind and devotion. Every act of great language, whatever its subject matter, illustrates an idea of order and a resonance of human possibility without which no man's mind can sense its own fullest dimensions.

As for rhythm and diction, so for imagery. To be sure, every word is at root an image, and poetic images must be made of words. Yet certainly there is in a well-constructed image an effect that cannot be said to rise from any one word choice, but from the total phrasing.

So for the sensory shiver of Keats' "The silver snarling trumpets 'gan to chide." So for the wonderfully woozy effect of John Frederick Nims' "The drunk clambering on his undulant floor." So for the grand hyperbole of Howard Nemerov saying that the way a young girl looks at him "sets his knees to splashing like two waves."

We learn both imagination and precision from the poet's eye. And we learn correspondences. Consider the following image from *Aereopagus* by Louis MacNeice, a poem as playful as it is serious, in which MacNeice describes Athens as a cradle of the western mind. Cradles, he makes clear, generally contain children, and all those boy-gods and girl-goddesses had their childish side:

> . . . *you still may glimpse*
> *The child-eyed Fury tossing her shock of snakes,*
> *Careering over the Parthenon's ruined playpen.*

It is a bit shocking to have the Parthenon spoken of as a playpen, but once the shock has passed, what a triumph there is in the figure: everything corresponds! Think how much would have been lost had the Parthenon a surviving roof, or had its general proportions or the placement of the pillars—slats—resisted the comparison. The joy of it is that, despite the first shock, nothing resists the comparison; and we find that the surprise turns out to be a true correspondence.

One of the poet's happiest—and most mortal—games is in seeking such correspondences. But what flows from them is more than a game. Every discovery of a true correspondence is an act of reason and an instruction to the mind. For intelligence does not consist of masses of factual detail. It consists of seeing essential likenesses and essential differences and of relating them, allowing for differences within the likenesses and for likenesses within the differences. Mentality is born of analogy.

Note, too, that the image-idea of "ruined playpen" does not simply happen, but is prepared for in "child-eyed." And note, further, the nice double meaning of "careering" as both "a wild rush" and "to make a career of."

A good extended image, that is to say, is made of various elements and is marked by both sequence and structure. Thus we have already touched upon the essence of the fourth element of the poet's trade: form.

There are many kinds of poetic form, but since all are based on pattern and sequence, let a tightly patterned poem illustrate. Here is Emily Dickinson's *The Soul Selects:*

> *The soul selects her own society,*
> *Then shuts the door;*
> *On her divine majority*
> *Obtrude no more.*
>
> *Unmoved, she notes the chariot's pausing*
> *At her low gate;*
> *Unmoved, an emperor is kneeling*
> *Upon her mat.*
> *I've known her from an ample nation*
> *Choose one;*
> *Then close the valves of her attention*
> *Like stone.*

Whatever the hunters of beauty and truth find for their pleasure in such a poem, the poet's joy will be in its form and management. He responds to the passion of the language for its own sparseness, to the pattern of rhyme and half-rhyme, to the flavor of the images (connotation), and to the way those flavors relate to one another. He responds to the interplay of the four-foot feminine lines (feminine lines end on an unaccented syllable) and the two-foot masculine lines (which end on an accented syllable).

And he responds, above all, to the way those two-foot lines develop in the last stanza into two boldly stroked syllables apiece (monosyllabic feet) so that the emotion held down throughout the poem by the sparseness of the language is hammered into sensation by the beat of those last two words: "Like stone"—thud! thud!

Beauty and truth are no irrelevancies, but they are abstractions that must remain meaningless to poetry until they are brought to being in the management of a specific form. It is that management the poet must love: the joy of sensing the poem fall into inescapable form, and therefore into inescapable experience. For the poet's trade is not to talk about experience, but to make it happen. His act of making is all he knows of beauty and truth. It is, in fact, his way of knowing them. His only way of knowing them.

As I. A. Richards, poet and scholar of the language, put it in a recent poem titled *The Ruins:*

> *Sometimes a word is wiser much than men:*
> *"Faithful" e.g., "responsible" and "true."*
> *And words it is, not poets, make up poems.*
> *Our words, we say, but we are theirs, too,*
> *For words made men and may unmake again.*

And now, at last, it is time to repeat the statement from which this long way round began. "In art," I said, "it does not matter what one pays attention to; the quality of the attention is what counts." It is time to amend that necessary false statement.

For it does matter where the poet fixes his attention. Attention must be to *something*. That something, however, is so casually connected with the subject of the poem that any reader will do well to dismiss the subject as no more than a point of departure. Any impassioning point of departure will do. The poet, being a man, must believe something, but what that something is does not matter so long as he believes it strongly enough to be passionate about it. What he believes, moreover, may be touched off by an image, a rhythm, or the quality of a word *in pursuit of which the subject is invented.*

The poem, in any case, is not in its point of departure, but in its journey to itself. That journey, the act of the poem, is its act of language. That act is the true final subject and meaning of any poem. It is to that act of language the poet shapes his most devoted attention—to the fullness of rhythm, diction, image and form. Only in that devotion can he seize the world and make it evident.

Further reading:
Ciardi, John: How Does a Poem Mean. Boston: Houghton Mifflin Co.; 1960.
Ciardi, John: 39 Poems. New Brunswick: Rutgers University Press; 1959.
Press, John: The Fire and the Fountain: An Essay on Poetry. New York: Oxford University Press; 1955.
Scott, A. F.: The Poet's Craft. New York: Cambridge University Press; 1957.
Valery, Paul: The Art of Poetry. New York: Pantheon Books, Inc.; 1958.

MORTON WHITE

[*Photograph by Sid Avery*]

Morton White, born in 1927, Harvard professor and author, associates himself with the analytic movement in contemporary philosophy: "Analytic philosophy can be broad in scope without abandoning standards of rigorous thinking and clarity. The two great dangers in philosophy are empty formalism and woolliness. One of my hopes is that philosophy will avoid extremes of trivial exactitude and vapid, pompous 'profundity.'" During 1959–60 Professor White was a Fellow at the Center for Advanced Study in the Behavioral Sciences, Stanford, California.

New Horizons in Philosophy

BY

MORTON WHITE

The most arresting and most distinctive feature of philosophy in the English-speaking world today is concentration
on linguistic and logical analysis. While dialectical materialism
is the official philosophy of the Soviet bloc, and Western Europe
continues to be strongly affected by existentialism, Britain and
the United States are primarily the homes of what is called
analytic or linguistic philosophy. Analytic philosophers are
neither sponsored nor controlled by any government or political
party, and they do not appeal to the Bohemian or the beatnik.
They invite both Marxist and existentialist scorn because they
spurn the pretentiousness and murk of much traditional philosophy. For good reasons analytic philosophy has never become
the favorite subject of the bistro or the *espresso* café, and it
needs no proof of its seriousness. It respects the values of the
reasonable man rather than those of the irrational man, though
it fully recognizes the existence of irrationality.

Analytic philosophy begins with an awareness of the fact
that philosophy is not a rival of science and that it cannot provide us with another way of studying the world with which
the scientist deals. When in the nineteenth century natural

591

science grew so highly specialized, it became evident that no-body could encompass the whole of knowledge. And so the drift of philosophy was away from encyclopedism, away from thinking that the philosopher was a superscientist, a universal genius, a know-it-all.

Not only did it become evident that universal knowledge was humanly impossible, but it was seen how grotesque it was to think that one could construct a system in which all our knowledge could be derived from a few philosophical principles, as the geometrical theorems of Euclid are deduced from his axioms. It was this mistake which resulted in the illusion that philosophers could dominate all knowledge through the command of a few pivotal truths. This may be called the metaphysical illusion, the product of a vast inflation of the powers and prospects of metaphysics, one of the oldest and most mysterious branches of philosophy.

According to tradition, metaphysics is the most fundamental of all disciplines. The first part of the word "metaphysics" is derived from the Greek *meta*, meaning "beyond," so that the subject was conceived as that which went beyond the problems of physics. Physicists, some metaphysicians said, deal with material things, biologists with living things, mathematicians with numbers, points and lines. But the metaphysician cuts a much wider swath; indeed he takes the whole cloth as his province, for he studies being *as such*. Not any particular being or limited class of beings, but just plain being, since the traditional metaphysician is the spectator of all time and eternity.

It took philosophers a long time to realize that the number of interesting things that one can say about all things in one fell swoop is very limited. When you lump together such different items as kings, cabbages, bits of sealing wax, numbers, thoughts and electrons in order to say what they all have in common, you are likely to discover that what they have in common is the fact that they exist. You lapse into emptiness through the effort to become supremely general.

Having reached this dour conclusion about the most central of philosophical disciplines, some philosophers asked themselves just what was left for them to do. If all of existence could be parceled out to different scientists who worked so effectively by specializing, and if the philosopher was unable to supply any significant first principles which could neatly order the tangled forest of modern science and information, what was the philosopher's function in the intellectual word? Once philosophy was everything. Now it threatened to become nothing.

Fortunately the story of philosophy did not end here. There were some who did not desert the battered, beleaguered ship. They knew that there were nonmetaphysical questions of large import which had always been asked by philosophers and which had to be asked more relentlessly than ever in an age of scientific specialization. One of these questions—short, but powerful— was "What do you mean?" The patron saint of philosophy, Socrates, had spent most of his time asking it, often to the discomfort of those with whom he conversed in Plato's *Dialogues* and to the immense delight of centuries of readers who watched Socrates puncture humbug and ironically examine ideas which could not stand the test of honest logical criticism. The question "What do you mean?" could be directed even at scientists. It was the tiny candle which had flickered since antiquity, which had never gone out even in philosophy's darkest days. It was used to light a philosophical bonfire by a generation of thinkers at the turn of the century—Ernst Mach, the Austrian philosopher-physicist who influenced Einstein; Bertrand Russell and G. E. Moore in England; Charles Peirce and William James in the United States. They sparked the various new explosive movements of the twentieth century—pragmatism in the United States, logical positivism in Austria, and Cambridge analysis, so called in honor of the English university where it first flourished.

No matter how far scientific specialization went it left the possibility of asking Socrates's question. In fact, the more the scientists specialized, the more their preoccupation with description, experiment, observation and prediction robbed them of the time and energy needed for the clarification of their fundamental concepts. Physicists before Einstein had failed to be sufficiently clear about the notions of space and time, and biologists were not always prepared to give comprehensible answers to the question "What is life?" Even mathematicians were foggy about the idea of number and had fallen into serious paradoxes. Here, then, was an opportunity for philosophers to co-operate with scientists in an effort to elucidate the basic concepts of special sciences, instead of pretending that the philosopher possessed a mysterious key to all scientific doors. The revival of the Socratic question "What do you mean?" as applied to the words of the scientist, thus preserved for the philosopher a central, if not regal, position. He was no longer a surveyor of everything, but rather a careful student of language who at this stage of the analytic movement tended to concentrate on the terms of natural science and mathematics. The most brilliant monument to this pre-World War I era in philosophy was the three-volumed *Principia Mathematica* of Russell and Whitehead.

After the First World War the harvest of this intellectual activity was reaped by younger philosophers who described themselves as logical positivists. Philosophy, they said in going beyond Russell and Whitehead, was nothing but the philosophy of science. And philosophy of science, as someone put it, was philosophy enough. A story was told of a philosopher of the old school who came into the office of his department during the '30's and overheard two of his younger colleagues arguing about the meaning of a physical theory. The disputants grew more and more intense, and just after one shouted, "What do you mean by saying that space is curved?" the other yelled, "What do you mean by saying it's not?" The first, not to be outdone, then produced that classic in philosophical oneupmanship: "What do *you* mean by 'mean'?" At this point the old professor could not contain himself and spoke up for his own generation as he interrupted the conversation to say, "Good morning, gentlemen. If that means anything to you."

The professor's greeting pointed a moral. It revealed a grave limitation in the conception of meaning itself. For the logical positivist a meaningful utterance was simply one that could be verified or falsified. And verifiability and falsifiability, it was said, were limited to scientific statements. Small wonder that a greeting like "Good morning" was said to be meaningless.

But much more than "Good morning" was at stake. For by these same narrow standards, poetry and ethics, in addition to metaphysics, were all nonsense.

At this point in its history analytic philosophy was at its furthest from the humanistic tradition. The verifiability theory of meaning was to the positivist in the 1930's what the guillotine was to the French Revolution, and like the guillotine it destroyed indiscriminately. It was one thing to attack metaphysics, another to say that every poetic or moral utterance was meaningless. And it did not help to add that moral and poetic language had what was called "emotive meaning," or the capacity to stimulate emotions. That was often a polite way of sweeping much of human language under the rug, to put it where the positivist could conveniently avoid it, indeed walk all over it while he puzzled about the meaning of space, time and number.

It soon became evident that the question "What do you mean?" had been conceived too narrowly. It tended to direct the philosopher's attention only to language in which knowledge was communicated. Under Plato's influence philosophers had identified the meaning of a term with an abstract concept, thinking of the word on the page as expressing a cloudy entity in Plato's realm of ideas. And therefore they tended to think that only declarative sentences, such as "Socrates is a man," had meaning as they conceived it. On this theory the command "Socrates, come here!" was strictly nonsensical. And so was the exclamation "Great Socrates!" because obviously it was hard to suppose that there was some weird resident of Plato's realm called "Great Socrateshood" which could serve as the meaning of the exclamation.

Partly because of these consequences and other more technical difficulties, and partly because of the intellectual mood created by the aftermath of the war, the influence of logical positivism waned perceptibly in the '40's. Unfortunately, however, the phrase "logical positivist" continued as an epithet which was wrongly applied to anyone with the faintest interest in the philosophy of language. For that reason an entirely different attitude in analytic philosophy has been hidden from public view. It is dominated by the idea that the philosopher should ask of utterances and writings not what their Platonic meaning is, but rather what their *use* is. This attitude is usually identified with the late Ludwig Wittgenstein, who was the leading philosophical figure at Cambridge University after the days of Russell and Moore, and who influences contemporary philosophy mainly through his posthumously published writings and through his loyal disciples.

As is so often the case in the history of ideas, a simple suggestion, undoubtedly present in the minds of many others who had failed to stress it sufficiently or to carry it out as brilliantly as Wittgenstein did, caught on among a great number of English and American philosophers after the Second World War. I am not a follower of Wittgenstein, and I regard a good deal of what he has said as dubious. But in the history of recent philosophy he is a liberating force. Once he said plainly and insistently that the main subject matter of the philosopher was the behavior of human beings trying to communicate with one another, a whole new world seemed to open up to the analytic philosopher, the many-sided world of language in all of its employments. Not just the language of scientific assertion and proof, for man does not communicate by assertion and proof alone. He greets, exclaims, exhorts, commands, judges, describes, promises and does many other things with words. And all of these linguistic activities have now become fair game for the philosopher who has abandoned the Platonic version of the question "What do you mean?"

What should the analytic philosopher do, now that he has been shown these new horizons, now that he has been freed from the restrictive idea that he is merely a logician of natural science? In the remainder of this article I should like to formulate and illustrate my own answer to this vital question.

Philosophers have an unprecedented opportunity to clarify the language which men use in the writing of history, in morality, law, religion, politics and education, to take the most challenging examples. And so I label my viewpoint "institutionalism" in order to suggest that one of the primary tasks of philosophy is to analyze, compare and contrast language as it is used for purposes of communication within these different institutions. While communicating in these situations, men use language in a variety of intertwined ways which express their beliefs, hopes, their needs and their values; and one job of the philosopher is to draw an intellectual map, to provide a coherent picture of the interconnections between these different modes of speech, feeling and thought.

Language is a cultural instrument, and it must be seen in its cultural setting. Those who fail to view it in this way and who instead regard it as a collection of dead sentences may fall into two related errors. One may be called formalism and the other essentialism. Formalism is the tendency to view language as if it were an inscription on a scroll or a monument rather than as the living, complex, subtle tool that it is. Essentialism is the idea that the philosopher can look at these dead words and, without attention to their use, summarize the essence of complex forms of communication. Philosophers given to such oversimplification have said that religion is merely a belief in God. Law has been defined as the command of the sovereign. History has been glibly summarized as the effort to report what actually happened in the past. Questions in each of these areas have been separated sharply from questions of morality. The icy hand of overabstraction guides the writing of those philosophers who think that merely by examining the *forms* of words, they can characterize the essence of religion, history or law. Their most common assumption is that by looking at any kind of language one can *always* single out those statements in it which are factual, objective and descriptive, and separate them sharply from statements of value. And this assumption, I think, is a mistake, notably when it is applied uniformly to the writings of historians and the language of lawyers. It is often the result of a failure to study the actual processes of law and historical writing, a failure which is encouraged by the formalism and essentialism of which I have spoken.

Of course, I do not wish to deny that *sometimes* we can make a distinction between statements of fact and evaluations in a given context. For example, two men can agree that someone has told a lie and yet judge his lying differently. In such

597

cases our conclusion about the lying may be reported in a conjunction of a factual statement and a moral statement: "Jones lied, and it was wrong of him to do so." Here another person is logically free to agree with the first or factual part of the conjunctive statement, while he denies the second if his moral viewpoint is different from ours. But a careful study of communication, especially in history and law, brings to light a kind of blended or hybrid language which defies any effort to decompose it into factual and moral parts that may be accepted or rejected independently. There are, I believe, uses of language which are simultaneously descriptive and evaluative, and which cannot be broken down into the assertion of a factual statement and an evaluative statement which may be judged separately. The person who speaks or writes in this way is doing two inseparable things at once, stating a matter of fact and evaluating, and therefore his audience must take or leave his speech as a whole. To acknowledge this possibility is to abandon certain conventional modes of classifying language which have dominated the history of philosophy.

My contention is that this hybrid kind of language is most commonly found in an institutional setting. It is too large, sprawling and complex for textbooks of logic, for they are too often dominated by a passion for neatness and an interest in classifying isolated statements. Therefore, in order to illustrate and clarify what I have in mind, I shall turn to a basic problem in the philosophy of history and another in the philosophy of law. History is an institution insofar as no civilized society can live without some image of its past. And no one can deny the pervasiveness of legal institutions.

One of the historian's concerns is to report particular facts, and another is to present a connected picture of the past. The first expresses itself in simple declarative statements, such as, "Caesar crossed the Rubicon," and the second in lengthy sequential narratives about the life of some person or the development of a society or a nation. And narrative is not usually studied by formal logicians. It is one thing to report the simple fact that Caesar crossed the Rubicon, but it is another to present

Caesar's biography or the history of Rome. By holding fast to this distinction between statement and narration one can see a profoundly important distinction between two ways in which value judgments operate in history. When the historian is assessing the evidence for individual statements of fact, his value judgments—whether on political or religious matters—are properly distinguished from his factual conclusions. But when he is forming his narrative, the historian is often unable to separate these two parts of his thinking. To show this let us consider some illustrations that are closer to home than Julius Caesar.

Historian Charles Beard once argued that President Franklin D. Roosevelt had planned to bring the United States into World War II soon after its beginning, had deceived the people into electing him for a third time by promising that he would keep us out of war, and had "maneuvered" Japan into attacking us at Pearl Harbor. Other historians have tried to refute these assertions by citing fresh evidence, by trying to discredit Beard's evidence, by suggesting that he deliberately neglected available evidence which did not fit in with his beliefs. I am not interested here in the historical details. But I do want to point out that the issue was simply whether Roosevelt did plan, deceive and maneuver in the manner alleged, and that in principle this can be settled in an objective way. We should not excuse anyone who would distort the facts. And no reference to the differing political values of historians should lead us to say that two contradictory views of Roosevelt's behavior are logically admissible, that because Beard and his critics operated with different value schemes, their contradictory views were equally valid from their different points of view. Either Roosevelt did or did not do the things attributed to him, and double talk should be ruthlessly excluded.

The situation changes dramatically, however, when we are asked to choose between two general narrative histories of the United States. Here we are not faced with a short question about one man's actions at a certain time. And here our values do play a part in determining which of two general histories we should write or prefer. Take, for example, the difference between general histories of the United States which take the Federalist point of view and those which are Jeffersonian in their slant.

Samuel Eliot Morison points out that sixty years ago it was difficult to find a general history of the United States that did not, as he puts it, "present the Federalist-Whig-Republican point of view, or express a very dim view of all Democratic leaders except Grover Cleveland." But by the middle of this century the fashion had changed and it was then equally difficult to find a good general history of the country "that did not follow the Jefferson-Jackson-Franklin D. Roosevelt line." Morison says that he was converted to the latter as a young man when he discovered in his first researches on New England Federalism that "the 'wise and good and rich' whom Fisher Ames thought should rule the nation were stupid, narrow-minded and local in their outlook." But isn't it clear that Morison's conclusion presupposed values which some other historian might not share? And is it not clear, therefore, that the historian who tells a story following a "line" is engaged in an undecomposable blend of description and evaluation?

Something similar is true of the history of philosophy. The historian of philosophy does not expound the views of any and all human beings who have philosophized. Consciously or unconsciously he adopts standards of philosophical excellence by which he judges who is to be admitted into his history. Doctrinal agreement with the historian is not the standard, but his history incorporates a judgment of importance and interest which rests on values that another historian of philosophy might easily reject. Any Catholic reader of histories of philosophy which skip lightly over the medieval period will understand what I mean.

When a historian believes that a certain political tradition is superior to another, he tends to see the history of the country as a development of that tradition. And when we see that history in terms of another tradition, we are no more in a position to say he speaks falsely than we would be if he and we were to see certain trick figures in psychology books differently. The reader may have seen the illustration that can at one moment be seen as a rabbit's head and at another as a duck's.

Duck or rabbit?

Well, the historian who tells the story of the United States in Jeffersonian terms because he admires that tradition, is a little like the man who always sees the duck-rabbit as a duck because he likes ducks more than rabbits. And we who evaluate his history are likely to praise it in the degree to which he sees the past as we see it in the light of our values. I think that opposing narrative historians sometimes confront each other as rabbit-loving rabbit seers confront duck-loving duck seers.

Some historians are loath to admit this because they view the problem absolutistically. They think of the general historian of the United States as confronted with an "actuality" whose main line is either Federalist or Jeffersonian and not both. They tend to assimilate the logic of narrative history to the logic of historical statement, and to hold that the general historian of the United States who is preparing to write his book is faced with just as objective an "either-or" as the historian who is trying to decide whether Caesar crossed the Rubicon. They argue that the Jeffersonian line or the Federalist line is *the* line which the main stream of American life has followed, and they refuse to allow that anything as ambiguous as the duck-rabbit turns up in their subject. But can they define the notion of a main stream in a completely objective manner? Can it be explained so as to make it possible for historians to converge on it in anything like the way in which scientific students of rivers locate *their* main streams? I doubt that it can, even though I am willing to grant that no one has said the last or even the next-to-last philosophical word on this subject. Until those words are spoken, historians should admit that one man's duck might be another's rabbit.

The historian must grant that in some parts of his work he engages in a blend of fact finding and evaluation, and that when he pretends in such cases to be recording merely what happened, he is not being accurate about the nature of his enterprise. Moreover, it is impossible to see what could be meant by saying that we can treat the narrative as a conjunction of factual statements and value judgments so that the reader can distinguish them and test them independently. It makes no sense to ask us to remove the Jeffersonian slant from a Jeffersonian history in order to see whether the remainder is factually true. And this is because the value orientation does not figure detachably in the narrative as it figures in the conjunction "Jones lied, and it was wrong of him to do so." The value orientation pervades or colors the narrative and he who would call the narrative a good one must be sympathetic to this coloring and orientation. He must therefore judge the history as a whole, simultaneously guided by the evidence and his values.

History is not the only mode of discourse in which the language of value and the language of fact are not related conjunctively. The law presents us with a similar kind of complexity. Take the case of a statute forbidding the entry of a vehicle into a public park. One might be tempted to say that whether anything is a vehicle is a question of fact, settled by purely empirical means and having nothing to do with the values of those who are trying to find out whether it is a vehicle. One dictionary at hand says, "VEHICLE: That in or on which a person or thing is or may be carried." But suppose that the statute had been enacted before the existence of roller skates. And suppose that a case were to come up in which it was necessary to decide whether a pair of roller skates was a vehicle. Surely the judge might hesitate before saying with a straight face that because a pair of roller skates is something "on which a person or thing is or may be carried" it should be excluded from a park by the statute.

When the judge reaches one of these puzzling examples, he might be moved to ask two questions. He might ask what the enactors of the statute would have said if roller skates had existed when they enacted the statute. This is a straightforward factual question of a kind that can rarely be answered with confidence. But even if it could be, its answer would not be decisive in all cases like this. The judge might more sensibly ask what social good or evil would be brought about by regarding a pair of roller skates as a vehicle and hence keeping it out of a public park. And this is a straightforward value question, the answer to which can play a vital part in the judge's effort to answer the question, "Are roller skates vehicles?" It shows that in the process of answering what is on the linguistic surface a question of fact, the judge can advert to his own values, to his own ideas of what is good for the community.

What shall we call this hyphenated process of looking-at-the-roller-skates-and-deciding-whether-it-is-good-to-call-them-vehicles? We may not have a simple name for it, but it is surely a mode of linguistic activity. It is not logically analyzable into two activities which may be judged independently, like walking and talking. It is not analogous to the combination of separable processes that lead us to the conjunctive conclusion, "Jones lied, and it was wrong of him to do so." If the judge in the roller-skate case were asked what he was doing, he might fairly reply, "Trying to decide whether roller skates are vehicles." And if asked to introspect further and to break down the activity into two separate processes, one of which was merely looking and another merely evaluating, he might be unable to do so.

What general significance should be attached to the existence of these hybrid processes in historical and legal thinking? First of all they show that when we turn to language in a complex cultural setting—the telling of stories and the settling of legal disputes are basic to most civilizations—we find uses of language that cannot be adequately understood if we remain prisoners of an exclusive and exhaustive dichotomy of language into the factual and the evaluative. Some linguistic activities are in a sense both. Reflecting on such modes of thinking and language makes the philosopher aware of a certain narrowness in the traditional philosophical classification of language. The case of the narrative shows that there are modes of discourse which

603

go beyond the simple, isolated statements treated by logicians who work with science and mathematics as their models. The philosopher of language who looks at law and history discovers modes of speech which require new philosophical categories.

This is not all. The philosopher who moves in this direction comes to see that the philosophy of language is not a dreary grammatical exercise. For once he begins to think about modes of discourse in a cultural setting, he will come to see that there are many others which transcend the word and the statement. The religious believer finds it impossible to characterize his religion merely by reference to a few propositions that he accepts. For religion is an organic unity of theological belief, moral attitude, emotional reaction to liturgy, view of human nature, and much more. Those who accept the same religion agree on many issues of value and fact which cannot always be separated.

The philosopher who tries to understand the use of religious language will meet in even more complicated form the sort of thing encountered in our discussion of history and law. He will find himself more and more concerned with the description and the evaluation of blends of thinking, feeling and doing. In short, with ways of life. And by dealing with ways of life he will come closer to the concerns of the ordinary man. The philosopher who begins by recognizing that a narrative is more than a mere conjunction of factual and evaluative statements, or who sees that some linguistic activities of lawyers fall under hybrid categories not usually acknowledged by philosophers, will soon see a whole new world of language opening up before his eyes. Philosophy of science is not philosophy enough. The philosopher must broaden his vision to civilization itself.

Such a philosophical student of human institutions need not be a mere reporter of linguistic behavior. He can also stimulate new ways of thinking and speaking. But the philosophic institutionalist should emulate the good and effective legislator who studies the customs of his land before he draws up new statutes. If the philosopher conceives of his function in this broad and generous way, he will help restore philosophy to its deserved central place in the intellectual world. Not through empty speculation about "being as such," but through a deeper understanding of man gained from a study of his ways of communicating with his fellow men.

Further reading:

White, Morton: THE AGE OF ANALYSIS. New York: New American Library of World Literature, Inc.; 1955.

White, Morton: RELIGION, POLITICS AND THE HIGHER LEARNING. Cambridge: Harvard University Press; 1959.

Meyerhoff, Hans: THE PHILOSOPHY OF HISTORY IN OUR TIME. New York: Doubleday Anchor Books; 1959.

Scheffler, Israel: PHILOSOPHY AND EDUCATION. Boston: Allyn and Bacon, Inc.; 1958.

DONALD J. HUGHES

Donald J. Hughes, senior physicist at Brookhaven National Laboratory, former director of the nuclear physics division of Argonne National Laboratory and internationally recognized leader in neutron research, died on April 12, 1960, at the age of forty-five, of a heart attack shortly after submitting the manuscript of this article. Active as a teacher and author of a number of scientific books and reports on neutron research, Doctor Hughes had profound social convictions on the proper use of atomic energy and capped his work with the Manhattan Project by signing the famous Franck report, which stated the scientists' case against the use of the first atomic bomb.

The editors wish to acknowledge the assistance of Dr. Harry Palevsky, friend and Brookhaven associate of Doctor Hughes, in the final editorial preparation of THE ELUSIVE NEUTRON.

ꡥꡥꡥꡥꡥꡥꡥꡥꡥꡥꡥꡥꡥꡥꡥꡥꡥꡥꡥꡥꡥꡥꡥ

The Elusive Neutron

BY

DONALD J. HUGHES

Since the beginning of the present century man has gradually come to know of the world of inner space, a strange world of the very small, where the "ultimate particles" of matter behave in ways completely alien to our everyday experience. Throughout the last several decades the dramatic revelation of this new world of matter has been dominated by a most remarkable subatomic particle—the neutron. The neutron's elusive nature and its many roles as a research tool have illuminated a few of the universe's most awesome mysteries and inspired some of man's greatest intellectual achievements.

The discovery of the neutron by Sir James Chadwick in 1932 marked a great step forward in understanding the basic nature of matter. More than twenty centuries ago the Greeks speculated that in spite of the wide diversity of matter it was all composed of minute particles which they called atoms to suggest their basic, individual character. Today, based not on speculation but on ingenious, indirect experiments, we know that atoms exist; we even know their sizes and shapes with accuracy, although they are invisibly small. The atomic scale of measurement staggers the imagination—100,000,000 atoms in a row would constitute a line only one inch long. Yet this realization is only the beginning, for we also know that the volume of each atom is practically empty, a void crisscrossed by electrons, eternally speeding about a small, heavy, central speck of matter—the nucleus. Though it is difficult to visualize an atom, its nucleus presents an even greater conceptual problem, for in extent the nucleus is only about one ten-thousandth the size of the whole atom. It is the nucleus which will provide the stage for much of the action to be described in this article.

Scientists who must enter the subatomic world constantly in their daily work learn to adjust their thinking to the world of the very small. As they do so, they gradually come to sense atoms and their constituent particles as though they were directly experienced. This perception of the atomic world is possible because mere smallness alone does not constitute an essential difference; the change is quantitative and not qualitative. This feeling of kinship with small objects is symbolized by a unit of nuclear size adopted, half in jest, by early researchers in the microcosmic world within the atom. To these physicists the nucleus of an atom was a concept that loomed "as big as a barn"; the measurement "barn," representing the cross-section area of an atomic nucleus, is still sometimes used as a unit of nuclear scale.

Though we can learn to visualize their size, we fail utterly when we witness the actions of atomic particles. For this involves not only another order of magnitude but qualitative differences as well. The laws governing the actions of atomic particles are completely alien to the everyday world. They are of two kinds— quantum mechanics governs the behavior of particles that are very small, and relativity applies to particles that are moving very fast. As these small particles move through a wide range of velocities, the full complement of strange behavior is encountered.

To illustrate this wide-ranging behavior, let us consider the application of quantum mechanics in the subatomic field. Normally we have no difficulty in distinguishing between a large particle of matter, such as a rolling marble, and a wave, spreading in all directions on a pond. The subatomic particles that are subject to quantum mechanics, however, act as both a particle and a wave. Each particle can act as if it is well localized, as a particle should; yet at the same time it can exhibit a wave length that increases as the particle moves more slowly. Man has not

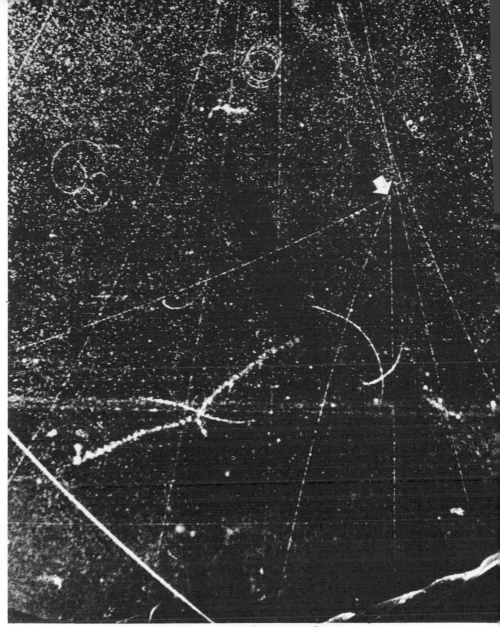

PORTRAIT OF A SUBATOMIC EVENT

Neutron-proton collision in a cloud chamber at the Brookhaven National Laboratory. The diverging tracks (arrow) show the impact of a highly accelerated neutron upon a proton, or nucleus of a hydrogen atom. While the neutron—invisible because it does not leave a path through the water vapor of the chamber—ricochets off its target, the proton shoots straight down toward the bottom of the photograph, and two pi mesons, particles with a life of only a millionth of a second, rebound at angles to the left. The other tracks in the picture represent particles not involved in the collision.

yet learned how to visualize an entity which shows concentration in space, as does a particle, and yet simultaneously spreads over large distances as a wave does. But in spite of our failure to visualize these things, they are demonstrable—small particles *are* waves and particles at the same time. We accept these complex laws of subatomic behavior as true, though we can neither understand nor visualize them through analogy with the phenomena of our everyday world.

The other laws at variance with common sense are those of relativity. These laws always involve one speed that is a fixed constant in nature, the 186,000 miles per second at which light moves. Relativity does not enter appreciably into our ordinary life, for speeds so far attained by man are insignificant relative to that of light. For subatomic particles, however, such speeds are common, and the strange principles of relativity emerge clearly, almost shockingly. As its speed increases, the weight of a particle grows, slowly at first, then enormously as its speed approaches that of light. Unquestionably the most striking property of relativity is the equivalence of matter itself to energy, the amount of energy involving again the fundamental constant, the speed of light. Expressed simply by the well-known Einstein equation, the relation is: $E = mc^2$. This equation, simple in appearance, yet distilling so much complex theory, gives the amount of energy (E) equivalent to the mass (m). Because the velocity of light (c) is such a large number—and its square, of course, is much larger yet—the amount of energy equivalent to a small amount of mass is prodigious. Einstein's equation indicates, for instance, that the energy resulting from the conversion of one pound of matter would equal that obtained by conventional power sources from 200,000,000 gallons of gasoline or 1,000,000 tons of coal!

What is the place and the role of the neutron among the so-called "fundamental particles" of matter? In structure the neutron is very much like the proton, the positively charged particle which forms the nucleus of the hydrogen atom. In fact, if the neutron is isolated in a vacuum so that it never comes into contact with any matter, the neutron will disappear of its own accord, and its place will be taken by a proton and an electron.

This process takes place so slowly—in approximately twelve minutes—that for the purpose of nuclear experimentation this spontaneous transformation can be ignored, for the time scale of experiments involves thousandths of a second or less. The essential difference between the neutron and the proton is that the neutron, as its name suggests, is neutral, bearing no electrical charge. This apparently trivial difference is the source of the astonishing diversity of the neutron's accomplishments.

The lack of electrical charge which distinguishes the neutron is vital because essentially all other components of matter are electrically charged; protons are positive, most electrons are negative and, on a larger scale, atoms are made up of positive nuclei surrounded by negative electrons. If the positively charged protons were shot into solid matter as probes, they would quickly be brought to rest by the repulsive forces of the other protons in matter—for like charges repel each other. The uncharged neutrons, on the other hand, pass easily into the innermost regions of the atoms which constitute matter, being unimpeded by the electrical charges of the constituents. Of equal importance is the fact that the neutron can penetrate matter at low particle velocities, enabling it to reveal to the observer the most striking properties of the subatomic world.

As the neutron penetrates solid matter, slipping easily through the electric fields of the atoms, its behavior at various velocities dramatically illustrates the strange laws of quantum mechanics and relativity which govern the world of the quick and the small. The two-sided nature of the neutron—its capacity for being either or both a particle and a wave—is best revealed at slow speeds. (It should be noted that a "slow" speed in neutron physics may be in the order of 1700 miles per hour and a "long" journey for a neutron might entail a transit of twelve inches of solid matter.) Having a definite mass and velocity, a slow neutron is expected to behave as a proper particle; surprisingly, it at the same time shows characteristics that are undeniably wavelike. The size of the wave, or the wave length of the neutron, varies inversely with its velocity, becoming larger as the speed of the neutron decreases. Thus we are forced to accept, common sense to the contrary, a penetrating particle with a size that increases indefinitely as its velocity decreases. As the neutron's speed drops, it becomes more and more like a light wave and less and less like a moving speck of matter.

The discovery that certain specially prepared metal surfaces would reflect neutrons as a mirror reflects light proved that slow neutrons are as truly waves as they are particles. For, in the act of reflecting from the highly polished surface, a neutron does not collide with a single atom of the surface; instead, as a very extended wave, it reflects from *all* the atoms in the entire surface, numbering many billions. But even as we observe the neutron in its wavelike motion, it can instantaneously change, behave as a typical particle, and further confound our common sense. Leaving the mirror, the reflected neutrons are detected by a gas-filled Geiger counter in which each neutron interacts with a single target nucleus of the gas, thus signaling the neutron's arrival. The neutron has collapsed from an extended wave capable of covering an entire mirror to a localized particle absorbed within a single nucleus!

The neutron's behavior also illustrates, simply and clearly, the central fact of relativity—the direct conversion of mass into energy. Unaffected by the negative electric charges of the electrons, neutrons pass through the shell of the atom and at times approach the central nucleus. Neutrons also penetrate the nucleus, unhindered by its positive electric charge. When such a penetration results in the stopping of a neutron in a nucleus, the process is called a neutron capture. When the neutron is captured by a nucleus, a large amount of energy is released—energy resulting from the disappearance of some of the excess mass added to the nucleus when the neutron is captured.

An example of this energy-producing process is found in the capture of a slow neutron by the nucleus of the metal aluminum 27, which in its stable form contains thirteen protons and fourteen neutrons. The additional (captured) neutron produces aluminum 28 with an unstable nucleus—a nucleus which spontaneously disintegrates with the emission of energy—containing thirteen protons and fifteen neutrons.

Though some neutron captures produce relatively modest amounts of energy others are self-perpetuating and result in awesome releases of energy. Such is the case in the fission process associated with neutron capture by the heavier elements, such as uranium 235. As the wave length or size of a neutron increases as its speed decreases, it is understandable that a very slow—and therefore large—neutron has the best chance of meeting and entering the nucleus as the neutron penetrates the atomic structure. When a slow neutron enters the U 235 atom and penetrates the nucleus, a tremendous agitation is produced which results in the explosive splitting of the nucleus into two approximately equal parts. The two parts weigh less than the original uranium atom, the vanished mass appearing as motion or kinetic energy involved in the separation of the severed parts. The same splitting process produces several additional free neutrons—we can understand them to be "boiled" off the two fragments of the original nucleus as they rush apart—which form the links of the "chain" which continues the splitting process with other U 235 nuclei. The emission of these additional neutrons poses no problem in a U 235 nucleus, which contains 143 neutrons and ninety-two protons.

The power implicit in the conversion of mass to energy is emphasized when we realize that, although only about a tenth of a percent of the mass of the uranium atom disappears in the process, it is sufficient to produce amounts of energy entirely unknown in the preatomic age, and millions of times greater than that produced by conventional high explosives. Actually two facets of the world of the very small are vital to the fission process—the triggering of the reaction resulting from the large wave length of the slow-moving neutron, a typical effect of quantum mechanics; and the enormous amount of energy that appears as a product of the relationship $E = mc^2$, the core of the relativity theory.

With this general understanding of the process through which neutrons are emitted or "liberated" through the fission of uranium nuclei in a reactor, it is time for us to examine the method by which these neutrons are controlled and put to various uses as research tools.

Neutrons can be produced for research, experimentation or industrial uses in several ways. One method, used mainly to produce a small supply of neutrons for experimental purposes, is to accelerate a charged particle such as a proton in a nuclear accelerator—a machine which speeds up the particle in a directed line of flight, investing it with tremendous energy. When the energized particle reaches sufficient speed it strikes a target nucleus in solid material placed in the proton's flight path. The proton is absorbed by the target nucleus, a process that excites the nucleus so that a neutron is emitted.

A more plentiful source of neutrons is the chain-reacting nuclear pile. This device uses the previously described fission process as the source of neutrons and sustains the chain reaction by means of moderating material which surrounds the fissionable fuel elements. The moderating material, generally highly purified graphite or water, serves to slow down the swiftly moving neutrons that are emitted in the fission process so that they may be readily absorbed by other fissionable nuclei, thus continuing the atom-splitting process.

Thus, neutrons in a reactor vessel may be thought of as a gas colliding with the atoms of the moderating material which surrounds the uranium metal that acts as fuel. Reactors are designed so that the neutrons are concentrated in the region of the uranium fuel in order that a chain reaction can be maintained. This is accomplished in part by surrounding the reactor with a wall of material which reflects escaping neutrons back into the reactor. The reflector is surrounded by a shield which absorbs those neutrons which penetrate the reflector. The main purpose of the shield is to reduce the radiation field to a safe biological value.

Neutron experiments can be carried out either inside or outside the reactor. Experiments inside the reactor utilize the intense flux of neutrons concentrated in the center of the atomic pile. Such experiments are usually performed to produce radioactive isotopes or to study the damage produced in materials subject to high radiation fields.

Beam experiments are carried on outside the reactor by opening a hole in the shield and allowing neutrons to escape in a beam from the central portion of the reactor. The intensity of neutrons available outside the reactor is typically 10,000 times smaller than that available on the inside. On the outside of the reactor very complex apparatus may be assembled to perform experiments that would be impossible inside the reactor.

The beam of neutrons emerging from the reactor includes neutrons of all energies or speeds—from the very-slow or low-energy particles to those with tremendous speed and high energy. Neutron energy can also be expressed in terms of temperature, which increases with the energy content of the neutron. Instruments are available which allow the experimenter to separate a small band of neutron energies from the broad distribution and then study the interaction of neutrons with matter.

Mechanical choppers use the particle properties of the neutron. These choppers are rotating disks which interrupt the beam of neutrons and periodically allow short bursts of neutrons to pass through the openings in the disks. The neutrons are then allowed to travel down the beam and are detected at some distance from the choppers. The high-energy neutrons, traveling at the greatest velocity, arrive first, and the slower low-energy neutrons lag behind and arrive at a later time. Thus the time it takes for a neutron to arrive at the detector after passing through the chopper is a measure of the neutron energy. The time interval is measured electronically.

Neutron spectrometers utilize the wave properties of neutrons. These instruments act in a way similar to an optical prism which separates white light into its various colors. The beam of neutrons is directed onto a single crystal of some material, usually copper or aluminum, and the crystal bends (diffracts) the neutrons through an angle depending on the neutron energy. By an arrangement of slits which define the various angles of diffraction, different energies in the incident beam may be separated. Beam experiments using such instruments are used to study the properties of the nucleus and the movement of atoms and molecules in solids and liquids.

In studying groups of atoms in matter, whether it be liquid, solid or gas, the principal task is one of determining the pattern of atoms relative to one another. The study of these atomic patterns, and the way in which they determine physical properties, such as hardness and color, is the concern of "solid-state physics." Research in this field can have enormous practical value, as shown recently by the development of the transistors which are replacing the vacuum tubes used in electronic circuits.

As atomic patterns change, so do the ordinary properties of materials. An outstanding example of the way in which differing atomic patterns result in different physical characteristics is the case of diamond and graphite—as the diamond in a ring and the graphite in your pencil. Both these materials are made of the same atoms, carbon; the difference in properties of the two materials results from the arrangement of the atoms within them.

There are several general methods of employing neutrons to study or to change the atomic patterns within material. Moderately fast neutrons directed through a crystalline structure—the fixed pattern of atoms in a solid material—collide with a certain number of the atoms and knock them out of their normal positions. Such a displacement can alter the basic properties of the material—characteristics such as its hardness and its facility for transmitting heat and electricity. Metals actually become harder after such neutron bombardment, a process which holds great promise for industry.

In order to study the arrangement of atoms in a crystal *without* disturbing the atomic pattern, it is necessary to use neutrons that are moving very slowly. It will be recalled that a neutron's wave length, or effective size, increases as its speed diminishes; for investigating atomic patterns the neutrons employed must have a wave length which matches the distance between the individual atoms of the crystal. As these slow and relatively large neutrons pass through material they are scattered by their collisions with the atoms; by studying the resultant deflection of the various neutron streams as they emerge from the material with a measuring device, we can analyze the atomic structure of the material. This procedure, called neutron diffraction, might be likened to rolling a stream of tennis balls down a bowling alley; a study of the deflection of the balls after they rolled in among the tenpins would suggest the pattern in which the pins were arranged.

As we move up the energy scale in neutron research, the fantastic little particle-wave becomes smaller and moves faster—

618

though it always retains its unique characteristic of having no electric charge. As you might expect, there is a point on this ascending energy scale where the fast neutron approximates the size of the nucleus of the atom. Despite the fact that the nucleus is a million million times denser than ordinary matter—such as a piece of granite, for instance—some of the fast neutrons which enter a nucleus re-emerge, leaving the nuclear particles unchanged. Others of the impinging neutrons are absorbed by the nucleus, just as "cloudy" glass is transparent to some light waves and opaque to others. This analogy has caused physicists to liken the nucleus to a cloudy crystal ball.

While we do not as yet understand how an alien neutron can pass through the closely packed neutrons and protons which comprise a nucleus, this process has made it possible for us to learn something about the structure of the nucleus; we know now, for instance, that nuclei are not the simple spherical objects we once supposed, but of various shapes ranging from spherical to elongated ellipsoids.

For the next step up the neutron-energy ladder we depend upon the large nuclear accelerators such as the cyclotrons, which can, by successive electrical pushes, speed up particles until they contain millions of volts of energy. Such high-energy neutrons not only penetrate a nucleus but also pull apart its strongly bound, constituent neutrons and protons. What still puzzles us about these tremendously cohesive forces—the same forces released in the fission process—is that they apparently do not operate until the particles involved practically touch each other.

By thus selecting neutrons with appropriate speeds, we can conduct large-scale investigations of materials comprising millions of atoms, or we can explore individual atoms, the nucleus of the atom or even the individual particles within that nucleus. It is the neutron's unique quantum mechanical change of size with speed that makes it possible to study phenomena of this enormous range in size.

The discerning reader may at this point wonder how the neutrons within the nucleus fit into such a relatively circumscribed area if, as we have postulated, their size increases in inverse ratio to their velocity. The answer is, of course, that all atoms and all the particles comprising atoms are continually in motion; within the nucleus the neutron is most energetic and moves very rapidly—vibrates, if you will—and thus has a wave length, or size, small enough to enable it to fit within the nucleus with plenty of room to spare.

At this writing the top of the energy ladder in neutron research is reached when we use the neutron not as an exploratory tool, but as an object to be explored. Within the last few years the giant new particle accelerators have provided us with enough energy—in the order of a billion electron volts—to penetrate the interior of the neutron itself. Using extremely energetic protons —the neutron's companion particle in the nucleus—as probes, scientists have exposed the internal structure of the neutron and found that it, in turn, consists of still-smaller particles, the mesons. A bewildering array of mesons, with various electrical charges, have been torn out of the neutron in this manner. The presence of mesons, originally discovered by cloud-chamber techniques in which the speeding particle left a track in water vapor, is now affirmed through the use of special particle counters.

The important role played by the meson in the structure of the neutron is strikingly revealed in the action triggered by the energetic protons. When such a "fast" proton passes near a stationary neutron, the proton transfers a positively charged meson to the neutron and, becoming itself a neutron, moves on with unabated speed. Meanwhile the neutron, having gained a positive charge, becomes a proton. This process of switching identity by exchange of mesons takes place constantly and rapidly within all nuclei, providing the mechanism for the force that binds the neutrons and the protons to each other.

Within the neutron, among the swarming mesons, contemporary physics has encountered two baffling puzzles. The first concerns the explanation of the observed properties of the neutron in terms of its constituent mesons. We might suppose that the neutron should consist of a positively charged core of matter surrounded by a rapidly moving negative meson—a model in miniature of the hydrogen atom with its positive nucleus and circumambient negatively charged electron. If this conjecture is valid, it should be possible, by delicate explorations in the space between the positive central core and the negative meson, to find some evidence of the electrical forces involved. Recent experiments performed at Brookhaven National Laboratory and at Stanford University revealed no evidence of a region in which separate charges exist. This presents us with a paradox; we know that mesons are present within the neutron because we can tear them out of the neutron, but we find no mesons when we probe inside the neutron.

The other puzzle brings up, once again, the old question— are there fundamental particles? Will we ever find the ultimate particle? With the enormous accelerators now building or in the planning stage, will we be able to split the meson only to find new submesonic members of our family of "elementary" particles? At the present time no scientist or philosopher has a valid basis for answering this question.

The practical application of the knowledge gained from research in neutron physics may benefit or menace society. The effect of the development of the fission A-bomb and the fusion thermonuclear bomb—which the A-bomb triggers—is surely potentially catastrophic. The employment of neutron activity in power-producing reactors, in radioisotopes for use in medicine, in food processing and in various industrial processes, on the other hand, promises a future that is beyond accounting—the use of radioactive tracers in United States industry alone already results in savings of $500,000,000 a year. The essential motivation for basic research in neutron physics, however, lies above and beyond all such social values; to the scientist the neutron is primarily a tool to be used for the better understanding of the structure and behavior of matter.

Further reading:
  Hughes, Donald J.: ON NUCLEAR ENERGY. Cambridge: Harvard University Press; 1957.
  Hughes, Donald J.: THE NEUTRON STORY. New York: Doubleday and Co., Inc.; 1959.
  Compton, Arthur Holly: ATOMIC QUEST. New York: Oxford University Press; 1956.

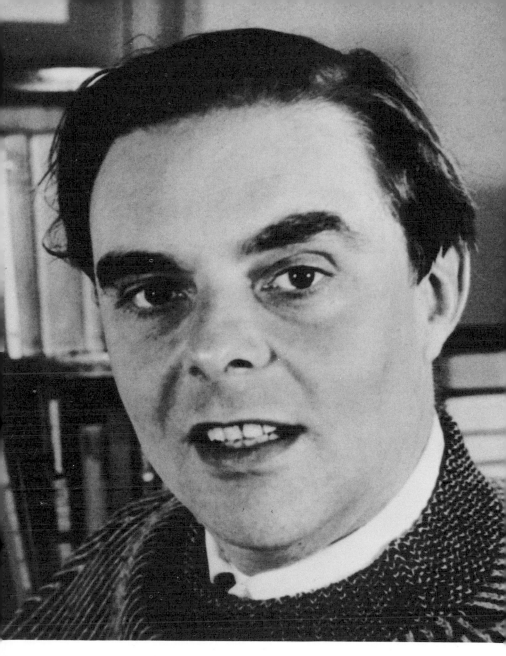

JOHN WAIN

As a writer John Wain was originally associated by the critics with England's "Angry Young Men," following the publication in 1953 of his first novel, Hurry on Down, *a mordant commentary on the English academic world. Though still a young man (36), he can no longer be considered "angry." After graduating from Oxford with First Class Honors, Wain lectured on English literature for eight years at the University of Reading. "I resigned," he says, "because I found that writing could not be combined with teaching except to the ruinous detriment of one or the other, but I have always kept my amateur's interest in education." Wain also writes poetry and critical essays. In 1960 he published his fourth novel,* A Travelling Woman.

The Dilemma of Youth

B Y

JOHN WAIN

In attitudes to education, as in most things, the world is divided. Many people in the West seem to believe that an educated person is somehow unworthy, little better than a traitor to the whole idea of education, unless he ranges himself pretty determinedly against the forces that propel his society along. This gives rise to the question, Can education legitimately aim at molding people into agreement with the basic assumptions of the society they live in, or is the only honourable role for the educated man that of rebel and disputant? Mr. David Riesman in a recent article has said roundly that "the relation of education to later life should be a dialectical and critical one." And speaking of the kind of student who makes the most favourable impression on faculty members, and finds himself recommended for fellowships, jobs, etc., he notes that the most favoured ones were 'a bit rebellious, a bit off-beat . . . these were the students apt to appeal to a faculty member who had not entirely repressed a rebelliousness of his own that had led him to be a teacher in the first place.'

The assumption here, that a main motive for devoting one's life to education is or can be 'rebelliousness,' is a widespread one in the West, though it must be virtually unknown in the Communist world, where the educational machine is seen as an assembly-line for producing good Communist citizens. But there are people in the West, also, who do not see education chiefly in terms of inciting people to challenge the society they live in, to overturn its assumptions, to rebel against its conventions. The word 'convention' means 'a coming together,' and in every society there are important areas of thought and feeling on which men have come together. What is education primarily useful for? To strengthen this cohesion—to bind a society more closely together by presenting its basic assumptions in an acceptable form—or to weaken them by encouraging, in every sphere and over every issue, 'rebellion'? Is the 'rebel' thinking too much of himself and too little of others? Are there some things more important than the purity of one's spotless little intellectual integrity? We must be careful—the answer may be No.

Some societies, both today and in the past, have gone so far along the road towards an official, orthodox education that the very question we are discussing would seem to them meaningless. In the Middle Ages, European education was dominated by the Roman Catholic Church; theology was 'queen of the sciences' in every scheme of learning, and the question of an unorthodox (or anti-orthodox) teaching simply never arose.

As a matter of fact, the Middle Ages offer an interesting point of comparison with totalitarian modern societies. Their literary and scientific culture was based on the Greek and Latin past; when the highly trained, subtle, disputatious mediaeval scholar engaged in historical or literary teaching, he was working with material which dated from before the rise of his own society with its all-pervading Christian beliefs and assumptions. This set a problem which, during the mediaeval centuries, called forth some heroic solutions. A mediaeval scholar who loved, say, Virgil—who responded to the majesty and beauty of Virgil's language and the nobility of his vision—was faced with the awkward fact that Virgil, having lived before Christ, was not a Christian writer, and therefore could not be used as an instrument of direct Christian teaching. If the mediaeval Christian scholars had been narrowly Philistine, they would have turned away from Virgil and concentrated entirely on their own Christian, neo-Latin culture. In fact, they did nothing of the kind; all the great Greek and Latin writers, in so far as the Middle Ages knew of their existence, were handed down with the utmost care, and every scrap of information about them was lovingly gathered.

To do this with the official backing of the Church was, of course, a matter of giving a Christian slant to the interpretation of the pagan classics, and this was accordingly done. Some of the interpretations we read about in a book like Comparetti's *Virgil in the Middle Ages* remind one of nothing so much as the efforts of present-day Soviet professors to 'prove' that Shakespeare or Goethe was 'progressive,' i.e. a Communist before his time. Their motive is a very strong one; being sensitive, intelligent readers, they want to go on being allowed to study these great poets and to spread a knowledge of them among their students; if this means dragging them across the ideological barrier, then drag they will. It is a mistake to mock at these men. If the Middle Ages had not performed the same service for Virgil and Ovid, not only would mediaeval culture have been much the poorer, but the works of these poets might have disappeared for ever.

The mediaeval church was no very hard task-master. In the absence of any strict standards of historical criticism, a scholar could get away with some very odd interpretations, if he had a strong enough motive to make him present his case vehemently. Thus, it was confidently asserted that the ancients were familiar with the Old Testament, so that they were already half-way to Christianity. Following on from this, the annotaters pounced on everything that would bear a Christian interpretation. Virgil's Fourth Eclogue, for instance, celebrates the prospective birth of a child to Pollio, a government official who was one of Virgil's early protectors. The poem pictures a new golden age of security and happiness which will date from this birth, and not unnaturally the early Christian commentators took this as a prophetic reference to the coming of the Messiah. It followed that Virgil must have been gifted with mystical powers of prophecy; and if he had them, might not others?

The important thing about the campaign is that it worked. Modern scholars are often puzzled to discern the exact degree of 'sincerity' behind the mediaeval policy of reading all literary texts as if they were allegories, and making them yield the 'right' meaning. Certainly they developed great skill at this kind of interpretation, and the exercise of that skill must have been a satisfaction in itself. But did the average mediaeval scholar, sitting down to expound a poem like the 'Aeneid' or Ovid's 'Metamorphoses' by splitting it up prismatically into a series of allegories, really believe that he was unwrapping a series of packages that had been deliberately tied by the author? Or did he not care about the author one way or another? Of course, the Middle Ages lacked the sense of history, as we now know it; they probably did not realise that an ancient Greek or Roman had an imagination attuned to a very different way of life from theirs, so different that the first step towards understanding his work would be to try to feel oneself back into his times. All they knew was that the ancients were 'pagan,' and must be made to yield a Christian message. Or was it 'all they knew'? Did some of the more sensitive among them realise, as they compiled their vast commentaries in which every detail of the text had its allegorical 'solution,' like a puzzle, that their labours were essentially irrelevant, that they erected a superstructure of their own on the base provided by the author's words?

I fancy this thought must have strayed into their minds now and again, just as it must stray into the minds of Communist critics whose life-work is to provide every literary classic with a protective awning of 'socialist realism.' Sometimes very subtle and perceptive work can be produced even under these conditions; I have read Marxist analyses of Shakespeare plays which certainly provide interesting sidelights; the young English art critic Mr. John Berger is not so utterly insensitive to painting as you would think from reading his bald statement that 'We can only make sense of art if we judge it by the criterion of whether or not it helps men to claim their social rights.' This is exactly on a level with the mediaeval view that, since Christian truth is the only truth, any writing which cannot be made to yield a direct Christian message is simply falsehood. And yet mediaeval literary criticism is often profoundly interesting. (My own view, by the way, is the exact inversion of the mediaeval one; I think that if Christianity is true, then every good poem or novel is 'Christian.' And if Marxism, with its economic explanations and its relentless emphasis on the class struggle, really offered a satisfying explanation of human history, then all good writing would be Marxist writing; it would relate, in its own way, to the truth as Marx proclaimed it.)

Much has been written in the West about Soviet education, and violent arguments have sprung up between those who warn us that it is already ahead of our own, and those who, at the opposite extreme, maintain that the Soviet Union, not being interested in the cultivation of intellectual freedom and the spirit of enquiry, has no such thing as 'education,' in our Western sense, anywhere within its borders. The first group point to the colossal State expenditure on schools and colleges; the second to the heavily-slanted, doctrinaire nature of Societ teaching.

Without wishing to open old wounds (for I have been involved in some of these arguments myself), I think it can be fairly said that Soviet education, admirably thorough as it is and enviably confident in the rightness of its own methods, is pre-eminently aimed at teaching its people to _know the answers._ All the answers: about medicine, about mathematics, about agriculture; about philosophy, about literature, about history and politics. The Soviet rulers do not encourage specialization, at any rate for undergraduates. They do not want historians or literary critics, they do not even want surgeons and engineers, who get on with the job according to their own lights, without much idea of the wider social implications of what they are doing. Their attitude is that all work is Communist work. A dam built by a Soviet engineer is not just a dam, it is a Communist dam. And so on down the line, until even the simplest tonsillectomy performed by a Soviet surgeon is a Communist tonsillectomy. Just as all literature, art and music produced by Soviet artists is required to be propaganda for the Soviet way of life, so all work is understood to be motivated first by a desire to serve that way of life and only secondly by love of the work itself.

This attitude, as everyone knows, is intensively fostered by Soviet teaching. The place occupied in eighteenth-century England by a simple assent to the Thirty-Nine Articles, which were drawn up by the English clergy in 1562 to unify Anglican worship, is occupied in the Soviet Union by a trio of formidable indoctrination courses, compulsory for all students, in whatever faculty, throughout the fifteen republics of the U.S.S.R. Thanks to the University of Michigan, we can now study the syllabus for these courses; in a thick pamphlet, *Administration of Teaching in Social Sciences in the U.S.S.R.*, they have published, in English translation, the requirements for three basic, compulsory courses: History of the Communist Party of the U.S.S.R., Political Economy, and Historical and Dialectical Materialism. The material is offered without comment, save for a short Introduction by Harlan H. Hatcher, setting out the circumstances —what the syllabi are, how they were obtained, and so forth. One sentence from this Introduction leaps into relief:

'Compulsory for all students, these courses constitute about eight to ten percent of the total instructional program of Soviet universities, technical schools, medical colleges and other institutions of higher education.'

Obviously a system which compels every trained person, from a marine biologist to a lawyer, to spend one hour out of every ten during his or her college years in getting by heart the official doctrines of the State is determined on one thing at least: no one among the intelligentsia is going to be able to plead ignorance on any question of dogma. If anyone fails to live up to the full doctrinal requirements, the responsibility is entirely on his own shoulders, since his professional career was not at liberty to begin until he had shown himself word-perfect in the orthodoxy.

All this, in general terms, one knew already. From conversations with Soviet students and bureaucrats, I had come away with the impression of a flawlessly rehearsed catechism. What the Michigan pamphlet does is to reveal, step by step, how the indoctrination is done. Each subject is divided into 'topics'; every topic has its official allotment of time, and its list of required reading. And the conclusions that must be reached are formulated in advance, there in the syllabus. Here, for example, is Topic 22 of the Political Economy course, 'Completion of Territorial Division of World Among Great Powers and Struggle for its Redivision. Formation and Basic Features of Imperialism's Colonial System.'

1. Imperialism as system of financial enslavement and colonial oppression. Completion of territorial division of world towards beginning of twentieth century. Struggle for redivision of divided world. Struggle of imperialists for world domination. Wars and militarization of national economy in capitalist countries.

2. Formation of imperialism's colonial system. Colonies and semi-colonies.

Role of colonies in era of imperialism. Colonies as spheres for investing capital. Colonies as markets for sales and as appendages supplying metropolitan countries with agricultural raw materials. One-sided character of development of national economy in colonial countries. Colonies as strategic military bases of imperialism.

And so on through two more articles.

That second section, when I read it, gave me a clue to the real nature of several conversations I had had in Moscow earlier in the year. Whenever 'imperialism' was mentioned, the same arguments came out, no matter whom you were talking to. The basic position was, in each case, that there is only one kind of imperialism, i.e. planting your flag on the soil of another country and then proceeding to 'exploit' that country. No distinction was admitted between old-style exploitation and modern mandate or protectorate systems; nor between countries which were being progressively educated towards self-government and those being held down by force. It was all 'imperialism'—whereas the Soviet annexation of, say, Latvia was not imperialism because it didn't involve running up the Soviet flag. And having read Topic 22, I see it all. If one urged that the British action in Cyprus, say, was motivated not by a wish to 'exploit' the Cypriots but by an obligation to NATO, that too had been forestalled, under the heading 'Colonies as strategic military bases of imperialism.'

I give this small and commonplace example to bring out the main point—that the Soviet educational system is succeeding

in the basic task its rulers have imposed on it, which is to re-
hearse its entire bourgeoisie in an elaborate question-and-answer
system of apologetics.

This is a form of 'education for orthodoxy' which it is easy
enough to reject as undesirable; one can't imagine any thoughtful person actually *wishing* to go in with such a system—though,
no doubt, once enclosed in it most people would resign themselves and keep their mouths shut. When I propose for examination the question with which I started, about education for assent or dissent, I naturally had no intention of seriously recommending a giant processing-machine such as the Soviet Union
has evolved. It isn't (in the West) necessary to muster all the
arguments against such a system, but if I had to choose one argument that contains all the others I would merely point out
that education is essentially a process of *launching*. An education, of whatever kind, has failed if it has not managed to stimulate in the student that kind of intellectual curiosity which will
naturally lead him, year by year, to extend his knowledge. And
also, it should go without saying, given him the necessary basic
information to build on; not only factual information, but
skills of a kind that do not show themselves in a parade of facts.
How to find the knowledge he wants; how to marshal information; how to consider a subject dispassionately, brushing away the
dust and cobwebs that will naturally form over any subject that
has lain in one's mind for a few years, among the lumber of one's
own prejudices and personal emphases. All this the student needs
before he can begin. And he begins on the day he leaves college,
just as the aviator begins on the day he first flies on his own.

By this test, the Soviet system of education fails. Its aim is
not to launch people on a lifetime of original and developing
thought, but to process them. By providing everyone with a
shared background of information and argument, they may paper over the cracks in the Communist system, and in some cases
actually cement them. But there is nothing here that can call itself education.

This kind of defect in the education of a totalitarian country is so glaringly obvious that one is sometimes driven close to
the opposite extreme. It is tempting, after a look at the results of

Communist orthodoxy in education, to throw the whole thing up and say that the sole duty of an educated person is to question, to probe, to protest, to rebel. Tempting, but in the end not satisfying.

All societies try to perpetuate themselves; we cannot deny them this right. Unless we take the extreme position represented by: 'Communism is evil. Therefore anything that helps to strengthen a Communist society is evil. Therefore Communist education is evil,' we can hardly quarrel with Russia or China for wanting to slant their educational systems towards orthodoxy. The West, naturally, does it too. In England, to take the example I know best, the State schools faithfully reflect the involvement of Church and Government which we symbolise by placing the Queen at the head of the Church of England. England is thus an 'officially' Christian country, in that the reigning monarch is identified with the Established Church. Proceeding downwards in a direct cause-and-effect chain, we get the compulsory religious teaching in schools. Every State run school has to have religious instruction; it is the only compulsory subject, whereas there is no law which compels a school to teach, say arithmetic. And every such school must assemble once every day, teachers and pupils together, for religious worship. Both the instruction and the worship must be 'undenominational'; there must be nothing to stir up the fierce warfare of the sects. But religion there must be. If a child's parents object—if they are Roman Catholics, or Orthodox Jews, or convinced atheists—the child is excused from these activities. But the school is not excused from the duty to provide them.

A Communist, then, could point out that we in England slant our education towards Christianity, which from his point of view is either a mere deception, aimed at keeping the poor in a proper state of resignation and holding back the wheels of change, or else a pitiable illusion. And however we chose to answer him, we could not deny that England has, in recent centuries, insisted on a definite show of orthodoxy from those entrusted with responsibility. The settlement of 1688, which came at the end of a long series of dangers and disasters provoked largely by Roman Catholic powers on the one hand, and the extreme revo-

633

lutionary forms of Protestantism on the other, found a solution in the Thirty-Nine Articles. The Church of England, as a middle way, was deliberately used as a political instrument. From the 1680's until within living memory, it was impossible to hold a responsible position in England without assenting to the Thirty-Nine Articles—in other words, belonging to the Church of England. Without that assent, no one could hold Government office, be a Member of Parliament, study at Oxford or Cambridge or hold a commission in the army or navy.

What is more, this system remained firmly in place until the historical circumstances that produced it had finally withered away. It was never overthrown by determined opposition from below; it simply faded away of its own accord when it became out-of-date. (One of the last people to run up against it, incidentally, was H. G. Wells. As a boy, already sceptical in his views, he wanted to become a pupil-teacher in order to carry on with his education. The Thirty-Nine Articles were demanded; he writhed, raged, but gave in for the sake of going on increasing his knowledge. As a result, he hated religions, churches and priests till his dying hour.)

It is beyond my competence to settle, or even profitably discuss, the question, Was England right in taking this action, or wrong? I can see, of course, that the country entered a period of political stability in the 1680's such as the world has seldom seen, and continued in it until the twentieth century. And it seems reasonable to guess that the price that had to be paid for this stability was the Thirty-Nine Articles. But, as I say, the question lies outside my competence. The stability may have had other causes. What matters for our present purpose is that England, a country always known as a stronghold of political freedom, did find it necessary for over 150 years to impose on its citizens, or on such of them as sought to win authority and influence, a kind of Loyalty Oath.

This decision, however, did not bear very directly on English education. You had to be 'Church of England' to get into Oxford or Cambridge, but once there you were not required to organize your studies along orthodox lines. (And if you were a Dissenter, there was, after the 1820's, the University of London offering first-class instruction—and there were always the Dissenting Academies, which play an honourable part in English educational history.) In other words, it was admitted that orthodoxy could not, in education, be forced on the student at every step. Compromise reigned; the comparison with modern Russia or China, or Nazi Germany, very soon breaks down. Shelley was sent down from Oxford for writing a pamphlet called 'The Necessity of Atheism;' but if he had restrained his impatience for print, and merely *talked* about this necessity, he would have been left in peace.

The battle, in short, was never violently joined. Since the Church was at the heart of English institutional life, successive governments protected themselves by the simple bargain of requiring assent to the Thirty-Nine Articles from those who directed, or studied at, the country's chief centres of learning; but they did nothing to hinder the setting-up of rival centres, nor did they indulge in witch-hunting among the accepted. Both orthodox and unorthodox proceeded along the same traditional lines. They saw education as a matter of imparting a traditional body of wisdom. The three Classical languages, Latin, Greek and Hebrew, would enable a man to study, in the original, most of the texts on which the culture and ethics of Western society were based. Then there were the principal modern languages. Then there was history—mostly European history, since Europe was, effectively, 'the world' until the twentieth century, just as 'philosophy' meant Western philosophy.

It was all rather like the process whereby old birds teach young birds to fly. The student was introduced to the texts in which the society's basic values were enshrined, and the implication was that if he made a mess of his life, or failed to be of use to the community, the responsibility would be his own.

Until the rise of mass communications, this system worked reasonably well. The target was a limited one; no attempt was made to educate an entire population, since it was assumed that decisions would be made by the educated class, and that values could be spread downwards, like butter soaking through a baked potato. Not until towards the end of the nineteenth century did successive shocks begin to weaken the traditional structure. First came industrialism with its demand for universal literacy. (No industrial society can be run by an illiterate working class.)

England, which became fully industrialized very early, was correspondingly early (1871) with compulsory free education, resulting in virtually 100% literacy. The ruling class of that time, like the Soviet ruling class of the present day, indulged in a good deal of boasting about its paternal generosity in teaching the people to read and write, but the more astute among them must have known that if they did not provide the funds for this instruction they would fall behind, in the race for trade, nations who *would* provide it.

From that hour, the older education was doomed. A literate people means a mass Press, challenging the values instilled by education with sensational and get-rich-quick values of its own. And within forty or fifty years, the Press was itself challenged by radio, cinema and, later, electronics. In every country where the entertainment and advertising industries are allowed a free hand, they spend money which makes the country's education budget look pitiable. They offer salaries to bright men which make the teacher's way of life, by comparison, reek of masochism. And they batter the minds of the people into insensibility before the vitalizing suggestions of literature, art or philosophy can begin to do their work.

It is at this point that we meet again, and in a sharper form, the initial question. Education for assent or dissent? For conformity or rebellion? In the East, there is no problem because both sides have been drawn into one central mass. The entertainment industry, the Press, the advertising copy-writers, have all been processed into the same solid block that contains the teacher and the writer. And Western visitors who feel disgust at the blatancy of their own ad-men and journalists often come back from Russia or China full of respect for the relative quietness and single-mindedness in the Communist atmosphere. Personally, I didn't. The bludgeoned conformity aroused my pity; the holier-than-thou attitude of official Communism, my impatience. This is not the way out. Better singing commercials than culture-squads raising hymns to Lenin by numbers.

And neither can that initial question admit of any simple answer. Should a society educate its members for assent?—Assent *to what?* The claim that a society can teach only 'the values that it has' implies that those values are widely recognised and can be stated easily. In the Communist world, this is true, at least as far as the official values are concerned. But in a free society, values are continually forming, evolving, emerging into consciousness. If we say, for instance, that the twin sources of Western civilisation are still, in spite of all modern changes, Christianity and the classics, that does not close the discussion. It opens it. We see the Christian thread running through various attempts at social justice—Welfare States and the like. And we see the classical thread running through the efforts to preserve intellectual freedom (the gift of the Greek) and impartial, universally recognised laws (the gift of the Roman). But having noted these broad outlines, we are no nearer to answering the enormous number of questions thrust on us by day-to-day life, and which all resolve themselves into one basic question: Given that our values are these, how do we apply them in this situation?—and this?—and that which is coming towards us? For liberal democracy, unlike Communism, has no answer-book; we do not claim, as the Communists do, that the truth is immediately obvious. John Donne has told us in his Third Satire that

> On a huge hill,
> Cragged and steep, Truth stands, and he that will
> Reach her, about must, and about must go,

and we believe him, and are willing to go about and about, toiling up to where Truth stands.

And this, of course, puts a great strain on the teacher. In our kind of society, the teacher—any kind of teacher, from kindergarten to graduate school—is in an almost impossible position. In a society inclined to be sceptical about the practical use of education, except in so far as it channels the young into well-paid jobs, the teacher, who has no well-paid job, has to stand as a witness that education does confer riches and happiness. However modest he is, sooner or later he has to make the claim, 'I have something to give your children. It will not bring them in big incomes and security; it will not solve their immediate personal problems. But I am offering it and I advise you to accept it on their behalf.' And if society, still sceptical, with an eye on the teacher's low salary, few possessions, modest living-quarters, answers with the sneer, 'You mean it will make them more like *you?*' then the teacher must find within himself, somewhere, the courage to say, 'Yes.' And let it go at that. Conscious as he is of his own inadequacies and limitations, of the many sacrifices he has accepted, of his own unsatisfied wants and irrational loves and hatreds, he must appear before the world as the representative of the free human mind. It is an almost impossible demand to make of anyone. And yet thousands accept it, and undertake the impossible, in every free country.

And having accepted it, they find themselves in the front line of attack. A society teaches 'the values that it has,' only by feeling its way concretely towards those values through the experience of living men and women. Both assent and dissent become merged in enquiry. For if we assent to the principle of intellectual freedom, we commit ourselves to fearless questioning. If we assent to the principle of the sacredness of the individual, we commit ourselves to the personal judgment. If we throw away the authority of the intellectual policeman on the corner, and substitute the right of appeal to the community of reasonable beings, we commit ourselves to respect for other people.

On either side of the fence, what we find is an education for assent. On the one side, assent to an authority which hands down values from above, and can alter them at will, and dictate exactly by what means they are to be put into practice. On the other, assent to a tradition of enquiry, of bringing even the least palatable truths into the open, and of making the practical application of those truths a matter for the individual conscience.

On the one side, assent to the tabulated and formally announced doctrines of a society. On the other, assent to the inner laws by whose authority the society came into being, and which, thwarted and fouled as they may be by individual acts of selfishness, still make themselves felt—as long as there is an education which frees the mind. To be free is, often, to be baffled by indecision; but a society whose education aims at banishing indecision will sooner or later find that truth, sanity and even loyalty have been banished as well.

C. P. SNOW

[*Photograph by Eugene Kammerman*]

Sir Charles Percy Snow, a scientist by training and a novelist by inclination, began his adult life as a molecular physicist upon his graduation from Cambridge in 1930 and entered upon a serious literary career in 1934 with The Search, *the story of an eminent scientist's rise and decline. During World War II Snow was chief of scientific personnel for the Ministry of Labor—a field in which he is still active. Sir Charles has now reached No. 7 of a projected eleven-volume novel sequence.* THE CONFLICT OF CULTURES *has been abstracted from the 1959 Rede Lecture delivered at Cambridge University, and since published by the Cambridge University Press as* The Two Cultures and the Scientific Revolution.

The Conflict of Cultures

BY

C. P. SNOW

B y training I am a scientist; by vocation I am a writer. For thirty years I have had to be in touch with scientists as part of a working existence. During the same thirty years I was trying to shape the books I wanted to write, which in due course took me among writers. It was through living among these groups and through moving regularly from one to the other and back again that I became occupied with the problem of what I call the "two cultures." For constantly I felt I was moving among two groups—comparable in intelligence, not grossly different in social origin, earning about the same incomes—who had almost ceased to communicate at all, who in intellectual, moral and psychological climate had so little in common that they might have inhabited different worlds.

As a result of this cultural dichotomy, I believe the intellectual life of the whole of Western society is increasingly being split into two polar groups. When I say the intellectual life I mean to include also a large part of our practical life, because I should be the last person to suggest the two can at the deepest level be distinguished. At one pole we have the literary intellectuals who, incidentally, while no one was looking, took to referring to themselves as "intellectuals" as though there were no others.

Literary intellectuals are at one pole—at the other, scientists; and, as the most representative, the physical scientists. Between the two lies a gulf of mutual incomprehension. The two groups have, moreover, a curious, distorted image of each other. Their attitudes are so different that even on the level of emotion they find little common ground.

Nonscientists tend to think of scientists as brash and boastful. Nonscientists have a rooted impression that the scientists are shallowly optimistic, unaware of man's condition. On the other hand, the scientists believe that the literary intellectuals are totally lacking in foresight, peculiarly unconcerned with their brother men, in a deep sense anti-intellectual, anxious to restrict both art and thought to the existential moment. Some of this subterranean backchat is not entirely baseless—though it is all destructive. Much of it rests on misinterpretations which are dangerous. I would now like to deal with two of the most profound of these misinterpretations.

First, concerning the nonscientists' impression that scientists are blankly optimistic. This accusation depends upon a confusion between the individual experience and the social experience, between the individual condition of man and his social condition. Most of the scientists I have known well have felt—just as deeply as the nonscientists I have known well—that the individual condition of each of us is tragic. Each of us is alone. Sometimes we escape from solitariness through love or affection or perhaps creative moments; but those triumphs of life are pools of light we make for ourselves, while the edge of the road is black. Each of us dies alone.

Some scientists I have known have had faith in revealed religion. Perhaps with them the sense of the tragic condition is not so strong. I don't know. With most people of deep feeling, however highspirited and happy they are—sometimes most with those who are happiest and most high-spirited—this tragic awareness seems to be in the fibers, part of the weight of life. That is as true of the scientists I have known as of anyone.

But nearly all scientists—and this is where the color of hope comes in—would see no reason why, just because the individual condition is tragic, so must the social condition be. Most of our fellow human beings, for instance, are underfed and die before their time. In the crudest terms, that is the social condition.

There is a moral trap which comes through the insight into man's loneliness; it tempts one to sit back, complacent in one's unique tragedy, and let the others go without a meal. As a group the scientists fall into that trap less than others. They are inclined to be impatient to see if something can be done and inclined to think that it can be done, until it's proved otherwise. That is their real optimism, and it's an optimism that the rest of us badly need.

In reverse this same spirit, tough and good and determined to fight it out at the side of their brother men, has made scientists regard the other culture's social attitudes as contemptible. That viewpoint is too facile; some of those attitudes are contemptible, but they are a temporary phase and not representative.

I remember being cross-examined by a scientist of distinction. "Why do most writers take on social opinions which would have been thought distinctly uncivilized and *démodé* at the time of the Plantagenets? Weren't they not only politically silly but politically wicked?"

The honest answer was that there was, in fact, a connection, which literary persons were culpably slow to see, between some kinds of early twentieth-century art and the most imbecile expressions of antisocial feeling. But though many of those antisocial writers dominated literary sensibility for a generation, that is no longer so, or at least to nothing like the same extent. Literature changes more slowly than science. It hasn't the same automatic corrective, and so its misguided periods are longer. But it is ill-considered of scientists to judge writers on the evidence of the period 1914–50.

Those are two of the misunderstandings between the two cultures. But is this arbitrary division defensible? Are these in reality two cultures? I believe the scientific culture is really a culture, not only in an intellectual but also in an anthropological sense.

The scientists' culture is intensive, rigorous and constantly in action. Their culture contains a great deal of argument, usually more rigorous and almost always at a higher conceptual level, than literary arguments—and even though the scientists cheerfully use words in senses which literary intellectuals don't recognize, the senses are exact ones. For example, "subjective," in contemporary technological jargon, means "divided according to subjects"; "objective" means "directed toward an object."

Remember, scientists are very intelligent men. Their culture is in many ways an exacting and admirable one. It doesn't contain much art, with the exception—an important exception —of music. It involves verbal exchange; insistent argument; long-playing records; color photography; the ear; to some extent the eye.

Of books, though, there is very little; of novels, history, poetry, plays, almost nothing. It isn't that scientists are not interested in the psychological or moral or social life. In the social life they certainly are interested, more than most of us. In the moral, they are by and large the soundest group of intellectuals we have; there is a moral component right in the grain of science itself, and almost all scientists form their own judgments of the moral life. It isn't that they lack the interests. It is more that the whole literature of the traditional culture doesn't seem to them to be relevant to those interests. They are, of course, dead wrong.

But what about the other side? The nonscientific culture is impoverished, too—perhaps more seriously, because it is vainer about it. The literary intellectuals still like to pretend that the traditional culture is the whole of culture, as though the natural order—the sciences—didn't exist; as though the exploration of the natural order were of no interest either in its own value or its consequences; as though the scientific edifice of the physical world were not, in its intellectual depth, complexity and articulation, the most beautiful and wonderful collective work of the mind of man. Yet most nonscientists have no conception of that edifice at all.

As with the tone-deaf, they don't know what they miss.

They give a pitying chuckle at the news of scientists who have never read a major work of English literature. They dismiss them as ignorant specialists. Yet their own ignorance and their own specialization is just as startling. A good many times I have been present at gatherings of people who, by the standards of the traditional culture, are thought highly educated and who have with considerable gusto been expressing their incredulity at the illiteracy of scientists. Once or twice I have been provoked and have asked the company how many of them could describe the Second Law of Thermodynamics. The response was cold; it was also negative. Yet I was asking something which is about the scientific equivalent of "Have you read a work of Shakespeare's?"

I now believe that if I had asked an even simpler question— such as, "What do you mean by mass, or acceleration?", which is the scientific equivalent of saying, "Can you read?"—not more than one in ten of the highly educated would have felt that I was speaking the same language. So the great edifice of modern physics goes up, and the majority of the cleverest people in the Western world have about as much insight into it as their neolithic ancestors would have had.

The reasons for the existence of the two cultures are many, deep and complex. I want to isolate one which is not so much a reason as a correlative, something which winds in and out of any of these discussions. It can be said simply, and it is this: If we ignore the scientific culture, then the rest of Western intellectuals have never tried, wanted or been able to understand the industrial revolution, much less to accept it.

All over the West the first wave of the industrial revolution crept on without anyone's noticing what was happening. It was destined to become in our own time by far the biggest transformation in society since the discovery of agriculture. In fact, those two revolutions, the agricultural and the industrial-scientific, are the only qualitative changes in social living that men have ever known. But the traditional culture didn't notice; or when it did notice, didn't like what it saw.

Almost none of the talent, almost none of the imaginative energy of the nineteenth century went back into the revolution which was producing the wealth. The traditional culture became more abstracted from it as society became more wealthy, trained its young men for administration, for the purpose of perpetuating the traditional culture itself, but never in any circumstances to equip them to understand the revolution or take part in it. Farsighted men were beginning to see, before the middle of the nineteenth century, that in order to go on producing wealth, society needed to train some of its bright minds in science, particularly in applied science. Few listened. The traditional culture didn't listen at all; and the pure scientists, such as there were, didn't listen very eagerly.

Thus the academics had nothing to do with the industrial revolution. So far as there was any thinking in nineteenth-century industry, it was left to cranks and clever workmen. The industrial revolution received very little educated talent. It had to make do with the guidance handy men could give it—sometimes, of course, handy men like Henry Ford, with a dash of genius.

Of course, one truth is straightforward—industrialization is the only hope of the poor. I use the word "hope" in a crude and prosaic sense. It is all very well for us, sitting pretty, to think that material standards of living don't matter. In fact, to deny this attitude is now to be accused of "materialism." It is all very well for one, as a personal choice, to reject industrialization. Do a modern Walden, if you like and, if you go without much food, see most of your children die in infancy; despise the comforts of literacy; accept twenty years off your own life—then I respect you for the strength of your aesthetic revulsion. But I don't respect you in the slightest if, even passively, you try to impose the same choice on others who are not free to choose.

The industrial revolution looked very different according to whether one saw it from above or below. To people who saw it from below there was no question that the industrial revolution was less bad than what had gone before. The only question was how to make it better.

In a more sophisticated sense that is still the question. In the advanced countries we have realized in a rough-and-ready way what the old industrial revolution brought with it—a great increase of population, because applied science went hand in hand with medical science and medical care; enough to eat, for a similar reason; everyone able to read and write, because an industrial society can't work without a broad base of literacy. Health, food, education—nothing but the industrial revolution could have spread them right down to the very poor.

Those are primary gains. There are losses, too, of course; one of which is that organizing a society for industry makes it easy to organize it for all-out war. But the gains remain. They are the matrix of our social hope. And yet, do we understand how they have happened? Have we begun to comprehend even the old industrial revolution, much less the new scientific revolution in which we stand? There never was anything more necessary to comprehend.

By the industrial revolution I mean the gradual use of machines, the employment of men and women in factories, the change from a population of agricultural laborers to a population largely engaged in making things in factories and distributing them when they were made.

Out of the industrial revolution grew another change, closely related to the first, but far more deeply scientific. This change comes from the application of real science to industry. I believe the industrial changes involving electronics, atomic energy and automation are in cardinal respects different in kind from any we have experienced before and will change the world much more. It is this transformation that, in my view, is entitled to the name of "scientific revolution." This is the material basis of our lives, or more exactly, the social plasma of which we are a part. And we know almost nothing about it.

Why aren't we coping with the scientific revolution? How are we going to meet our future, both our cultural and practical future? I believe both phases of the question lead to the same conclusion. If one begins by thinking only of the intellectual life or only of the social life, one comes to a point where it becomes manifest that our education has failed us.

I don't pretend that any country has got its education perfect. In some ways the Russians and Americans are both more actively dissatisfied with their educational establishment than the English—at least they are taking more drastic steps to change it. That may be because they are more sensitive to the world they are living in. I have no doubt that, though neither of them has got the answer right, they are a good deal nearer than we in England. We do some things much better than either of them. In educational tactics we are often more gifted than the Russians or the Americans. In educational strategy, in contrast, we are only playing at it.

The differences between the three systems are revelatory. The English teach a far smaller proportion of their children up to the age of eighteen, and take a far smaller proportion even of those they do teach up to the level of a university degree. The old pattern of training a small elite has never been broken, though it has been slightly bent. Within that pattern the English have kept their national passion for specialization, and we work our clever young up to the age of twenty-one far harder than the Americans, though no harder than the Russians. At eighteen English science specialists know more science than their contemporaries anywhere, though they know less of anything else.

The American strategy is different in kind. They take everyone, the entire population up to eighteen, in high schools and educate them very loosely and generally. Their problem is to inject some rigor—in particular, some fundamental mathematics and science—into this loose education. A very large proportion of the eighteen-year-olds then go to college; and this college education is, like the school education, much more diffuse and less professional than its English counterpart. At the end of four years the American young men and women are usually not so well-trained professionally as their English equivalents—though I think it is fair comment to say that a higher proportion of the best of them, having been run on a looser rein, retain their creative zest. Real severity enters with the Ph.D. At that level the Americans suddenly begin to work their students much harder than the English do.

The Russian high-school education is much less specialized than the English, much more arduous than the American. It is so arduous that for the nonacademic it seems to have proved too tough, and they are trying other methods for students from fifteen to seventeen. The general method has been to put everyone through a kind of continental *lycée* course, with a sizable component, more than 40 per cent, of science and mathematics. Everyone has to do all subjects. At the university this general education ceases abruptly; and for the last three years of the five-year course the specialization is more intensive than that found in either England or America.

With some qualifications, I believe, the Russians have judged the situation sensibly. They have a deeper insight into the scientific revolution than the English or the Americans. The gap between the cultures doesn't seem to be anything like so wide as it is in the West.

The Russians have judged what kind and number of educated men and women a country needs to come out on top in the scientific revolution. I am going to oversimplify, but their estimate, and I believe it's pretty nearly right, is this: First of all, as many alpha-plus scientists as the country can produce. No country has many of them. Provided the schools and universities are there, it doesn't matter much what you teach these individuals. They will look after themselves.

Second, a much larger stratum of alpha professionals—these are the people who are going to do the supporting research, the high-class design and development. Third, another stratum educated to a college-degree level. Some of these will do the secondary technical jobs, but some will take major responsibility, particularly in the human jobs. The proper use of such men depends upon a different distribution of ability from the one that now holds. As the scientific revolution goes on, the call for these men will be something we haven't imagined —though the Russians have. They will be required in thousands upon thousands and they will need all the human development that a university education can give them. It is here, perhaps, most of all that our insight has been fogged.

Fourth and last, politicians and administrators—an entire community—who know enough science to have a sense of what the scientists are talking about.

That, or something like that, is the specification for the

scientific revolution. I want now to go on to an issue which will, in the world view, count more. That issue is that the people in the industrialized countries are getting richer, and those in the nonindustrialized countries are at best standing still; so the gap between the industrialized countries and the rest is widening daily. On the world scale this is the gap between the rich and the poor.

Among the rich are the United States, the white Commonwealth countries, Great Britain, most of Europe and the U.S.S.R. China is betwixt and between, not yet over the industrial hump, but probably getting there. The poor are all the rest. In the rich countries people are living longer, eating better, working less. In a poor country like India the expectation of life is less than half what it is in England. In all nonindustrialized countries people are still working as laboriously as they have always had to work, from neolithic times until our own. Life for the overwhelming majority of mankind has always been nasty, brutish and short. It is so in the poor countries still.

This disparity between the rich and the poor has been noticed. It has been noticed most acutely by the poor. And because they have noticed it, it won't last long. Whatever else—in the world we know—survives to the year 2000, that won't. Once the trick of getting rich is known, as it now is, the world can't survive half rich and half poor.

The West has got to help in this transformation. The trouble is that the West with its divided cultures finds it hard to grasp just how big and, above all, just how fast the transformation must be.

The comforting assurances, given from top to bottom, that in 100 or 200 years things may be slightly better for have-nots only madden. Pronouncements such as one still hears from old hands on Asia or on Africa—"Why, it will take those people five hundred years to get up to our standard!"—are both suicidal and technologically illiterate.

The fact is, the social enrichment of a poor country has already been proved possible. Someone said when the first atomic bomb went off that the only important secret is now let out—the thing works. After that, any determined country could make the bomb, given a few years. In the same way, the only secret of the Russian and Chinese industrialization is that they've brought it off. That is what Asians and Africans have noticed. It took the Russians about forty years, starting with something of an industrial base—czarist industry wasn't negligible—but interrupted by a civil war and then the greatest war of all. The Chinese started with much less of an industrial base but haven't been interrupted, and it looks as though it would not take them much more than half the time.

The Russian and Chinese transformations are being made with inordinate effort and with great suffering. Much of the suffering was unnecessary; the horror is hard to look at straight, standing in the same decades. Yet these examples have proved that common men can show astonishing fortitude in chasing tomorrow.

The transformations have also proved something which only the scientific culture can take in its stride. It is simply that technology is rather easy. Or more exactly, technology is the branch of human experience that people can learn with predictable results. For a long time the West misjudged this very badly. Somehow we've made ourselves believe that the whole of technology was a more or less incommunicable art. It's true enough that we start with a certain advantage, not so much because of tradition, I think, as because our children play with mechanical toys. They are picking up pieces of applied science before they can read. That is an advantage we haven't made the most of.

The curious thing is that none of that seems to matter much. For the task of totally industrializing a major country, as in China today, it takes only will to train enough scientists and engineers and technicians. Will, and quite a small number of years. There is no evidence that any country or race is better than any other in scientific teachability; there is a good deal of evidence that all are much alike. Tradition and technical background seem to count for surprisingly little.

There is no getting away from it; it is technically possible to carry out the scientific revolution in India, Africa, Southeast Asia, Latin America and the Middle East within fifty years.

There is no excuse for Western man not to know this, and not to know that this is the one way out through the three menaces which stand in our way—H-bomb war, overpopulation and the gap between the rich and the poor. This is one of the situations where the worst crime is innocence.

Since the gap between the rich countries and the poor can be removed, it will be. If we are shortsighted, inept, incapable either of good will or enlightened self-interest, then it may be removed to the accompaniment of war and starvation—but removed it will be. The questions are how and by whom.

To those questions one can only give partial answers; but that may be enough to set us thinking. The scientific revolution on a world scale needs capital first and foremost—capital in all forms, including capital machinery. The poor countries, until they have got beyond a certain point on the industrial curve, cannot accumulate that capital. That is why the gap between rich and poor is widening. The capital must come from outside.

There are only two possible sources. One is the West, which means mainly the United States, the other is the U.S.S.R. Even the United States hasn't infinite resources of such capital. If the West or Russia tried to do it alone, it would mean an effort greater than either had to make industrially in the last war. If they both took part it wouldn't mean that order of sacrifice—though in my view it's optimistic to think, as some wise men do, that it would mean no sacrifice at all. The scale of the operation requires that it would have to be a national one. Private industry, even the biggest private industry, can't touch it, and in no sense is it a fair business risk.

The second requirement, and as important as capital, is men. That is, trained scientists and engineers adaptable enough to devote themselves to a foreign country's industrialization for at least ten years out of their lives. Here, unless and until the Americans and the English educate themselves both sensibly and imaginatively, the Russians have a clear edge. This is where their educational policy has already paid big dividends. They have such men to spare if they are needed. The English haven't, and the Americans aren't much better off. Imagine, for example, that the United States and British governments had agreed to help the Indians to carry out a major industrialization, similar in scale to the Chinese. Imagine that the capital could be found. It would then require something like 10,000 to 20,000 engineers from the United States and England to help get the thing going. At present we couldn't find them.

That is the size of the problem—an immense capital outlay, an immense investment in men, both scientists and linguists, most of whom the West does not yet possess—with rewards negligible in the short term, apart from doing the job, and in the long term most uncertain.

People will ask me, "This is all very fine and large. But you are supposed to be a realistic man. Can you possibly believe that men will behave as you say they ought to? Can you imagine a political technique in parliamentary societies like the United States or England by which any such plan could become real?"

This is fair comment. I can only reply that I don't know. I confess, and I should be less than honest if I didn't, that I can't see the political technique through which the good human capabilities of the West can get into action. The best one can do, and it is a poor best, is to nag away. That is perhaps too easy a palliative for one's own disquiet. For though I don't know how we can do what we need to do, or whether we shall do anything at all, I do know this—if we don't do it, the Communist countries will in time.

If that is how it turns out we shall have failed, both practically and morally. At best, the West will have become an enclave in a different world. Are we resigning ourselves to that? History is merciless to failure. In any case, if that happens we shall not be writing the history.

Meanwhile, there are steps to be taken which aren't outside the powers of reflective people. Education isn't the total solution to this problem, but without education the West can't even begin to cope. All the arrows point the same way. Closing the gap between our cultures is a necessity in the most abstract intellectual sense, as well as in the most practical. When those two senses have grown apart, then no society is going to be able to think with wisdom. For the sake of the intellectual life, for the sake of the Western society living precariously as rich among the poor, for the sake of the poor who needn't be poor if there is intelligence in the world, it is obligatory for the English and the Americans and the whole West to look at our education with fresh eyes. This is one of the cases where the English and the Americans have the most to learn from each other. We have each a good deal to learn from the Russians, if we are not too proud. Incidentally, the Russians have a good deal to learn from us too.

Isn't it time we began? The danger is that we have been brought up to think as though we had all the time in the world. We have very little time. So little that I dare not guess at it.

A NOTE ON THE TYPE

This book was set on the Linotype in ELECTRA, designed by the late W. A. Dwiggins (1880–1956). The Electra face is a simple and readable type suitable for printing books by present-day processes. It is not based on any historical model, and hence does not echo any particular time or fashion. It is without eccentricities to catch the eye and interfere with reading—in general, its aim is to perform the function of a good book printing-type: to be read, and not seen.

The book was composed by Kingsport Press, Inc., Kingsport, Tennessee, printed by Livermore and Knight Co., Providence, Rhode Island, and bound by The Plimpton Press, Norwood, Massachusetts. The paper was manufactured by S. D. Warren Co., Boston. Typography by Vincent Torre.